MEDIEVAL DUBLIN V

Medieval Dublin V

Proceedings of the
Friends of Medieval Dublin Symposium 2003

Seán Duffy

EDITOR

FOUR COURTS PRESS

Typeset in 10.5 pt on 12.5 pt Ehrhardt by
Carrigboy Typesetting Services, County Cork for
FOUR COURTS PRESS LTD
7 Malpas Street, Dublin 8, Ireland
e-mail: info@four-courts-press.ie
and in North America for
FOUR COURTS PRESS
c/o ISBS, 920 NE 58th Avenue, Suite 300, Portland, OR 97213.

A catalogue record for this title is available
from the British Library.

ISBN 1–85182–801–x hbk
ISBN 1–85182–802–8 pbk

This book is published with the active support of
Dublin City Council/Comhairle Chathair Átha Cliath.

Dublin City
Baile Átha Cliath

Printed in Ireland by ColourBooks Ltd, Dublin.

Contents

Contributors

SEÁN DUFFY is a fellow of Trinity College, Dublin and chairman of the Friends of Medieval Dublin.

ALAN J. FLETCHER is a senior lecturer in the English Department, University College, Dublin and a member of the Royal Irish Academy.

RAYMOND GILLESPIE is a senior lecturer in the Department of Modern History at NUI, Maynooth.

ALAN HAYDEN is a director of Archaeological Projects Ltd.

ROSANNE MEENAN is a freelance consultant archaeologist.

EMMETT O'BYRNE is a post-doctoral fellow at the Micheál Ó Cléirigh Institute for the Study of Irish History and Civilisation, UCD.

JOHN Ó NÉILL at a research assistant at the Centre for Archaeological Fieldwork, Department of Archaeology and Palaeoecology, Queen's Univeristy, Belfast.

MICHAEL O'NEILL holds a doctorate in architectural history from Trinity College, Dublin.

PÁDRAIG Ó RIAIN is Emeritus Professor of Old Irish at University College, Cork.

LINZI SIMPSON is a senior archaeologist with Margaret Gowen and Co. Ltd.

Editor's Preface

The fifth annual symposium on medieval Dublin was held by the Friends of Medieval Dublin in Trinity College on Saturday 17 May 2003 and this volume presents revised versions of almost all the papers delivered on the day, as well as some additions: Alan Hayden spoke at the previous year's symposium, but his paper was held over to this year's volume for technical reasons, while neither Alan Fletcher nor Linzi Simpson addressed the symposium on this occasion, but made their papers available, for which we are very grateful.

Besides holding the annual symposium and publishing its proceedings, this has been a busy year for the Friends of Medieval Dublin. Established in 1976 in response to the Wood Quay crisis, individual members of the group have campaigned to secure the preservation of Carrickmines Castle, and have been delighted by the vindication of the actions of all those, popularly known as the 'Carrickminders', who sought to prevent the castle's destruction to make way for an 'interchange' on the M50 motorway: on 27 January the Supreme Court found that the protestors had established grounds for an appeal against the order by the Minister for the Environment, Heritage, and Local Government approving his own grant of consent to the demolition of the castle, and on 29 January a judicial review in the High Court overturned the ministerial order. It is to be hoped that rather than, literally, bulldozing through the legal and other obstacles that stand in the way of its plans for Carrickmines, those charged with responsibility for the nation's heritage will learn that the bulldozer is not the solution.

The Friends have continued to make their concerns felt in other areas, by, for example, making a submission to the draft city development plan. They have a strong presence on the group established, in an enlightened move, by Dublin City Council to produce a conservation plan for the city walls. During the Wood Quay affair an indispensable map was prepared on behalf of the Friends by Howard Clarke, and *Dublin c.840 to c.1540: the medieval town in the modern city* (Dublin: Friends of Medieval Dublin and the Ordnance Survey, 1976) has now gone into its second, significantly revised edition (Dublin: Royal Irish Academy, 2002). This is a work mainly for scholars. Therefore, this year, in association with Dublin City Council, the Friends have launched a brochure (written and designed by Dr Clarke, Ruth Johnson and Linzi Simpson) which illustrates three walks around the remains of the medieval city, and we hope that this will prove informative and entertaining for Dubliners and visitors alike.

This year's annual symposium (the sixth) has been designed to coincide with a series of lectures in Christ Church cathedral to mark the opening of a

major expedition of its surviving medieval manuscripts. The Friends look
forward to the publication in 2005 of the proceedings of the symposium as
Medieval Dublin VI. We are thankful to Dublin's City Manager, Mr John
Fitzgerald, and the City Council for their continued support, which allows us
to publish the proceedings of the symposia at an affordable price. As ever, we
owe a great debt of gratitude to the staff of Four Courts Press (especially
Martin Fanning) for their ongoing commitment to the series.

SEÁN DUFFY
Chairman
Friends of Medieval Dublin

Excavations on the southern side of the medieval town at Ship Street Little, Dublin

LINZI SIMPSON

ABSTRACT

The small-scale excavation at the corner of Ship Street Little (nos 1–7) and Bride Street has revealed evidence of the original channel of the river Poddle on the southern side of the medieval town, in the tenth/eleventh century. Even at this early date there was evidence of human activity in the form of structural elements to contain the river (a stone revetment and post-and-wattle fence), domestic debris and at least one rubbish pit. These early river levels, which were aceramic, also produced a very fine bone motif-piece, which can be dated stylistically to the tenth/eleventh century (see Appendix).

The channels were subsequently infilled as part of the Anglo-Norman refortification works in the late twelfth century, which included the construction of a huge city moat into which the flow of the Poddle was then redirected, forming a water-filled defence. After infilling and consolidating the original river channel, and diverting the river from its original route, the land in Ship Street Little then became available for habitation and the partial footprints of a total of five post-and-wattle structures, as well as a possible tanning pit and stone drain, were found during the excavations. The sixth building in the sequence was part of a sill-beamed house, dated by dendrochronology to c.1285. The final phase of structural activity was industrial in nature and was identified as a tanning complex, probably late medieval in date, which included a rectangular timber pit and three barrels. The area was subsequently infilled in the eighteenth century in preparation for the construction of Georgian houses.

INTRODUCTON

This small site lies just outside the medieval city walls, in the southern suburb, on the corner of Ship Street Little and Bride Street (plate 1). As archaeological testing (Scally 1992; Hayden 1993) had located potential timber structures, part of the resolution of the site included the excavation of a small area (Licence no. 93E132: planning no. 0083/93), measuring 7.50m east-west by 4.50m wide and positioned approximately 3m south and 14.50m east from the Ship Street Little and Bride Street frontages respectively. This area was selected as it had originally formed a laneway leading into the Georgian

Plate 1 Excavation from the east

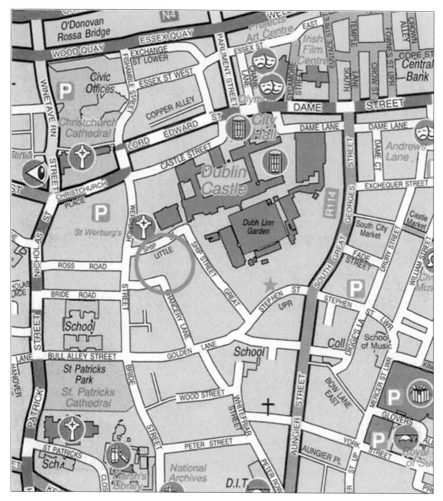

1 Site location

houses on this side of the street and, as a result, the archaeological deposits had not been removed by cellars as elsewhere but survived to a total depth of 4.50m. The writer directed the excavation with a team of six, from Margaret Gowen and Co. Ltd from 17 August to 24 September 1993. The work was carried out on behalf of Zoe Developments (now Danninger Ltd).

THE HISTORICAL AND ARCHAEOLOGICAL SETTING

The site is located in a much under-researched part of the medieval landscape and, although small in size, the results give good detail about the development in this area, especially when taken in conjunction with other excavations

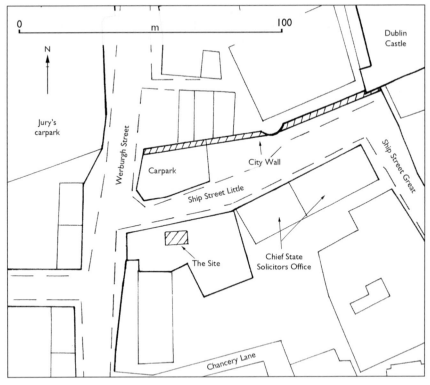

2 Site detail

(figs 1–3). It lies just beyond the two (or possibly three) clay and earthen embankment defences, which encircled Dublin from the mid- to late tenth century and which were subsequently replaced by a stone wall in *c.* 1100 (fig. 3). Several sections of these banks have been found to the northwest of the site, at Werburgh Street, and, on a larger scale, to the west in the important excavations at Ross Road (Hayden 2002; Walsh 2001).

This early town of Dublin was positioned on high ground but was protected on three sides by water: on the south and east by the Poddle, which snaked through the low-lying valley to the south, and on the north by the main river of Dublin, the Liffey. Ship Street Little, in the Poddle valley, lay immediately west of a large natural pool or lake, known as the *Dubh Linn* or Black Pool from which Dublin takes its name (fig. 3). This pool was tidal, fed *via* the Liffey and Poddle, and was originally quite large, stretching over as far as South Great George's Street. However, it gradually silted up, a problem that is documented as early as the fourteenth century, although it probably began considerably earlier. By the early seventeenth century, the pool had all but dried up but was never built on in succeeding centuries, because, according to local tradition, the ground was too

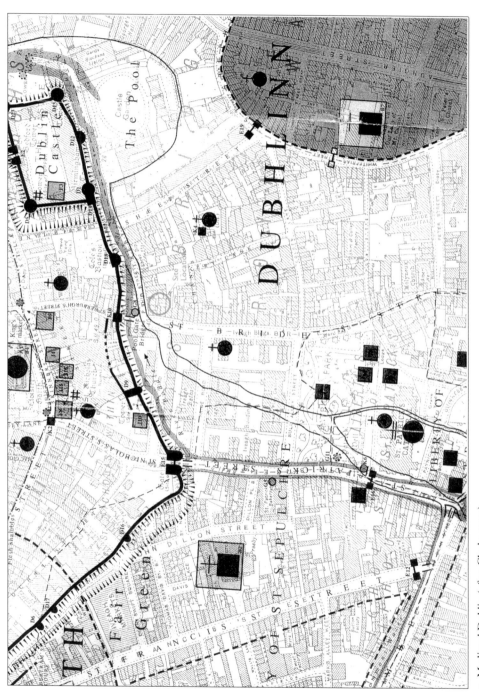

3 Medieval Dublin (after Clarke 2002)

soft. It now forms part of the Castle Gardens, now called appropriately the *Dubh-linn* Gardens (fig. 1).

At some time *c*.AD 1100 the clay embankments around the town were replaced by a strong city wall, possibly built under the auspices of Irish king Muirchertach Ua Briain, who controlled Dublin at this date. This new wall represented a considerable expansion of the defended town as it also included a large swathe of land running along the high ground to the west, along High Street. The wall was a substantial edifice, which had at least three mural gates (east, west and south) guarding each entrance into the city and this advance in the defences, from clay to stone, probably marks the zenith of the flourishing Hiberno-Norse port, which came to an abrupt halt when the Anglo-Normans, under Strongbow, attacked and successfully took Dublin in 1170. After seeing off a surprise return by the expelled Hiberno-Norse king, Ascall Mac Turcaill, the new Dubliners set about refortifying their city, which involved rebuilding parts of the wall, especially on the exposed southern side, close to the site under discussion.

The excavations at Ross Road to the west demonstrated that in some locations the city wall was rebuilt entirely, as a new wall was located 12m south of the old wall (Walsh 2001, 112). A new city moat was also constructed at this time, running outside the wall, and this must have been an impressive earthwork as it measured approximately 18m in width and, on average, 7m in depth. Excavations along various sections of this ditch indicate that it can be dated to the Anglo-Norman period (Simpson 2000, 44–5). The site at Ship Street Little is positioned 31m to the south of an extant section of the city wall but it is not known if it represents the original *c*.1100 wall or a later Anglo-Norman replacement, as no investigations have been carried out there to date. If the city ditch is approximately 18m wide in this location, this suggests that the southern lip of the ditch lies just 13m north of the site under discussion, with Ship Street Little running in between.

The Poddle

The Poddle river rises in Greenhills, Tallaght, and approaches the city from the Poddle valley in the south. In the early period it flowed in two separate channels around the little church of St Patrick *in insula* (later to become a cathedral) before continuing in the direction of Dublin Castle and the Black Pool, the low-lying nature of the ground perhaps suggesting that the entire area was wet at this time (O'Neill 1950, 4; Simms 1979, 25–41). It is certainly of note that, as late as the sixteenth century, the land between St Patrick's Cathedral and Bride Street was documented as being of little use because of the wet and marshy conditions there (Ronan 1927, 45). From an early date the Poddle was utilised in Dublin's defences, providing a natural water barrier on the eastern and southern side of the embanked town. The excavations at Ross Road, to the west of the site under discussion, demonstrated that there was a channel of the Poddle river running along the base of what appeared to be a facing of stone (0.80m in height by 1.20m in width), which extended for over 4m in length. This may possibly have been a defensive feature on the river, which was subsequently replaced, the excavator suggests, by the city wall *c.*AD 1125 (Walsh 2001, 108).

Despite this early activity, it was the arrival of the Anglo-Normans in Dublin, which was to a have a huge impact on the topography of the southern suburb, including the actual course of the river Poddle. The monks of St Thomas's abbey, established in the late twelfth century some distance to the southwest of the walled town, were the first to divert this important river to flow in a circuitous route around their extensive lands, in order to power their lucrative water mills (Simpson 1997, 22). The continuation of the Poddle further north was also channelled artificially to run along the west side of Patrick Street, within the archbishop's manor of St Sepulchre, and remains of this channel, confined within timber revetments, were located during the excavations of the Poddle watercourse at Patrick Street (Walsh 1997, 27). These revetments were dated dendrochronologically to *c.*1202, but, as over 1m of silt had already accumulated in the base of the channel, the excavator estimated that the original diverted channel could probably be dated to *c.*1180 (ibid., 27).

The excavations located the remains of a mill which is called 'Shyreclappe' when first mentioned in the documentary sources *c.*1230, and this may have been the purpose of the diverted channel (Simpson 1997, 28), as the Poddle was brine as far as the Cross Poddle (the junction of Patrick Street and Kevin Street and the Coombe, just opposite the cathedral). However, the channel was also fed directly into the city ditch, a substantial earthwork, which was probably first constructed in the late twelfth century (ibid. 2000, 44–5). The utilisation of this branch of the Poddle in a civic and communal way suggests that the creation of a water-filled defence was of primary importance. However, the knock-on effect was an improvement in the general drainage of the area, which then became available for occupation. This is also suggested by the fact that, further west at Ross Road, the mural tower known as Geneville's Tower was built over the line of the abovementioned early Poddle channel, sometime in the first part of the thirteenth century (Walsh 2001, 112).

Ship Street Little and Bride Street
The excavation evidence at Ship Street Little certainly suggests activity in this area in the eleventh century and this is not surprising as excavations to the southeast of the site, at the site of the church of St Michael le Pole, suggest human occupation as early as the eighth century. The graveyard was certainly in use in the eleventh century, culminating in the construction of a stone church in *c.*1100 (Gowen, 2001). Other early activity was found further to the southwest during excavations at Bride Street, which included a series of rubbish pits and a rectangular structure could be dated (by carbon dating) to between

the eight and tenth century. These were subsequently sealed by a phase of
burials (Mc Mahon, 2002).

It was probably the re-diversion of the channel of the Poddle that fundamentally altered the landscape in the area, which was certainly occupied by
the late twelfth century. The location of the site, just south of the river, made
it an attractive place for various industrial processes especially tanning, as the
results of the excavation suggests. This was usually carried on outside the main
area of settlement, and often banned inside the walls because of the noxious
smell generated by the use of urine in the tanning process. The latter also
needed plenty of water. The Poddle however, as stated above, was brine at
least as far as St Patrick's Cathedral, and this perhaps suggests that there were
other artificial watercourses on the eastern side of Patrick Street, which
channelled fresh rather than salty water in the direction of Ship Street Little.

The 'Polla'

Ship Street Little is an early route, which led from Bride Street (on the west)
into South Great George's Street (which curved around the eastern side of
the pool), and from there northwards into the eastern Viking suburb that is
now the Dame Street/College Street area. It ran parallel to the city moat, the
sharp turn into Ship Street Great reflecting the western edge or rim of the
pool, and thus the present street-layout reflects much earlier topographical
patterns. The city wall and ditch lay directly north of the site and the main
access into the city from this side was *via* the mural gate-tower known as the
'Pole gate' or 'Pool gate', which stood in the middle of Werburgh Street. The
church of St Michael le Pole, where evidence of early activity has been found,
lay to the east while the church of St Brigit, probably a second early site, lay
to the west.

The presence of the pool evidently had a major impact on the placenames
and this entire suburb was known as 'Polla' throughout the medieval period.
This affixation was in use at least by the late twelfth century, if not earlier, as a
documentary reference records a land-grant dated *c.*1180 in which a 'Pulle-
Street' is named somewhere in the parish of St Brigit (McEnery and Refaussé
2001, no. 4). St Brigit's and St Michael's both had 'of the pool' attached to
their names (ibid. nos 88, 498), while the mural gate-tower in Werburgh Street,
as already stated, was called 'Pool gate', and there were mills known as the
'Pole mills' along the Poddle watercourse. That 'Pole' came to be used for the
general area is also demonstrated in the documentary sources: for example,
between 1231and 1242 a land grant refers to a road (presumably Bride Street),
which extends from the north of St Patrick's cathedral 'eastwards to Polla'
(McNeill 1950, 68), while in *c.*1270 a road (in the parish of St Patrick) is
described as extending to the east towards 'Pollo' (Brooks 1936, 143, 103, 144,
104). Similarly, a mid-fourteenth century deed refers to the watercourse in the
'Poll' (McEnery and Refaussé 2001, no. 617, 662) while in 1318 Gilbert de

Twyford received a plot of ground in 'le Poll', somewhere in the general area (Gilbert 1889–1944, i, 117).

Ship Street Little is not named in the documentary sources, although, as stated earlier, it probably does represent an early route, as it reflects the presence of the pool and may also have been the 'Pulle-Street' mentioned above. A land grant dated to 1356 describes both Bride Street and Little Ship Street as 'the cross-ways, of which one goes towards St. Brigid's church [Bride Street] on the south, and the other goes towards the "Poll" mills on the east [Ship Street Little]' (McEnery and Refaussé 2001, no. 662). However, in 1370 the place-name 'Schepe Street' (Sheep Street) is recorded when a 'curtilage' or property plot is described as being located in the parish of St Michael (ibid. nos 245, 281). Despite this usage, the name is not consistently used as, *c.*1499, a grant of land in the parish of St Brigit is still described by reference to Bride Street on the west and 'the street from the bridge to the "poll" mill on the north' (McEnery and Refaussé 2001, no. 1110), while in 1557 it is described as 'the lane going to the "Poll Myll"' (ibid. no. 1245).

The ownership of some of the lands can be traced in the documentary sources. In *c.*1255 Gilbert fitz Daniel (written Gilbert *de la Polle* on the appended seal) granted land to a man called 'Ralph the cook', which was close to St Brigit's church (McEnery and Refaussé 2001, no. 498). Ralph was evidently amassing land in the suburb as, *c.*1258, Slany, wife of the late Gillepatrick the butcher, also granted land to Ralph, which is described as being in the parish of St Brigit, 'between the land formerly belonging to Eustace de Taunton, and that of the Hospital of St John without the new gate of Dublin, and extending from the street to the Pool water' (ibid., no. 88). One reference may actually identify the owner of the excavation site at Ship Street Little: in 1356, Sir Thomas son of Elias de Ashbourne (a prominent Dublin citizen) granted to Richard de Heygreve lands 'in the Poll', which are described as being 'in the corner, beyond the Pole Gate, on the cross ways, of which one goes towards St. Brigid's church on the south, and the other towards the "Poll" mills on the east' (ibid. no. 662).

The Pole mills

Ship Street Little led, not only to Ship Street Great, but also to the mills on the Poddle watercourse, although each would have had their own mill-races. The Pole mill, held by the priory of the Holy Trinity at Christ Church, probably dates to the thirteenth or fourteenth century, as it does not appear in their early confirmation grants. The priory leased it out and in 1338 Sir Elias de Ashbourne, mentioned above, leased the mill to a chaplain called Walter Mareschal, along with its watercourse, having received them from Elias de Heyford (McEnery and Refaussé 2001, no. 617). By 1356, there were two mills listed and Robert son of Sir Elias de Ashbourne granted them, along with numerous other properties, to the abovementioned Richard de Heygreve (ibid. no. 661). The property is described as containing two mills with their ponds and watercourses in 'the Poll' and Richard was convenanted to repair and rebuild them and surrender them in good condition at the end of the term (24 years). Interestingly, Sir Thomas received one mark of the rent, while the commons of the city received two marks, probably because they were located on the communal waterways.

By the fifteenth century the mills are named as the Pole and the Wode mills and appear frequently in the documentary sources (McEnery and Refaussé 2001, nos 379, 694, 886, 1190, 1245). The term 'woad' is interesting as it refers to a blue dye, which was imported in Dublin in the medieval period, for use in the cloth manufacturing. This suggests that there was a second industry involving dyeing cloth on the banks of the Poddle, which was also taking advantage of the availability of water. In 1477 the priory of the Holy Trinity granted the mills to John Kenane, miller, who was bound to provide 'cogges' and 'ronges' for the mill wheels and 'all other necessaries which pertain to the miller according to his art' (ibid. no. 1012). That Kenane repaired the mill is evident from a reference in a confirmation charter granted to the priory of the Holy Trinity dated to 1504, in which the 'the mill de Pollo in the suburb with its waters' is mentioned. This is presumably the same mill depicted on Speed's map of Dublin, dated 1610, located to the north of the site (McNeill 1950, 256; fig. 4).

The tanning house
The discovery of tanning activity during the excavations can probably be tied into a reference in the late fifteenth century, which alludes to a tanning house in what appears to be the same location. In 1485 John Warynge, parson of Mulhuddart, and Sir Thomas Laundey, chaplain, received from John Estrete 'a messuage and a tan-house with a bawn and haggard place without the Pole gate in St. Bride's parish where John Browne dwells, and an orchard called Paradise adjoining' (McEnery and Refaussé 2001, no. 348). John Warynge was archdeacon of Dublin by 1488 and in this year he and his co-grantee Thomas Laundey, granted this property back to John Estrete (ibid. no. 352). This is a very important grant as it gives details as to the location of the property, which place it very close to if not at the site under discussion. The property was described as 'outside the Polegate and lying between the land of John Benet on the east, the land of St. Brigid on the west, the street in front leading to the Pole mill on the north, and the street leading from the Polegate to St. Brigid's church [Bride street] on the south and rear' (ibid.). Incidentally, the location of 'Paradise', the garden, can also be identified as a large garden on the eastern side of Bride Street, known originally as Ascall's Garden. As Ascall can be identified with the last Hiberno-Norse king of Dublin, this suggests that the garden is pre-Norman in date (Simpson 2002, 68).

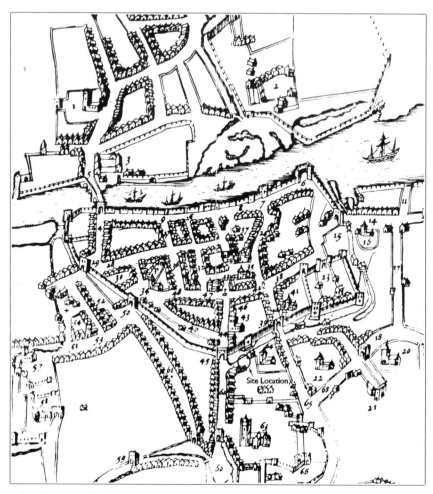

4 Speed's map of Dublin

Speed's map of Dublin (1610)

Speed's map of Dublin allows us a last glimpse of what Dublin must have looked like before it was fundamentally altered in layout and population in the first half of the seventeenth century. A combination of the Civil and Cromwellian Wars had devastated Dublin by the mid-seventeenth century and was responsible for the destruction of three quarters of all existing buildings. This rapid de-population was succeeded by an influx of Dutch and Flemish Quakers, followed by protestant Huguenot refugees, which probably increased the population of Dublin tenfold. Thus Speed's map freezes what was essentially the remnants of medieval Dublin. Speed depicts the curving line of Ship Street Great, which dominates the street pattern around the Ship Street

Little area, taking its line from the edge of the pool; the latter, although largely dried up by this date, was originally bounded on the east by the rear wall of the properties along South Great George's Street and Stephen Street.

The southern side of Ship Street Little, including the site under discussion, is built up by this date and occupied by houses, presumably cage-work or timber-framed pitched buildings. The Poddle watercourse or city moat is clearly visible to the north, as are the mills on the southern lip of the moat. What is evident from the map is that the area around Ship Street Little was very developed by the early seventeenth century and was evidently part of the core of the town.

THE EXCAVATION

Summary of Levels

Level I   Early channels of the river, tenth/eleventh century.
Level II   Substantial channel, tenth/eleventh century-late twelfth century.
Level III   Diversion of the river and the first post-and-wattle structure, late twelfth century.
Level IV   Posts-and-wattle structures and occupation.
Level V   Possible tanning complex and post-and-wattle structure, early-late thirteenth century.
Level VI   Sill-beamed house, late thirteenth century.
Level VII   Tanning complex, probably fourteenth/fifteenth century.
Level VIII   Infilling of the site in the eighteenth century.

LEVEL I

The excavation revealed several water channels at the lowest levels, 4.50m below ground level, which were presumably associated with the river Poddle and could probably be dated to the tenth/eleventh century (fig. 5). These channels were cut into natural deposits, that is, a distinctive limestone mudstone (F68) at the eastern end of the site, overlain by a sterile grey silt deposit (F62) at the western end. The earliest channel, which was at least the full width of the cutting (4.50m), was composed of heavy river gravel (F66), and was over 0.30m in depth, the coarseness of the gravel suggestive of rapid movement. However, this early channel partially sealed a large pit (F67) indicating that it did not represent the first activity on site. This pit, which was over 1m in diameter and 0.30m in depth, was found, on closer examination, to be a domestic refuse pit, which contained fragments of wattle, as well as shell (razor and hazelnut) and three timber posts. It was evidently cut into dry land, suggesting that the site did not lie originally within a wide river channel but in an area subject to flooding.

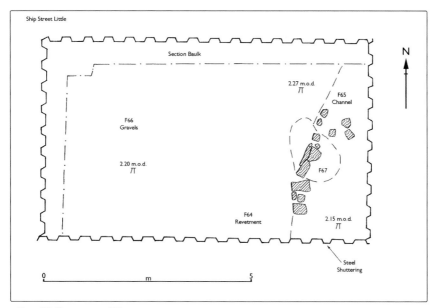

5 Level I, Revetment F64

The stone revetment, F64 Efforts were evidently made to try to control the
water flow in the area from an early date, presumably because people were
living in the immediate vicinity. The pit (F67) was sealed, not only by the
gravel (F66), but also by what was originally a second smaller channel (F65),
which was orientated north-south. This channel measured 1.80m wide at the
upper level, narrowing to 0.75m at the base and was filled with large rounded
stones, gravel and silt, over 0.50m in depth. It was bordered on the west by a
light stone revetment (F64), which survived for 2.40 metres in length by
0.15m in height but was truncated at the northern end by a later channel
(F54–61/F70–71). Only two courses of the revetment survived, composed of
small angular limestone measuring, on average, 0.20m by 0.18m by 50mm but
with no evidence of any mortar (fig. 5).

Discussion of Level I The lowest levels of the excavation were evidently
close to the original bed of the Poddle but in ground that was not originally
under water, as the presence of the domestic pit (F67) demonstrated. The
area was then flooded as the deposition of the gravel (F66) suggests, and the
result of this was a series of succeeding water channels, which dominated the
general area. The north-south orientation of the channel (F65) may suggest
that this was not the main Poddle bed but fed into it somewhere to the north.
These channels, unfortunately, did not produce datable material but the
evidence from the later stratigraphy suggests that they probably dated to the
tenth or eleventh century.

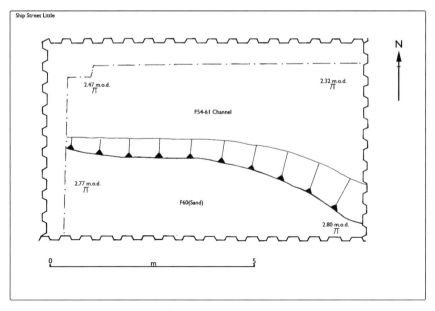

6 Level II, Phase I, The Channel F54–61

LEVEL II

Phase 1

The lower channel F54–61 After the F65 channel went out of use, a more substantial channel (F54–61) replaced it, the southern side of which was located
within the cutting, indicating that it was orientated east-west (fig. 6). It was
substantial in size and measured at least 4m in width, cut on the southern side
into a gritty sandy deposit (F60), which had built up over the gravel (F66).
The channel was 0.50m in depth and was filled with dense coarse river gravel,
as well as lenses of sand and silt, again suggestive of intermittent fast-flowing
water. This gravel also contained a large number of butchered animal bones at
the upper levels, one of which was identified as a motif-piece (see Appendix).
The blade of a small tanged knife was also retrieved from this level but was in
very bad condition.

The channel must have been open and easily accessible to the people living
close by, as it became a dumping ground for general domestic waste, identified
by the highly organic deposit (F63), which sealed the channel at the eastern
end. This was at least 0.40m in depth and contained a high number of shells,
butchered animal bones and wattle fragments. The remainder of the channel
was then sealed by a black gravel layer (F57), 0.20m in depth, which extended
beyond the southern limit of the channel, suggesting that the entire area was
swamped at some stage by a great flow of water, presumably a flash flood.

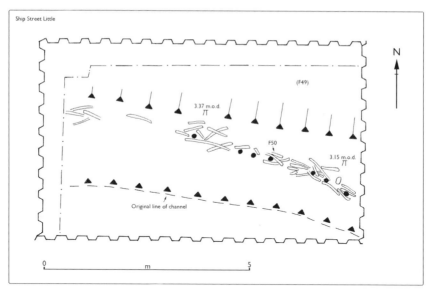

7 Level II, Phase II, F70/71 Channel

Most importantly, however, this deposit was the first to produce pottery, the sherd of Ham Green A suggestive of a date in the early twelfth century.

Phase 2

The channel was re-established (F70/71), however, after the flash flood, and was of a similar size and orientation, although it also began to silt up (fig. 7). The western end became filled with gravel and silts (F58, F59 and F56) measuring collectively 0.25m in depth, while the eastern end was filled by a single deposit of gravel and organic refuse material (F49), containing animal bone and shell, which suggested that some of the infilling was deliberate. A substantial post-and-wattle fence, F50, was then used to delineate the southern bank of the channel and this extended for over 7m in length, the posts measuring between 50mm and 80mm in diameter and standing on average 0.30m in height. The wattle was best preserved at the eastern end where it stood to over 0.30m in height but it may not have been in use for a long time as only a thin layer of gravel and silt deposit built up against the northern side.

The fence then burnt down and was subsequently sealed by a substantial silt and sand deposit, F55, which formed the main upper fill of the channel at the western end. This contained a thin layer of black gravel/shale (F48), the finds from which included a sherd of Ham Green B pottery. An extensive coarse gravel layer (F51) then sealed the rest of the channel, again suggestive of a massive influx of water or flash-flood and this produced a collection of pottery (Minety ware, Saintonge and Ham Green B), which suggests that this event occurred not before the late twelfth century/early thirteenth century.

Dating and discussion of Level II The deep east-west channel (F54–61) appears to indicate the presence of a far more extensive water-channel than the north-south gully (F65), and this was probably the river Poddle proper, evidently a convenient place in which to dump household rubbish. Thus, this probably forms part of the Poddle river found further west at Ross Road. The earliest levels did not contain pottery and can therefore be presumed to date to the pre-Norman period, a conclusion that is supported by the finding of the motif-piece, which was found in the substantial gravel deposits. This attractive piece, which contains thirty-three patterns, has been examined by Dr Ruth Johnson and dated stylistically to the tenth century/early eleventh century (see Appendix). She concluded that it drew heavily on the traditions of Irish art, while adopting elements of the Anglo-Saxon, Manx and Scandinavian repertories, which were current in the tenth and early eleventh centuries. These hybrid style reflected Dublin's status as an advanced urban colony and trading emporium, making it susceptible to cultural interchange. The gravel from the channel produced few additional finds apart from a small tanged knife blade, which is, unfortunately, impossible to date. A fragment of human bone was also found and a study by Dr Barra Ó Donnabháin identified it as a single fragment of the side of the skull of an adult. Although it was not possible to determine the sex of the individual, Ó Donnabháin suggests that it was probably from a younger adult (Ó Donnabháin 1994, 2).

The deposit that sealed the early channel contained early twelfth-century pottery, providing a *terminus post quem*. The excavation evidence also suggests that the area was subject to flash-flooding at this date and the re-establishment of the channel (F70–71) supports this, the fence (F50) clearly representing an attempt to delineate it. Similar fences were found further west at Ross Road where the early Poddle channel was also located during the extensive excavations there (Walsh 2001). The post-and wattle fences were cut into the riverbed in a similar manner and were probably associated with the section of stone-revetted bank mentioned previously (0.80m in height by 1.20m in width) on the northern side of the channel, which extended for over 4m in length (ibid., 108).

LEVEL III

The area appears to have undergone a complete change in land usage after the final flooding episode suggested by the deposition of the gravel (F51) sometime in the late twelfth century. From this level on, there is no more evidence of water-borne activity and a concerted effort appears to have been to infill and actually occupy the land.

Structure I This first attempt was represented by the construction of some sort of a post-and wattle structure, Structure I, at the southern end of the

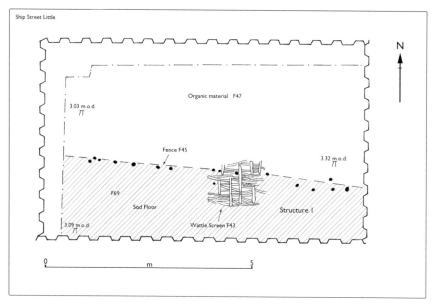

8 Level III, Structure I

cutting, which was orientated east-west and measured at least 6m long by at least 2.60m wide (fig. 8; plate 2). The northern wall (F45) was the only wall within the cutting and this was originally very strong, suggested by the fact that the posts were driven to over 0.65m in depth (although the wattle did not survive). The posts were substantial in size, the diameters ranging from 40mm and 60mm, and included birch, as well as several hazel posts and two of ash. The floor of the building was a distinctive beige/brown sod (F69), which was consistently 0.20m in depth, respecting the line of the northern wall. A wattle screen (F43) probably originally formed part of this floor, although it must have been knocked slightly out of position. This measured almost 1m square, and was composed of hazel and birch rods, and tightly woven wattle (the diameters of the posts and the general spacing make it unlikely that this represented part of the main wall of the structure F45). The deposits to the north of the building (F47) were organic in nature and contained a large amount of animal bone and shell, suggesting that they probably represent dumped rubbish from the building.

The structure was comprehensively sealed by what appears to be three reclamation or infill deposits, F37, F44 and F40, which were deliberately laid, probably to consolidate the ground. All these deposits produced pottery, which included Ham Green B, and S.E. Wiltshire and at least one roof tile. F37 produced three sherds of S.E. Wiltshire, three roof-tiles and one sherd possibly from Bristol, as well as abundant animal bone, charcoal fragments and shell. F44 also produced human bone.

Plate 2 Level III, Structure I, from the south

Dating and discussion of Level III Level III represents a fundamental change in the usage of land in Ship Street Little in the late twelfth century, from an area that was originally within the flood plain of the Poddle to solid ground, suitable for building and habitation. This exploitation of the land can be directly related to the refortification programme of the city, which got underway soon after the Anglo-Normans captured Dublin in 1170. This refortification programme included rebuilding parts of the city wall, excavating a city ditch and establishing extra-mural gate towers on all the major approaches to the city. The south side of the city was particularly vulnerable and the excavations at Ross Road established that the Anglo-Normans built an entirely new wall just twelve metres south of the old wall (at Ross Road). However, it was the excavations at Patrick Street that revealed evidence that may help explain what was happening in the Ship Street Little area at this date. Sometime in the 1180s the Poddle river was ingeniously used to bolster the defences in Dublin by being channelled along the west side of Patrick Street into the newly-constructed city ditch, the first reference to which may be in *c.*1186, when a 'new ditch' is described somewhere in the immediate vicinity (Simpson 1997, 27). This work probably resulted in the land in the Bride Street/Sheep Street area being dried out and made available for settlement.

Structure I represents the first of what were probably many flimsy buildings put up in the newly-drained area, which was still relatively boggy, as suggested by repetitive efforts to infill the area. The size of the fence suggests that it was a structurally strong building but not enough was within the cutting to establish exact type or dimensions. However, it can be dated to the late twelfth-early thirteenth century by the deposits that sealed it, which produced Ham Green and S.E. Wiltshire pottery. One of the deposits (F44) also produced a well-preserved lower mandible or jaw bone, which was identified by Ó Donnabháin as being from a child whose age at death was between eight and nine years. He also identified defects suggestive of some sort of biological upset occurring when the child was about three to four years of age, which was probably the result of late weaning (Ó Donnabháin 1994, 3–4). Other parts of this child's skeleton were found in the succeeding levels in F39, where this clay was evidently exploited for use as a later floor (Structure II).

LEVEL IV

Structure II The remains of a second post-and-wattle structure, Structure II, were cut into the infill deposits (F40 and F44), which sealed Structure I but this new building was orientated north-south rather than east-west and measured at least 3.60m north-south by at least 3.70m wide (fig. 9). The western wall was a solid post fence (F38), the posts (mostly hazel and birch, as well as one ash and one oak) measuring between 40mm and 50mm in diameter

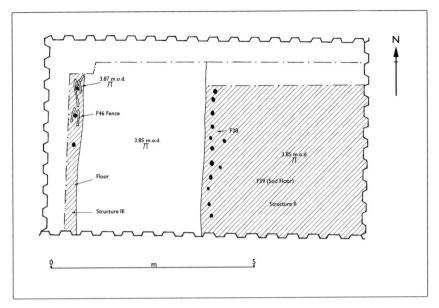

9 Level IV, Structure II and III

by between 0.10m and 0.20m in height. This building also appears to have been involved in a fire, as most of the posts were burnt. The floor of the building (F39) was represented by a trampled surface of timber chips and fragments, and this contained numerous animal and human bones, shells and flecks of charcoal, as well as Minety ware, Ham Green and Dublin wares. This floor surface was set in a sub-floor or foundation of sod (F39.1), which was over 0.20m in depth, extending slightly beyond the line of the F38 fence.

Structure III The eastern side of a third flimsy structure, Structure III, was tentatively identified in the west corner of the cutting, lying approximately 3.20m west of Structure II but badly damaged by a later pit (F42) (fig. 9). The structure was suggested by the presence of an insubstantial post-and-wattle fence, F46, which was orientated north-south but only survived for a short stretch measuring 1.50m in length. Only three posts and fragmentary wattle survived, the posts measuring on average 30mm in diameter and standing to 0.30m in height. The posts did, however, contain what appeared to represent a pure brown/grey sod floor layer (F53), extending westwards beyond the limit of excavation. This evidently represented a floor level in what was probably a small outhouse. After the building went out of use it was sealed by a substantial organic deposit (F32), which appears to have been laid deliberately in one single event and was probably part of the ongoing reclamation and consolidation of the area. This deposit produced a large number of pottery sherds and probably represents dumped domestic refuse.

Dating and discussion of Level IV Both Structure II and III appeared to be contemporary but Structure III was evidently very flimsy, only the sod layer suggesting that it may originally have represented a building. Structure II to the east, however, was evidently more substantial in size, although there was no indication of any internal roof supports, as one would expect. The floor (F39) did produce a variety of pottery sherds including Ham Green, Minety ware and local wares, along with numerous animal bones, shell and charcoal. Surprisingly, the floor deposit also produced a total of twenty five disarticulated human bones, which were examined by Ó Donnabháin and identified as a juvenile, who was aged between eight and nine at the time of death. The child suffered from iron deficiency anaemia (hypoferraemia), which was common in medieval populations but the bones showed no other pathological changes. The infill deposit (F44), on which the building was founded (Level III), also produced the jaw of a child who had an age-of-death of between eight and nine years and Ó Donnabháin suggests that this may represent the same child. This would suggest that the infill clay deposits were reused as a floor within Structure II. Other bones identified within F39 were dog and mouse (Ó Donnabháin 1994, 2).

The substantial deposit that sealed Structure III indicates a time when there were no structures in the area, which was then used for dumping domestic refuse. This deposit (F32) produced a total of fifty-two pottery sherds, all of were representative of a date from the late twelfth/thirteenth century onwards. A fragment of roof tile and a bronze pin were also recovered from this level.

LEVEL V

Structure III was eventually sealed by a deep deposit of organic material, F29, which included layers of pure cess, cockle and hazel-nut shells, animal bones and charcoal, as well as medieval pottery (local ware, S.E. Wiltshire and Ham Green A). This deposit was substantial in depth, measuring over 0.60m at the eastern end, and it comprehensively sealed Structure II in one event. A second phase of dumping, however, was represented by a series of clay, lime-stone and organic deposits, F26, F25, F30, F23 and F22, the latter of which produced a total of twenty-seven pottery sherds, including Minety ware, Saintonge, Ham Green B, as well as Dublin local wares.

Structure IV The remains of a substantial fence, F17, at the eastern end of the cutting and associated with a wood-chip floor (F18), suggests the presence of a structure or building, Structure IV, built over the shale deposit (F23) but only a small section, 0.55m in width, lay within the cutting (fig. 10; plate 3). The fence was relatively substantial, surviving for 1.80m in length and composed of posts (mostly birch) measuring between 60mm and 80mm in

Plate 3 Level V, Structure VI, from the west

diameter. The wattle, although standing to 0.20m in height, was in a very fragmentary state and, although there was no evidence of internal independent
roof supports, the west wall did have at least two larger posts inside the line of
the fence, which may have acted as subsidiary roof supports. The associated
floor (F18), on the eastern side of the fence, was represented by a dense wood-
chip layer, which contained large numbers of animal bones and, most noticeably, many small leather fragments and offcuts, as well as several planks. The
planks probably originally made up part of the floor.

The structure was bordered on the west by a mixed sod layer (F16), which
produced a collection of medieval pottery including Saintonge and Ham
Green A, the sequence of deposits indicating a date in the thirteenth century.
A scatter of small posts (F17.1), eight in all, were noted to the west of the
structure at a similar level but these were all relatively flimsy, measuring
between 20mm and 30mm in diameter with no trace of wattle.

The drain F27 The western side of the site was occupied by a stone-lined pit
(F42) and drain (F27), which are suggestive of the tanning industry and these
structures can probably be related directly to Structure IV, where the leather
offcuts may suggest that some sort of leather-working was also taking place

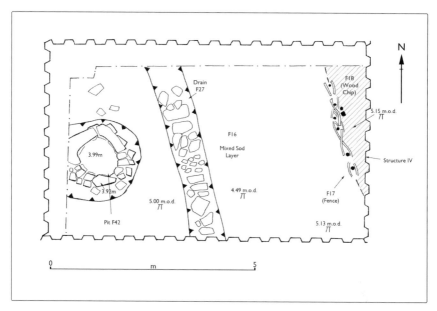

10 Level V, Structure IV, drain

(fig. 10; plates 4 and 5). The stone drain was orientated north-south and was set at the base of a deep trench that measured 0.80m in width by 0.75m in depth. It was neatly constructed of limestone, and measured internally 0.40m in width by 0.27m in height, capped by large limestone slabs (0.60m by 0.30m). The drain, which had no defined base, was filled with a loose brown organic silty deposit, which was 60mm in depth and the drain cut had been backfilled with a similar organic deposit, F28.

The stone-lined pit, F42 The drain was constructed at the same time as a stone-lined pit (F42), which was topped by a barrel and this was positioned on the extreme western side of site (fig. 10; plate 5). The entire cut for the pit measured internally 0.80m in diameter by 1.55m in depth, and the base was lined with uncut limestone block to a height of 0.55m. The masonry, which was neatly faced internally, had no mortar and the base was identified as a single flat stone. The pit was originally topped with a barrel, F36, which gave a combined depth of 1.30m, but unfortunately only two wooden hoops survived (birch/hazel, 70mm in width), which suggested that the staves had been physically pulled out, possibly for reuse. The cut (F33) for the barrel was then infilled with loose organic material and the upper section was backfilled filled with sticky grey clay (F52), which contained numerous fragments of shale. The pit was filled at the lower levels with a deposit of wattle and dense wood-chip, which was then sealed by two distinctive fills, a layer of sticky clay, and a second layer of loose organic material, which was also full of wood-chip. The

Plate 4 Level V, drain F27, from the west

pit and drain complex was eventually sealed by a mixed organic material (F21), which was very compact and contained lenses of pure brown organic cess material, mixed with rotten limestone chips. This layer, 0.55m in depth, sealed both the drain and well, and produced medieval pottery, indicating a date in the thirteenth century.

Dating and discussion of Level V The deposition of deep deposits of organic and clay material (F26/F29), as well as dumps of limestone chippings, F25 and F23, represents a deliberate and concerted effort to build up and consolidate the ground, perhaps because it was still wet and marshy. The combination of shale/limestone and sticky clay would have provided a very solid surface on which to build and this is what subsequently happened in this area. The F29 infill deposit produced a total of eleven sherds of medieval pottery including imported and local wares while the only artefact recovered was a plain bronze pin (from F22). This area was then suitable for occupation, although the primary use appears to have been industrial in nature, represented by the stone drain and the stone-lined pit in the western side of the site, probably relating to tanning. The post-and-wattle building may lend credence to this as the wood-chip floor (F18) produced numerous small fragments of leather off-cuts suggesting that there was small-scale working of leather. The

Plate 5 Level V, pit F42, from the west

clay deposit (F16), to the west of the building, was very consistent in type and may have represented some sort of planned surface, producing a total of seventeen sherds of predominantly local wares, with only one sherd each of Ham Green and Saintonge. A small iron blade also came from this level.

The western side of the site was evidently open plan and, while the drain was a typical type of medieval stone drain, the combination of the stone-lined pit and barrel was rather more unusual. While it was originally thought to have represented a well, it is more likely to have formed part of a tanning complex for which firm evidence was found in Level VII, although it could not be dated (see below). The pit and barrel were very similar in type to a stone-flagged stave-lined pit found during excavations along Patrick Street, to the west of the site under discussion (Walsh 1997, 40–1). The Patrick Street pit, however, was larger in size measuring 1.60m in diameter and had a wooden bucket in the middle. More importantly, it also had the base of a large wooden barrel sitting in a similar position to the Ship Street Little example.

The Patrick Street pit was also associated with several lime deposits and this is often found at tanning complexes where it was used in de-hairing hide. A number of horns, either derived from the hides or the residue from associated horn-working, were also uncovered at this site (ibid., 40). The pit at Ship Street Little, however, did not produce lime deposits at this level (see

Level VII) but the base of the pit was filled with a dense wood-chip deposit, possibly associated with extracting 'tannin', the natural residue used in the tanning process. The pit was very small in size measuring only 0.80m in depth making it unlikely that it was used to soak entire hides or skins, as a total length or diameter of 1.20m is usually needed for soaking skins while hides require a larger pit, measuring at least 1.80m (Serjeantson 1989, 135).

The pit at Patrick Street was dated by dendrochronology to the fourteenth century but the example at Ship Street Little was probably late thirteenth-century in date, as it was sealed by a sill-beamed house, which was dated by dendrochronology to *c.*1285. Pottery, including Ham Green B and S.E. Wiltshire ware, was recovered from the lower fill of the pit and also from the deposit (F21) sealing the drain.

LEVEL VI

The post-and-wattle building, Structure IV, was replaced by a sill-beamed building (F5), Structure V, which was probably a domestic house but only a small section was within the cutting (plates 6 and 7).

Structure V The complete plan of Structure V was not within the cutting, the excavated dimensions measuring 3.40m north-south by 3.20m in width (figs 11 and 12). As a result only one wall, the western wall (F5), was exposed sitting directly on the clay surface (F16) (plate 7). It was composed of two oak base-plates (F5.5 and F5.6), which were scarfed together to form one continuous wall-plate held in position and levelled off by a series of well-positioned packing stones. The wall plate measured collectively almost 4m in length by 0.16m wide by 70mm in depth and had a centrally-placed through-mortise at either end. Both mortises still had an oak dowel in position, 25mm in diameter, driven in from the western side. The wall-plate was laid from south to north and the scarf joint measured 0.27m, secured by three nails, set in a triangular pattern.

A series of overlapping planks formed the main wall and this shuttering was in relatively good condition, positioned at the western side of the mortises. However the uprights, which would originally have sat in the mortises and supported the plank walling, had clearly been robbed out, as the planks were extensively damaged in and around the mortises. The planks were of oak, and measured on average between 0.50m and 0.60m in length by between 0.18m and 0.20m in width by 20mm in depth. A good section of the upper level survived where it had collapsed, the remains of iron nails indicating it had originally been bolted onto the uprights. The planking was also held in position by a series of narrow uprights or laths positioned on the western side, which were up to 0.60m in height by between 45mm and 65mm in diameter. One of the laths was set in a crude angled lap-joint thus the lath was

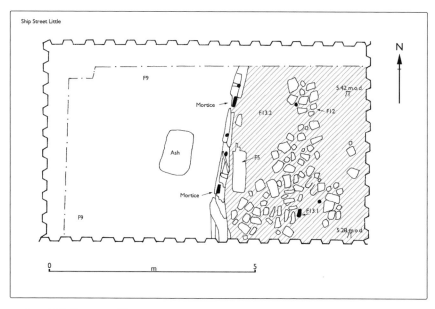

11 Level VI, Structure V

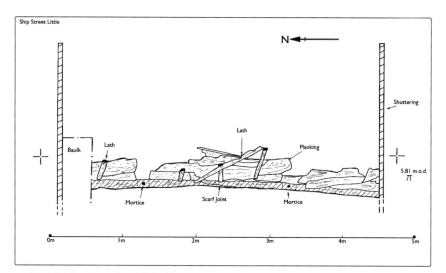

12 West Facing Elevation of F5 (Structure V)

positioned diagonally rather than vertical and held in place at the base by a nail. The laths appear to represent a secondary support system, added later as they were driven into crude little roughly-hewn mortises, which were cut into the west side of the wall place (i.e., independent of the mortises). This, coupled with the excessive over-lapping of the shuttering, suggests that this wall was repaired at some date.

Plate 6 Level VI, Structure V, from the north

The roof support, F13.1 A large oak rectangular post, F13.1, was located approximately 1.60m east of the wall-plate, at the southern end. This measured 0.20m north-south by 90mm wide by 0.24m in height, supported at the base by a series of large packing stones. A second smaller rectangular post (F13.2) lay 2.30m to the north and this may have also represented some sort of roof support, although the post only measured 70mm north-south by 40mm wide by 0.18m high.

The floor levels, F12 and F6 A rough stone surface (F12) was laid within the building, although this was probably not the floor proper but rather represented some sort of a sub-floor or foundation layer (plate 6). It was composed of irregularly-shaped angular limestone, averaging 0.20m by 0.15m, which nevertheless did form a relatively flat surface, best preserved at the southern end of the site. The sub-floor was sealed by a trampled timber and wattle surface (F6), which consisted of a mix of loose brown organic material, which contained dense concentrations of timber chippings and wattle fragments. This produced fragments of leather, as well as animal bone and shell.

The deposits outside Structure V on the western side suggest that the occupants of the building dumped domestic refuse in this area. The F9 deposit consisted of a brown woody organic layer, which had a small concentration of

Plate 7 Level VI, Wall of Structure V, from the west

ash in the centre, presumably from the hearth, which was not located within the excavated area. The spread of ash was substantial, measuring 0.80m north-south by 0.40m wide by at least 0.20m in depth, but was clearly not burning *in situ*, as it was mixed through with the woody organic deposit, which showed no evidence of burning. The F9 layer was sealed by F8, which contained twigs and wattle fragments and was similar in type to the F6 habitation level within the structure but was not as compact or trampled.

Dating and discussion of Level VI Structure V represents the last medieval building to survive on the site and dendrochronological dating indicates a date of AD 1289 +/–9 (Queen's University, Belfast) for its construction (fig. 11). The surviving wall (F5) indicates that it was a sill-beamed house, and the relatively substantial large post (F13.1) probably represents some sort of internal roof support, although this is not certain. The rough stone surface, F12, was laid as a foundation, most likely in an attempt to keep the ground dry and the succeeding trampled surface, F6, is typical for a house of this type with the detritus of everyday life clearly represented. Although the F6 trampled surface produced only one sherd of Dublin-type fine ware and several fragments of weaved rope, the deposits that built up against the west face of the wall, F8 and F9, probably originating in the structure, produced a large assemblage of pottery dating to the thirteenth century, as well as one bronze pin with a decorated head. Of most interest was the dump of ash, which, while probably not representing the actual hearth, suggests that the latter was nearby.

The sill-beamed house was built on the site of the earlier tanning complex (Level V) and was then succeeded by a second tanning complex (Level VII), probably suggesting that Structure V was also involved in this process. The floor of the house was certainly composed of timber chips and fragments of leather off-cuts were found within the building, which were similar in type to the leather recovered from Structure IV (Level V). Structure V is representative of the new order in Dublin after the Anglo-Normans arrived in 1170, and which saw the introduction of the new type of timber-framed building that in some instances replaced the older post-and-wattle structures (Simpson 2000, 59). This new type of building dispensed with most of the internal roof supports and replaced the non-load bearing post-and-wattle walls with timber planking, set in a strong base-plate made of the more durable oak, of which there was a plentiful supply in Ireland (Wallace 1981, 251). The new medium demanded new carpentry skills and these are probably best demonstrated in the timber revetments found at Wood Quay during the extensive excavations there (ibid.).

Structure V can be directly paralleled with a very important excavation carried out at Back Lane in Dublin, in which two types of sill-beamed buildings were identified (Coughlan 2000, 220–5: Structures G and H). Structure G was a large building that measured 12.60m in length by 4.60m in width, divided into a front room, back room and side passage. The walls were composed of wall-plates scarfed together and the roof was supported by large corner uprights, which were earthfast, a throw-back to the post-and-wattle technique. The internal divisions of the house were also of wall-plate and plank construction. Structure G also had a timber drain within the house, which extended along the north wall and, at first glance, this may appear to be paralleled to Structure V in Ship Street Lower. However, the drain (F27) lay outside Structure V and was comprehensively blocked by the deposit F21, which also sealed the stone-lined tanning pit. Thus it is unlikely (although not impossible) that the drain was still functioning while the house was in use.

The second sill-beam structure found Back Lane, Structure H, was a similarly constructed house (measuring 7m long by 5.80m wide) but within a specially-dug pit, rendering it semi-sunken. The type of walling used can be directly paralleled to Structure V in Ship Street Little, most notably the use of the vertical laths. Like Ship Street Little, in Back Lane the use of these supports appears to represent repairs, designed to give extra support where the wall was failing slightly. A second similarity was the use of the internal roof support (F13.1) as Structure H also had internal roof supports (as opposed to posts at the corner). However, these roof supports were much larger, centrally placed and founded on distinctive pad-stones (Coughlan 2000, 211).

The building at Ship Street Little can also be compared with other sill-beam buildings found in Dublin, at High Street, Christchurch Place, Wood Quay, and a second excavation at Back Lane (Simpson 2000, 61–2). At High Street one of the buildings was relatively small, measuring 5m square, but the only surviving wall was a substantial mortised wall-plate, which contained two vertical posts and traces of planking, similar to the Ship Street Little example. A second example, which was slightly sunken, had a planked wall set in a wall-plate, which survived to 1.50m in height (similar in type to Structure H in Back Lane) (Murray 1981, 175–7). A second excavation at Back Lane (on the north side of the street) also located the remains of a sill-beamed building, which was similar in type to Structure G (Back Lane south) (Bennett 1993, no. 46).

The sill-beamed houses found in the other major cities in Ireland are all similar in type. During excavations in North Gate, Cork, the sill-beam houses were dated to the late thirteenth/early fourteenth century, a similar date to that obtained for Structure V in Ship Street Little. However, the Cork examples were founded on stone walls, which provided a firm foundation (Hurley 1997, 51). Sill-beamed houses were also found in Waterford, in Peter's Street, High street and Arundel Square, where they were earlier in date, dating from the mid-to-late twelfth century onwards. This type again was similar to the Back Lane type, but had grooved sill beams, into which the staves were set, while the Back Lane examples were rebated. The roofs in the Waterford examples were supported by large vertical posts, which formed part of the wall and were usually located in opposing pairs at regular intervals along the wall (Hurley and Scully 1997, 104).

LEVEL VII

A second phase of tanning activity was identified in Level VII, which was probably a continuation of Level V. This complex consisted of three sunken barrels and a rectangular pit, all of which were associated with lime deposits (fig. 13; plate 8).

The barrels F36 and F35 The remains of two horizontal hoops and one vertical stave are all that remains of the barrel (F36), which was located at the western end of the cutting. This barrel, which measured 0.80m in diameter, was evidently removed, perhaps with a view to reusing the timbers. The barrel (F34), located in the southwest corner, was similar in type but was truncated by the site shuttering, and was later sealed by the tanning pit (F14) (see below). This barrel measured at least 0.60m in diameter by 0.62m in depth but only seven staves survived, measuring between 0.50m and 0.74m in length by between 0.12m and 0.14m in width. A total of four hoops also survived and these were of ash, averaging between 50mm and 60mm in width. A rectangular

Plate 8 Tanning pit F14, from the west

oak timber post, F35 (70mm by 40mm), was located on the northeast side of the barrel and this may have been associated with it, although its function was not clear. The barrel was filled with an organic deposit, which contained a large amount of wood chippings.

The third barrel, F24, was located centrally and this measured 0.74m in diameter by 0.62m in depth with a total of six staves surviving, averaging between 0.14m and 0.16m in width. Three ash hoops were also identified, although in a fragmentary state. The barrel was filled with a brown sticky organic deposit at the very base (F31), which had heavy charcoal fill, and this was sealed by a deposit of pure sticky lime. The upper level comprised a loose organic deposit, which was 0.32m in depth.

The lime deposit The sticky lime deposit found within the barrel (F24) was also found elsewhere in the cutting in a number of spread (F11–15), the largest of which measured 1.80m east-west by 1.05m wide by between 50mm and 0.15m in depth (fig. 13). A second large spread was associated directly with the barrel (F24). The lime was an off-yellow colour and some of it was crumbly to touch, while other clumps were rock hard. It was sealed by the deposition of a dark grey stoney clay deposit, F19, which appears to have been laid down deliberately after the complex went out of use (see below).

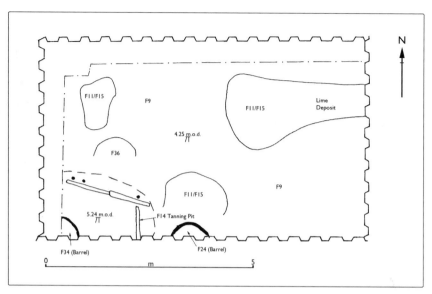

13 Level VII, Tanning Complex

The tanning pit, F14 The lime deposit was clearly associated with a shallow rectangular timber pit, which was located in the southwest corner and which would have sealed the barrel (F34) (fig. 13). The pit was in a very fragmentary condition with only the eastern and northern walls exposed, the remainder extending beyond the shuttering. It measured at least 1.80m east–west by at least 1.40m wide and consisted of planks (0.80m by 0.10m by 10mm) set vertically along their edge surviving to between 50mm and 0.15m in height. The planks, which were of oak, were held in position by at least three stout square pegs, 50mm square, which were driven into the ground along the external face of the walls. The pit was cut into a highly organic woody layer (F20), which had crushed shell and lenses of black organic material, and extended for 1.15m north of the pit. This was almost 0.20m in depth and had a highly obnoxious smell, suggesting that it was derived from the tanning process, which uses urine.

Dating and discussion of Level VII The timber-lined pit, barrels, and spreads of lime suggest that the possible tanning processes identified in Level VI continued into Level VII, but unfortunately there was no dating evidence from this phase. The lime deposits extended over the habitation deposits associated with the late thirteenth century sill-beamed house but it was not clear if the area had been scarped or levelled off at any stage. The use of the barrels is similar to a medieval complex containing at least five barrels found at Patrick Street but both rectangular and round pits have been found (Walsh 1997, 40). However, subsequent monitoring along the line of the city ditch also produced a second complex, which could be dated to the post-medieval period and this contained a rectangular pit very similar in type to F14, as well as three buckets and a drain (ibid., 75). On balance, the lack of post-medieval finds may suggest a late-medieval date for Level VII at Ship Street Little and this fits in with the general sequence of the site.

The substantial and deep lime-deposits suggest that initial de-hairing was carried out on the site and, although there was no trace of any hides, this is often the case. The pit or trough (F14) was not exposed in its entirety but was at least 1.80m in length, the length indicating that it was large enough to accommodate hides (Serjeantson 1989, 135). The trough sealed one of the barrels, indicating that there were at least two phases in this complex, which probably extended for a greater area. Although the complex was not securely dated, it probably represents the 'tanning house' mentioned in the documentary sources.

LEVEL VIII

Level VIII could be dated firmly to the eighteenth century and this was characterised by the deliberate deposition of substantial deposits of sticky clays (F7, F2, F3 and F4). These solid sticky clay layers were extremely hard and compact, and extended across the site to a depth of 1.80m. F7 was the first of these layers to be thrown down and this was sticky grey silty clay, which extended directly over the wall (F5) of Structure V (Level VI), buckling the planks and encasing the lime deposits, F11 and F15, of Level VII. The F19 clay deposit, at the western side of the site, which sealed the F14 pit, was similar in type. Both these deposits were then sealed by a succession of clays (F2, F3, F4), which were tipped in from east to west, building up the ground level artificially by nearly 2m.

Dating and discussion of Level VIII The final phase of activity recorded on the site represents an attempt to infill the area and build up the ground level in the eighteenth century in preparation for construction of the Georgian houses. The excavation cutting, however, was located in what was originally an arched access, and as a result there were no cellars in this location so that the full depth of clay survived, unlike elsewhere on the site. The clays produced both medieval (Dublin wares) and post-medieval pottery (tin-glazed ware, blackware and North Devon gravel-tempered ware), the mixed nature suggesting that some of the clays were originally from a medieval context. In addition to the pottery finds, the F2 deposit also produced two fragments of the skull of a younger adult, examined by Ó Donnabháin and thought to relate to the same individual, although it was not possible to identify the sex. Ó Donnabháin noted that the young adult had suffered from iron deficiency anaemia, probably as a result of the body's response to invasion by disease (Ó Donnabháin 1994, 1, 4).

SUMMARY AND CONCLUSIONS

The excavations at Ship Street Little have provided us with an insight into the development outside the city walls, on the southern side of the settlement, an area where little work has been done to date. Although the excavation was very small in size, it was sited very strategically to take advantage of the well-preserved deposits in this area, which were over 4.50m in depth. The earliest levels, dating to the tenth/eleventh century, can be related directly to the original line of the Poddle and its many channels, and the early attempts made to define these, using a stone revetment, followed by a post-and-wattle fence. This area was inhabited, as the dumped refuse containing animal bone and shell was evidently associated with people living nearby, as was the fine motif-piece. This is not surprising as excavations at the site of the church of St Michael le Pole, directly to the southeast, have documented activity as early as the eighth century, although the church itself was built in *c.*1100 in an area that was already a burial ground (Gowen 2001). Similarly, excavations between Bride Street and Chancery Lane also located evidence of habitation that could be dated to some time between the eighth and tenth century (Mc Mahon 2002).

The excavation also corroborates the results of the Patrick Street excavations, where the evidence indicates that the Poddle was artificially channelled in a ditch to flow along the west side of Patrick Street, before emptying into the city moat. This channel was later augmented by timber revetments, which were dated dendrochronologically to *c.*1202. This refortification work can be documented in the Ship Street Little excavation by the infilling of the river channels, and the subsequent occupation of the area as the land was now available for settlement. This was demonstrated by a sequence of at least four post-and-wattle structures, although only a small section of each lay within the excavation cutting. The building sequence culminated in the construction of a sill-beamed house, a type of house usually associated with the Anglo-Normans in Dublin: unsurprisingly, this house was dated by dendochronology to *c.*1289 +/− 9.

There was also evidence of contemporary industrial activity in the form of the well-built stone-lined pit and barrel and drain, which were probably used in the tanning process. A second late phase was identified, which can probably be related to the 'tanning house' mentioned in the documentary sources, dating to the fifteenth century. This complex included barrels and a large rectangular timber-lined pit, which, judging from its dimensions, was possibly used for soaking hides. Unlike the earlier possible 'tanning' phase, this phase was also marked by the deep deposit of lime, which is known to have been used in the de-hairing process. The greatest intervention to the area can be dated to the eighteenth century when the entire area was infilled to a depth of almost two metres with sticky clay. This was evidently intended to consolidate the ground, possibly in preparation for the construction of Georgian buildings, which fronted out onto the street.

The site is now occupied by a modern apartment block but was built on piled foundations combined with a specially-designed thick floor slab. This effectively means the new building 'rafts' over the *in situ* archaeological deposits, the two metres of eighteenth-century clay acting as a protective buffer zone. This helps preserve the underlying archaeological levels which were not removed during the development.

APPENDIX
A Viking-Age bone motif-piece from Ship Street Little, Dublin
(NMI, reg. no. 93E132) by Dr Ruth Johnson

Motif-pieces or trial-pieces are 'small portable raw pieces of scrap material with carved or incised positive patterns comprising art motifs sporadically positioned over the surface' (O'Meadhra 1973). They are generally found in Hiberno-Norse levels in Dublin, although they have also been found at indigenous Irish sites in pre-Viking contexts, e.g. Nendrum, in Viking-Age Scandinavia and in other parts of the Viking world, notably York and London. There has been much speculation about the function of motif-pieces but the accepted explanation is that they were primarily learning attempts or working drawings of craftsmen working in some other medium, such as metal or wood.

Description (figs 14–15; plates 9–10)
Portion of an incomplete rib-bone of unknown species with breaks at one end and at one side. Thirty-three patterns were identified, 15 on Side A and 18 on Side B. The patterns are grouped centrally on the flattest parts of the bone. Several patterns are incomplete where the bone is broken and identification of these is based either on comparison with complete patterns on the same piece or with motifs from other Irish pieces. A number of other motifs have presumably been lost from the right end (see layout) of the bone.

Methodology For this study, the motif-piece from Ship Street Little was illustrated, photographed and described according to the scheme of classification and method-ology devised by O'Meadhra, who compiled a corpus of all motif-pieces known from Ireland by 1973. The faces of the bone were labelled A and B respectively. Patterns were read from left to right according to the layout on the drawings and a pattern number was given to each discrete set of markings. Where distinct blank field lines occur they are also isolated as patterns. This study was conducted using the photo-graphic and drawn record only. The emphasis of this paper is on the art-historical analysis alone and the construction method of the motif range.

Find Details The motif-piece was found at the bottom of a trench in an aceramic layer of river gravel, interpreted as a channel associated with the river Poddle. The con-textual information implies a deposition-date for the piece sometime before the early twelfth century.

Abstract Ornamentation

The abstract patterns vary in their stage of completion, giving an insight into the methods of construction. Incised marks indicate that abstract designs were carefully laid out according to geometrical rules. Cutting typically began with a field line (B1). Several of these field lines contain roughly incised geometrical setting-out marks which the craftsman intended to use as a guide for the development of various knot motifs (A1, A3, A4, A6, A10, A14, A15 and B2, B13). A further stage of pattern development is found in A7, A11, and B3, B4 and B7, where cutting has begun within the setting-out marks but where the pattern is unfinished.

A number of the patterns are well formed and appear to be complete, though this is always a subjective judgment. Variations of the double duplex occur in different stages of construction on both sides (A6, A9 and B4, B5). On Side A, a fully worked version of this motif can be seen alongside the marking-out lines for the same pattern. The duplex enjoys longevity of use in Ireland and is found in various forms on motif-pieces. Pattern A9 is a well-formed double duplex formed by two pairs of lentoid rings placed crosswise and set diagonally in a square field. Here, the central portion of the motif has been carved in false-relief using a technique termed chip-carving, characterised by the use of sharply angled cuts producing a faceted surface. Patterns B10, B11 and B15 also use the duplex motif as a grid for simple chip-carving in rectangular field lines.

A complete and well-formed chip-carved cross motif with expanded terminals occurs on both sides of the piece (A13, B6, B9, B12 and B14). The basis of this pattern is a square field containing a diagonal cross with a ring at each corner of the field and a square figure with rounded corners set diagonally to the field line. Pattern A7 illustrates how this motif was constructed with the central cross portion and background to the field near the boundary being recessed prior to cutting within the circles. Patterns A8, A14, A15 and B17 and B18 are hard to interpret because they are broken. A common feature of A8 and A15 is the use of a series of parallel vertical bands at the ends of the field. A variation of this pattern occurs with a rectangular hatched frame, on a motif-piece from Lagore crannóg, Co. Meath, which has been dated to the eighth–ninth century (NMI W.29).

Most of the patterns on the Ship Street Little piece are simple cord-plaits or cruciform knotwork figures. Interestingly, certain techniques and patterns common to the motif-pieces from other Dublin sites are not represented here, for instance, key or fret patterns and triquetra knots, which were noted on numerous examples from Fishamble Street (Johnson 1993). Furthermore, there is no interlacing of the bands on the knots or cord-plaits. The chip-carving technique is also relatively rare on motif-pieces, a notable exception being the Lagore piece and some of the Fishamble Street pieces. Ó Floinn has suggested that the link between such pieces and metalworking may be very close (Youngs 1989, 76).

Zoomorphic Ornamentation

From an art-historical point of view, it is the zoomorphic representations on the Ship Street Little piece that are most diagnostic. On Side A, there are two rectangular fields containing animal ornament of similar form but in mirror image (A2 and A12). Pattern A2 is a reverse S-shaped backward looking creature with its head at the top

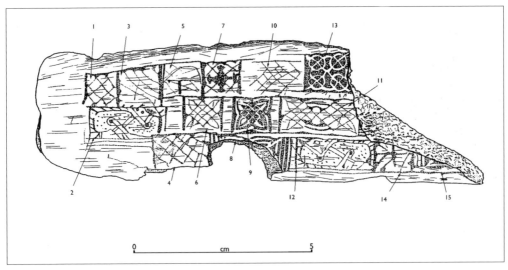

14 Motif Piece, Side A

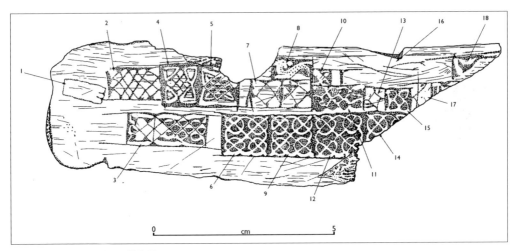

15 Motif Piece, Side B

right of the field and two cloven feet at the bottom left. Its incised snake-like body is set around two shallow drilled pivot points. The width of the body is not uniform and it is speckled with bifurcating rows of dots possibly acting as a guide for a double contour. A double band cuts across the width of the body at the neck, waist and hoof. The creature has a round eye and a small open jaw; an ear or lappet is attached to the head in the top right hand corner of the field and diagonal hatching fills the background area at the left corner. Figure A 12 is very similar in design except for the small upturned snout and the eye, which instead of being drilled, is square in shape and roughly carved in false relief.

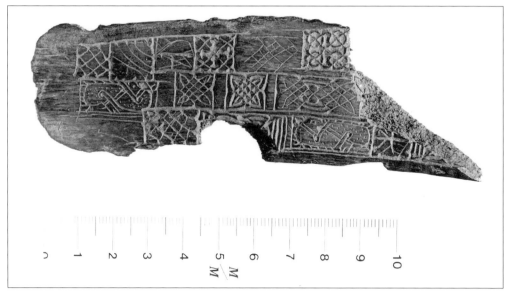

Plate 9 Motif piece, Side A (Photo by B. Dempsey, TCD)

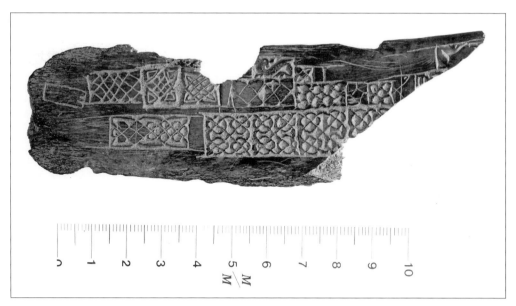

Plate 10 Motif piece, Side B (Photo by B. Dempsey, TCD)

Interpretation A2 and A12 These figures pose problems in their interpretation because they are unfinished. Two hind legs are discernible on each animal but the intended position of the forelegs is unclear. It seems unlikely, however, that the craftsman intended the beasts to be bipedal. The bands segmenting the body may indicate the path for an irregularly interlacing lappet or tail. This is a feature common to the

Viking art style known as Jellinge, but they are ambiguous and could equally be a decorative element derived from the ninth century Anglo-Saxon Trewhiddle style, wherein double nicks were sometimes used to give definition to the contours of animals.

The Jellinge style overlapped with the Borre style in Scandinavian art, dying out by the year 1000. An Anglo-Scandinavian variant of the style developed in Northern England during the tenth century, combining Borre and Jellinge elements. In Ireland, examples of the Borre style are relatively rare and the Jellinge style does not appear on any motif-pieces previously studied (Rosedahl 1991, 231). The classic Jellinge style animal as defined by Wilson (1980, 97) has a head shown in profile with an open mouth, lip lappet, almond-shaped eye and a head lappet or pigtail, which interlaces with the body. The ribbon body is double-contoured and filled with transverse billeting. The foreleg extends from a spiral hip and has two claws on each foot.

Although the animals on the Ship Street Little piece do not display all of these defining features, overall the animals do relate to the Jellinge Style. This animal is then probably best described as a Hiberno-Saxon variant of the Jellinge style relating to the art of the Manx crosses and to the Yorkshire school of sculpture in the tenth century. Ó Floinn (pers. comm.) suggests a Manx influence for these creatures and a parallel can be seen on a fragment of Odd's cross-slab from Kirk Braddon in the Isle of Man. The slab depicts two opposed S-shaped four legged beasts with spiral hips and double contours. Their bodies are filled with pelleting and their interlacing limbs cross their bodies at the neck, waist and leg.

Certain aspects of style and form of the Ship Street Little zoomorphic patterns also relate to a poorly-executed beast motif on a cross shaft at Middleton in Yorkshire, which is a regional variation of the Jellinge style (Wilson 1984, 144). The Middleton animal is an S-shaped backward looking beast, set around two pivotal points, with a double contour and cross-bands interlacing with the snake-like body. Scholars are divided as to the origin of the Scandinavian Jellinge style, some suggesting that it derived from insular prototypes. There was a native insular tradition of animal art with interlace, which no doubt influenced and was influenced by the incoming Viking style.

Description B8 The animal on Side B (8) is of a different form and appears to be finished. It is carved in profile in low relief with a backward-looking head, open jaws and a pointed eye. Lappets or ears extend from the back of the head but some detail here has been lost where the bone has been broken. The neck curves gently and the body is arched greyhound-fashion with the back leg extended in a gentle curve. A short, blunt tail points towards the top right corner of the field and the rather large feet lie at the bottom of the field. Like the animals on Side A, the body is speckled with rows of small dots. Field B18, which is incomplete, shows the hind portion of a similar beast, which is upside down according to the layout on the drawings.

Interpretation B8 These beasts do not have any clear parallels in the animal art of Ireland or of Scandinavia. They are simple in execution and semi-naturalistic and there is no interlacing of the limbs or of lappets. In Anglo-Saxon metalwork of the ninth century, however small animals occur on a number of items from Trewhiddle in Cornwall. The animal ornament found on items in the Trewhiddle hoard varies according to the shape and size of the field. They are usually speckled and have a characteristic square snout and well-formed hip, a triangulate body and three-toed feet. Sometimes a bump can be seen on the forehead and the eye is often set on a stalk. Although similarities between the animal of the Ship Street Little piece and the type fossils seem tenuous, it should be remembered that Hiberno–Saxon craftsmen were skilled in the integration of new ideas with traditional forms. Interpretations also varied according to patronage, regional traditions and the development and degeneration of insular styles.

Ship graffiti At first glance Pattern A5 appears to be composed of random indistinguishable marks but, when viewed upside down, it may be read as the outline of a ship with a mast. Less distinct are diagonal lines that may be taken as stays or billowing sails. If accepted as such, it is a very crude sketch and best termed graffito. Examples of ship graffiti have been recognised elsewhere in the material assemblage from Winetavern Street and Christchurch Place, but these are executed at a larger scale on reused wooden planks, and are more intricate and detailed. In his study, Arne-Emil Christensen (see Wallace (ed.) 1988) interpreted the latter examples as representations of vessels of Nordic type and compared them satisfactorily with similar finds from Scandinavia and elsewhere in the Viking world. As Christensen noted, the Dublin ship representations are unusual in that they show the complete hull and rigging rather than a stylised prow, which is more common. The ship on the motif-piece also differs from the Winetavern Street and High Street depictions in that it does not clearly display the double-ended high stem and stern typical of Viking ships. A wooden gaming-piece found at High Street also bears a highly stylised ship under sail on the obverse. The design of this object, which may have been based on a coin of the Birka-Hedeby series, is at a more comparable scale to the pattern size on the Ship Street motif-piece.

The significance of Viking and medieval graffiti is notoriously difficult to interpret (see Blindheim, 1985). Graffiti are common in coastal districts of Scandinavia reflecting the maritime tradition surviving from the Viking Age until the seventeenth century. Ships carved on wood were found in ship burials at Gokstad and Oseberg and are common on stave churches of the eleventh century and later. Ships were also found incised on slates at Jarlshof, Shetland. However, as far as I am aware, ships are not represented on any other motif-pieces from Ireland or elsewhere, making the Ship Street Little example unique. The proximity of the site to the natural harbour or Black Pool, formed by the confluence of the River Poddle and the River Liffey, might therefore serve to explain the unusual choice of motif on this piece.

Conclusion

Stylistic analysis and comparisons allow for a tentative dating centring on the tenth century, although it is equally feasible that the piece could be an eleventh-century product. The main stylistic influences seem to be Viking, Anglo-Saxon and Manx. A close relationship can be seen between the work on this piece and the motifs and techniques used to decorate the fine metalwork of this period.

ACKNOWLEDGEMENTS

The author would like to thank Kevin Weldon and Lindsay Rafter, of Margaret Gowen and Co. Ltd. Pottery identification was by Clare Mc Cutcheon and wood identification by Tim Coughlan.

BIBLIOGRAPHY

Backhouse, J., Turner D.H. and Webster L. (eds) 1984 *The golden age of Anglo-Saxon art 966–1066*. London.
Bennett, I. (ed.) 1993 *Excavations 1992: summary accounts of archaeological excavations in Ireland*. Bray.
Blinheim, M. 1985 *Graffiti in Norwegian Stave Churches*, c.*1150–1350*. Oslo.
Brooks, E. St J. (ed.) 1936 *Register of the hospital of S. John the Baptist without the Newgate*. Dublin.
Christensen, A. 1988 Ship graffiti and models in P.F. Wallace (ed.) *Miscellanea* 1 1988 13–26. Dublin.
Clarke, H.B. 1990 The topographical development of early medieval Dublin. In H.B. Clarke (ed.) *Medieval Dublin: The making of a metropolis*, 52–9. Dublin.
— 2002 *Dublin part 1, to 1610*. Irish Historic Towns Atlas. Dublin. Royal Irish Academy.
Coughlan, T. 2000 The Anglo-Norman houses of Dublin: evidence from Back Lane. In S. Duffy (ed.), *Medieval Dublin I*, 203–33. Dublin.
Curtis, E. and Mc Dowell, R.B. (eds) 1943 *Irish Historical Documents, AD 1172–1922*. London.
De Courcy, J.W. 1996 *The Liffey in Dublin*. Dublin.
Duffy, S. 1996 The historical background. In *Archaeological excavation at 33–34 Parliament Street/Exchange Street Upper*. Unpublished stratigraphic report by Georgina Scally lodged with the Heritage Service, Department of the Environment. Dublin.
Gilbert, J.T. (ed.) 1889–1944 *Calendar of ancient records of Dublin*. 19 vols. Dublin.
Gowen, M. 2001 Excavations at the site of the church and tower of St Michael le Pole, Dublin. In S. Duffy (ed.), *Medieval Dublin II*, 13–52. Dublin.
Hayden, A. 1993 Unpublished report on archaeological test-trenching of a potential development site at Werburgh Street/Little Ship Street, lodged with the Heritage Service, Department of the Environment. Dublin.
— 2000 West side story: archaeological excavations at Cornmarket and Bridge Street Upper – a summary account. In S. Duffy (ed.), *Medieval Dublin I*, 84–116. Dublin.
— 2002 The excavation of pre-Norman defences and houses at Werburgh Street: a summary. In S. Duffy (ed.), *Medieval Dublin III*, 44–68. Dublin.
Henry, F. 1967 *Irish art during the Viking invasions (800–1020 A.D.)*. London.
Hurley, M.F. and Scully, O. 1997 *Late Viking age and medieval Waterford*. Waterford.
Hurley, M.F. 1997 *Excavations at North Gate, Cork, 1994*. Cork.
Lynch, A. and Manning, C. 2001 Excavations at Dublin Castle, 1985–7. In S. Duffy (ed.), *Medieval Dublin II*, 169–204. Dublin.
Johnson, R.C. 1993 A group of Viking-age bone motif-pieces from Fishamble Street, Dublin. Unpublished BA dissertation (University College, London).
Laing, L. 1987 *Later Celtic art in Britain and Ireland*. London.
Lang, J.T. 1988. *Viking-age decorated wood: a study of its ornament and style*. Medieval Dublin Excavations 1962–81, Ser. B vol. 1. Dublin. Royal Irish Academy.
McEnery, M.J. and Refaussé R. (eds) 2001 *Christ Church deeds*. Dublin.
McMahon, M. 2002 Early medieval settlement and burial outside the enclosed town: evidence from archaeological excavations at Bride Street, Dublin. *R.I.A. Proc.*, 102C (4), 65–135.
Murray, H. 1983 *Viking and early medieval buildings in Dublin*, BAR, Ser. 119. Oxford.
Ó Donnabháin, B. 1994 Report on human remains from Ship Street Little, Dublin. Unpublished report lodged with the Heritage Service, Department of the Environment. Dublin.

O'Meadhra, U. 1979 *Early Christian, Viking and Romanesque art: motif-pieces from Ireland*. Stockholm.

— 1987 Irish Insular, Saxon and Scandinavian elements in the motif-pieces from Ireland. In M. Ryan (ed.) *Ireland and Insular art A.D. 500–1200*, 159–65. Dublin.

Ronan, M.V. 1927 The Poddle river and its branches, *RSAI Jn.* 57, 45.

Ryan, M. (ed.) 1987 *Ireland and Insular art A.D. 500–1200*. Dublin.

Rosedahl, E. 1991 *The Vikings*. London.

Scally, G. 1992 Unpublished archaeological report on test-trenches at nos 1–2, 6–7 Ship Street Little, Dublin. Submitted to the Heritage Service, Department of the Environment. Dublin.

— 2002 The earthen banks and walled defences of Dublin's northeast corner. In S. Duffy (ed.), *Medieval Dublin III*, 11–33. Dublin.

Serjeantson, D. 1989 Animal remains and the tanning trade. In D. Serjeantson and T. Waldron (eds), *Diet and craft in towns*. BAR British Series 199, 129–46.

Simms, A. 1979 Medieval Dublin: a topographical analysis. In *Irish Geography* 12, 24–41.

Simpson, L. 1997 The historical background. In C. Walsh, *Archaeological excavations at Patrick, Nicholas and Winetavern Streets, Dublin*.17–33. Dingle.

— 2000 Forty years a-digging: a preliminary synthesis of archaeological investigations in medieval Dublin. In S. Duffy (ed.), *Medieval Dublin I*, 11–68. Dublin.

— 2002 History and topographical survey. In M. Mc Mahon (ed.) Early medieval settlement and burial outside the enclosed town: evidence from archaeological excavations at Bride Street, Dublin. In. *RIA Proc.*, 102C (4), 67–70.

Speed, John 1610 *Dublin, from theatre of the empire of Great Britain*. Reproduced, Phoenix maps (1988), Dublin.

Swan, D.L. 2000 Archaeological excavations at Ushers Quay, 1991. In S. Duffy (ed.), *Medieval Dublin I*, 126–58. Dublin.

Sweetman, H.S. (ed.) 1875–86 *Calendar of documents relating to Ireland, 1171–1307*. 5 vols. London.

Wallace, P.F. 1981 Anglo-Norman Dublin: continuity and change. In D. Ó Corráin (ed.), *Irish Antiquity*, 247–66. Dublin.

Walsh, C. 1997 *Archaeological excavations at Patrick, Nicholas and Winetavern Streets, Dublin*. Dingle.

— 2001 Dublin's southern defences, ten to fourteenth centuries: the evidence from Ross Road. In S. Duffy (ed.), *Medieval Dublin II*, 88–127. Dublin.

Wilson, D.M. and Klindt-Jensen, O. 1980. *Viking art*. London.

Wilson, D.M. 1984 *Anglo-Saxon Art*. London.

Youngs, S. (ed.) 1989 *'The work of angels': masterpieces of Celtic metalwork, 6th–9th centuries AD*. London.

Dublin's oldest book?
A list of saints 'made in Germany'

PÁDRAIG Ó RIAIN

INTRODUCTION

Between the years 853 and 860, Bishop Ado of Vienne in France compiled a martyrology, or list of saints' feast-days arranged according to the calendar, of a type called historical.[1] This kind of martyrology, which the Venerable Bede († 735) had first devised, provided some account of the circumstances of the death or martyrdom of its saints, thus setting itself apart from the earlier type styled Hieronymian.[2] The latter type, with its stark and unremitting lists of bare names, has been deservedly described by the Bollandist, Victor de Buck, as one of the most horrible books ever produced in Antiquity.[3] Ado's much less horrible historical martyrology quickly became one of the most popular texts of its kind. Within ten years of its composition it had already formed the basis of the even more popular Martyrology of Usuard.[4] Thereafter, together with the latter, it served as the principal liturgical source of information on the feast-days of the saints for over seven hundred years, until it was finally superseded by Pope Gregory's Roman Martyrology in 1584.

Curiously, despite its rapid rise to popularity throughout Latin Christendom, no copy of Ado's martyrology appears to have reached Ireland for well over 150 years. About 830, some twenty-five years before Ado had composed his text, two martyrologies had been prepared at the monastery of Tallaght near Dublin, both of them Hieronymian in character.[5] One was an abbreviated prose version of the Hieronymian Martyrology, sometimes called the Martyrology of Jerome, of a type whose antecedents, as I have shown elsewhere, can be traced to Lindisfarne in Northumbria.[6] The other Tallaght text was a metrical

1 J. Dubois and G. Renaud (eds), *Le martyrologe d'Adon: ses deux familles, se trois recensions: texte et commentaire* (Sources d'histoire médiévale; Paris, 1984). 2 For a discussion of the various kinds of martyrology, see R. Aigrain, *L'hagiographie, ses sources, ses méthodes, son histoire* (Paris, 1953, repr. as Subsidia Hagiographica 80; Brussels, 2000, with bibliographical supplement by R. Godding), 32–106, 406–14; J. Dubois, *Les martyrologes du moyen âge latin* (Typologie des sources du moyen âge occidental; Turnhout, 1978). 3 L.M. Rigollot (ed.), *Ad acta sanctorum supplementum* (Paris, 1875), p. iv. 4 J. Dubois (ed.), *Le martyrologe d'Usuard: texte et commentaire* (Subsidia Hagiographica 40; Brussels, 1965). 5 For these texts and their date, see P. Ó Riain, 'The Tallaght martyrologies, redated', in *Cambridge Medieval Celtic Studies*, 20 (1990), 21–38. 6 P. Ó Riain, *Anglo-Saxon Ireland: the evidence of the martyrology of Tallaght* (H.M. Chadwick Memorial Lectures 3; Cambridge, 1993).

version of the prose text named, after its author, the Martyrology of Óengus.[7] As far as can now be judged, these two texts satisfied whatever need there was in Ireland for written sources of information on the feast-days of the saints for at least 200 years. Indeed, the earliest documentary evidence we possess of the influence thereafter of an external martyrology on an Irish text dates from as late as the period immediately after 1150, when a fresh copy was made, probably at Terryglass in Co. Tipperary, of the ninth-century Tallaght prose text.[8] This fresh copy reveals slight traces of the influence of Ado's work, mainly in marginal annotations, but also in supplementary entries added, albeit very sparingly, to the lists of the body of the text.[9] Soon afterwards, in the period 1168 x 1174, just as the English invasion of Ireland was beginning, Ado's martyrology was again used, this time quite extensively, in the preparation of at least three new native martyrologies, which are now commonly referred to as Gorman, the Commentary on the Martyrology of Óengus, and Drummond.[10] The first of these was written by the abbot of the Augustinian priory of Knock near Louth, the other two were compiled, I believe, at Armagh.[11]

Comparison of the Martyrology of Drummond with the only surviving full Irish copy of Ado's work, the thirteenth-century Martyrology of Christ Church, Dublin,[12] now Trinity College MS 576, fol. 75–132, reveals that both texts depended on a common source which had already been adapted to suit Irish preference.[13] The two texts regularly agree to differ with Ado in the spellings of saints' names, in the inclusion of additional saints, in the omission

7 W. Stokes (ed.), *Félire Oengusso Céli Dé: the martyrology of Oengus the Culdee* (Henry Bradshaw Society 29; London, 1905; repr. Dublin, 1984).   8 R.I. Best and H.J. Lawlor (eds), *The martyrology of Tallaght* (Henry Bradshaw Society 68; London, 1931).   9 P. Ó Riain, 'A Northumbrian phase in the formation of the Hieronymian martyrology: the evidence of the martyrology of Tallaght', in *Analecta Bollandiana*, 120 (2002), 311–63; at 325–6.   10 For these texts, see W. Stokes (ed.), *Félire hÚi Gormáin: the martyrology of Gorman* (Henry Bradshaw Society 9; London, 1895); idem, *Félire Oengusso*; P. Ó Riain (ed.), *Four Irish martyrologies: Drummond, Turin, Cashel, York* (Henry Bradshaw Society 115; London, 2003), 1–120.   11 P. Ó Riain, 'Die Bibliothek des Verfassers des kommentierten *Félire Óengusso*', in E. Poppe and H.L.C. Tristram (eds), *Übersetzung, Adaptation und Akkulturation im insularen Mittelalter* (Münster, 1999), 87–104; at 93–6; idem, *Four Irish martryologies*, 4–9.   12 For the text, see J.C. Crosthwaite and J.H. Todd (eds), *The book of obits and martyrologies of the cathedral church of the Holy Trinity, commonly called Christ Church, Dublin* (Dublin, 1844). For the manuscript, see M.L. Colker, *Trinity College Library Dublin: descriptive catalogue of the medieval and renaissance manuscripts* (London, 1991), 1038–40. Cf. W. Hawkes, 'The liturgy in Dublin, 1200–1500: manuscript sources', in *Reportorium Novum*, 2.1 (1957–8), 33–67; at 57–8. The manuscript, which also contains a calendar, necrology, and copy of the rule of St Augustine was the chapter book of Christ Church. Colker dated the main hand of the martyrology to shortly after 1200, but a date in the mid- to later thirteenth century is indicated by the inclusion of some feasts, the subject of the latest of which, that of Peter the Martyr at 29 April, did not die until 1252 and was canonized in 1253.   13 G.H. Forbes (ed.), *The ancient Irish missal in the possession of the Baroness Willoughby de Eresby, Drummond Castle, Perthshire* (Edinburgh, 1882), p. vi; Ó Riain, *Four Irish martyrologies*, 16–22.

of saints, in the wording of entries, in the selection of saints' days, and in the precedence given to certain saints.[14] However, their dependence on a common source adapted to Irish requirements is made most clear by their shared rewording of Ado's three entries on Irish saints, viz. Patrick, Brigit and Columba. Thus, at 1 February, the Irish versions agree almost word for word in reading *Item apud Hiberniam, dormitatio beatissimae uirginis Brigidae ueneranter hodie commemoratur*, against Ado which reads: *Item apud Scotiam, sanctae Brigidae virginis, cuius vita miraculis claruit.*[15] Similarly, at 17 March, the words *Apud Hiberniam, Occiani insolam, natale sancti Patricii archiepiscopi Scottorum*, common to both Drummond and Christ Church, may be compared to Ado's *In Scotia, natale sancti Patricii episcopi et confessoris.*[16] Finally, at 9 June, the Irish versions read *Item eodem die, apud Hiberniam, natale sanctorum confessorum Columbae abbatis et Baithini sucessoris eius* whereas Ado has *In Scotia sancti Columbae presbyteri et confessoris*. Since the Martyrology of Drummond can be dated to the 1170s, the source version of Ado that it shares with the Christ Church text is obviously earlier still. The purpose of this paper is to show how the textual history of the Irish version of Ado throws light not only on the early liturgical history of Hiberno-Norse Dublin but also on the wide geographical spread of the external contacts cultivated by the town's early Christian authorities.[17]

FEASTS ADDED IN IRELAND AFTER 1200

Fortunately for modern scholars, medieval copyists of martyrologies could rarely resist the temptation of adding entries of more local or communal interest. The successive scribes of the Christ Church text were no exceptions to this rule. Thus, despite the fact that almost all the additions to Ado are now in the hand of the manuscript's main scribe, several separate layers can still be identified, each of which can be peeled away, almost effortlessly. The most straightforward procedure is to identify each of the layers more or less in the reverse order of its addition, and this is what I propose to do here, beginning with the additions made in the margins by (usually very much later) hands, with, wherever possible, an approximate dating of the hand in question:

14 For examples, see Ó Riain, *Four Irish martyrologies*, p. 18n.   15 Both the Christ Church text and Ado added further, but quite distinct, comments.   16 As at 1 February, both the Christ Church text and Ado added further, but quite distinct, comments.   17 Since its publication in 1844, with a long introduction by J.H. Todd, the text of the martyrology has attracted very little attention. In fact, only John Hennig returned to the text, in two important articles, 'The sources of the martyrological tradition of non-Irish saints in medieval Ireland', in *Sacris Erudiri*, 21 (1972/3), 407–34; at 416–24, and 'Deutsche Ortsnamen in der martyrologischen Tradition', in *Archiv für Kulturgeschichte*, 54 (1972), 223–40; at 232–5. However, Hennig did not attempt to establish a date and provenance for the various layers of the text.

February: 23 *In Anglia apud Wenloc; sancte Milburge uirginis* (14th-cent. hand).
April: 3 *In Anglia sancti Ricardi episcopi* (16th-cent. hand). 28 *In Iberna sancti Roberti* (16th-cent. hand).
May: 9 *Translacio sancti Nicholai* (13th-cent. hand using red ink). 13 *Sancte Sithe uirginis* (14th-cent. hand). 20 *In Anglia apud Herefordiam beati Aethelberti regis et martiris* (14th-cent. hand).
July: 31 *De reliquiis sancti Patricij Hiberniensium apostoli. Item de reliquiis sancti Laurencij Dublinie archiepiscopi* (added in 13th-cent. hand to list of relics).
August: 1 *In Britannia maiori foras murum ciuitatis Exonie; uigilia sancte Satiuole, uirginis et martiris* (16th-cent. hand).
October: 2 *In Anglia; sancti Thome He[re]fordi,*[18] *episcopi* (14th-cent. hand). 13 *Translacio sancti Eduuardi regis et confessoris, apud Westmonasterium* (13th-cent. hand).

As might be expected of a community which, by the early to mid-thirteenth century, had become predominantly English in its racial character, almost all of the entries by later hands reflect a concern with English cults. A particular concern with Hereford underlies two fourteenth-century entries, one on Ethelbert (20 May), titular of Hereford cathedral, the other on Thomas (2 October), bishop of the see. Although Thomas's relics were already translated in 1287, the saint was not canonized until 1320, which provides a suitable earliest date for this addition.[19] The three latest additions of this kind concern the feasts of Bishop Richard of Chichester († 3 April 1253), Abbot Robert of Molesme († 28 April 1110) and the vigil of the feast of the early English virgin, Sidwell of Exeter (1 August), all of which were added by a sixteenth-century hand.

The second-latest layer of additions, this time in the hand of the main scribe, consists of a number of feasts datable to the thirteenth century:

January: 19 *Et apud Wigorniam, sancti Wlstani episcopi et confessoris* († 1095, cn. 1203).
April: 29 *Eodem die, sancti Petri martiris apud Melan de ordine Predicatorum* († 1252, cn. 1253).
May: 10 *Eodem die, translatio sancti Laurentij Dublinie archiepiscopi* († 1180, cn. 1225, trs. 1226). 25 *Eodem die, translatio sancti Francissi* († 1226, cn. 1228, trs. 1230).
June: 13 *Eodem die, sancti Antonii confessoris fratrum minorum* († 1231, cn. 1232).
July: 7 *In Anglia, translatio sancti Thome martiris Cantuariensis archiepiscopi* († 1170, cn. 1173, trs. 1220).
October: 4 *Eodem die, natalis sancti Francissi confessoris* (trs. 1230).

---

18 Trimming of the upper margin during binding resulted in the loss of some suspensions, but the final *i*, which is absent in the published edition, can still be detected.   19 Dates in the late thirteenth century are indicated by the entries on Richard of Chichester (3 Apr.),

November: 14 *Eodem die, natalis sancti Laurencii archiepiscopi et confessoris* († 1180, cn. 1225). 16 *Eodem die, sancti Eadmundi, Cantuariensis archiepiscopi* († 1240, cn. 1246).

Although the entries on Laurence – who had, of course, a very close connexion with Christ Church – Thomas Becket, and the Franciscan entries (Francis, Antony) reflect dates shortly before or after 1230, those relating to Edmund of Canterbury and the Dominican Peter the Martyr cannot have been made before their respective dates of death and canonization in 1240/46 and 1252/3. This has a bearing on the date of the scribe, who, despite Colker's assignment of the hand to about 1200, must have been at work in or after the latest relevant date, in this case 1253.

ENGLISH FEASTS ADDED IN IRELAND BEFORE 1200

So much for the thirteenth-century and later additions; those made in the twelfth century again comprise two layers, the later of which relates mainly to English cults:[20]

February: 28 *Eodem die, sancti Oswaldi episcopi et confessoris.*
March: 1 *Eodem die, sancti Dauid.*[21] 2 *Eodem die, sancti Sedde* (recte *Cedde*) *episcopi et confessoris.* 18 *Eodem die, in Britannia, natalis sancti Eadwardi regis et martiris.*
April: 19 *Cantuarie, passio sancti Elphegii archiepiscopi et martiris.*
May: 19 *Eodem die, sancti Dunstani, archiepiscopi Anglorum.*
June: 21 *Eodem die, translatio sancte Uurburge uirginis.* 25 *et apud Glouerniam sancte Keneburge uirginis.*
July: 2 *Eodem die, sancti Swithini episcopi et confessoris.* 6 *In Britannia, sancte Sexburge uirginis.* 7 *In Anglia, translatio sancti Thome martiris Cantuariensis archiepiscopi.* 17 *Eodem die, sancti Kenelmi, regis et martiris.*
August: 24 *Apud Rotomagum, depositio sancti Audoeni, episcopi et confessoris.*[22]
September: 24 *Item sancti Ceolfrithi, abbatis et confessoris.*
October: 19 *Eodem die, Oxonie; sancte Fretheswide uirginis.*
November: 20 *Eodem die, sancti Eadmundi, regis et martiris.*
December: 29 *Cantuarie, passio sancti Thome, eiusdem ecclesie archiepiscopi* († 1170).

who was canonized in 1262, and King Edward (13 Oct.), whose remains were moved to Westminster in 1269.   **20** With one exception, all of these additions were placed last in their respective lists. The exception; at 7 July, concerns the feasts of Thomas Becket and Máel Ruain of Tallaght, which are respectively second last and last. A possible explanation for this is the local character of the latter cult, which could have led to its later insertion. In three instances (28 Feb., 25 June, 19 Oct.), Irish additions occupy penultimate position, ahead of English ones.   **21** Interest in the Welsh saint would probably have been prompted by his position as patron of the principal Welsh see. See Ó Riain, *Four Irish martyrologies*, p. 6. **22** Although not English, this entry was doubtless added because of the proximity to Christ Church of St Audoen's. Relics of the saint are also included in the Christ Church list at 31 July.

Werburgh of Chester (21 June), whose feast is shared by the Drummond martyrology, must have been added before the others. The origins of the Dublin
church named after her, which is usually dated to 1172 x 1178, may well have
been earlier, as Howard Clarke has pointed out,[23] and this possibility seems now
to be borne out by the presence of the saint's feast in both the Drummond and
Christ Church texts. At this period, Chester was Dublin's closest overseas trading
partner, which would explain local interest in the cult.[24]

With the exception of Thomas Becket († 1170), the English entries relate to
long-established, mainly southern English cults, whose addition I would date to
the period between 1180 and 1212. The see of Dublin was then held by the royal
clerk, John Cumin, Laurence's successor as archbishop, who is known to have
taken a particular interest in the religious practices of the diocese.[25] A native
of Somerset, Cumin had previously been archdeacon of Bath and warden of
Glastonbury, and this would explain the southern English bias of the additions.

IRISH FEASTS ADDED IN IRELAND BEFORE 1200

The second, slightly earlier, layer of twelfth-century additions made in Ireland
comprises over thirty feasts of Irish saints, most of which are also contained in
the Martyrology of Drummond:

January: 9 *Et apud Hiberniam, Felan ad Christum migrauit.* 31 *Eodem die, sancti
Edani episcopi.*

February: 6 *Episcopus Mel.* 11 *Eodem die, episcopi Etchani.* 16 *Eodem die, sancti
confessoris Berchani.* 19 *Eodem die, sancti confessoris Baithini.* 21 *Eodem die, sancti
confessoris Fintani.* 28 *Eodem die, confessoris Sillani.*

March: 15 *Eodem die, sanctorum filiorum Nessani.* 19 *Eodem die, Auxilli et Lactani.*

April: 21 *Et in Britannia, sancti confessoris Maelrubai.* 30 *Eodem die, sancti
confessoris Ronani.*

May: 9 *Eodem die, sancti episcopi Sanctani.* 22 *Hybernia, sancti Boetheni abbatis et
confessoris.*

June: 11 *Eodem die, sancti Mectail.* 13 *Eodem die, sancti confessoris Me[c]nisi.* 18
Eodem die, sanctorum confessorum Baithini et Furudrani.

July: 7 *Et in Hibernia, sancti Maelruein confessoris.*[26]

---

23 H. Clarke, 'Conversion, church and cathedral: the diocese of Dublin to 1152', in J. Kelly
and D. Keogh (eds), *History of the Catholic diocese of Dublin* (Dublin, 2000), 19–50; at p. 47.
24 Ibid. p. 39.   25 For Cumin, see A. Gwynn, 'Archbishop John Cumin', in *Reportorium
Novum*, 1 (1956), 285–310; A. MacShamhráin, 'The emergence of the metropolitan see:
Dublin, 1111–1216', in Kelly & Keogh, *History of the Catholic diocese*, 51–71; at 62–71; M.
Murphy, 'Archbishops and anglicisation: Dublin, 1181–1271', in ibid., 72–91; at p. 78.
26 An attempt has been made to change the second *e* of *Maelruein* to *a*.   27 This word was

August: 19 *Et in Hybernia, sancti*[27] *Mocthei confessoris.* 23 *Eodem die, sancti confessoris et episcopi Eogani.*[28] 25 *Eodem die, sancti Michee episcopi, confessoris.*[29] 31 *Item, ipso die, sancti Edani, episcopi et confessoris.*

September: 2 *Eodem die, sanctorum Lomani et Colmani et Macnisi.* 3 *Et in Hibernia, sanctorum confessorum Colmani sotiorumque eius.* 6 *Eodem die, Maculini episcopi et confessoris.*

October: 19 *In Hibernia, sancti Auxilii, episcopi et confessoris.*

November: 3 *In Galliis, monasterio Claraualle, depositio beati Malachie, episcopi et confessoris* († 1148, given papal approval in 1190).[30] 9 *Et in Hibernia, sancte uirginis Sinche.* 17 *Eodem die, sancti Dulech confessoris.* 25 *In Hibernia, sancti confessoris Finnchua.* 27 *Eodem die, sancti Secundi, episcopi et confessoris, qui Longobardorum nobili genere ortus, beatum Patricium ad Hiberniam secutus, post eum primus episcopatum tenuit. Ibique recto morum tramite exempla illius perfecte complens, quieuit in pace.*

December: 18 *In Hibernia, sancti Maigneni confessoris.*

Almost all of the Irish additions are shared by the Martyrology of Drummond, which effectively means that the layer must have been added before 1170 or so.[31] Furthermore, a large number of the churches associated with the saints shared by the two texts are located at or near foundations of the canons regular of St Augustine. This means that an Augustinian canon is likely to have been responsible for the bulk of the Irish additions. The regular canons were already in Ireland by 1137 and, in the period between 1140, when Malachy of Armagh visited Arrouaise, and 1148, when he died in Clairvaux, the reformed Arroasian observance had begun to be widely adopted here.[32] By about 1146, there were already Arroasian canonesses in Dublin and, although there is no direct evidence to show that Christ Church's canons had become either regular or Arroasian before 1162, when Laurence (Lorcán Ua Tuathail), who had previously introduced the rule to Glendalough, was consecrated archbishop of Dublin, the environment for such a change seems to have been already in place before Laurence's predecessor Gregory (Gréne) died in 1161. I suspect that Gregory at least prepared the way for the insertion of the considerable Irish element into the text, and I shall be returning to this point later. In the meantime, we can proceed to a discussion of the two earliest and perhaps most fascinating of all layers added to the text, at two separate centres on the Continent, Metz on the river Mosel and Cologne on the Rhine.[33]

added later above the line.   28 Not *Cogani* as misread in the published edition.   29 For the enigmatic Michan, patron of a prebendary church of Christ Church, who may not have been Irish, see Hennig, 'The sources of the martyrological tradition', p. 420.   30 This feast is already entered in the martyrology of Gorman (Stokes, *Martyrology of Gorman*, p. 211) on the previous day, as was first customary.   31 For the full list of shared Irish entries, see Ó Riain, *Four Irish martyrologies*, p. 20n.   32 A. Gwynn and R.N. Hadcock, *Medieval Religious Houses: Ireland* (London, 1970), p. 146.   33 For a much more detailed discussion

FEASTS ADDED IN METZ

Unlike my procedure up to now, I shall begin with what I consider to be the earlier of the two added continental layers, that made in Metz, whose diocese at the time formed part of the ecclesiastical province of Trier. Both continental layers are also present in a closely related martyrology, now kept in the University Library of Lund, Sweden, which formerly belonged to the cathedral of St Laurence, historically the metropolitan see of *Dania* (Denmark), and, in the early twelfth century, of the whole of Scandinavia.[34] Some entries in the Christ Church text are absent from the Lund manuscript and vice versa. Entries unique to one or other manuscript are identified as such in footnotes. The bracketed entries relate to churches either within Metz, although unstated, or elsewhere within the ecclesiastical province of Trier, including Rheims, Toul, Verdun and Trier itself:[35]

January: 8 *Metis ciuitate, depositio sancti Pacientis episcopi et confessoris.* 16 [*Sancti Fursei confessoris atque abbatis*].

February: 16 *Eodem die, Metis ciuitate, natalis sancti Symeonis episcopi et confessoris.* 18 *Metis, depositio sancti Legoncii ipsius urbis episcopi et confessoris.* 21 *Eodem die, Metis ciuitate, natalis sancti Felicis episcopi et confessoris. Qui sedit annos quadraginta duos et menses sex.*

May: 11 [*Eodem die, depositio beati Gengulfi egregii martiris.*][36]

June: 2 [*Sancti Algisi confessoris*].

July: 6 [*Eodem die, depositio sancti Goaris confessoris.*][37] 8 [*Sancti Kiliani martyris, cum sociis suis Othmanno et Thothimanno. Et sancti Wlfradi confessoris.*][38] 25 *Metis, sancte Glodesindis uirginis, cuius sepulchrum crebris miraculis illus-*

of these layers, see P. Ó Riain, 'Das Martyrologium der Kölner Klöster Groß St. Martin und St. Pantaleon und St. Symphorian zu Metz aus dem frühen 11. Jahrhundert: Textzeugen aus Irland und Dänemark, in *Archiv für Liturgiewissenschaft* (2004, forthcoming). The priority of the Metz element is indicated textually by the entry at 15 Nov., where the reference to a church in Metz precedes a Cologne addition. This is the only day on which Metz and Cologne additions coincide but precedence of Metz entries over Irish (16, 21 Feb., 10 Aug., 4 Sep.) and other additions is regular. **34** The manuscript is now Lund, University Library, Medeltidshandskrift 7 (previously Bibl. Ms. H. L. a); the text has been published in C. Weeke (ed.), *Libri memoriales capituli Lundensis. Lunde Domkapitels Gaveboge*r ('*Libri datici Lundenses*') (Copenhagen, 1884–1889). I am indebted to Professor John McCulloh, Kansas State University, for drawing my attention to this very important source. **35** Hennig, *Sources of the martyrological tradition*, 421–3, already drew up an (incomplete) list of the additions in the Christ Church text relating to French churches, including those of Metz. **36** The beginnings of the cult are traced to Lorraine. **37** The church of St Goar, whence the German town of that name, came into the possession of the Benedictine monastery of Prüm in 765. Prüm is also the subject of an entry here; at 26 July. Both centres lay within the archdiocese of Trier. See M. van Uytfanghe, 'Goar', in *Lexikon des Mittelalters*, 4 (1989), col. 1528. **38** Apart from the Christ Church and Lund texts, this feast is, to my knowledge, found only in the twelfth-century martyrology of St Simeon in Trier; see A. Rosenthal, *Martyrologium und Festkalender der Bursfelder Kongregatio*n (Münster, 1984), p. 34. **39** See previous note.

trantur. 26 [*Et dedicatio sancti Saluatoris in Prumia.*][39] 27 *Metis, depositio sancti Fronimi, episcopi et confessoris.*

August: 10 *Metis ciuitate, depositio sancti Auctoris, episcopi et confessoris.* 16 *Eodem die, Metis, natalis sancti Arnulfi, episcopi et confessoris, admirande uirtutis uiri.* 29 *Ipso die, Metis, depositio sancti Aldelfi, episcopi et confessoris.*

September: 3 [*Ciuitate Tullensi, festiuitas sancti Mansueti, episcopi et confessoris, qui ibidem sepultus, creberrimis pollet miraculis.* 4 [*Eodem die, apud Uirdunum, Mauri et Siluani, sanctorum, confessorum atque pontificum.*] 9... *Post multum uero temporis, sanctissimum corpus eius* [Gorgonii] *hinc rursus translatum est ad Gallias, positumque iacet in loco qui dicitur Gorzia, sexto miliario ab urbe Metensi.* 14 [*Treuiris, sancti Materni, episcopi et confessoris.*][40] 27 *Metis ciuitate, depositio sancti Petri, episcopi et confessoris.*

October: 1 [*Treuiris, sancti Nicecii, episcopi et confessoris.*] 3 [*Eodem die, depositio dompni Madaluei, Uirdunensis episcopi.*] 11 *Eodem die, natalis Sanctini, Virdunensis episcopi.*[41] 14 *Eodem die, sancti Celestis episcopi et confessoris, discipuli beati Petri apostoli, qui cum sancto Clemente et Felice ad urbem Metim ueniens, post primum in eadem urbe episcopus constitutur, celestem uitam duxit, et ad Christum feliciter migrauit.* 15 [*Remis ciuitate, depositio sancti Basoli confessoris.*] 28 *Eodem die, Metis civitate depositio sancti Terentii episcopi et confessoris.*[42] 31 [*passio sancti Foilani martiris*].

November: 7 *Metis ciuitate, depositio sancti Ruphi, episcopi et confessoris.* [*Hasternaco monasterio, depositio sancti Willibrordi, episcopi et confessoris.*] 15 *et dedicatio sancte Marie iuxta murum Metensium.*[43] 23 *Eodem die, Metis ciuitate, depositio sancti Clementis, primi Metentium pontificis.*

December: 1 [*Item, eodem die, in ciuitate Uirdunensis, natalis sancti Agerici episcopi.*] 8 [*Treueris depositio Eucharii episcopi.*] 14 [*Remis, natale sancti Nichasii episcopi, qui capite truncatus est.*]

As far as can be judged from the stratification of the additions, the earliest detectable interference with the base text of Ado took place at Metz, where not only entries relating to local cults were added but the text appears also to have been collated with versions of the Martyrologies of Jerome and Florus.[44] From this flurry of scribal activity some dating evidence might be expected to emerge, especially from the additions relating to local cults. In this regard, the addition at 15 November, which commemorates the dedication of the convent of Sainte-Marie 'near the wall' of Metz is of considerable assistance, since this took place during the episcopate of Adalbero II († 1005).[45] This supplies a useful earliest probable date of about 1000 for the additions made at Metz. Given the subsequent itinerary of the exemplar of the Christ Church text,

This is omitted from the Lund text, which shows little interest in church dedications.
40 Omitted from Lund.   **41** Omitted from Christ Church.   **42** Omitted from Christ Church.
43 Omitted from Lund.   **44** I propose to discuss the Hieronymian entries elsewhere.   **45** See N. Gauthier, 'Province ecclésiastique de Trèves (Belgica Prima)', in *Topographie chrétienne des cités de la Gaule des origines au milieu du viiᵉ siècle*, I (Paris, 1986), p. 47.

from Metz to Dublin via Cologne, it is scarcely a coincidence that, about fifty years earlier, Irish influence in Metz had increased dramatically through the arrival there of the Irish-educated, Scottish-born, St Cathróe († 953) who was given the task of reforming the Benedictine monastery of St-Félix (later St-Clémens) by Bishop Adalbero I († 962). Cathróe completed the task in close co-operation with the noted Benedictine reformer, John of Gorze.[46] The so-called Gorze reform, which was based on rigorous conventual discipline, a common life, and an efficient management of monastic estates, was then at its height. Moreover, it was centred, as the added entry for 9 September shows, in a monastery not far from Metz. The later bishop of Metz, Adalbero II († 1005), also promoted Irish influence by appointing Cathróe's successor, an abbot named 'Fingenius' (Fíngen) to the headship of the reformed Benedictine monastery of St-Symphorien. A possibly forged diploma attributed to Otto III decreed that this was to be under the control of Irish abbots for as long as possible; and that monks of other nations were to be admitted only when there were no Irish.[47] It is scarcely an accident, therefore, that the Metz additions to the Christ Church text include one each relating specifically to St Felix (21 February) and St Clement (23 November), respectively the third and first bishops of Metz, while another, on the second bishop, St Celestis (14 October), refers in passing to the other two. Furthermore, of the bishops of Metz, only Felix is accompanied by the precise number of years that he held the see in a form that corresponds exactly to an entry in an eleventh-century list of bishops of Metz, now Paris, Bibliothèque Nationale, MS Lat. 5294, but previously kept at the monastery of St-Symphorien in Metz.[48]

What is possibly the strongest pointer of all to Irish involvement at Metz in the early transmission of the Christ Church text is the fact that all of the additions that specify the city, save three (25 July, 9 September, 15 November), concern early bishops of the see. The significance of this lies in the fact that the two reformed Benedictine monasteries which housed the episcopal *martyria* of Metz, St-Félix/St-Clément and St-Symphorien, were under the control of a single Irish abbot in the period about 1000.[49] Another pointer to Irish

---

46 For the Irish in Lorraine and, more specifically, in Metz, see D.N. Dumville, 'St Cathróe of Metz and the hagiography of exoticism', in J. Carey, M. Herbert, P. Ó Riain (eds), *Studies in Irish hagiography: saints and scholars* (Dublin, 2001), 172–88; J.–M. Picard, 'The cult of Columba in Lotharingia (9th–11th centuries): the manuscript evidence', in ibid., 221–36; L. Weisgerber, 'Eine Irenwelle an Maas, Mosel und Rhein in Ottonischer Zeit?', in J. Knobloch and R. Schützeichel (eds), *Leo Weisgerber Rhenania Germano-Celtica* (Bonn, 1969), 359–77; at 366–7. Cf. M. Parisse, 'Remarques sur les fondations monastiques à Metz au moyen âge', in *Annales de l'Est*, 31 (1979), 193–224; at 201–2.   **47** For the most recent discussion of the circumstances, see Dumville, 'St Cathróe of Metz', p. 181n.   **48** For the list of Metz bishops, see O. Holder-Egger (ed.), 'Nomina pontificium Mettensis sedis et actus catalogi episcoporum Mettensium', in *Monumenta Germaniae historica, scriptores*, 13 (1881), 305–6; H. Leclercq, 'Metz', in *Dictionnaire d'archéologie chrétienne et de liturgie*, 11 (1933), cols. 822–3.   **49** See Picard, 'The cult of Columba', p. 233.

authorship of the Metz additions is the fact that the entry on Mansuetus of Toul (3 September) refers to ongoing miracles at his tomb. In a Life written for him shortly before 1000, Mansuetus had, quite wrongly, been declared an Irishman.[50] Much the same fate befell Algisus (2 June), who was reputed to be a companion of Fursa's; his relics were kept in Waulsort which, through its founder Cathróe, had a close association with Metz. The presence of Algisus, together with Fursa (16 January) and his brother, Fáelán (31 October), in both Christ Church and Lund texts was thus also very probably due to an Irish monk based in Metz. This may also be true of the entry on Killian and his associates, who are commemorated in both texts on 8 July.[51]

On balance, therefore, a strong case can clearly be made for an involvement of the Irish at Metz – about the beginning of the eleventh century, when their influence was at its highest – in the composition of the version of Ado that eventually reached Dublin and Christ Church. Before reaching Dublin, however, the text was to make one detour, to Cologne, in the process receiving once more a substantial number of local additions.

FEASTS ADDED IN COLOGNE

Although devoid of any specific mention of Cologne, I take the bracketed entries to have also been added there. However, some of these may already have been added in Metz.[52]

January: [15 *Eodem die, natalis sancti Mauri abbatis, discipuli sancti Benedicti abbatis.*][53]
February: [6 *Eodem die, transportatio reliquiarum sancti Pantaleonis et Quirini martyrum.*][54]

---

50 See *Acta sanctorum*, Sept. 1 (1868), p. 639 (*Mansuetus, transmarinis partibus nobilium quidem Scotorum clara progenie genitus*). Cf. J. Choux, 'Mansueto', in *Bibliotheca sanctorum*, 7 (1966), cols. 632–5. **51** This could just as easily have been added in Cologne. **52** For a previous listing of the entries specifying Cologne, see Hennig, 'Deutsche Ortsnamen in der martyrologischen Tradition', p. 233. As far as the textual stratification of these additions is concerned, those relating to Cologne or its associated churches are in first place twice, in final position 14 times, and, where followed by other entries, four times ahead of English additions, twice ahead of Irish entries, and three times in front of additions drawn from a copy of the Hieronymian martyrology. The principal authority for the feasts celebrated in Cologne is G. Zilliken, 'Der Kölner Festkalender. Seine Entwicklung und seine Verwendung zu Urkundendatierungen. Ein Beitrag zur Heortologie und Chronologie des Mittelalters', in *Bonner Jahrbücher: Jahrbücher des Vereins von Altertumsfreunden im Rheinlande*, 119 (1910), 13–157. **53** Zilliken, 'Der Kölner Festkalender', 38–9. For a discussion of the entry, see Hennig, 'The sources of the martyrological tradition', p. 419; Hennig did not realise that the corresponding entry in the martyrology of Tallaght, which he took to be earlier than that of the Christ Church text, in fact derives from the latter. **54** The Benedictine abbey in Cologne, under Irish control in the early eleventh century, was dedicated to St Pantaleon, with Quirinus as co-patron. This feast is neither in the Lund text nor is it listed in Zilliken's 'Der Kölner Festkalender'.

March: 27 *Apud Coloniam, sancti Evergisli episcopi.*[55]

April: 16 *In Colonia, translatio sancti Albini martyris.*[56] 23 [*Eodem die, natalis sancti Adelberti martiris.*][57] 30 [*Rome, uia Appia, passio sancti Quirini martiris.*][58]

May: 23 *In Colonia prope murum, dedicatio basilice sancti Martini confessoris in monasterio eiusdem.*[59]

June: 10 *In Colonia, passio sancti Maurini abbatis et martyris. Qui peracto agonis sui triumpho, domus tumuli celo tantum notus, et angelici tantum obsequii reuerentia ueneranda habitauit, usque ad incarnati uerbi annum nongentesimum quinquagesimum septimum. Nam quia non potuit latere sub modio lucerna ardens coram domino, dum ponendo fundamento basilice sancti Pantaleonis terra effoditur, loculus gloria tibi Christe Maurini abbatis inuenitur; ac primo peruidetur locum lapis claudens, inscriptus martiris nomine, et officio, et martirii eius die et loco. Hic requiescunt ossa bone memorie Maurini martiris, qui in atrio ecclesie martirium pertulit, sub die quarto idus Iunii.*[60] 21 [*Ipso die apud Mogontiam, passio sancti Albini martiris.*]

July: 9 *Eodem die, in Colonia sancti Heriberti episcopi et confessoris.*[61]

September: 3 [*Eodem die, sancti Remacli, episcopi et confessoris cuius corpus requiescit super fluuium Amblauia.*][62]

October: 10 *Apud Coloniam Agrippinam, natalis sanctorum martirum, Gereonis, cum aliis trecentis decem et octo. In Troia, Uictoris, cum trecentis triginta. In Uerona, Cassii et Florentii, cum aliis septem. Quos ferunt Theobeos fuisse, et cum legione illa beati Mauricii, iussu Maximiani imperatoris, in Galliis transitum fecisse, atque circa Reni litora consedisse, et funestum tyranni imperium*[63] *respuendo, pro uera pietate colla pacienter gladiis subdidisse.*[64] 11 *Item, ipsa die, depositio beati*[65] *Brunonis, Agripinensis archiepiscopi, cuius uita gloriosa et illustris fuit.*[66] 13 *In Colonia, inuentio corporis sancti Maurini martiris.* 15 … *sanctorum Maurorum … cum numero trescentis sexaginta …* (instead of *numero quinquaginta* in Ado). 16 [*In castro Sollercii, sancti Eliphii martiris. Alibi … et depositio sancti Galli confessoris.*][67] 21 *In Colonia, undecim milia uirginum.* 23 *In Colonia, sancti Seuerini, episcopi et confessoris.*

---

55 Omitted from Christ Church.   56 Omitted from Lund.   57 The cult of Adalbert of Prague, who was martyred in 997, quickly spread to Germany. Zilliken, 'Der Kölner Festkalender', 64–5.   58 See note 54.   59 This is omitted from the Lund text, which had little time for church dedications.   60 The Lund text has only the first sentence. 61 Omitted from Christ Church.   62 Remaclus is best remembered for his posthumous intervention on behalf of his church against the wishes of Archbishop Anno of Cologne; M. de Somer, 'Remaclo', in *Bibliotheca sanctorum*, 11 (1968), cols. 124–7; A. Legner, *Kölner Heilige und Heiligtümer: ein Jahrtausend europäischer Reliquienkultur* (Cologne, 2003), 30–1. 63 This word was wrongly read as *impium* in the published edition of the text.   64 Ado placed this entry (or series of entries) in his list for 9 October. However, his version does not specify Troia (Xanten, near Cologne) and Verona (Bonn). Cf. Hennig, 'Deutsche Ortsnamen in der martyrologischen Tradition', p. 233. The Lund text does not contain the Cologne addition to this entry.   65 This is wrongly read as *sancti* in the published edition. 66 Omitted from Lund.   67 Zilliken, 'Der Kölner Festkalender', 106–7.

November: 1 [*Rome, natalis sancti Cesarii martiris.*][68] *In Colonia, sancti Euergisi, episcopi et confessoris.* 12 *In Colonia, sancti Cunberti,*[69] *episcopi et confessoris.* 15 *et sancti Benedicti in Colonia.* 16 [*Et depositio beati Otmari, episcopi et confessoris.*][70]

December: 22 [*In ciuitate Spolitana, passio sancti Gregorii martiris.*][71]

In the case of the Christ Church martyrology, the Cologne additions, which are by any standards considerable,[72] can be dated to the period between about 1000 and 1050. The more recent date is calculated on the basis of the lack of any trace of a number of cults known to have been introduced to Cologne churches about or after 1050. These include the famous cult of the Three Holy Kings, which was brought from Milan to Cologne on 23 July 1164. Likewise absent from the Christ Church text are the feasts of Ulrich of Augsburg, which was proclaimed for the diocese of Cologne by Archbishop Hermann († 1056), and that of Agilolf, an eighth-century bishop of Cologne, whose relics arrived back there through the good offices of Archbishop Anno in 1062.[73] The earlier date of *c*.1000 is based on a number of indications. First, several entries reflect the well-known concern of Archbishop Bruno († 965) – whose own *natalis* (11 October) is also recorded here – with relics.[74] Among the relics brought by Bruno to Cologne were those of Evergisel, whose day (1 November) uniquely falls here on the octave of his usual feast in Cologne, and of Gregory of Spoleto (22 December). Bruno's immediate successor, Folkmar, was responsible for discovering the remains of Maurinus in 966, which prompted the long entry at 10 June. This entry is in word-for-word agreement with an account of the discovery written by Stephanus of Cologne between 990 and 1000.[75] Similarly, the relics of Albinus, whose translation is commemorated on 16 April, were brought to Cologne by the

68 Zilliken, 'Der Kölner Festkalender', 110–11; Legner, *Kölner Heilige*, 141–3.   69 The published edition wrongly reads *Cumbert*.   70 Zilliken, 'Der Kölner Festkalender', 114–15. F. Caraffa, 'Gregorio di Spoleto', in *Bibliotheca sanctorum*, 7 (1966), cols. 212–13.   71 Ibid., 124–5.   72 Largely on the strength of the references in the Christ Church text, Hennig, 'Deutsche Ortsnamen in der martyrologischen Tradition', p. 234, stated: 'Von keiner anderen deutschen Stadt lässt sich so originelle irische Kenntnis nachweisen wie von Köln'.   73 F.W. Oediger, *Die Regesten der Erzbischöfe von Köln im Mittelalter* (Publikationen der Gesellschaft für rheinische Geschichtskunde 21, Bonn, 1954), I, p. 227 (Nr. 775); ibid., p. 257 (Nr. 889).   74 Bruno's biographer, Ruotger, specifically referred to the archbishop's activity in this area. See G.H. Pertz (ed.), 'Ruotgeri Vita Brunonis', in *Monumenta Germaniae historica, scriptores*, 4 (1841), 252–75; at p. 266; H. Kallfelz, *Lebensbeschreibungen einiger Bischöfe des 10.–12. Jahrhunderts* (Darmstadt, 1973), p. 225.   75 L. de Heinemann (ed.), 'Ex translatione S. Maurini auctore Stephano', in *Monumenta Germaniae historica, scriptores*, 15 (1888), 683–6.   76 Zilliken, 'Der Kölner Festkalender', 62–3, suggested, wrongly, that the translation commemorated here was that of 1186. For Theophanu, see H.E. Stiene, 'Kölner Heiligenlegenden im 10. und 11. Jahrhundert', in A. von Euw, P. Schreiner (eds), *Kaiserin Theophanu: Begegnung des Ostens und Westens um die Wende des ersten Jahrtausends* (Cologne, 1991), I, 125–35; at 127–31.

Byzantine empress, Theofanu, between 983 and 991.[76] Finally, the entry concerning St Adalbert of Prague, whose cult was very strong in Germany, could not have been made earlier than the year of his martyrdom in 997.[77]

An even narrower dating of the Cologne additions to the Christ Church text seems possible by reference to the lack of any mention of the feast of Archbishop Heribert who died on 16 March 1021.[78] Having succeeded to the see of Cologne in 999, Heribert founded the Benedictine monastery of Deutz in the suburbs of the city in 1002, and already during his lifetime he had gained a reputation for sanctity. However, although his cult did not receive official approval until after 1046–8, the fact that a piece of his clothing is among the relics listed in the Christ Church text at 31 July indicates not only that he was already dead when the relics were brought together, but that he had also become the subject of a local cult. We may infer from this that the Cologne element was added to the text in the little more than twenty years that elapsed between Heribert's death in 1021 and the approval of his cult in 1046–8.

The same *terminus post quem* of roughly 1000 applies to the Cologne additions to the Lund martyrology. However, some additions – for example, the feasts of Ulrich of Augsburg (4 July) and Archbishop Heribert (16 March) – must have been made about or after 1050. This would suggest that the exemplar of the Lund text had remained on in Cologne when that of the Christ Church text had already left.

COLOGNE'S 'IRISH PERIOD'

Where in Cologne were these entries added and how did the text come to be preserved in Ireland? All the indications are that the additions to both the Christ Church and Lund texts were made at the two 'Irish churches' of Cologne. One of these was the church of St Pantaleon, whose 'irische Periode' has been placed precisely between the years 1019 and 1042, when it was governed by an Irish abbot, Elias (Irish Ailill).[79] Elias, who was one of Heribert's closest associates, was called to the bishop's bedside in 1021 to administer the last rites. The other Irish church was Gross St Martin, which was likewise governed by Elias and which, according to the chronicler, Marianus Scottus, had been placed under Irish control in the 970s.[80] There

---

77 M.C. Cellettti, 'Adalberto', in *Bibliotheca sanctorum*, 1 (1962), cols. 185–90; Zilliken, 'Der Kölner Festkalender', 64–5.   **78** For Heribert, see H. Müller, *Heribert, Kanzler Ottos III. und Erzbischof von Köln* (Veröffentlichungen des kölnischen Geschichtsvereins e. v., Cologne, 1977); idem, 'Die Kölner Erzbischöfe von Bruno I. bis Hermann II. (953–1056)', in von Euw, Schreiner, *Kaiserin Theophanu*, 15–32; at 25–8.   **79** H.J. Kracht, *Geschichte der Benediktinerabtei St Pantaleon in Köln 965–1250* (Siegburg, 1975), p. 56.   **80** G. Waitz (ed.), 'Mariani Scotti chronicon', in *Monumenta Germaniae historica, scriptores*, 5 (1844), 481–564; at p. 555.

are two entries that bear out this provenance. One, at 6 February, although not mentioning Cologne as such, uniquely records the translation of the relics of Pantaleon and Quirinus, repectively patron and co-patron of the monastery of St Pantaleon, whose community would have had a particular interest in the event.[81] The other, at 23 May, equally uniquely commemorates the dedication of the basilica of St Martin *in monasterio eiusdem* in Cologne.[82] Several entries in the Christ Church text are otherwise attested only in manuscripts particular to St Pantaleon. These include the translation of the relics of Albinus (16 April), which, having been brought from Rome by Empress Theophanu between 983 and 991, were presented to St Pantaleon.[83] Similarly, the entry at 15 November, which reads *et sancti Benedicti in Colonia*, is rendered *dedicatio s. Benedicti (in claustro)* in the only other manuscripts, all of them from St Pantaleon, to have recorded what is clearly a commemoration of the transformation of this church into a Benedictine abbey.[84] We may conclude, therefore, that the exemplar of the Christ Church text had been previously kept at the Irish monastery of St Pantaleon in Cologne.

IRISH FEASTS ADDED IN COLOGNE

As we have seen, a number of feasts of Irish saints active on the Continent were added to the martyrology, probably while this was still in Metz.[85] Also added, again apparently in Metz, were some continental saints who were thought to be of Irish origin.[86] It is not altogether surprising, therefore, that at least nine purely Irish feasts should also have been added to the martyrology.[87]

May: 10 *In Hybernia, natalis sancti Comgalli abbatis et confessoris.* 16 *In Hybernia insula, natalis Brendani.*

June: 3 *In Hybernia, natalis sancti Coemgini abbatis et confessoris.* 9 (added to the feast of Columba, which is already in Ado) *et Boethini succesoris eius.* 25 *In Scocia, natalis sancti Lugudi abbatis et confessoris.*

August: 10 *Et in Scotia, sancti Blani, abbatis.*

81 The particular interest in Quirinus is corroborated at 30 Apr., where a notice of the saint's martyrdom was added to the text.   82 The alternative feast of the dedication of Gross St Martin's on 1 May, which is preserved in the church's memorial book of 1316, must have related to a later building; see C. Kosch, *Kölns Romanische Kirchen: Architektur und Liturgie im Hochmittelalter* (Regensburg, 2000), p. 81.   83 Zilliken, 'Der Kölner Festkalender', p. 62.   84 Ibid., 114–5.   85 See above at p. 62.   86 Perceived links with Ireland or Iona may also explain the presence in both the Christ Church and Lund texts of the two Northumbrian saints, Bede (26 May) and Oswald (5 August). The presence of Botulf (17 June) of Ikanho may be due to the practice of presenting him iconographically in Benedictine garb. Finally, Olaf (29 July) of Norway, who died in battle in 1030, may have been introduced to each text separately.   87 Six Irish feasts are in Lund only, viz. Tigernach (4 April), Máel Dóid (13 May), Cairnech (16 May), Tigernach (16 May), Ciarán

September: 4 *Et in Hibernia, sancti Ultani, episcopi et confessoris.* 25 *Et in Hibernia, sancti episcopi et confessoris Barri.*

December: 12 *Et in Hibernia, sancti Finniani, episcopi et confessoris.*

Some of these were no doubt added in Metz. For example, Lugaid of Lismore and Blaan of Dunblane may owe their inclusion to the known Scottish element among the Irish of Metz, which, while principally exemplified by Cathróe, may also have involved others.[88] Metz interest in Comgall of Bangor is otherwise shown by a marginal addition to the Metz copy of the Hieronymian Martyrology, now Bern Stadtbibliothek 289.[89] For the rest, the additions are just as likely to have been made in Cologne. Certainly, the presence in the Lund martyrology of the feast of Máel Dóid of Muckno in modern County Monaghan can scarcely be unconnected with the Irish background of Elias (Irish Ailill), abbot of Gross St Martin and, after 1019, of St Pantaleon. As is shown by his obit in the Annals of Ulster, Ailill had previously belonged to the church of Muckno.[90]

THE CHRIST CHURCH LIST OF RELICS

Internal textual evidence shows, then, that the Cologne exemplar of the Christ Church martyrology must have been kept at the Irish Benedictine house of St Pantaleon in the first quarter or so of the eleventh century. The significance of this finding is enhanced by the fact that it fits very neatly into a scenario recently put forward by Raghnall Ó Floinn to explain the composition of the list of relics which Christ Church claims to have held.[91] The list was twice copied into the composite Trinity College manuscript 576, first as an entry contained in the martyrology itself (31 July), then, separately, as a preamble to the later section of the manuscript containing a Book of Obits. The relevant part of the 31 July entry reads:

> *Reliquie sanctorum, que a tempore Donati, primi Dublinie ciuitatis episcopi, usque ad tempus Gregorii eiusdem urbis episcopi, in quadam capsa latuerunt, in uno cum ... capsa posite sunt scrinio; scilicet ... De baculo sancti Petri, et de cathena eius ... De reliquiis undecim milium sanctarum uirginum. De reliquiis sancte Pinnose, uirginis et martiris ... et de reliquiis sancti Benedicti ... De uestimento Herberti, Coloniensis episcopi ...*

(9 September), Adamnán (23 September).   **88** See Dumville, 'St Cathróe of Metz'. **89** The other saints were Patrick and Brigit. See *Acta sanctorum*, Novembris II/1, p. [x]. **90** S. Mac Airt and G. Mac Niocaill (eds), *The Annals of Ulster (to A.D. 1131)* (Dublin, 1983), s.a. 1042 [henceforth AU].   **91** R. Ó Floinn, 'The foundation relics of Christ Church cathedral, Dublin', in D. Bracken, J. Hawkes, P.S. Hellmuth, D. Ó Riain-Raedel

Having drawn attention to the presence of a number of relics clearly relating to Cologne, including not only a piece of Archbishop Heribert's clothing but also (pieces of) the staff and chains of St Peter, relics of the 11,000 virgins, and relics of Pinnosa, one of the few virgins known by name, amounting to at least five of the eighteen relics listed, Ó Floinn concluded that the collection of relics originated in Cologne. Furthermore, relying on the claim in the list itself that the relics had been in Christ Church since the time of the first bishop of Dublin, Donatus (Irish Dúnán, † 1074), who had already acceded to the see in 1028,[92] Ó Floinn further argued that the relics are likely to have been procured in the first place in order to mark the foundation of the cathedral church of Christ Church, which is dated to about 1030.[93] A pilgrimage to Rome undertaken in 1028 by the putative founder of the church, Dublin's Hiberno-Norse king, Sitriuc III (Silkbeard), in the company of Flannacán Ua Cellaig, king of Brega (now roughly Counties Meath and North Dublin), would have provided the opportunity of travelling to (or from) the Eternal City via Cologne, or *Sancta Colonia*, as it was then known.[94] Accommodation in the city would naturally have been sought and received from either St Pantaleon or Gross St Martin or from both. Procurement of the relics and martyrology from a centre then renowned for its collection of relics would have been regarded as a most natural and fitting means of marking the beginnings of Dublin's cathedral church. Moreover, Ó Floinn's novel but, in the circumstances, natural suggestion that Dublin's first bishop is likely to have previously been a member of one or other of the Irish Benedictine communities in Cologne, before returning with Sitriuc, is worthy of consideration.[95] At the very least, one can imagine Donatus's presence in Cologne in the company of Sitriuc when both relics and martyrology were no doubt ceremoniously and solemnly handed over.

The various other strands of the case made by Ó Floinn do not concern us here. Suffice it to state that the internal evidence of the Christ Church

(eds), *Peregrinatio: pilgrimage in the medieval world* (Dublin, forthcoming). Ó Floinn's findings were originally announced at a conference on pilgrimage held in University College Cork in 2000.   **92** For Donatus, see A. Gwynn, 'The first bishops of Dublin', in H. Clarke (ed.), *Medieval Dublin: the living city* (Dublin, 1990), 37–61; at 37–40; Clarke, 'Conversion, church and cathedral', 38–40.   **93** Traditionally dated to 1038, the year of the foundation was revised backwards by A. Gwynn, 'The origins of the see of Dublin', in G. O'Brien (ed.), *The Irish church in the eleventh and twelfth centuries* (Dublin, 1992), 50–67; at 58–67 (originally published in *Irish Ecclesiastical Record*, 57 (1941), 40–55, 97–112). Cf. Clarke, 'Conversion, church and cathedral', p. 35.   **94** For Sitriuc's pilgrimage to Rome, see AU s.a. 1028.   **95** His name would indicate a possible connexion, perhaps as eponym, with the ecclesiastical family of Uí Dúnáin, which was based at Tuilén (Dulane) in Brega. It is unlikely to be a coincidence, therefore, that Cairnech, patron of the church of Dulane, is among the Irish saints now present in the Lund martyrology. For the Uí Dúnáin, see D. Ó Corráin, 'Mael Muire Ua Dúnáin (1040–1117), reformer', in P. de Brún, S. Ó Coileáin, P. Ó Riain (eds), *Folia Gadelica: essays presented by former students to R.A. Breatnach* (Cork, 1983), 47–53.

martyrology bears out his interpretation of the relic list as evidence of a close relationship between a church in Cologne, very probably that of St Pantaleon, and Christ Church. Indeed, it would appear permissible to conclude that the relics, accompanied by a copy of the Martyrology of Ado, arrived in Christ Church in the year 1028, perhaps on 31 July, unless this was the day of their re-enshrinement by Donatus's successor, Gregory.[96]

In addition to relics and martyrology, some architectural ideas may also have been brought back to Dublin from Cologne. Tadhg O'Keeffe notes the similarity between the treatment of polygonal apses in Lotharingian churches, in association with square or near square transepts, and the pre-Norman architecture of the Christ Church crypt. Citing the example of similarly constructed *Langchorkrypten* and *Querschiffkrypten* in Cologne, O'Keeffe concludes that 'if one were to slip an unmarked and un-notated plan of the Christ Church crypt into a folder of 11th-century Lotharingian crypt plans, it might not leap out immediately as an Irish interloper'.[97]

CIRCULATION OF THE CHRIST CHURCH MARTYROLOGY IN IRELAND

Whether or not the architecture of the Christ Church crypt can be put down to German influence, the textual evidence presented here would place the arrival of a copy of Ado in Dublin, from Cologne, in the early part of the eleventh century. However, there is no textual evidence to show that the value of its presence in Christ Church was fully realized, either in Dublin or elsewhere in Ireland, for well over a century afterwards. Certainly, as we saw above, no local additions were made to the text until after 1150, when there was a re-awakening here to the need for liturgical renewal. Indeed, once in Dublin, the martyrology would appear to have been laid aside for well over a hundred years – together with the Cologne relics – before being taken out at the beginning of the second half of the twelfth century, dusted down and – while also being used as a source of entries by a new generation of Irish martyrologists – brought up to date and refurbished through the addition of entries reflective of the position and newly found affiliations of Christ Church.

When is this new awakening to the value of the text in their possession likely to have affected the community of Christ Church? The answer to this may well lie in the martyrology itself and, more particularly, in that part of the list of Christ Church relics at 31 July that concerns the Hiberno-Norse prelate, Gregory (Irish Gréne, † 1161).[98] Although Gregory's appointment to

---

96 An entry concerned with relics may already have been on this day in the Cologne exemplar. The Lund martyrology refers, albeit in a marginal addition, to the feast of relics in two Lund churches on 31 July.   97 T. O'Keeffe, *Romanesque Ireland: architecture and ideology in the twelfth century* (Dublin, 2003), at p. 101.   98 See above at p. 67.

the see of Dublin had originally reflected local opposition to the diocesan and metropolitan arrangements agreed in 1111 at the synod of Ráith Bressail, by 1152, when he received the *pallium* of the newly created archdiocese, the bishop had clearly come to terms with the post-Ráith Bressail arrangements.[99] By having the effect of breaking the connexion of Dublin with Canterbury,[100] this development was clearly a watershed in the history of the diocese. Moreover, although at this stage an old man, Gregory's stated concern with re-enshrinement of the cathedral's relics, together with the box or casket (*quadam capsa*) in which they had lain since the time of Donatus, shows that he was very much affected by, and party to, the then mounting awareness of the need for liturgical reform. Although no date is mentioned for the translation of the relics, its circumstances would indicate that some of the measures 'enjoining rule and good conduct' on the Irish Church that were promulgated at the synod of Clane in 1162,[101] had already been the subject of discussion ten years earlier at Kells-Mellifont.

Be this as it may, there is external evidence to support the view that Gregory was also responsible for rescuing the martyrology from the relative obscurity in which it had lain, and initiating a process that brought it to much wider attention. The several new or 'revised' martyrologies that were produced in Ireland in the period between 1150 and 1180 show signs of having drawn on a copy of Ado's work. The earliest example of this process are the notes and other interpolations added by Áed Mac Crimthainn to the Book of Leinster version of the Martyrology of Tallaght some time after 1150.[102] By comparison with his later contemporaries who drew much more heavily on external sources, Áed's use for his copy of Ado was very limited. However, there are a few indications to show that he was using the Christ Church copy. For example, among seven additions for December/January is the description of Maurus (15 January) as *discipulus Benedicti* which, although present in the Christ Church text, is not in Ado. The fact that this entry caught the attention of the commentator on the Martyrology of Óengus at Armagh between 1170 and 1174 would suggest that he, too, was drawing on the Christ Church text, and this is confirmed by a misplacement of the feast of Marius and Martha, common to Christ Church and the Commentary at 19 January, as against Ado's 20 January.[103] Indeed, although hitherto misunderstood in this matter by both John Hennig and myself, the Commentator may have explicitly drawn the attention of his readers to precisely this dependence on the Christ Church text in his entry for 19 January, as well as on no fewer than nine other

---

99 MacShamhráin, 'Emergence of the metropolitan see', 51–5.   **100** F.J. Byrne, 'Bishops, 1111–1534', in T.W. Moody, F.X. Martin, F.J. Byrne (eds), *A new history of Ireland* (Oxford, 1984), IX, 264–332; at p. 311.   **101** B. Mac Carthy (ed.), *Annála Uladh: Annals of Ulster* (Dublin, 1893), II, s.a. 1162 [henceforth AU].   **102** Ó Riain, 'A Northumbrian phase', 325–6.   **103** Stokes, *Félire Oengusso*, 42, 48. For a discussion of the entry, see Hennig, 'The sources of the martyrological tradition', p. 419.

occasions, by describing his source as the (Roman) martyrology of a certain Gregorius.[104] No pope of the name is known to have been concerned with a revision of the 'Roman' martyrology, prior to Gregory XIII, whose floruit (1572–85) is much too late for consideration here. Therefore, it would now seem that the person intended was none other than Gregory, archbishop of Dublin, who, having 'rediscovered' the text, would have been responsible for bringing it to the attention of other churches, most notably Armagh. There, it (or a copy) would have been used both by the Commentator on Óengus and, much more extensively, by the compiler of the Martyrology of Drummond which, as I have already stated, drew on a Christ Church-type text for the vast majority of its non-Irish saints.[105]

Although this would raise the question as to how they found their way back into the Christ Church text, some 'improvements' to the martyrology may also have been made at Armagh, which was accorded a form of imprimatur over the work of all other Irish schools at the synod of Clane in 1162.[106] The lively interest of the Christ Church text in St Patrick is exemplified by use of the title *archiepiscopus Scottorum* at 17 March. This is followed by a long commentary, now only in this text, together with an extensive note on Patrick's follower, Secundinus, at 27 November which bear the hallmarks of rewriting at Armagh, most likely in the Augustinian house of SS Peter and Paul. Indeed, the use of the title *archiepiscopus Scottorum* reflects, or antici-pates, the re-affirmation at the synod of Clane in 1162 of the orders of 'archbishop of Ireland' to the successor of St Patrick.

Examination of the Martyrology of Gorman confirms the view that the Christ Church text was then circulating in southeast Ulster. Although mainly relying on a copy of Usuard for its non-Irish saints, Gorman occasionally also used Ado. Moreover, as both Hennig and Dubois have previously noted,[107] a number of entries relating to Metz were drawn by Gorman from a copy of Ado, which, although neither scholar was aware of it, was obviously the Christ Church text.[108] In sum, therefore, the indications are that the version of Ado in circulation in Ireland in the period 1150–1180 was the text that had arrived in Christ Church from Cologne shortly before 1030.

CONCLUSION

The reception of Ado in Ireland, then, seems to have turned on the quite fascinating fortunes of a single copy. Originating, as far as one can judge,

---

104 Ó Riain, 'Die Bibliothek des Verfassers', 93–6; J. Hennig, 'The notes on non-Irish saints in the manuscripts of *Félire Oengusso*', in *RIA Proc.*, 75C (1975), 119–60; at p. 125. 105 Ó Riain, *Four Irish martyrologies*, 16–22. 106 AU s.a. 1162. Cf. Ó Riain, 'Die Bibliothek des Verfassers', 93–6. 107 J. Dubois, 'Les sources continentales du martyrologe irlandais de Gorman', in *Analecta Bollandiana*, 100 (1982), 607–17; at p. 614; Hennig, 'Sources of the martyrological tradition', 422–3. 108 Ó Riain, 'Das Martyrologium der Kölner Klöster'.

about the year 1000 in a foundation under Irish control in the city of Metz, either St-Félix (alias St Clémens) or St-Symphorien, a copy of the text first passed to Cologne, where it remained, apparently at the monastery of St Pantaleon, which had well-attested Irish associations, until 1028. It was then presented, in the original or in a copy, to the Hiberno-Norse royal pilgrim, Sitriuc Silkbeard, together with a satchel-full of relics, for placement in the cathedral church which the king was about to found back in Dublin. There it lay, probably together with the Cologne relics, for well over a hundred years, until after 1150, when it again attracted the attention of reform-minded clerics. At that point, it went into circulation as a source for the several new martyrologies then being written. In the process, the Christ Church text received a new layer of additions, either in Dublin, or at Armagh, or in both centres. Finally, about the middle of the thirteenth century, it was recopied in the form in which it now survives, subject to a few additions made between 1253 or so and the reformation which took effect in Christ Church only very gradually after the middle of the sixteenth century.

As to the claim that this is Dublin's oldest known book, I have been unable to discover evidence for any earlier one. Sitriuc's father had already converted to Christianity, and literacy among the Hiberno-Norse of Dublin is, of course, already attested in crude inscriptions on coins, the earliest of which dates, appropriately enough, to Sitriuc's reign.[109] To this in itself impressive feather in Sitriuc's cap may now be added a second, the distinction of having brought its first known book to Dublin, a German copy of the Martyrology of Ado, to mark the opening chapter of the diocesan history of Ireland's capital city.

ACKNOWLEDGEMENTS

I am indebted to my colleagues, Drs Diarmuid Ó Murchadha and Kevin Murray, for having read and commented on this paper. I am also indebted to Professor John McCulloh, Kansas State University, for having drawn my attention to the Lund martyrology.

109 W. O'Sullivan, *The earliest Irish coinage* (Dublin, 1961), p. 2.

Excavations at Longford Street Little, Dublin: an archaeological approach to Dubh Linn

JOHN Ó NÉILL

INTRODUCTION

The excavations at Longford Street Little lie within the putative enclosure around the church of St Peter and the church of St Stephen, to the southeast of the medieval town of Dublin. The site of the excavation is bounded to the south by Longford Street Little, and backs onto properties that front onto Digges Lane (to the east), Stephen Street Lower (to the north) and Aungier Street (to the west). A small alleyway, Dawson Court, provides access to the site from Stephen Street Lower. Around the same time as the Longford Street Little excavation, five test trenches were also opened on the area adjoining the site and fronting onto Digges Lane (see fig. 1).

A preliminary phase of testing was undertaken by the author for Margaret Gowen & Co. Ltd in April 2000 in response to a proposal by the Salvation Army to build a hostel on the site. This was followed by full excavation in February and March 2001. The Longford Street Little excavation was undertaken by the author along with Simon Dick, Nuala Hiney, Peter Kearns, Kara Ward, Chris Dempsey, Georg Schilcher, Robbie McPherson, Dotre Danner Lund, Esteban Hernández and Rosaline Hainsworth. The following paper outlines the results of the excavation at Longford Street Little in the context of wider issues associated with archaeological approaches to early phases of settlement at medieval Dublin. In particular, the issues of the ecclesiastical enclosure around St Peter's and the possibility of identifying pre-Norse settlement are discussed.

BACKGROUND

The identification of an ecclesiastical enclosure within the modern streetscape and the general historical and archaeological background to the area have been rehearsed previously in *Medieval Dublin* and do not need to be restated in full here (Simpson 2000; Coughlan 2003). References to Dublin, or *Dubh Linn*, prior to the first Viking raids, are confined to two annalistic entries. The Annals of the Four Master make reference to a St Bearaidh, abbot of Dubh Linn, who died in 650 (O'Donovan 1851, 265), while the death of another

73

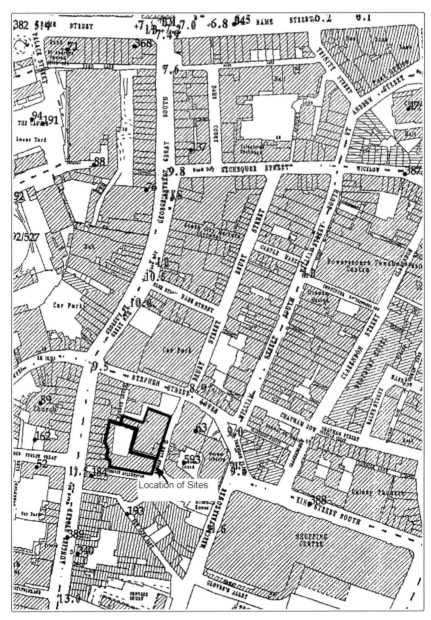

1 Location map showing the boundaries of the area of excavation at Longford Street, with the main excavated area in white, Digges Lane site also shown.

abbot, Siadal, is recorded in 790 in the Annals of Ulster (Mac Airt and Mac Niocaill 1983, 247). It is believed that Vikings occupied the *Dubh Linn* enclosure in setting up their *longphort* or ship-enclosure in 841 (Clarke 2000, 31).

Since the observation of a 'rath-like' street pattern on the southeastern side of the tidal pool (i.e. the *Dubh Linn*) by Myles V. Ronan in 1940 (Ronan 1940, 482), there has been a growing belief that the modern streetscape is merely a fossilization of earlier landscape units (e.g., Clarke 1977). The location of St Peter's church can be identified from a series of maps from the seventeenth century and later and lies at the apex of the reputed enclosure where it is closest to the pool. The exact location of the church is unclear, but the churchyard was partly subsumed by a new theatre designed by Sir Edward Lovett Pearce, facing onto Longford Street, and opened in 1733 (e.g., Stockwell 1938, 65). A triangular plot beside a small east-west building lies behind this theatre on Rocque's map of 1756 and is indicated as a graveyard on subsequent maps by the Ordnance Survey and appears to be the site of the medieval church. An account of the Convent of Discalced Carmelites in *An historical guide to the city of Dublin* (Wright 1825) states that '... the friars of this order performed divine service in a small inconvenient building behind the houses on the south side of Stephen-street, near Aungier-street', suggesting that a building on the site of St Peter's may have even continued in use until the early nineteenth century. Of the churches south of the Liffey that can be located today, only Christ Church (founded *c.*1030) pre-dates 1121, when St Peter's and a number of other churches first appear in the documentary record, in a poem in the Book of Uí Maine (Macalister 1942).

Archaeological excavations within this enclosure include four separate areas, listed in the synthesis of previous research in *Medieval Dublin I* as site-numbers 16, 16A, 25 and 38 (Simpson 2000, 67–8) and totaling some seventeen individual excavations. Since the publication of that article, further testing and excavations within the enclosure have been undertaken by the author (for Margaret Gowen Ltd), Nóra Bermingham (for IAC Ltd: see Bermingham 2001), James Eogan (for ADS Ltd: see Eogan 2001), Audrey Gahan (for ADS Ltd: see Gahan 2001), Melanie McQuade (for Margaret Gowen Ltd: see McQuade forthcoming), Franc Myles (for Margaret Gowen Ltd: see Myles forthcoming) and Dermot Nelis and Tim Coughlan (for IAC Ltd: see Coughlan 2003). To date, all archaeological work within this area has been focused on properties which are the subject of development proposals. The excavations at Longford Street Great (Coughlan 2003), which also took place in 2001, and the Longford Street Little excavations presented a fresh opportunity to examine areas with the potential to shed light on this issue.

THE EXCAVATION: LONGFORD STREET LITTLE

The initial testing of the site had revealed one main area, to the north of the property, where archaeological deposits were likely to be disturbed during construction. Cellars had removed the archaeological deposits along the

Plate 1 Pre-Norman ditch during excavation.

Longford Street Little frontage. Excavation revealed a series of phases of activity on the site. The detailed phasing, with a complete outline of the stratigraphic relationships, is included in the report submitted following the excavation (Ó Néill 2001). For the purposes of this paper (and ease of understanding), this information is presented as a series of phases of occupation.

The earliest is possibly pre-Norman in date, and is characterised by a curving, stepped ditch. The next phase represents episodes of activity following the Anglo-Norman occupation, when a new north–south boundary was introduced to the site in the late twelfth century. This layout of the site continues to the mid-fifteenth century, by which time the suburbs of medieval Dublin were in decline, and is only replaced during Aungier's redevelopment of the area in the 1660s (see Burke 1972).

Pre-Norman

Stratigraphically, the earliest feature identified during excavation was a ditch (F130), which was only identified in the northeast corner of the site (plate 1) and could be traced for some 6–7m, curving beyond the eastern boundary of the excavation and below the Bakery on Digges Lane (see fig. 2). The subsequent testing on the Digges Lane site revealed that the ditch continued into that site. Basements along the Longford Street Little frontage had removed all

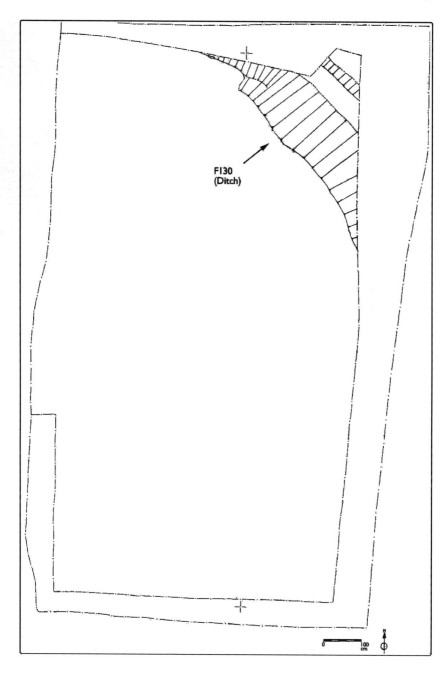

2 Plan of the pre-Norman Ditch.

Plate 2 Traces of thirteenth century bank and surface during excavation.

traces at this location. Due to the proximity of the ditch to the adjoining
buildings, the base of the ditch was not uncovered. The width of the ditch was
not exposed in Longford Street Little, but was identified as 6m wide in the assessment at Digges Lane. The lowest recorded level was at 7.81m OD, with the
ditch having been cut from around 9.60m, giving a minimum depth of 1.79m.
Animal bone and a curved roof tile in the DCTT fabric (Wren 2001) were recovered from the silty clay fill of the ditch. The roof tile is likely to be of eleventh-
century date. No other features could be clearly identified with the ditch.

Late twelfth to thirteenth century
After the ditch had become completely backfilled, a further episode of activity
was evidenced by a wall slot, bank and stone surface (see plate 2 and fig. 3).
These features overlay the silty clay which filled the whole of the pre-Norman
ditch. The rough stone surface rested directly on the natural clays and was
identified across an area measuring 13m (north-south) by 7.5m (east-west). A
number of later features had disturbed this stone surface, which also appears
to have been churned up during use. At the southern end of the site where the
stones were less compact, the surface appears to have been exposed for longer
and was contaminated with later finds including sherds of Dublin-type wares,

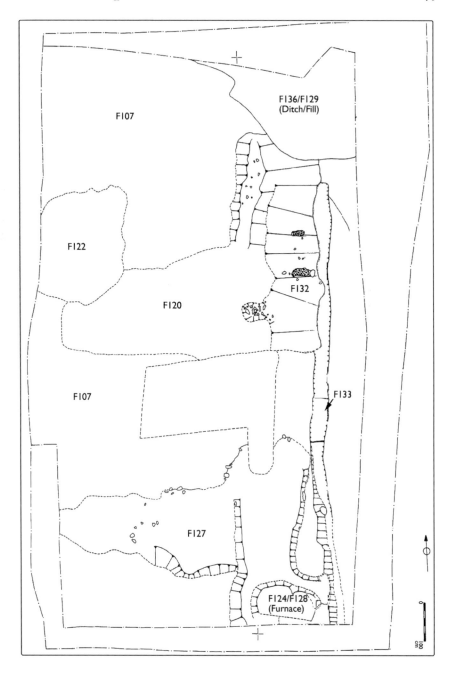

3 Plan of features dating to the late-twelfth, thirteenth and fourteenth century.

Saintonge, Sgraffito and clay pipe fragments. Finds at the more compact northern end included a glass bead, and a heavily corroded coin which was not identifiable after conservation. Medieval pottery from the excavation included Minety-type, Ham Green B, Leinster Cooking Ware, various Dublin-type wares and Saintonge, producing a very mixed picture (McCutcheon 2001).

A north-south boundary was established close to the eastern side of the site during this phase. Initially an 11m slot (F133) was opened at the eastern limits of the stone surface F109/F110. This slot was around 0.40m wide and 0.20–0.30m deep, with a possible gap around 5.4m from the northern end. This feature was initially opened as a trench intended to contain a fence line or hedge, although no evidence of posts or timbers was identified in the fill, other than a single nail. This property boundary does not follow the orientation of the pre-Norman ditch. After the slot went out of use, its components either decayed, or were deliberately removed, since no shadow remained in the fill (F134) on excavation. A layer of silt (F135), similar to that which filled the ditch (F130), sealed the top of the slot, suggesting a short period of disuse. A small number of sherds of Dublin-type wares (McCutcheon 2001) were recovered from the fill of this slot, suggesting a late twelfth- to mid-thirteenth-century date.

A bank of compact clay (F120/F127) was constructed on a north-south alignment placed onto the earlier stone surface F109/F110. This bank slightly overlay the wall slot (F133) and the layer of silt (F135), although it was unclear if they had been constructed as a unit or sequentially, with the bank replacing the wall slot. This bank was not continuous and the separate components (F120 and F127) did not join up. The northern section was present for some 4.20m, and was 2.60m in width. The bank rested directly on the infill of the ditch (F131) as well as the stone surface F109/110, and survived to a height of 0.30m, or to around 9.82m OD. At its southern limit, the bank turned to the west and tapered off towards the western limit of the site.

At the southern end of the site, a similar bank (F127) was present for some 4m, and was at least 2.60m in width. At this end of the site it survived to a height of around 0.25m, or 9.84m OD. At its northern end, the bank turned to the west and tapered off towards the west, similar to the northern section of the bank, forming a 2.50m-wide gap between the two, which was present for up to 4m. This suggests that some form of entranceway existed between the two banks, at the same location as the earlier gap in the wall slot (F133). There was much disturbance in this area. Some sherds of Dublin-type wares were recovered from the banks, along with a floor tile and some glass, which may be intrusive.

Thirteenth and fourteenth centuries

A series of features was identified as post-dating F120 and/or F127. These included the remains of some form of furnace F124/F128 (plate 3), a deposit of silty clay quite similar to floor material (F122), and a number of possible postholes represented by voids (F132) or traces of charcoal overlying the

Plate 3 Thirteenth- or fourteenth-century furnace.

north bank (F127). A ditch (F136) was opened on roughly the same alignment as the earlier ditch, but extending east/west rather than curving towards the south. This ditch truncated F127 and was roughly perpendicular to the line of the banks. At the northern end of the site, a new ditch was opened, on an east/west alignment and in the same place as the earlier ditch, F130. The portion that was within the area of the excavation indicated that this ditch was U-shaped and measured 1.50m across at the top, and was around 1.00m deep (i.e., from around 9.30m OD to 8.30m OD).

The remains of a furnace were found at the southern end of the site, dug into the bank F127. This was roughly hourglass-shaped, although the southern side was not fully exposed. The furnace was around 1.44m in length, between 0.80m and 0.45m in width and 0.25m in depth. A rough lining of grey-green clay was present around the edges and two voids identified at the western end may have originally contained stakes. The inner fill of the furnace contained no charcoal and only traces of a metallic residue, suggesting that the whole furnace had been emptied on its last use. An irregularly shaped piece of slate with a drilled hole in the centre was recovered from the fill. This may have functioned with a tuyére as part of the furnace. A sherd of Dublin-type ware and a line-impressed floor tile were also recovered from the fill, suggesting a late thirteenth- or fourteenth-century date.

Plate 4 Medieval lintelled drain.

A deposit of silty green clay was found over an area of 2.60m (north/south) by 1.60m (east/west) and extending beneath the western limits of the site. It partially covered the western tail of the northern bank (F120). There was no evidence for an enclosing feature or any other clear indication of the origin of this feature, although it did clearly resemble a floor deposit. A single sherd of Dublin-type ware was recovered and the feature was completely sealed by the clay deposit F107.

Fourteenth century to late seventeenth century
The later ditch was allowed to silt up with a deposit of clayey soil (F129), which began forming across the whole site (F107). Some fragments of Dublin-type wares, Saintonge green glazed wares, Ham Green wares and medieval floor tile were recovered from the ditch suggesting that this happened in the thirteenth or fourteenth centuries. A stone-lined and lintelled drain (F119) was constructed through the garden soil (F107) that had begun to develop (see plate 4). This drain was subsequently dismantled and became backfilled by F107, the garden soil deposit continued forming, and then sealed the medieval activity on the site. This was disturbed during the seventeenth-century activity on the site and there was some contamination of F107 with later finds. Medieval artefacts recovered from F107 included Dublin-type wares, Saintonge, floor tiles, copper alloys and other finds. At least one fragment of a human femur was recovered from this level (information from Laureen Buckley), although no burials were identified anywhere on the site in the course of excavation.

The drain was constructed to the east of the bank (F120/F127), which would have still been clearly visible on the site. The drain was traced for the whole length of the site, some 14m (north/south) and measured around 0.20m in width (internally). It was around 0.25m in height, from the base lining to the top of the lintels. The base dropped from 9.40m OD at the southern end to 8.95m OD at the northern end. The drain was constructed of drystone walls of limestone cobbles, pushed into the sides of an earth-dug trench (around 0.50m in width). Limestone flagstones were used to line the base and as lintels, some of which survived intact. A fragment of a moulded mullion was used as part of the side wall of the drain. This piece of window tracery, with roll and fillet mouldings and a hollow chamfer, was carved from a hard, fossiliferous limestone and retained some traces of limewash on the worked surfaces. This is probably fifteenth-century in date (information courtesy of Dr Rachel Moss) and may have emanated from a building in the area.

The drain was deliberately dismantled, as the majority of the lintels had been removed and the clay soil (F107) had penetrated the drain. Line-impressed floor tiles, Saintonge and Dublin-type wares suggest a possible early fifteenth-century date for the period of use of the drain. Floor tiles in the DT3 Fabric include motif numbers L20 (4-tile cusped circular band enclosing foliage) and

L43 (Double Quatrefoil in a circle). This fabric has been dated to the late fourteenth and fifteenth centuries (Wren 2001).

By the time of Speed's map of Dublin (1610) a single boundary is indicated between St Stephen's and St Peter's, probably corresponding to Digges Lane.

Late seventeenth century and later
The acquisition and development of the site by Francis Aungier in the 1660s is evidenced by the introduction of a series of properties fronting onto Angier Street and orientated east/west. At least one pit and a number of wall footings could be dated to this period. Further evidence of the late seventeenth-century and early eighteenth-century development of the area was recorded during excavation. A considerable quantity of post-medieval pottery was recovered. Notable finds included a Frechen mug with a stamped medallion containing the mark of Pieter van der Ancker and a porcelain tea bowl of the Ming Emperor Chenghua (1465–87) which is probably a fake (McCutcheon 2001).

DISCUSSION

The excavated evidence from the Longford Street Little site is unremarkable in itself. Taken in the context of its location, to the southeast of the Poddle tidal pool from which the modern city takes its name, it highlights a number of relevant issues. These are discussed below.

The putative ecclesiastical enclosure around St Peter's
As indicated in Coughlan's paper (2003, fig. 5), the ditches identified during the two 2001 excavations may be associated with an enclosure of twelfth-century date (or earlier). The orientation of the earlier ditch at Longford Street Little and Digges Lane suggests that it curves inside the line of Stephen Street to the north and the angled turn of Digges Lane, to the south (for the historical maps of Dublin, see Clarke 2002). The northern portion of the latter street may be the boundary between St Peter's and St Stephen's as shown on Speed (1610). If St Peter's was surrounded by a ditched enclosure, it is not difficult to place the laneway, which is now Digges Lane, outside this enclosure. The excavations on the opposite side of Digges Lane produced no evidence of occupation earlier than the late twelfth or early thirteenth century (Buckley and Hayden 2002).

If we take Rocque's map of 1756 as an accurate base map for the street pattern in the eighteenth century (fig. 4), it can be argued that the angled section of Goat Alley (now Digges Lane), immediately north of its junction with Beaux (Bow) Lane, would have allowed Goat Alley to continue on a line to intercept White Friars Lane. The latter is named as White Friars Alley on de Gomme's map of 1673. Entries in the parish register for years such as 1670

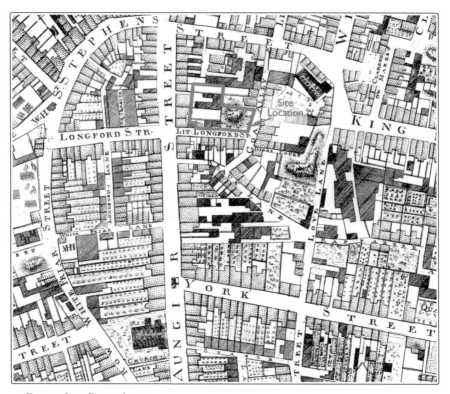

4 Extract from Rocque's map.

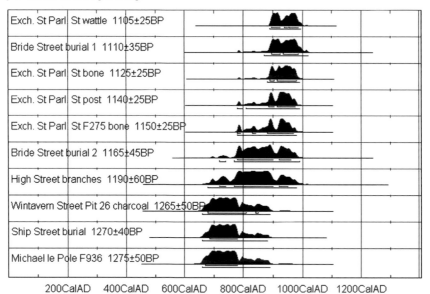

Exch. St Parl St wattle 1105±25BP						
Bride Street burial 1 1110±35BP						
Exch. St Parl St bone 1125±25BP						
Exch. St Parl St post 1140±25BP						
Exch. St Parl St F275 bone 1150±25BP						
Bride Street burial 2 1165±45BP						
High Street branches 1190±60BP						
Wintavern Street Pit 26 charcoal 1265±50BP						
Ship Street burial 1270±40BP						
Michael le Pole F936 1275±50BP						
200CalAD	400CalAD	600CalAD	800CalAD	1000CalAD	1200CalAD

Calibrated date

5 Selection of radiocarbon dates from Dublin (various sources).

include addresses at streets such as Bow(e) Lane (e.g., Mills 1911, 14) that are not shown on de Gomme. Phillips's survey of Dublin from 1685 shows a street where Digges Lane should be, but does not indicate Bow Lane. Brooking's *Map of the city and suburbs of Dublin* (1728) does show Bow Lane (as Elbow Lane), but indicates that Longford Street Little was intended to continue to King Street (this is also shown on Phillips's 1685 map and survives as a cul-de-sac entered off Digges Lane in Campbell's map of 1811).

The Aungier Street development seems to have led to the establishment of plots perpendicular to the frontage, with the added need for changes to the street grid. The peculiar orientation of the street layout to the east of Aungier Street would suggest that it was superimposed on more organic, earlier land divisions and, possibly, laneways. Locational references to streets and roads are scarce in the thirteenth and later centuries and almost non-existent before that date.

Archaeological approaches to Dubh Linn
The character and location of the pre-Viking settlement of Dublin should be of great importance to our understanding of the interaction of the Gaelic and Norse communities and the development of the urban centre. The substance of archaeological discussions of this issue is the neat division of the material record into 'Gaelic' and 'Norse' categories, based on comparative morphology and occasionally radiocarbon or other dating techniques. While this is largely unproblematic, it does preclude the existence of a middle ground reflecting contemporary ambiguities in identity and allegiance and, effectively, the coalescing of biological, cultural and political identities is largely taken as read. In the case of Coughlan's Longford Street excavations and those at Longford Street Little, no artefactual material was recovered that indicated a date for the enclosing ditch, other than suggesting a date in or before the twelfth century (see above). In reality, there are few common diagnostic finds that would have clearly indicated a significant date contemporary with the pre-Norse annalistic references rather than the aftermath of 841. The fact that the primary deposits could not be identified at Longford Street Little precluded a sensible dating programme, but highlighted the potential importance of applications such as radiocarbon dating.

The relevance of radiocarbon dating can be seen in the various burial traditions found in the vicinity of Dublin, including inhumation burials with grave goods, generally regarded as Norse, and inhumations in long cists and lintel graves, generally regarded as Gaelic. These two assertions of identity can be reinforced using radiocarbon dates such as at Ship Street which is regarded as Norse (Linzi Simpson, pers. comm.) and Bride Street and Michael le Pole which are not regarded as Norse (e.g., Gowen 2001; McMahon 2002). In effect, radiocarbon dating may become the primary tool for establishing more than the presence of pre-Viking settlement in Dublin. In historical periods it is often employed as a tool for differentiating various aspects of identity as seen through the excavated record. As a preliminary to future work in this area, it is appropriate to consider some of the problems and limitations of radiocarbon dating with specific reference to the issues under discussion.

Some problems in identifying pre-Viking settlement around Dublin
There is a growing corpus of dated samples from the excavations around Dublin city centre. Allied to the information recovered by archaeological excavation, the dates can be considered within the context provided by the documentary evidence for the development of the town. Unfortunately, the constraints of radiocarbon are considerable and, within the framework of the historical chronology of Dublin, it can be shown that only where optimal conditions apply will radiocarbon dating provide significant results. These constraints fall into two categories: samples and calibration. Recent work on examining the nature of samples submitted for radiocarbon dating has shown that the inaccuracy produced by certain categories of sample is greater than previously realised (Ashmore 1999). Since the dating technique measures the rate of decay since the death of an organic entity, the incorporation of more than one entity into the sample could inadvertently lead to an inaccurate result in the event of a chronological variation in the time of death of the entities. Thus, the dating of a human or animal bone can be considered as representing an estimation of the date of death of the individual from which the bone was obtained. The same assumption cannot be made for a date obtained from a number of bone fragments that cannot be demonstrated to come from a single individual. Similar problems exist for dates obtained from a number of pieces of charcoal, as opposed to a single piece of wood (and are compounded by the potential age variation in wood from a single tree, with the inner rings capable of being up to 200 years or more older than the outer rings). In light of these problems, dates obtained from more than one entity must be treated with extreme caution, if not discarded altogether.

The calibration of radiocarbon dating is the statistical apparatus by which a calendar date is estimated for the measured sample. Revision and analysis of this apparatus and developments in computer programming have led to increasingly useful analytical tools, such as the OxCal programme (Bronk-Ramsey 2000). In figure 6, a series of simulated dates is plotted. Each date-range is an estimation of the statistical range that would be provided by radiocarbon dating for a sample which died in the calendar year indicated in the left-hand column. Two calendar dates, the year 795 for the first Viking raids, and the year 841 for the Dublin *longphort*, demonstrate the problems with calibrated radiocarbon dates for Dublin. To produce a calibrated radiocarbon date that clearly precedes the Viking raids, a sample pre-dating 700 would be required. Similarly, pre-*longphort* activity would need to be at least mid-eighth century in date to produce a calibrated range that clearly precedes the *longphort*. Thus, to obtain a radiocarbon date that clearly predates 841 one would have to recover materials from settlement dating from the period 650–750, the century following the Annals of the Four Masters reference.

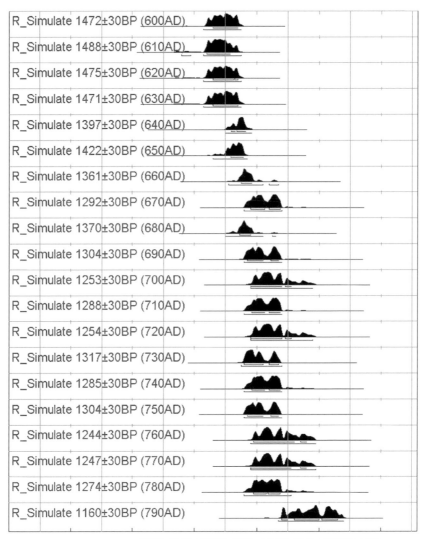

400CalAD 600CalAD 800CalAD 1000CalAD

6 Plot of simulated radiocarbon dates from 700 to 840.

CONCLUSIONS

So, where is Dubh Linn? The excavated evidence from Longford Street Little
suggests that an enclosing ditch was present and that it possibly relates to that
identified on Longford Street in 2002 (Coughlan 2003). There was no evidence

of the original date of the enclosure, although it can be demonstrated to pre-Norman.

Another potential candidate for the location of Dubh Linn, such as the site of the church of St Michael le Pole, has produced an early date (Gowen 2001; McMahon 2002). This date is a mixed charcoal sample that calibrates in the range 660–890 AD. The quality of this sample would no longer be considered as sufficient and it must be disregarded. This is not to dismiss St Michael le Pole as a candidate since the presence of an enclosure with a diameter of 100m to 200m has also been argued for this site (McMahon 2002, 82). An enclosed area of this size would be typical for an ecclesiastical site of some importance (e.g., Swan 1985, 97). This argument could equally be applied to the St Peter's enclosure since the area enclosed by the Longford Street and Longford Street Little ditches measures around 150m in diameter. On the basis of the toponymic '*le Pole*', St Michael le Pole would seem the more likely location.

The pre-841 community seems to have occupied a location along the southern side of the pool, the Dubh Linn. The earliest Norse settlement, on the other hand, seems to have been on the opposite, northern, side of the pool, although it was fairly unstructured until after 917 (Simpson 2000). The survival of the name *Dubh Linn* suggests that, in its earliest stages, the pool was the focus of the general settlement, with the Norse developing the opposite side of the Poddle to the existing Gaelic settlement. The tenth century town then shifted its attention towards the Liffey, with the subsequent development of a transpontine suburb in the eleventh century. This theory may be put to the test in future excavations.

REFERENCES

Ashmore, P.J. 1999 Radiocarbon dating: avoiding errors by avoiding mixed samples. *Antiquity* 73, 124–43.

Bermingham, N. 2001 Longford Street Little. In I. Bennett (ed.) *Excavations 2000*. No. 270.

Bronk-Ramsey, C. 2000 *OxCal Program v3.5*.

Buckley, L. and Hayden, A. 2002 In S. Duffy (ed.), *Medieval Dublin II*, 13–52. Dublin.

Burke, N. 1972 An early modern suburb: the estate of Francis Aungier, earl of Longford. *Irish Geography*, VI, no. 4; 365–385.

Clarke, H.B. 1977 The topographic development of early medieval Dublin. *RSAI Jn.* 109, 33–47.

—2000 Conversion, church and cathedral: the diocese of Dublin to 1152. In J. Kelly and D. Keogh (eds) *History of the Catholic diocese of Dublin*, 19–50. Dublin.

—2002 *Dublin part 1, to 1610*. Irish Historic Towns Atlas, no. 11. Dublin. Royal Irish Academy.

Coughlan 2003 Excavations at the medieval cemetery of St Peter's church, Dublin. In S. Duffy (ed.), *Medieval Dublin IV*, 11–39. Dublin.

Eogan, J. 2001 Mercer Street. In I. Bennett (ed.) *Excavations 2000*. No. 277.

Gahan, A. 2001 Mercer Street. In I. Bennett (ed) *Excavations 2000*. No. 276.

Gowen, M. 2001 Excavations at the site of the church and tower of St Michael le Pole. In S. Duffy (ed.), *Medieval Dublin II, 13–52*. Dublin.

Mac Airt, S. and Mac Niocaill G. 1983 *The Annals of Ulster (to A.D. 1131)*. Dublin.

Macalister, R. 1942 *The Book of Ui Maine, otherwise called the book of the O'Kellys. Facsimile*. Dublin.

McCutcheon, C. 2001 Medieval and post-medieval pottery from Longford Street Little. Unpublished report.

McMahon, M. 2002 Early medieval settlement and burial outside the enclosed town: evidence from archaeological excavations at Bride Street, Dublin. *RIA Proc.*, 102C, 67–135.

McQuade, M. *forthcoming* Bow Lane. In I. Bennett (ed.) *Excavations*.

Mills, J. 1911 *The register of the parish of St Peter and St Kevin, Dublin, 1669–1761*. Parish Register Society of Dublin, vol. IX. Exeter and London.

Myles, F. *forthcoming* Stephen Street Upper. In I. Bennett (ed.) *Excavations*.

O'Donovan, J. (ed) 1851 *Annala rioghachta Eireann: Annals of the kingdom of Ireland by the Four Masters from the earliest period to the year 1616*. 7 vols, Dublin.

Ó Néill, J. 2001 Excavations at Longford Street Little. Unpublished report submitted to the Heritage Service, Department of the Environment. Dublin.

Ronan, M.V. 1940 Lazar houses of St Lawrence and St Stephen in medieval Dublin. In J. Ryan (ed.) *Féilsgribhínn Eóin Mhic Néill*, 480–89. Dublin.

Simpson, L. 2000 Forty years a-digging. In S. Duffy (ed.) *Medieval Dublin I*, 11–68. Dublin.

Stockwell, L. 1938 *Dublin theatres and theatre custom, 1637–1820*. Kingsport, Tennesse.

Swan, L. 1985 Monastic proto-towns in early medieval Ireland: the evidence of aerial photography, plan analysis and survey. In H.B. Clarke and A. Simms (eds), *The comparative history of urban origins in non-Roman Europe*, 77–102. BAR Series 255i. Oxford.

Wren, J. 2001 Ceramic building materials from Longford Street Little. Unpublished report.

Wright, G. 1825 *An historical guide to the city of Dublin*. 2nd edn. London.

The excavation of pre-Norman burials and ditch near St Michan's church, Dublin

ROSANNE MEENAN

INTRODUCTION

Construction of new premises for the Bar Council of Ireland necessitated excavation of a site at the junction of Church Street and May Lane, Dublin 7. The excavations were carried out on behalf of Archaeological Development Services Ltd and were financed by the Bar Council of Ireland.

HISTORICAL BACKGROUND

The earliest known monument in this part of the early town is St Michan's church. The traditionally-quoted date for its foundation is *c.*1090. Tradition relates that St Michan may have been a Dublin Viking who converted to Christianity; the church was founded on land that, it has been suggested, may have been granted by Muirchertach Ua Briain (Bradley 1992, 50–1). St Michan's and the land on either side was held by the priory of Holy Trinity (Christ Church) in 1202 (Purcell 2003, 196–8). St Michan's was the only parish church serving the city on the north side of the Liffey until the end of the seventeenth century.

The bridge over the Liffey leading northwards from the developing town may possibly have been in position as early as 1014 although it is first mentioned only in 1112 (Bradley 1992, 51). The Slige Midluachra, the main road from Ulster, may have approached the crossing of the Liffey by way of Bow Street (Clarke 1990, 57–8). Church Street has been variously referred to as the 'Great Street', 'High Street', 'the King's Way', 'the Great Street of Oxmantown' and 'Oxmantown Street' and was certainly in existence in the thirteenth century (Clarke 2002, 13). By the fourteenth and fifteenth centuries it was the main thoroughfare from the north into the city. May Lane was previously known as Comynes' Lane first recorded in 1470 (Clarke 2002, 15). Robert Blancheville was granted Comyn's Lane provided that he built a gate at the end of it (Purcell 2003, 200).

The area north of St Michan's and west of Church Street appears to have been an area of craftworkers and merchants in the fourteenth and fifteenth centuries. The development of landownership here is discussed by Purcell in

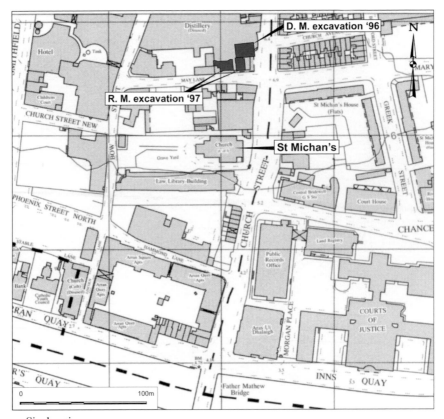

1 Site location map

a general history of Oxmantown (2003, 220–3). She traced ownership of the plot between St Michan's and May Lane; it came into the hands of the Barnewalls *c*.1498 who still owned it in 1576 (ibid., 221–2). Houses are marked along Church Street on John Rocque's map of 1756. There are, however, no houses marked on the May Lane frontage of the excavation area on Rocque's map. Buildings are marked on the May Lane frontage on the 6–inch first edition of the Ordnance Survey.

PREVIOUS EXCAVATION

The site was excavated in two phases. Declan Murtagh carried out the first phase in 1996. This was in the middle of the development site where evidence for the earliest activity, dated to the mid-late thirteenth century, was represented by a cobbled surface and stone-lined lime pit. A series of slightly later pits dated from the thirteenth-fourteenth centuries (Bennett 1997, 21). These features produced a range of pottery including Ham Green, Minety ware and

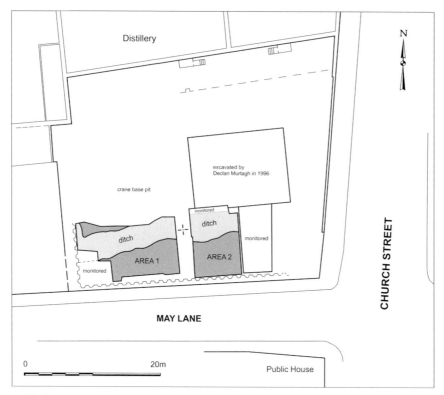

2 Site layout

Dublin-type coarse and the Dublin-type wares. A phase of later medieval activity consisted of a stone-lined pit interpreted as a lime pit. The presence of sixteenth-century material such as Beauvais, Merida-type ware and late Valencian lustre-ware in a number of the pits indicated activity in that period in the area (Declan Murtagh, pers comm.).

Monitoring was carried out on the excavation for the crane pit immediately to the south of the above site. Following the discovery of human bone in the section face of the pit, further excavation was requested. This second phase of investigation took place in January 1997 over four weeks and this paper describes the results of those excavations (licence no. 96E384).

THE SITE

The site is located on the northern corner of Church Street and May Lane (fig. 1). The houses fronting onto May Lane had no basements and therefore there was no disturbance below street level along that frontage. However, the houses fronting onto Church Street had basements resulting in the loss of material along that frontage. The OD level on the footpath on May Lane was 7.48m (Malin). The site extended for 24m from west to east and was 11.5m wide at its widest (fig. 2). The boundary along the north side was formed by the void created by the excavation of the crane pit; the boundary along the south was formed by sheet piling along the May Lane frontage. The limits at the east and west ends were set down by space constraints. The excavation was carried in two stages; Area 1 to the west was the first area to be excavated while Area 2 was opened on the completion of Area 1. A baulk separated the two areas.

THE EXCAVATION

Approximately 2m of overburden and rubble were removed by machine before hand-excavation commenced. Underlying natural levels (F26) comprised gravels interspersed with deposits of sand. The gravel varied from a very heavy loose coarse type to layers of fine pure sand which varied between grey and orange in colour. These glacial deposits are prevalent on the north side of the Liffey. The gravel was overlaid along the southern length of the site by a layer of fine natural orange clay (F8), which was quite distinctive both by its colour and by its fine texture. Two phases of medieval activity were identified.

Phase 1 (fig. 3; plate 1)
The earliest feature exposed on the site was a ditch (F35) cut into the fine orange clay, gravels and sand. It ran from the southwest corner of the excavated area in a north-easterly direction. The northern edge of the ditch survived only at the west end of Area 1 as it had been removed elsewhere during the excavation of the crane pit. The profile of the ditch varied. At the east end the base was square in profile. In other areas the base was V-shaped or U-shaped in section. The width at the base varied between 300mm and 600mm. The OD level at the base in the west end of Area 1 was 3.03m (Malin). There was a slight shelf along both sides of the ditch just above the base; this was continued along its entire length. There was an interruption in the southern slope at the east end of Area 2. Otherwise the sides sloped down gently from edge to base. In patches there was a green patina to the gravel on the sides of the ditch. This may have been where the surfaces were exposed to air when the ditch was open in antiquity. There was only one length where original edges on both sides could be seen to have survived. It stretched for about 3m in length in the middle of Area 1. Here the ditch was 4m wide from edge to edge.

Elsewhere both original edges were not available, either because of earlier destruction or because the baulks had to be stepped out for security. The cut through the fine orange clay was located some 2m south of the cut through the gravel, thereby forming a shallow shelf along the south rim of the ditch. However, the deposit of orange clay was much less substantial in the eastern

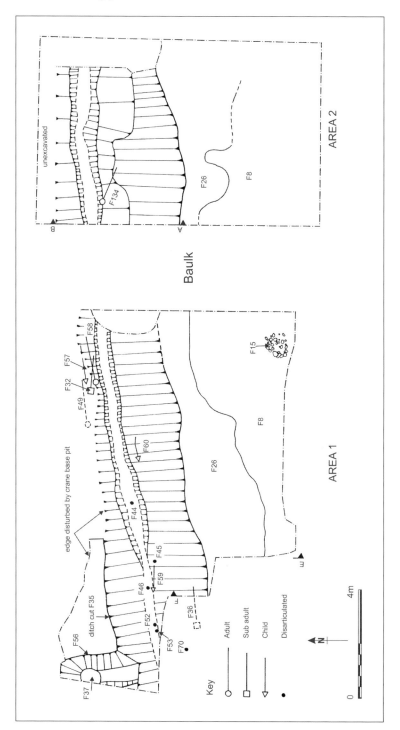

3 Plan of ditch showing location of burials. Phase I

Plate 1 Ditch in area 1, looking west

portion of Area 1 and in Area 2 and therefore the cut through it for the ditch was less obvious in those areas. There was no evidence for upcast from the digging of the ditch (this would have been distinctive as re-deposited gravel). There was no evidence for it on the surviving edge of the ditch on the north side. If the ditch was associated with St Michan's church, it would be expected that the upcast would have been thrown to the south side of the ditch, forming a bank inside the ditch. There was no evidence for this.

At the lowest level the fill comprised a layer of very loose large water-rolled stones (F136). The layer was 200mm deep and was very difficult to excavate out. The stones were interpreted as having fallen in from the sides of the ditch, originating from the natural gravel layer. At the west end of the ditch the stones were not lying in a silt matrix, nor was there a silt layer overlying the natural sands. A possible explanation for the absence of silt here was that the drainage through the sand was such that silt did not have the opportunity to accumulate. A silt lens (F138) was present in the ditch in Area 2; it overlay the stone layer and was approximately 100mm thick. The main fill of the ditch was an orange/brown clay (F25); this was gritty and stony in places but on the whole it was quite fine. The clay was consistently flecked with charcoal and there was a high animal-bone content. There were lenses of stonier material contained within it but the layer was removed as one. In Area 2 it had a lower stone content at a lower level (F137). The ditch fill was distinctive, in the sense that it came away cleanly from the natural sands and gravels.

From the fill layer 169 sherds of medieval pottery were recovered. They were present down to the bottom of the fill and comprised Ham Green, Dublin-type coarse ware, Dublin-type ware, Dublin cooking ware and North Leinster cooking ware (Sandes 1997, 8).

The burials
Human bone was recovered from the surface of the natural gravel underlying orange/brown clay (F25). There was a minimum of 10 individuals present (one of these (F70) was recovered during removal of a baulk under archaeo-logical supervision at a later date). There were six almost complete burials, another two were burials which may have been disturbed by later activity and the remainder were groups of disarticulated human bones. Three of the complete burials and one of the disturbed burials were located within 3m of each other on what was the north slope of the ditch. It was the discovery of these bones in the section face of the crane pit which led to the requirement for the excavation and they had suffered a small amount of damage as a result of the mechanical disturbance. The other burials were placed further apart, one of them located in Area 2. All of the burials were placed within the line of the ditch. None were found in the natural layers outside the ditch. The burials did not yield clear evidence for grave cuts but one of them (F32) showed faint evidence for a cut. There was no evidence for timber lining of

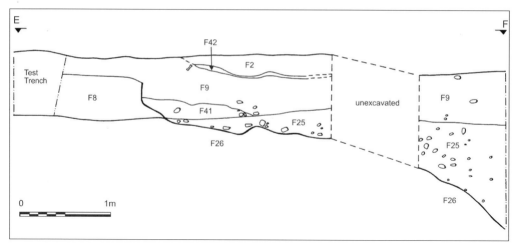

4 East facing section through ditch F35. West end of area 1

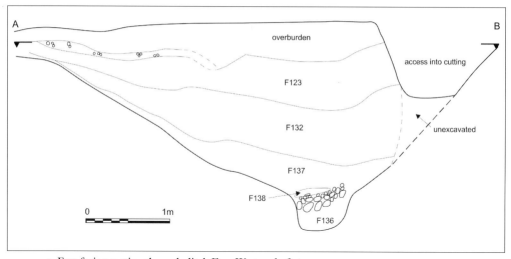

5 East facing section through ditch F35. West end of area 2

the grave or for shrouds. There were no grave goods associated with the skeletons.

    Where the burials were complete or almost complete it was clear that the orientations were east/west with the heads at the west. They were supine, apart from one of the adults, which lay on its side. One had flexed legs while the rest were extended. They were all located in the bottom of the ditch or lying on the surface of the slope of the ditch. One (F59) was lying on top of the stone layer at the bottom of the ditch and was very badly fragmented. The ten individuals consisted of two middle-aged men, one of whom suffered from osteoarthritis; three adolescents (aged 16–20 years), one of which was male and two female; four

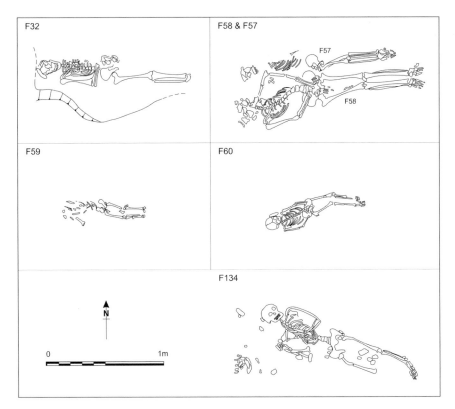

6 Plans of burials

juveniles (three 5–9 years and one 10–16 years) and one infant (4–11 months at time of death (F70)). There was a high proportion of adolescents and juveniles in the assemblage. One of the middle-aged men (F58) was buried alongside the 10–16 years old juvenile (F57). There was evidence for nutritional deficiencies in the form of linear hypoplasia on the tooth enamel and also in the form of cribra orbitalia and porotic hyperostosis. These are caused by iron-deficiency anaemia, possibly caused by lack of Vitamic C or by a parasitic infestation of the gut (Buckley n.d., 4). One juvenile (F60) had suffered a chronic infection in the jaw, which was probably exacerbated by nutritional deficiency.

Two samples of bone were subjected to radiocarbon dating (see Appendix). The bone from F60 produced a radiocarbon determination of 990 +/– 40 BP (Before Present) giving a calibrated date of AD980–1160 (95.4% probability). Bone from F134 produced a radiocarbon determination of 1072 +/– BP giving a calibrated date of AD 890–1030 (95.4% probability).

In summary, these burials were all placed inside the line of the ditch. F32 was the only instance where there was a suggestion of grave cut. In the other cases it was impossible to distinguish cuts in the coarse gravel. It is doubtful if

Plate 2 Burials F57 & F58 in ditch F35

the group of burials could be considered as a cemetery. While there was a cluster in the vicinity of F57 and F58, the rest of the burials were placed much further apart from each other. There is a possibility that they were placed in the ditch as a consequence of some calamitous event (see below). In addition there were two cases where pairs of legs were found in what looked like undisturbed circumstances. There were seven finds of disarticulated human bones. These were three separate finds of human skull, the disarticulated remains of a child's left femur along with possible adult skull fragments, fragments of a child's skull, human jaw bone found with animal bone and a collection of disarticulated sub-adult remains comprising pelvis and skull. Some of them gave the appearance of having been gathered together and tidied up. The origin or purpose of these deposits of bone was not clear.

Other Phase 1 activity
There were several other poorly preserved signs of medieval activity, all of which were cut through the natural sands and gravels. The insertion of sheet piling along the western boundary cut through a complex of pits. F56 was a small trench or gully running NNW/SSE, which was cut into the natural gravel. Its excavated length north/south was 2.10m and it was 1.20m wide at the south end where it opened out into the main ditch. It was not clear whether it had been constructed either at the same time as or after the main ditch or whether it had been cut by the main ditch. Its fill was the same orange-brown clay as in the main ditch. An area of crude cobbling (F15), roughly circular, was exposed lying directly on top of the fine natural orange clay (F8), south of

Plate 3 Burial F134 in ditch F35

the ditch cut. It is possible that the area of cobbling had been greater and this patch was all that remained.

Phase 2 (fig. 7; plate 4)

A phase of later medieval activity was represented by a layer of grey silty clay (F9) that overlay the ditch and its fill. This layer was most significant at the west end of Area 1 and became shallower towards the east. Its upper levels were contaminated by the overlying post-medieval material but its lower levels contained some stones, charcoal, animal and shell and medieval pottery. Several pits were cut into the grey clay. These did not relate to each other and were only associated in so far as they were cut down from the same level. They all bottomed in the natural gravels and contained a range of animal bones and medieval pottery. They were similar to the pits found on Murtagh's excavation. A crude setting of stones (F28) lay at 5.14m OD. It consisted of two parallel lines of stones 400–450mm apart running in an east/west direction with a few other stones associated with them. However the feature was not well preserved and it may not have had archaeological significance.

A complex of three pits (F 20, F30, F31) was exposed at the east end of Area 1 extending under the baulk which separated Areas 1 and 2. They were all dug through the southern slope of the ditch (F35), resulting in its total destruction here. The fills of the different pits were difficult to distinguish but they contained animal bone, charcoal and medieval pot-sherds. The complex was further disturbed by a post-medieval pit (F54) which contained a

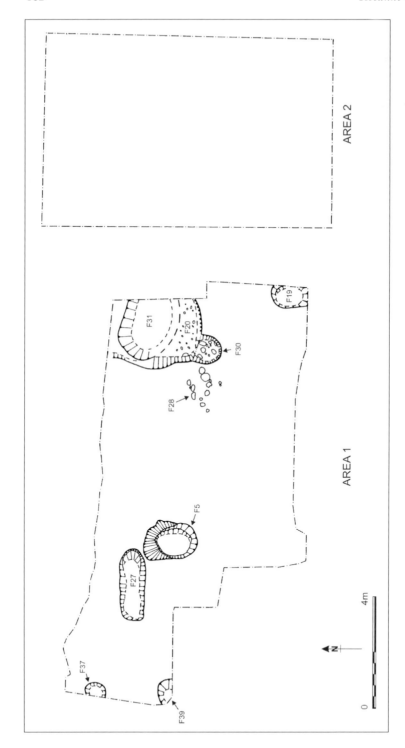

7 Phase 2

Plate 4 Phase 2 pits (F5 in foreground, F27 behind)

concentrated deposit of large animal bones within a matrix of loose black soil. Phase 2 pits were not exposed in the eastern end of the site. This horizon did not produce evidence for dwelling houses.

Phase 3 (fig. 8)

The features dating to the post-medieval period in Area 1 were dotted around the site while those found in Area 2 related to the backs of the houses fronting on to Church Street or possibly were related to the houses on May Lane. The sheet piling along the west side cut a pit (F11) which had two layers of fill, both of them with brick, slate, animal bone and pottery, some of which was tin-glazed earthenware, probably dating to the 17th century. This feature was cut by a rectangular cobbled feature (F24) which was surrounded on three sides by the bottom of a stone footing (F18) and which was cut by the sheet piling on the west side. This was interpreted as a structure used in the tanning process. Tanning was an activity carried out in this area throughout the medieval period and into the early post-medieval period (Purcell 2003, 221).

The remains of a stone-built flue (F17) were exposed along the north side of the cutting and a portion of it may have been removed during the excavation for the crane pit. It was situated above the cluster of burials here and may have been responsible for disturbance of some of the bones. The feature consisted of a stone-built passage with a flagged floor; the walls of the passage splayed outwards towards the north. The entire structure was square in plan so that the passage was contained within the square. The structure

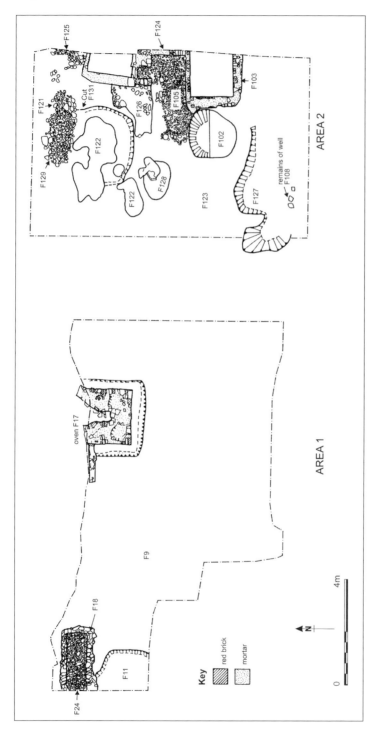

8 Phase 3

survived to a sufficient height to suggest that there had been a domed roof over the end of the passage or the chamber but there was no such evidence concerning the short stretch of passage. It was built primarily of stone but brick was also present. A rectangular pit had been excavated for the structure; the pit bottomed on the orange gravel (F25). A sherd of mottled ware (late seventeenth-eighteenth century) was found in the fill of the pit. The function of this feature was not clear but it is likely that it served some kind of industrial purpose, although there was no waste material present. It was not possible to relate stratigraphically the kiln/oven directly with the houses along Church Street or those on May Lane but it is probably safe to assume that they were related.

Some features survived in Area 2 which were presumably once associated with the houses. These were pits, a well, remains of walls and cobbled features and a deposit of grey clay which was mixed with layers of possible iron pan. One of the brick-lined pits (F103) was probably associated with the remains of outhouses at the rear of the Church Street frontage. It yielded a large quantity of late eighteenth-century pottery, comprising mainly cream ware and locally-produced black-glazed ware. Wine bottles were also found and the facetted stems of two wine glasses refined the dating of the pottery to 1775–1790. The eastern limit of the excavation was set 10–12m west of the Church Street frontage. This bank of material was reduced by machine under archaeological supervision a couple of months later and it was clear that basements in the houses and the series of pits at their rear had removed all traces of the earlier stratigraphy.

RESULTS OF EXCAVATION

The construction of St Michan's has been traditionally dated to *c.*1096 (Bradley 1992, 50). It served the population of Oxmantown which may have grown in size as a suburb of Dublin once the bridge over the Liffey was built. Church Street would have become a thoroughfare after the construction of the bridge.

It is reasonable to attempt to identify the ditch found on this excavation as a ditch enclosing St Michan's (fig. 9). The distance between the church and the arc of the ditch is 70–80m. This would produce an approximate diameter of 140–160m for the enclosure assuming that it was circular, that the present church structure was built on the site of the earlier church, and that the church stood in the middle of the enclosure. Alan Hayden, during testing on the south side of St Michan's in 2000, found two medieval ditches one of which he suggested may have formed the southern boundary of the property occupied by St Michan's (Bennett 2002, 82). This ditch would lie approximately 80m south of the church. Excavation is taking place at the time of writing on the Maguire & Patterson site which may yield further information on the presence or absence of an enclosing feature here. Cia McConway

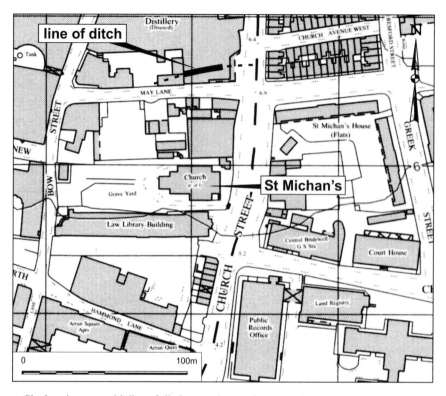

9 Site location map with line of ditch super-imposed on street layout

found human remains during testing on the north side of St Michan's church, between the church and May Lane, in 1996. She found no evidence for an ecclesiastical enclosing feature on the site that she tested and suggested that the enclosure may have been located further to the north, closer to May Lane (Bennett 1997, 29). Enclosing ditches around ecclesiastical foundations in the environs of the early town are found, for example, at the site excavated by Coughlan on Stephen Street Upper (Coughlan 2003, 11–39)

The presence of the burials within the line of the ditch was the most interesting feature of the excavation. No burials were found outside its line. The burials were found lying on the natural deposits, either on the sides or at the bottom. They were all aligned east/west. Interestingly, small groups of disarticulated bone were also found as if they had been gathered up and tidied away. Burials were deposited in cemeteries associated with churches at this time, for example, at St Michael le Pole's where radiocarbon dating of one skeleton produced a slightly later date in the early twelfth century (Gowen 2001, 36). Ó Donnabháin and Hallgrímsson, in their paper on Viking-Age burials in Dublin, discuss atypical groups of burials at Wood Quay and Temple Bar and are of the opinion that they were a response to some sort of

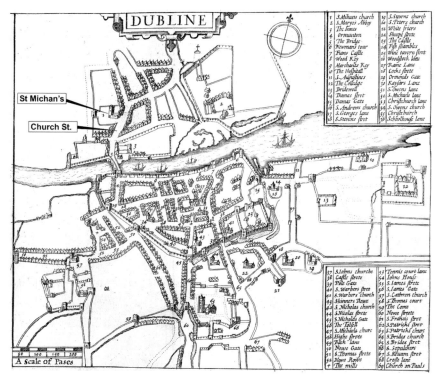

10 Dublin 1610, by John Speed

calamitous situation (Ó Donnabháin and Hallgrímsson 2001, 70). Such untypical burial places may also have been a response to a shortage of space in a time of rapid urban expansion (ibid.). The burials in Church Street must be considered an atypical group.

The two radiocarbon dates are not helpful in providing precise information on the dating of the ditch. However, if it had been constructed for a defensive or enclosing function, it would appear that that function may have become redundant or obsolete by the time the burials were inserted, although it is likely that it was still open at that time. There was no evidence to suggest for how long the ditch had been open, although F60 was buried on top of the layer of stone that seemed to have rolled down from the sides. It is unlikely that there was much or any water in the ditch when the burials were inserted as there would have been a fear that the burials would have been exposed or swept away. Therefore, if the ditch was associated with a church on the site and the ditch had become redundant by the time the burials were inserted, this would tend to suggest that the church was founded earlier than the traditional date of 1090.

There is no evidence to indicate the identity of the people who were buried there. While Oxmantown is associated with the movement of people from the

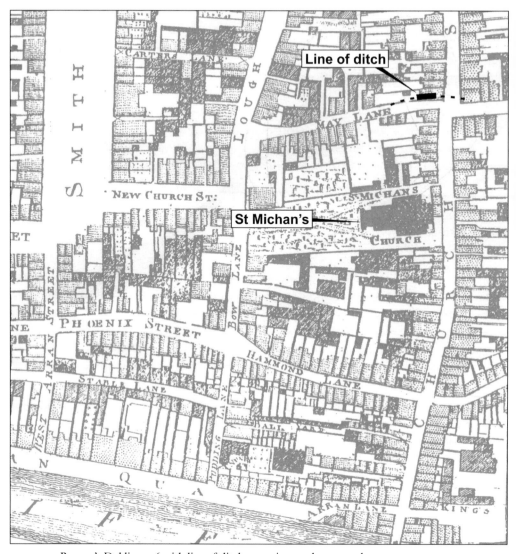

11 Rocque's Dublin 1756 with line of ditch super-imposed on street layout

south side of the river to the suburb, the burials cannot be identified as having been Scandinavian in origin. However, the nature of the burials suggests that the individuals were Christian. Green-glazed pottery was present in the fill of the ditch down to its bottom level. This suggests that the ditch was filled at a time after the arrival of the Anglo-Normans. It might be argued that the ditch was so thoroughly back-filled that the memory of its existence had disappeared when the street pattern in the area was established. For instance, there is no trace of it on Speed's map of 1610 (fig. 10).

If the ditch was not associated with the church there is no surviving evidence to suggest what else it may have been associated with. The excavated section of ditch was very short and it is difficult to extrapolate its exact orientation. Street patterns elsewhere in the vicinity do not appear to retain the footprint of a circular enclosure (fig. 11). Church Street itself does not observe a possible curve around a pre-existing circular enclosure. The extrapolated curve of the ditch would suggest that the ditch and the Church Street alignment would intersect just north of the present-day junction of Church Street, May Lane and Mary's Lane. It has been suggested, however, that the ecclesiastical enclosure may have straddled Church Street, if indeed Church Street represents an ancient main thoroughfare.

Although the site lay within the area known as Oxmantown, a large area of settlement, no archaeological evidence for dwelling houses was exposed during the excavation, even if medieval activity was shown by the presence of the pits. The conduct of commerce and industrial activities such as tanning is referred to above, so that it is clear that people did live on or in the vicinity of the site in the later medieval period.

APPENDIX

Radiocarbon Report from Oxford University Radiocarbon Accelerator Unit:
F 60
OXA–10527: 990+/– 40BP
68.2% probability
990 AD (41.4%) 1050 AD
1090 AD (16.6%) 1120 AD
1140 AD (10.2%) 1160 AD
95.4% probability
980 AD (95.4%) 1160 AD

F134
OXA–10528: 1072+/–39BP
68.2% probability
900 AD (15.5%) 920 AD
960 AD (52.7%) 1020 AD
95.4% probability
890 AD (95.4%) 1030 AD

ACKNOWLEDGMENTS

I wish to thank Katie Hyland, Archaeological Development Services Ltd, for her drawings and Eoin Halpin for his advice.

REFERENCES

Bennett, I. 1997 *Excavations 1996*. Bray.
—2002 *Excavations 2000*. Bray.
Bradley, J. 1992 The topographical development of Scandinavian Dublin. In Aalen, F.H.A.
    and Whelan, K. (eds) *Dublin city and county. From prehistory to present.* 43–56. Dublin.
Buckley, L. n.d. Church Street, Dublin: skeletal report. Unpublished specialist report.
Clarke, H.B. 1990 The topographical development. In H.B. Clarke (ed.) *Medieval Dublin.
    The making of a metropolis,* 52–60. Dublin.
—2002 *Dublin Part 1, to 1610.* Irish Historic Towns Atlas no. 11. Dublin. Royal Irish
    Academy.
Coughlan, T. 2003 Excavations at the medieval cemetery of St Peter's church, Dublin. In
    S. Duffy (ed.) *Medieval Dublin IV,* 11–39. Dublin.
Gowen, M. 2001 Excavations at the site of the church and tower of St Michael le Pole,
    Dublin. In S. Duffy (ed.) *Medieval Dublin II,* 13–52. Dublin.
Ó Donnabháin, B. and Hallgrímsson, B. 2001 Dublin: the biological identity of the
    Hiberno-Norse town. In S. Duffy (ed.) *Medieval Dublin II,* 65–85. Dublin.
Purcell, E. 2003 Land use in medieval Oxmantown. In S. Duffy (ed.) *Medieval Dublin IV,*
    193–228. Dublin.
Sandes, C. 1997 Church Street II, Dublin: the medieval pottery. Unpublished specialist
    report.

Cultures in contact in the Leinster and Dublin marches, 1170–1400

EMMETT O'BYRNE

During the late 1160s English troops, at the invitation of Diarmait Mac Murchada (MacMurrough), landed on the Leinster coast to restore him to his kingdom. By the time of Mac Murchada's death in May 1171, he had succeeded largely in his aims, bringing the Leinster aristocracy and the Ostman king of Dublin to their knees. The death of Mac Murchada brought Henry II of England to Ireland on 18 October 1171. Henry II, a masterful politician, had more tools of conquest at his disposal than just brute force, knowing full well that fine wines and flattery could do more for men's attitudes than the naked edge of the sword.

With this in mind, Henry set to wooing the Irish princes and drawing them into the Plantagenet social orbit by inviting them to come to Dublin for the Christmas season. At Dublin the conqueror sought, on his terms, to forge a 'community of outlook' among the Irish princes and newcomers, revealing a deliberate strategy of peace and coexistence to bed the colony down. Henry, plying the Irish with liberal doses of flattery, as well as drink and food from 'the sumptuous and plentiful fare of the English table', won them over. Indeed, it can be argued that these Christmas feasts were the midwife for the birth of an Anglicised native elite in Leinster. Whether any of the Irish realised it at the time, these feasts glossed over their junior status in this arrangement, each of them now owed feudal obligations to Henry. The depth of Henry's illusion became even more profound as the relationship gradually became more defined, attracting and entangling the Irish in it. Thus, the feudal noose was steadily placed around the necks of the Irish princes. This paper focuses on the period between 1171 and 1400, and examines the emergence of an Anglicised Irish elite in Leinster. It also attempts to trace the interaction of the Welsh, Irish, and Ostman communities of the Dublin marches and the nearby mountains of Wicklow that originally made up Henry II's 'community of interest'.

Even before the arrival of Henry II, the Leinster princes by 1170 knew their world had changed forever. Brutality was not, of course, the monopoly of the newcomers, as the Leinstermen took the opportunity to return the favour whenever it presented itself. The cultivation of the image of Richard de Clare (better known as Strongbow) as a conqueror was crucial to the subjection of Leinster. As Robert Bartlett and Rees Davies point out, this sort of strategy demanded acts of brutality designed to create a psychology of inferiority and dependence among those resisting conquest. In Leinster, the English made examples of Irish leaders who resisted: in early 1172 Murchad Mac Murchada (brother of Diarmait and king of Uí Chennselaig) was killed by the troops of Henry II, but Strongbow reserved his worst for Murchad Ua Broin (O'Byrne), Diarmait Mac Murchada's deadly enemy. After capturing Ua Broin and his son in 1172, Strongbow conveyed them to the Mac Murchada capital of Ferns for execution and, in a carefully calculated act, fed their bodies to his hounds, sending a brutally effective message to the Leinster nobility.[1] By late 1172 the English conquest in Leinster had the upper hand, but subduing those Leinster nobles opposed to Strongbow proved a bloody business. Even so, the killing of many of their fellow Christians in Leinster disturbed the consciences of the conquerors. Among those uneasy with the slaughter in Leinster was Gerald of Wales, churchman and English apologist. In a probable reference to the harrowing of Kildare during the 1170s, Gerald balked at the killing, remarking searchingly about 'the new and blood-stained acquisition of land, secured at the cost of great bloodshed and the slaughter of a Christian people'.[2]

But to the medieval mind the right to rule was often acquired legitimately through conquest. Accordingly, the conquest was the legal basis of the emerging new order in Leinster, a point not lost on Henry II of England. A medieval king was also a lawgiver. This meant that Henry II was unrestricted by native tradition or law, entitling him to destroy the old establishment in Leinster and raise up a new order.[3] In fact, Henry II was more preoccupied with braking Strongbow's ambitions than annihilating the old Leinster aristocracy. Indeed, the emergence of a hybrid and Anglicised Irish elite has largely been neglected in the histories of the period. The origins of some of this community lay firmly within the old client-base of the now deceased Leinster king, Diarmait Mac Murchada. Prominent among them was Diarmait's natural son, Domnall Cáemánach (Kavanagh), seneschal of the Irish of Leinster between 1172 and 1175.[4] Another important figure was Diarmait's son-in-law, Domnall Mac Gilla Mo-Cholmóc, king of Uí Briúin Chualann. Others were Diarmait's enemies, having been intimately involved in the great Leinster rebellion of summer and autumn 1171, men such Fáelán Mac

1 R. Bartlett, *The making of Europe* (London, 1994), pp 85–6; R.R. Davies, *Domination and conquest: the experience of Ireland, Scotland and Wales, 1100–1300* (Cambridge, 1999), p. 51; W.M. Hennessy and B. McCarthy (eds), *Annála Uladh: annals of Ulster*, 4 vols (Dublin, 1887–1901), s.a. 1172; G.H. Orpen (ed.), *The song of Dermot and the earl* (Oxford, 1892), p. 158. 2 Giraldus Cambrensis, *Expugnatio Hibernica: the conquest of Ireland*, ed. A.B. Scott and F.X. Martin (Dublin, 1978), pp 156–7; J. O'Donovan (ed), *Annala rioghachta Eireann: Annals of the kingdom of Ireland by the Four Masters from the earliest period to the year 1616*, 7 vols (Dublin, 1851), s.a. 1171 [hereafter AFM]. 3 D. Sunderland, 'Conquest and Law', *Studia Gratiana*, xv (1972), pp 45–6. 4 *Song of Dermot*, p. 161.

Fáeláin of Uí Fáeláin, the lieutenant in West Leinster of the high-king Ruaidrí Ua Conchobair (O'Conor), and Muirchertach Mac Murchada, Diarmait's own kinsman.

However, after Strongbow broke Ruaidrí Ua Conchobair's siege of Dublin in September 1171, these Leinster princes found themselves completely exposed to the resurgent English. With the English hot on their heels and bereft of Ruaidrí's protection, these princes acknowledged political reality, falling over themselves to welcome Henry II during the winter of 1171–2. As the English king made his triumphant progress through Leinster to Dublin, he was met by a throng of Leinster princes, including Fáelán Mac Fáeláin and the Uí Tuathail (O'Tooles), eager to avail of his protection from Strongbow.[5] Another of these pragmatic princes was Domnall Mac Gilla Pátraic, king of North Ossory. He had put up considerable resistance to Mac Murchada and Strongbow between 1169 and 1171, but in the autumn of 1171 he pragmatically submitted to Strongbow and became his vassal. He was allowed to hold North Ossory, gaining the benefits of Strongbow's protection from the threat of Domnall Ua Briain of Thomond. Domnall Mac Gilla Pátraic was nobody's fool, and he doubly ensured his position by bending his knee before Henry II in the winter of 1171.[6] In fact, the only part of North Ossory given to the settlers belonged to the Uí Cháellaide (O'Keallys), Domnall's bitter enemies. Domnall was to render feudal service to Strongbow by campaigning for him in 1173, 1175 and 1176, a service that dovetailed perfectly with his agenda.[7] This arrangement proved mutually advantageous to both Mac Gilla Pátraic and the English until Domnall's death in 1185.[8]

Diarmait Ua Dímmusaig (O'Dempsey) of the Offaly sub-kingdom of Clanmaliere was another example of the pragmatic Leinster prince. In spite of initial opposition, Diarmait (described as lord and defender of Offaly in 1172) seemingly allied himself to the English about 1173. This elevated him beyond his traditional vassal status to one of superiority over his Ua Conchobair Failge (O'Conor Faly) overlord. Other facts confirm this: hitherto virtually unknown, he was able to found the Cistercian house at Monasterevin in 1178. Diarmait's political domination of the O'Conor Falys was such that he was lauded as lord of Offaly at his death in 1193.[9] To the south of Clanmaliere, Cú Chríche Ua Mórda (O'More) of Laois was rich enough to establish the Cistercian abbey of Abbeyleix in 1183. However, alliance with the English could also have untoward effects: in 1196, Domnall Ua Mórda was killed while defending the colonists from the O'Conors of Connacht, and Mac Murchada and Ua Conchobair Failge dynasts fell during an English

5 *Expugnatio*, pp 94–5; M.T. Flanagan, 'Henry II and the kingdom of Uí Fáeláin', in J. Bradley (ed.), *Settlement and society in medieval Ireland* (Dublin, 1988), p. 233.   6 Ibid., pp 95, 161–3.   7 E. O'Byrne, *War, politics and the Irish of Leinster, 1156–1606* (Dublin, 2003), p. 41.   8 AFM, s.a. 1185.   9 O'Byrne, *War, politics and the Irish of Leinster*, p. 17.

expedition to Ulster that same year.[10] Thus, from early on it is clear that many of the Leinster Irish sought to integrate themselves within the system, but, as Geoffrey Hand points out, these belonged to a privileged class.[11]

Leaving the nobility of greater Leinster to one side, there is also evidence for the English accommodation of Irish princely families near Dublin. Here we find ourselves on fertile ground, as the decisions of these elites to come to the terms with the newcomers ensured their survival. After the breaking of the Irish siege of Dublin in September 1171, the self-seeking Domnall Mac Gilla Mo-Cholmóc, Mac Murchada's son-in-law and king of Uí Briúin Chualann, accepted the overlordship of his brother-in-law, Strongbow. In the winter of 1171–2, Domnall doubly secured his future in the new order by submitting at Dublin before Henry II. Although the Meic Gilla Mo-Cholmóc lands at Santry, Raheny and Clontarf in north Dublin were granted to Englishmen, the upshot of Domnall's submission to Henry II was that the dynasty's remaining lands were held directly of the king. In effect, Domnall and his kinsmen were now outside the power of the grasping Strongbow. Now blanketed by royal protection, Domnall set his dynasty on a course to span the ethnic divide. And during the lifetime of Domnall's son, Diarmait, the Meic Gilla Mo-Cholmóc transformed themselves into the fitz Dermots, adopting the nomenclature of the English. Instead of being christened Domnall, Diarmait or Donnchad, their young men now bore names such as John, William, Robert and Ralph, the forenames of the conqueror.[12] The only recorded trouble with the settlers occurred in the late twelfth century or perhaps in the early thirteenth, then a Donohoe (Donnchad) Mac Gilla Mo-Cholmóc (perhaps Diarmait's brother) killed a Roger fitz Gilbert.[13] By 1276, the descendants of the Meic Gilla Mo-Cholmóc, the fitz Dermots, were indistinguishable from the settler aristocracy. Then Domnall Mac Gilla Mo-Cholmóc's great-great-grandson, Ralph fitz Dermot was paid for defending the Vale of Dublin from January to November 1276 against the MacMurroughs and O'Byrnes, whereupon Edward I gave them his seal of approval, rewarding Ralph with a knighthood that completed the family's metamorphosis.[14]

The reaction of the Meic Gilla Mo-Cholmóc to the English can be contrasted with that of the ruling Ostman elite of the city-state of Dublin. The fall of Dublin to Mac Murchada on 21 September 1170 and the ejection of its king, Ascall Mac Turcaill, transformed the political order of the city.

10 AFM, s.a. 1196; W.M. Hennessy (ed.), *Annals of Loch Cé*, 2 vols (London, 1871), s.a. 1196.   11 G. Hand, *English law in Ireland, 1290–1320* (Cambridge, 1967), pp 205, 209. 12 F.J. Byrne, *Irish kings and high-kings* (London, 1973), p. 151; J.T. Gilbert (ed.), *Chartularies of St Mary's abbey, Dublin*, 2 vols (London, 1884–5), i, pp 31–7; K.W. Nicholls, 'Anglo-French Ireland and After', *Peritia*, i (1982), pp 381–2.   13 C. McNeill (ed.) *Calendar of Archbishop Alen's register* (Dublin, 1950), p. 110.   14 H.S. Sweetman (ed.), *Calendar of documents relating to Ireland, 1171–1307* (London, 1874–85), ii, no. 1496, p. 285; *Cal. docs. Ire.*, ii, no. 2344, p. 562.

From exile in the Western Isles, Ascall gathered a fleet and troops and plotted his restoration. In an attempt to restore the old order, Ascall landed near Dublin in July 1171 to retake his city, but he was defeated and captured. This defeat sounded the death knell of the Mac Turcaill kings of Dublin, but it was given effect when the English decapitated a captive but truculent Ascall in his own assembly hall.[15] After the beheading of Ascall, Walter de Ridlesford I was granted the dynasty's lands stretching from Tully to Bray and inland to Glencullen in the southern Dublin marches.[16] Furthermore, the Meic Turcaill lost their extensive north Dublin holdings at Portrane, Malahide, Portmarnock and Kilbarrack. However, by 1174 Hamund Mac Turcaill and his brothers had sufficiently rehabilitated themselves to have their Kinsealy lands confirmed to them.[17]

The partial restoration of the Mac Turcaill lands is consistent with the favour displayed by the English to other Ostman communities, for example, Edward I's confirmation of Henry II's charter of 1172 to the Ostmen of Waterford.[18] Such English favour towards the Ostmen of the Dublin marches was evidenced by their incorporation at a higher social level than most Irish, as illustrated by the thirty-six identifiable rents paid by Ostmen for lands in the Vale of Dublin.[19] The major Harold lineage based at Kilgobbin was one of the most prominent Ostman families of the south Dublin marches. After the conquest of 1170, the Harolds like the Meic Turcaill lost their lands to the newcomers. But it is distinctly likely that the Harolds were rehabilitated alongside their old Mac Turcaill masters around 1174, a process probably acknowledged by the Ostman gift of Kilgobbin to the priory of Holy Trinity.[20]

The ending of the Mac Turcaill hegemony allowed the Harolds and their fellow Ostmen, the Archbolds, to become more important in the marches. Significantly, the Harold leaders came to see opportunity in the Mac Turcaill implosion, opportunity to advance their ambition. The leading and most influential branch of the Harolds was based at Kilgobbin, and in the decades that followed the English conquest of Dublin, two important leaders emerged from that family. These were John Harold and Elias Harold (sometimes known as 'de Muta'), perhaps brothers or at least very close kinsmen. As the most powerful of the surviving Ostman lords and the owner of Kilgobbin, John Harold filled the role vacated by the Meic Turcaill as the natural leader

15 *Song of Dermot*, p. 181.   16 *Cal. docs. Ire.*, i, no. 355, p. 53.   17 *Chartul. St Mary's, Dublin*, i, no. 61, pp 83–4; no. 244, p. 477; no. 269, pp 504–5; nos 216–17, pp 233–4; *Alen's register*, pp 28–9.   18 J. Davies, *A discoverie of the true causes why Ireland was never entirely subdued nor brought under obedience of the Crown of England* (London, 1612), pp 105–6. 19 L. Simpson, 'Anglo-Norman settlement in Uí Briúin Chualann', in K. Hannigan and W. Nolan (eds), *Wicklow: history and society* (Dublin, 1994), p. 203.   20 *Alen's register*, p. 28. The text says that the Ostmen made a gift of Theachatan by reason of their forfeiture. See also E. O'Byrne, 'A much disputed land: Carrickmines and the Dublin marches', in S. Duffy (ed.), *Medieval Dublin IV* (Dublin, 2003), pp 231, 235 [hereafter O'Byrne 'A much disputed land'].

of the Ostmen of the southern Dublin marches.[21] And it was his successors who eventually occupied a territory stretching from Saggart to Kilmashiogue (near Marlay Park), later known as Harolds' Country.[22] Like their contemporary and neighbour Domnall Mac Gilla Mo-Cholmóc of Uí Briúin Chualann, the Harold leaders steered their large and extended lineage on a course of accommodation with the settlers. And from early on their labours bore fruit, as they were soon incorporated within the feudal settlement, particularly on the lands of the archbishops of Dublin and of the priory of Holy Trinity, and also on the royal manors.[23]

Not to be outdone by John, Elias served successive archbishops of Dublin as an administrator of their extensive estates. At some point between 1181 and 1212 we find Elias witnessing Archbishop John Comyn's grant of the tithes of Newcastle McKynegan (east Wicklow) to the church of Grace Dieu,[24] while, during the pontificate of Henry de Londres as archbishop of Dublin between 1212 and 1228, Elias served as seneschal of the lands of the archbishopric and as a judge in its courts. He was also an important landowner, holding ten carucates at Haroldstown otherwise known as villa Elye Harold in Coillache (now Three Castles near Blessington, Co. Wicklow) in the archbishopric's manor of Ballymore.[25] Upon Elias's death in the early decades of the thirteenth century, his lands at Haroldstown passed to his cousin Sir Geoffrey Harold of Kilgobbin, a collector of rents in the Vale of Dublin. In turn, these lands passed to Sir Geoffrey's son Peter, sheriff of Dublin during the early 1330s.[26]

There were also other Ostman communities scattered throughout the northern and eastern foothills of the Wicklow mountains, as well as in the adjoining coastal plain. Harolds and Archbolds could be found from Glencree in the north to the fitz Gerald town of Wicklow in the south. Moreover, the Harolds and Archbolds living in the fitz Gerald barony of Wicklow, then part of Kildare, were recognised feudal tenants. In 1308 George de la Roche, one of the co-heirs of the barony of Wicklow, brought an action before the Dublin bench. He complained that the rents due to him from his portion were forcibly taken from him by a combination of Irish, settlers and Ostmen. Of the Ostmen, he named Ankedal son of Richard Carragh Harold, John son of

21 F.E. Ball, *A history of the County Dublin*, iii (repr., Dublin, 1995), p. 66; see also E. Curtis, 'The clan system among the English settlers in Ireland', *E.H.R.*, xxv (1910), p. 118. 22 Ibid., p. 58. 23 K.W. Nicholls, 'Críoch Branach: the O'Byrnes and their country', in C. O'Brien (ed.), *Feagh McHugh O'Byrne: the Wicklow firebrand* (Dublin, 1998), p. 17; *Alen's register*, p. 31; J. Mills et al. (eds), *Calendar of the justiciary rolls of Ireland*, 3 vols (Dublin, 1905–56), i, p. 306; *Cal. justic. rolls*, ii, p. 476; *Cal. justic. rolls*, iii, p. 285; NAI, RC 7/13 (iv), pp 22–4; *Cal. docs Ire.*, ii, no. 1577, p. 313; *Chartul. St Mary's, Dublin*, ii, p. 349. 24 *Alen's register*, p. 31; *Cal. docs. Ire.*, i, no. 656, p. 101. 25 Ibid., pp 123, 168, 191. There was still a Harold family living at Three Castles during the late 1540s and early 1550s, see *The Irish fiants of the Tudor sovereigns* (repr. Dublin, 1994) *Edw VI*, nos 226, 347, 472. 26 Ball, *A history of the County Dublin*, iii, p. 57; *Cal. docs. Ire.*, iii, no. 180, p. 86; *Cal. docs. Ire.*, iv, no. 612, p. 291. no. 613, p. 295.

Askyl Harold and John son of Robert Archbold in particular.[27] Moreover, it is strongly suggested that the Archbolds were the dominant Ostman lineage before 1170 at Wicklow and in the surrounding district, for, much earlier on 13 March 1190, Pope Clement III confirmed to Archbishop John Comyn of Dublin 'the land of Wickingelo that Archibald held', reflecting Strongbow's grant of about 1173 to Walter de Ridlesford I of Ostman lands, including 'Brien and the land of the sons of Thorkill with appurtenances'.[28]

Besides the mix of Irish, Ostmen and English of the marches, another layer of ethnic diversity can be detected amid the marchlands of south Dublin and Wicklow. Even before the 1160s, the Leinster coast always acted as a magnet for the Welsh. In previous centuries the kingdoms scattered along the Leinster coast had many political and commercial links with Wales. To demonstrate this point, Dr Ailbhe MacShamhráin has shown the occurrence of British names among the genealogies of the Leinster princes. Furthermore, the cult of St Kevin was also exported successfully to the Isle of Man, while Welsh and Cornish saints figure prominently in the hagiography of Glendalough. And, as shown by other scholars, there can be no doubt as to the strength of the connection between the Ostman city-state of Dublin and the North Welsh kingdoms before 1169. For example, the eleventh-century Ostman kings of Dublin appear to have settled an exiled Welsh dynast from Gwynedd and some of his followers at Cloghran in north Dublin, a community that evolved into the Fitzrery family of Cloghran.[30] About the same time, the Ostmen also appear to have planted some of the men of Gwynedd at Carrickmines in the Vale of Dublin. These Welshmen were most probably the ancestors of the later Howels and the Walshes of Carrickmines.[31]

The English conquest of Leinster created a whole host of new ties with Wales. Many English lords of Leinster, such as the Bigods, de Valences, de Bohuns, de Clares and Mortimers, held lands in Wales, while lesser marcher lords such as the Blunds, Roches, fitz Rhyses, Lawlesses, de Valles and Pencoits were all Cambro-English in origin. On the Leinster coast there seem also to have been communities of Welsh merchants at Arklow and Wicklow.[32]

---

27 NAI, RC 7/13 (iv), pp 22–4; Nicholls, 'Anglo-French Ireland', p. 373.   **28** *Alen's register*, p. 17. That the Archbolds originated in the barony of Wicklow is further confirmed by their appearance in the crown pleas of Kildare on 28 April 1314, see *Cal. justic. rolls*, ii, p. 314; *Report of the Deputy Keeper of the public records in Ireland* (Dublin, 1869–), no. 39 (1907), p. 66 [hereafter *DKR*].   **29** A. MacShamhráin, *Church and polity in pre-Norman: the case of Glendalough* (Maynooth, 1996), pp 68, 124.   **30** E. Curtis, 'The Fitzrerys, Welsh lord of Cloghran, Co. Dublin', in *Louth Arch. Soc. Jn.* (1921), pp 13–15; S. Duffy, 'Ireland and the Irish sea region, 1014–1318', unpublished Ph.D. thesis (University of Dublin, 1993), pp 4, 109–11, 231; M.T. Flanagan, 'Historia Gruffud vab Kenan and the origins of Balrothery', in *Cambrian Medieval Celtic Studies*, no. 28 (1994), pp 71–94.   **31** O'Byrne, 'A much disputed land', pp 231–4; see also idem, 'On the frontier: Carrickmines Castle and Gaelic Leinster', *Archaeology Ireland*, vol. 16, no. 3 (Autumn, 2002), pp 13–5.   **32** S. Duffy, 'Ireland and the Irish sea region, 1014,1318', p. 135; P.

These Welsh colonists spearheaded the colonisation of the Dublin marches and the Wicklow mountains. To the forefront of this colonising drive were the Welsh marcher lineages of fitz Rhys and Lawless. The fitz Rhyses were followers of Walter de Ridlesford I. He, after the defeat of the O'Tooles of Uí Muiredaig in 1177–8, pushed into Imaal in pursuit of the more belligerent Uí Tuathail branches.[33] And it was to Rhys son of Philip, the fitz Rhys progenitor, that de Ridlesford entrusted the task of hammering down Imaal, granting him the half of Imaal in Uí Muiredaig for the service of a knight. Between 1185 and 1193 John, lord of Ireland, confirmed de Ridlesford's donation to Rhys son of Philip.[34] The fitz Rhys lordship in Imaal lasted just over a hundred years, ending with Geoffrey fitz Rhys's grant of his holdings to Sir Theobald Butler on 2 November 1294.[35] Even so, the fitz Rhys arrival in Imaal birthed a colonist community still existent there in the late 1350s. Although the fitz Rhyses forcibly created their lordship of Imaal, establishing a borough at Donaghmore with a large protecting motte at Castleruddery, they fostered links with the defeated O'Tooles.[36] Before 1256 Philip fitz Rhys granted lands to Moriertagh O'Toole (Muirchertach Ua Tuathail), allowing the Irish to participate in the feudal settlement of Imaal.[37] For their part, the O'Tooles displayed some affection for their new masters, incorporating the forenames Geoffrey, David and Elias into their nomenclature.

If the fitz Rhyses of Imaal were the most powerful Welsh lineage in west Wicklow, the Lawlesses came to dominate much of east Wicklow. In comparison to the fitz Rhyses, the Lawlesses do not seem to have belonged to the first wave of newcomers. Instead they probably arrived in Ireland during the early years of the thirteenth century. They are first mentioned living on the lands of the archbishopric of Dublin during the 1212–28 reign of Archbishop Henry de Londres, indicating that they may have been his clients originally. And it was not long before they were in trouble. Between 1212 and 1228 a Walter fitz Hugh Lawless lost his life in a fatal entanglement with two

Becker, 'Dublin Merchant Guild Roll, *c.*1190,1265', unpublished MPhil (University of Dublin, 1995), p. 125. **33** W. Stokes (ed.), 'The annals of Tigernach', *Revue Celtique*, 16–18 (1895–7), repr. in 2 vols (Felinfach, 1994), s.aa. 1177, 1178. **34** E. St John Brooks, 'The de Ridlesfords', *RSAI Jn.*, 81 (1951), pp 116–29; L. Price, 'The grant to Walter de Ridlesford of Brien and the land of the sons of Turchill', *RSAI Jn.*, 84–5 (1954–5), p. 74; *Expugnatio*, n. 113, p. 305; E. Curtis (ed.) *Calendar of Ormond deeds*, 6 vols (Dublin, 1932–43), i, no. 8, p. 4; *Cal. docs Ire.*, i, no. 1757, p. 262. For Theobald Butler's grant of the lands of Kilrenner to Rhys son of Philip, see *Ormond deeds*, i, no. 113, p. 48. **35** For Geoffrey fitz Rhys's grant to Butler see *Ormond deeds*, i, no. 321, p. 131. See also his earlier dealings and grants to Butler of 29 October 1292 and 31 October 1294, see *Ormond deeds*, i, no. 319, p. 130, no. 320, p. 131. See also Eustace le Poer's grant of probably the late thirteenth century of the manor of Donaghmore in Imaal to Edmund Butler , see N.B. White (ed.), *The Red Book of Ormond* (Dublin, 1932), p. 89. See Geoffrey fitz Rhys's grant of lands in Imaal to Archbishop John de Sandford in January 1288; see *Ormond deeds*, i, no. 288, p. 112. **36** E. Grogan and A. Kilfeather, *Archaelogical inventory of County Wicklow* (Dublin, 1997), p. 177. **37** *Alen's register*, p. 141.

Irishmen, while Simon Lawless, a poacher in the royal forests, was fined half a mark by the royal courts of justice in 1228. Indeed, Simon was not alone in his offence. Five others of Ostman and Irish ancestry also faced similar charges and varying fines, including the son of Obonechan Macnabboth and MacLauchelin Othothel.[38] Over time, the Lawlesses spread out from the lands of the archbishopric of Dublin into the royal manors and to the fitz Gerald cantred of Wicklow. In 1229–30, Adam, the abbot of St Thomas's, made a grant of lands at Killiskey to William Lawless so that he might build a home there, a charter witnessed by Simon Lawless and John Lawless, along with Thomas of Killoughter and Thomas of Rathnew, presumably kinsmen of the grantee.[39] Considerable coexistence can also be demonstrated between the Lawlesses and the Irish, for many Lawless holdings in east Wicklow lay close to Irish lands. To illustrate this point, Archbishop Luke (1228–55) confirmed the woods of Killiskey, previously held by Lorcán Ua Tuathail, to Meyler Ua Tuathail. In all probability, Meyler's forests must have virtually adjoined the Killiskey lands of William Lawless. And, before 1256, John Lawless shared the townland of Killadreenan (near present-day Newtownmountkennedy) with other Ua Tuathail landowners.[40] The Lawlesses were to build five stone houses for the defence of the region between Wicklow town and Newcastle McKynegan, a territory later known as Lawlesses Country.[41]

The proximity of Irish and settler holdings in the Dublin and Wicklow marches confirmed the emerging partnership between the English, the Irish and the Ostmen of the medieval county of Dublin. Indeed, this partnership was to facilitate greatly the bedding down of the feudal settlement in east Leinster. As has been shown, after the conquest many Irish families sought actively to fit into the feudal settlement. Another example of a pragmatic dynasty was the O'Tooles of Uí Muiredaig. After the English killed Dúnlaing Ua Tuathail in 1178, many O'Tooles fled to the sanctuary of the mountainous regions of Imaal, Glenmalure and to other lands of the bishopric of Glendalough. There Archbishop Lórcan Ua Tuathail of Dublin, Dúnlaing's brother, seems to have created a safe haven on church land for them through a grant of land to the local priory of St Kevin.[42] The O'Tooles seemingly spilt into two families, one based in Kildare and the other in the Wicklow mountains. Like most of the Irish nobility of East Leinster, both families gradually adopted a more conciliatory attitude to the English and sought to carve a place within the new order.

38 *DKR*, no. 35 (1903), p. 31.   39 J.T. Gilbert (ed.), *Register of the abbey of St Thomas, Dublin* (London, 1889), pp 180–81.   40 *Alen's register*, p. 123; L. Price, *The placenames of County Wicklow*, 7 vols (Dublin, 1945–67), p. xlvii [hereafter Price, *Placenames*]. 41 Nicholls, 'Críoch Branach', p. 17; P. Connolly (ed.) *Irish exchequer payments 1270–1446* (Dublin, 1996), p. 320.   42 *Alen's register*, p. 8; O'Byrne, *War, politics and the Irish of Leinster*, pp 17, 27.

Walter Ua Tuathail is a good example of this accommodation. He was a man of some importance with access to common law. The enfranchisement of Walter was through a charter granted to his great-grandfather Gilla Pátraic in 1209 by William Marshal, lord of Leinster. Furthermore, an extent of the Kildare barony of Kilkea taken on 4 October 1311 reveals that Walter (probably the same as the fourteenth-century Walter Dubh Ua Tuathail of Leinster, father of the heretic Adam Ua Tuathail) held seven carucates there.[43] Walter's cousins living in the Leinster mountains were also especially favoured, particularly by the archbishops of Dublin. They retained their tenure of the abbacy of Glendalough; Thomas and Tadeus Ua Tuathail were abbots between 1170 and 1228.[44] Also, the English archbishops of Dublin were prudent enough to cultivate alliances with the O'Tooles. In the early thirteenth century, they focused their attention upon Lórcan, the youthful Ua Tuathail leader. Their fostering of relations with Lórcan was a shrewd move, as he probably dwelt at Glenlorkan, an area adjoining Glendalough. Further confirmation of Ua Tuathail favour in the eyes of the archbishops was the presence of Lórcan on the west Meath campaign of the justiciar, Archbishop Henry de Londres, in 1214 against Máel Sechnaill Óg Ua Máel Sechnaill (O'Melaghlin) and Ua Conchobair Failge, a decision which cost him his life.[45] After Lorcán's death, relations prospered between the archbishopric and the O'Tooles. The latter continued to serve as important officials of the archbishopric, becoming progressively more Anglicised, adopting forenames such as Agatha, Meyler, David, Henry, Nicholas, Elias, Richard, and Walter.[46] In comparison to the warfare raking the midland colony from the 1210s, the different ethnic communities of East Leinster co-existed peacefully. In East Leinster the colony prospered, with these different communities living cheek by jowl, resulting in mutual toleration, promoting mutual indulgence and a long-lived peace. But if the peace between native and newcomer in East Leinster ever broke down, the close cohabitation of the Irish and the colonists spelt mortal danger for the latter.

On the other hand, it would be naive to think that considerable tensions did not bubble beneath the outwardly tranquil surface of East Leinster. Peace in East Leinster, it should be stressed, was entirely dependant upon the continued coexistence of native and newcomer. Many Leinster princes still nursed considerable grievances about the new order, brooding how the conquest cost the loss of ancestral lands. Added to this potent mix of loss and land was the hotly contentious matter of the legal status of the Irish. By the

---

43 Nicholls, 'Anglo-French Ireland', p. 376; *Cal. justic. rolls*, i, p. 271; for the extent of Imaal on 2 October, 1311 see *Red Bk Ormond*, pp 15–6. 44 *Alen's register*, p. 76; MacShamhráin, *Church and polity in pre-Norman*, pp 164–5. 45 D. Murphy (ed.), *The annals of Clonmacnoise* (Dublin, 1896), s.a. 1214; Glanlorkan was among the Glendalough possessions of the priory of All Hallows on 30 August 1604: see *Irish patent rolls of James I* (Dublin, 1966), no. xix, p. 65. 46 *Alen's register*, pp 81–2; Nicholls, 'Anglo-French Ireland', p. 382.

early thirteenth century, the question of access to the common law was proving divisive, leading to the gradual weakening of the position of those Anglophile Leinster nobles. Indeed, the access of the English of Ireland to the law of England became a badge of cultural and racial superiority. For the English of Ireland, access to the law became more than an ethnic birthright, evolving into a triumphant affirmation of their own Englishness. In turn, this begat an exclusive mentality among the settlers, leading to a growing lack of toleration and the development of an offensive attitude towards the Irish. As early as 1228, a problem was emerging in homicide cases. Then it was noted that when juries found that the deceased was Irish, an accused Englishman could walk free without censure. In terms of access to the law, such glaring racial prejudice was becoming obvious.[47]

In that same year, the Cistercian chapter-general authorised Stephen of Lexington, abbot of the English Cistercian house of Stanley, to undertake the reform of the Irish order. While Stephen was quite right to reestablish the internationalism of the order, there was an ethnic aspect to his work. For he was to note: 'How can anyone love cloister or book who knows only Irish?'. In spite of this, the Irish of East Leinster remained remarkably peaceful in contrast to the turbulent condition of the midlands. But the extinction of Marshal lords of Leinster in 1245 and the subsequent division of their lordship seems to have proved a decisive point for the Leinster Irish. In 1246 Henry III confirmed the rapid advance of royal law, ordering that the laws of England be observed in Ireland.[48] By 1253 the chillier climate of great selectivity was evident in Leinster. Then the Leinsterman Malmorth Offorthiern and his brother Rothericus, in obvious difficulties, sent a letter to Henry III. In it, they said that they and their ancestors were always loyal to the English and they should not be prevented from selling their lands.[49] Two years later, in 1255, the archbishop of Tuam wrote to the pope, telling him that the barons of Ireland were preventing the faithful Irish from bequeathing chattels.[50] A year later Pope Alexander IV took Henry III to task in a letter, attacking the English for their attitude towards the Irish, and asked that both races be judged by the same law.[51]

---

47 R.R. Davies, 'The peoples of Britain and Ireland, 1100–1400, III: Laws and customs', *Transactions of the Royal Historical Society*, 6th ser., 6 (1996), pp 5–6; idem., 'The peoples of Britain and Ireland, 1100–1400, II: Names, boundaries and regnal solidarities', ibid., 5 (1995), pp 19–20; Hand, *English law in Ireland*, pp 201–2.   48 O'Byrne, *War, politics and the Irish of Leinster*, 32–3.   49 *Calendar of close rolls 1251–3*, pp 458–9; R. Frame, 'Les Engleys nées en Irlande, the English political identity in medieval Ireland', *Transactions of the Royal Historical Society*, 6th ser., 3 (1993), p. 88; in November 1281 Art Mac Murchada and Caruel Alfortien got safe conduct to visit Earl Roger Bigod of Norfolk, see *Cal. docs Ire.*, ii, no. 1873, p. 405.   50 A.J. Otway-Ruthven, 'The native Irish and English law in medieval Ireland', *I.H.S.*, 7, no. 25 (March, 1950), p. 12; on 30 July 1255, Henry III wrote to his son Edward about the alleged abuses of the law, see *Cal. docs Ire.*, ii, no. 460, p. 74. See also *Cal. papal letters, 1198–1304*, pp 75, 283.   51 G.O. Sayles (ed.), *Documents on the*

The Irish elite in East Leinster was now under pressure, but that most of them still operated within the system shows that many English marchers were more pragmatic than the royal officials. Indeed, Roger Bigod, lord of the liberty of Carlow, patronised his Mac Murchada cousins, employing them as officials of his lordship. As ever, among the most ardent protectors of the Irish were the archbishops of Dublin. Indeed, the inquisition held at the archbishopric's castle at Castlekevin between 1257 and 1263 was an effective demonstration of the relatively benign rule of the archbishops and the hybrid world of the frontier. The ethnic composition of the jury further illustrates this point. Along with Richard and Thomas Lawless, there were ten Irish jurors, including Elias and Simon Ua Tuathail.[52] Indeed, Nicholls noted in 1982 that the law practised in the archbishop's courts differed substantially from the common law, describing it as 'an older stratum of Anglo-French legal practice'. Quite clearly the law of the archbishopric's courts predated the imposition of common law and was at odds with judgments of the royal courts. Importantly, the courts of the archbishopric accepted compensation for theft and the killing of Englishmen.[53] For example, in the case of Donnchad Mac Gilla Mo-Cholmóc, the killer of Roger fitz Gilbert, Bishop William Piron of Glendalough elected to accept compensation for his unlawful killing rather than press for the full implementation of the law. Another case from Archbishop Henry de Londres's pontificate (1212–28) again shows this. Then, Doneiult and Convye MacDeneuilt killed Archbishop Henry's tenant, Walter fitz Hugh Lawless, but, after appearing before the archbishop and his Ostman seneschal Elias Harold, the pair paid money for having killed Lawless.[54]

The mounting tensions between the Irish and English of East Leinster finally snapped in 1269. Fighting seems to have broken out between the Irish and English of the archbishopric of Dublin, before engulfing the southern lands of the medieval county of Dublin and the fitz Gerald barony of Wicklow. Famine seems to have been the spark. This, combined with worsening weather and poor English decisions, resulting from the probable initial insensitivity of Archbishop Fulk de Sandford towards the Irish, shattered the long-lived coexistence of native and newcomer in the region. Although Henry of Almain temporarily put down the rising, it flared up again and continued into 1270.[55] From the scale of the violence, Archbishop Fulk's hold over his Irish tenants had weakened considerably since the death of Muirchertach Ua Tuathail early in the year 1264.[56] Muirchertach's failure to sire a male heir played a

affairs of Ireland before the king's council (Dublin, 1979), p. 3.   **52** *Alen's register*, p. 110.
53 Nicholls, 'Anglo-French Ireland', p. 376.   **54** *Alen's register*, pp 110–11; this compensation method of atoning for unlawful killing did not only pertain to Irishmen. During Archbishop Luke's reign, 1228–55, the Englishman Robert Passauant paid a fine for his killing of Long William Lawless in the archbishopric's tenement of Kilmacberne: see *Alen's register*, p. 112.   **55** O'Byrne, *War, politics and the Irish of Leinster*, pp 58–9.   **56** Ibid., p. 59.

crucial factor in the developing conflict. His death had profound and far-reaching effects, creating a power vacuum in the mountains at a time when tensions were plainly rising. The new Ua Tuathail leaders were probably from the leading family of Imaal, a much more volatile lineage than Muirchertach's followers. They linked up with Gerald Ua Broin, lord of the O'Byrnes, ensuring the swift spread of war throughout the Leinster mountains.

Indeed, Archbishop Fulk's initial ignorance of the plight of the Irish also contributed to the growing crisis in Wicklow, culminating in a directive from England in July 1270 to the king's justiciar, James de Audley, to suppress the revolt. About winter 1270–71 Archbishop Fulk changed tack, adopting a much softer approach towards the Irish, sending his brother John de Sandford to treat with them for peace. The fragile peace was lost after Fulk's death on 6 May 1271. The reign of his absentee successor, John of Darlington, resulted in a prolonged archiepiscopal vacancy that led to the disastrous extension of common law into the Wicklow mountains. The full application of the common law represented an intensification of royal overlordship in the mountains, involving an unacceptable erosion of the position of the Irish. The threat to the authority and status of the Irish leaders provoked a new rising, preventing a return to the *status quo ante*. The intrusion of the royal officials into the Wicklow mountains also coincided with a serious deterioration of the weather, exposing the already restless Irish to further hardship. On this occasion, the O'Byrnes and O'Tooles were joined by the Ostman Harolds, indicating that resentment towards the government was widespread. In the summer of 1271, the alienation of the Harolds from the government was confirmed, as a Stephen Harold languished with three Ua Tuathail hostages and an Ua Broin in government custody.[57]

While the O'Tooles and the O'Byrnes continued to wage war upon the government, the MacMurroughs remained aloof from the struggle until 1274. But the movement of the loyal Muirchertach Mac Murchada in 1274 to adopt the leadership of the war was a serious development. In contrast to their fitz Dermot cousins (formerly the Meic Gilla Mo-Cholmóc), the MacMurroughs had largely preserved their status among the Irish of Leinster. The late entry of Muirchertach into the war during 1274 could also be construed as an attempt to preserve his position against ambitious vassals such as the O'Byrnes. Indeed, Muirchertach's impact was immediate and dramatic, inflicting a devastating defeat upon a large English army at Glenmalure.[58] Despite the capture of Muirchertach at Norragh during 1275, the war in the Leinster mountains raged on unabated. In Muirchertach's absence, Art Mac Murchada now assumed the leadership of the Leinster war, routing the justiciar Geoffrey de Joinville at Glenmalure at 1276. However, de Joinville's successor as justiciar, Robert de Ufford, successfully ended the war in July 1278.[59]

---

57 *Cal. docs Ire.*, ii, no. 1577, p. 313.   **58** R. Flower, 'The Kilkenny chronicle in Cotton MS', *Anal. Hib.*, 2 (1932), p. 332.   **59** O'Byrne, *War, politics and the Irish of Leinster*, p. 61;

Although the Irish had been forced to submit, their grievances remained as bitterly felt as ever, centring upon their severe legal difficulties. It was not only the Leinster princes who wanted a remedy to the situation, many other Irish potentates also evinced a strong desire for a grant enfranchising them with access to the common law. In that same year, 1278, the justiciar Robert de Ufford reported to Edward I that the Irish offered 7,000 marks for a grant of English law.[60] Indeed, the English king thought it a good idea that a grant be made to the Irish, saying: 'it seemed meet to them that a grant of common law of the English should be made, because the laws which the Irish use are detestable to God and so contrary to all that they ought not to be deemed law'.[61] These efforts originated in the attempts, dating from 1274, of Archbishop David MacCarwell of Cashel, and several other prelates, to gain a grant of law for the Irish of Leinster and Munster. But Edward I was unprepared to go ahead with the enfranchising of the Irish without hearing the opinions of the English of Ireland. Accordingly, de Ufford was instructed to ascertain their views. Finding their responses unfavourable, the plan was shelved, as it was again in 1290.[62]

Some aspects of brehon law were imported into English statutes in recognition of the limitations of common law in the borderlands of Ireland. In 1278, the Irish parliament enacted a statute that contained the principle of kin liability (*cin comfhocuis*). According to Geoffrey Hand, this made Irish leaders of semi-autommous areas responsible for their followers.[63] An example of this principle of kin liability on a larger scale can be seen in Muiris Mac Murchada's submission of July 1295 at Castlekevin in the Wicklow mountains. The terms of the submission reveal that Muiris was the acknowledged leader of the Leinster Irish. Muiris promised on behalf of Murchad Ua Broin and Fáelán Ua Tuathail to keep the peace, pledging to punish the O'Byrnes and O'Tooles if they rebelled. But even for a committed Anglophile lord such as Walter Ua Tuathail, the disadvantageous legal status of the Irish proved a constant reminder of inferiority. Before the justiciar, John Wogan, Walter took a legal action against William son of David and Jordan le Palmer at the Kildare assizes on 13 July 1299, claiming that the pair had tried to deseise him of some lands at Corbaly Otothill near Tancardestown, Co. Kildare.[64] The

J.T. Gilbert (ed.), *Facsimiles of the national manuscripts of Ireland*, ii (Dublin, 1878), plate lxxvi, no. 3; *Annals of Clonmacnoise*, s.a. 1276. **60** A. Gwynn, 'Edward I and the proposed purchase of English law for the Irish *c.*1276–80', *Transactions of the Royal Historical Society*, 5th ser., 10 (1960), pp 111–26. **61** *Cal. docs Ire.*, ii, no. 1400, p. 263; no. 1408, p. 265. **62** A.J. Otway-Ruthven, 'The request of the Irish for English law, 1277–80', *I.H.S.*, 6 (1948–9), pp 262–70; B. Murphy, 'The status of the native Irish after 1311', *Irish Jurist* (1967), p. 119; Davies, *A discoverie of the true causes*, p. 144. **63** Hand, *English law in Ireland*, p. 203; G. Mac Niocaill, 'The interaction of laws', in J. Lydon (ed.) *The English in medieval Ireland* (Dublin, 1984), p. 110. **64** *Cal. justic. rolls*, i, p. 271; *Red Bk Ormond*, pp 13–15. On 3 October 1311, Jordan le Palmer held Carrig in the barony of Kilkea; he must have been a close neighbour of Walter Ua Tuathail. John Wogan was the feudal overlord of

Englishmen answered that they did not have to answer him as he was a *Hibernicus*, making the plea of the exception of Irishry. This plea had the same effect as the plea of alienage in England. Under English common law, the alien was rightless. For example, the alien could not hold or inherit land, sit on juries, and was incapable of suing at law. In consequence many aliens tried to obtain charters of denizenship, allowing them access to the protection of the law.[65] In making the plea of the exception of Irishry, the two Englishmen made a preemptory attempt to shut Walter Ua Tuathail out of the case on grounds of his Irish blood. As Irish blood was the equivalent of unfree blood, if the plea was proved the pleader would not have to answer such a rightless person. But if it should fail, there could be no reply or further defence and the pleader was shut out.[66] However, the most clear-cut and effective reply to the exception was the production of a charter of enfranchisement or a grant of English law.[67] In the case of Walter Ua Tuathail, he went to his charter box and proved he had access to the law through the production of the charter that William Marshal had granted to his great-grandfather, Gilla Pátraic Ua Tuathail, in 1209.[68] Another such case dated from 1356. Then William Newlagh pleaded that Simon Neal of Clondalkin was Irish and he should not have to answer him. Neal, though, was able to prove successfully that he was descended from the O'Neills of Ulster, one of the five bloods enfranchised by Henry III with a grant of English law in 1219.[69]

The submission of the Irish of Leinster at Castlekevin in July 1295 ushered in an uneasy six-year peace between the Wicklow Irish and the settlers. Early in 1301 the O'Byrnes and the O'Tooles were joined by Muiris Mac Murchada, king of Leinster, in the sack of Wicklow and the castle of Rathdown belonging to the loyal fitz Dermots.[70] The English response was devastating, defeating the Irish completely as well as carrying off their cattle. Although the Irish had suffered a serious reverse, they continued to raid the settlements into the autumn, compelling the English to bring another expedition against them. From government records it is clear that the war had engulfed the whole region, stretching from the north Wicklow coast to Carlow. Between 1 January and 12 February 1302, Walter Wogan received expenses for maintaining 10 men at arms and 24 footmen for the defence of Ofelmeth against the O'Byrnes and the MacMurroughs, while Brother William of Ross, deputy-justiciar of Ireland, relieved Wicklow and the royal castle of Newcastle McKynegan.[71]

both Walter and the le Jordans. **65** Significantly, only the alien's children born after the grant of such a charter could benefit from it. For a comparison of the legal status of Irish with that of an alien, see Davies, *A discoverie of the true causes*, p. 102. **66** Murphy, 'The status of the native Irish after 1311', p. 119. **67** Hand, *English law in Ireland*, p. 200. **68** *Cal. justic. rolls*, i, p. 206. **69** Otway-Ruthven, 'The native Irish and English law in medieval Ireland', pp 5–6; Davies, *A discoverie of the true causes*, p. 103; see also *DKR*, no. 53 (1926), p. 30. **70** *Chartul. St Mary's, Dublin*, ii, pp 330. **71** Connolly (ed.), *Irish*

In 1305 the contraction of the colony was evident. Then Newcastle McKynegan, close to the Wicklow coast, was described as 'a very weak and small castle in a strong march'.[72] Placing Newcastle McKynegan in further peril was the rising unrest of the local Ostman lineages of Archbold and Harold. North of Newcastle McKynegan, the Harolds seized large chunks of the royal manors as the power of central government and the fitz Dermots receded. By 1305 the fitz Dermots had sold their remaining lands in Uí Briúin Chualann to Nigel le Brun, while their lands in the Glencapp and Glencree uplands were under pressure, as evidenced by the killing in December of John Shilgry, the king's sergeant of Glencry (probably Glencree) by Richard son of Reginald Harold.[73] Indeed, the Harolds received sterling assistance from their Archbold kinsmen in their scramble to salvage whatever they could from the wreck of the royal manors, as a glance at a list of felons from December 1305 confirms.[74]

Another figure determined to exploit the situation was the mercurial Murchad son of Gerald Ua Broin (*c*.1265–1338), lord of the O'Byrnes. An ambitious figure, he, appeared as leader of the O'Byrnes in July 1295 during the submission of the Leinster Irish at Castlekevin. Murchad realised that if his lordship was to survive, he had to seize the fertile lands occupied by the settlers of east Wicklow. To achieve his goals, Murchad was prepared to court Ostman discontent. This set him on a collision course with that other great figure of Wicklow politics, Sir Hugh fitz Hugh Lawless, leader of the Lawlesses. Hugh Lawless is first mentioned in 1286 when he and his associate Thomas Karrek were each fined a mark for failing to appear before the courts, before becoming Sir Theobald Butler's attorney in the region in 1292.[75] The alliance with the Butlers was fruitful, for Hugh was sergeant of both the manor of Arklow and the cantred of Wicklow in 1297, inferring that the Butlers now held the barony of Wicklow from the fitz Geralds. After the death of Theobald Butler in 1299, Hugh entered the service of his brother Lord Edmund Butler, also the son-in-law of the justiciar John Wogan.[76] As Hugh posed as the defender of the landed interests of Wogan and Butler in east Wicklow, he was exposed to the hostile intentions of the neighbouring O'Byrnes.

Having said that, Hugh proved a resourceful figure, reaching a temporary understanding with Murchad Ua Broin, as the following incident in 1305 demonstrates. A party of Englishmen led by the Burrokes, clients of Nigel le Brun, the escheator of Ireland, took twelve oxen from Kilpoole near Wicklow town. It was subsequently adduced in evidence that eight of the oxen belonged to Murchad Ua Broin, while the other four were the property of

exchequer payments, 1270–1446, p. 165.   **72** *Cal. docs Ire.*, v, no. 335, p. 117.   **73** *Cal. justic. rolls*, i, p. 476.   **74** *Cal. justic. rolls*, ii, pp 484–5.   **75** *Cal. docs Ire.*, iii, no. 271, p. 122. Thomas Karrek and Hugh Lawless were recorded in 1326 as holding lands near Powerscourt: see *Alen's register*, p. 195; Price, *Placenames*, p. lviii.   **76** *Ormond deeds*, i, no. 448, p. 176.

Hugh Lawless. Accordingly, Hugh and his brother Walter, accompanied by the O'Byrnes, pursued the Burrokes and their men to le Brun's manor of Rathbo near Dublin. After a confrontation, the Burrokes surrendered to the sheriff of Dublin, causing the cattle to be impounded. That the O'Byrnes claimed to be 'the faithful *Hibernici* of Edmund [Butler]' indicates that they may have reached some form of understanding with the Butlers. In their defence, the Burrokes stated that the O'Byrnes were the hostile Irish of Kilpoole, killers of several of their kinsmen. In fact, they added that Kilpoole belonged not to Edmund Butler but to the prior of Conall. The evidence of the Burrokes was accepted by the jury, resulting in a finding that the O'Byrnes were not faithful and therefore outside the law.[77]

It was not long before Hugh Lawless fell out with the Irish, probably due to the continuance of Butler territorial ambition in Wicklow.[78] One of the first signs of trouble was the execution on 17 March 1306 of Macnochi (mac Eochaid) Ua Tuathail and two of his sons along with Lorcan Oboni, described as a strong thief. They had earlier been captured close to the castle of Newcastle McKynegan by Thomas de Suerterby, constable of that castle and a former royal justice.[79] In May the O'Mores of Laois burnt Ballymore in the western Wicklow mountains, leading the justiciar John Wogan to punish Murchad Ua Broin for its sack. Testimony to the growing coordination between the Irish of east and west Leinster was their victory over Wogan's army at Glenealy in the Ua Broin lordship later in 1306. The 'Book of Howth', mentioning this victory, records that Irish came from other parts of Ireland to aid the Irish of Leinster.[80] The fighting continued in 1307, affecting aspects of everyday life for the settlers of east Wicklow. Indeed, the records of the county of Kildare show considerable disorder in the town of Wicklow. All the townsmen of Wicklow, except John Balestre, Simon Lawless, William Cornwaleys and John Lawless, were in heavy mercy, owing considerable fines for trespass.[81]

West of Wicklow town, the situation for the settlers in the mountains was complicated by the outbreak of a famine and the vacancy in the Dublin archbishopric. After the death of Archbishop Richard de Ferings on

77 *Cal. justic. rolls*, ii, pp 479–80.   78 Edmund Butler held Imaal by October 1311: see *Red Bk Ormond*, p. 15.   79 *Chartul. St Mary's, Dublin*, ii, p. 334; 'The Book of Howth', in J.S. Brewer and W. Bullen (eds), *Calendar of the Carew manuscripts*, v (London, 1871), p. 169; Robin Frame, 'The Dublin government and Gaelic Ireland, 1272–1361', unpublished Ph.D. thesis (University of Dublin, 1971), pp 70–71; for de Suerterby's legal career, see Connolly (ed.), *Irish exchequer payments 1270–1446*, pp 123, 125, 129, 130, 131, 134, 137, 139. De Sueterby had served against the Irish of Wicklow during 1294–5, seeing action at Glenmalure, Castlekevin and Newcastle McKynegan: see ibid., p. 125.   80 'Book of Howth', p. 127; *Chartul. St Mary's, Dublin*, ii, pp 333.   81 *Cal. justic. rolls*, ii, p. 336; *DKR*, no. 42 (1911), p. 41. De Suerterby with 36 hobelars and 113 footmen had been based at Newcastle McKynegan in October 1307: see Connolly (ed.), *Irish exchequer payments 1270–1446*, p. 198.

18 October 1306, the government took the archiepiscopal lands into the king's hand until the election of a new archbishop. The election resulted in a prolonged and bitter struggle between Nicholas Butler, brother of Edmund Butler, and the eventual archbishop, Richard de Havering.[82] Like earlier in 1271 royal officials again harassed the Irish living on archbishopric's mountainous lands and interfered among churchlands in the mountains. And, as in 1271, the behaviour of these royal officials helped to provoke the O'Tooles to further violence. In response the Dublin government, in early April 1307, reinforced the garrison of Castlekevin. Evidence of the seriousness of the situation was the government's transfer of Thomas de Suerterby from Newcastle McKynegan to Castlekevin. There he took up the office of constable of Castlekevin, receiving reinforcements of 30 hobelars and 80 footmen as well as food and 1,000 quarrels for crossbows. Aware that the settlers were still unprepared to fight both the O'Byrnes and O'Tooles, the Dublin council now sought to divide them. On 9 April the council offered Murchad Ua Broin the Glenealy lands of Richard Ua Tuathail. In addition, it granted Hugh Lawless Kilfee (in the Devil's Glen above Ashford) belonging to David McGilnecowil Ua Tuathail.[83] While Murchad and Hugh accepted happily, the O'Tooles were still far from being subdued. Their attack came between 18 and 22 April, resulting in a large force under Nigel le Brun engaging them in a series of encounters. On the other hand, the O'Tooles on the other side of the mountains had placed themselves at the service of Thomas Butler of Tullow in 1307, becoming heavily involved in his bitter feud with Arnold le Poer for control of Kynnegh church in Carlow. There, Fáelán Ua Tuathail of Imaal and his kerns guarded the church for Butler against le Poer's forces, and intimidated his candidate for the mastership of the church.[84]

At the same time, considerable turmoil was raging in the barony of Wicklow. The tenants of the barony of Wicklow had withheld feudal services from their overlords. The principal malcontent was Murchad Ua Broin, but the discontent also extended to the Ostman Harolds and Archbolds and settlers such as Amaury de Beaufo of Ennereilly. Either in late 1307 or early 1308 George de la Roche, one of the co-heirs of the barony of Wicklow, exercised his right to seize goods and chattels from the lands of his tenants to compensate himself for his losses. The tenants gave chase, overpowering the bailiffs at Wicklow, taking back their chattels and goods, leaving de la Roche to begin a suit before the Dublin bench. In spring 1308 the ongoing Ua Tuathail revolt increased its ferocity, resulting in the reinforcing of the garrison at Newcastle McKynegan. On 12 May William O'Kinaghan and Cuygnismio Ua Tuathail burnt Castlekevin, sacked Courcouly before threatening Newcastle

82 J. Dalton, *The memoirs of the archbishops of Dublin* (Dublin, 1838), p. 118; T.W. Moody et al. (ed.) *A new history of Ireland* (Oxford, 1976–, in progress), ix, p. 310.   83 *Cal. justic. rolls*, ii, pp 354–5.   84 *Cal. justic. rolls*, ii, pp 353, 353; *Cal. justic. rolls*, iii, pp 14–5.

McKynegan some days later.[85] But on 8 June 1308 Murchad Ua Broin joined the O'Tooles and helped to defeat the army of Justiciar Wogan in Glenmalure. Eight days later the Irish followed up their success, descending upon the English of west Wicklow, burning Dunlavin, Tobber and other towns. On 21 August the English had a measure of revenge for their terrible summer. Then William O'Kinaghan, now a prisoner and described as 'that strong thief and murderer' was brought before the justiciar at Dublin and was condemned to be drawn and hanged.[86] In spite of O'Kinaghan's execution, the war continued. On 23 October William de Burgh, deputy of Lord Lieutenant Piers Gaveston, led another expedition against the Irish of mountains. Its impact must have been generally ineffective, for late that year the Irish captured and demolished Castlekevin yet again.

The perilous state prevailing in the marches demanded further government intervention. In spring 1309 Lord Lieutenant Piers Gaveston led an army of about 1,500 into Wicklow to rendezvous with the forces of the marchers and those of the loyal Irish. The support of the marchers and the local knowledge of Henry Ua Tuathail were to prove invaluable for Gaveston's campaign against the O'Byrnes. Other Irish loyalists such as John son of Ralph fitz Dermot of Rathdown would not serve against the O'Byrnes, opting to pay instead a scutage fine of 1*l*. 3*s*. 4*d*. for the service of a knight and a foot sergeant. After Gaveston's subjugation of the O'Byrnes, the lord lieutenant demonstrated his appreciation for the service of Henry Ua Tuathail, rewarding him with £6 'for certain business done'. Against the will of the Irish, between April and June Gaveston had Castlekevin rebuilt and Newcastle McKynegan repaired and cut a pass from Castlekevin to Glendalough.[87] After Gaveston's army returned to Dublin, the O'Byrnes joined Maurice de Caunteton, supporting his rebellion in east Leinster and threatened the whole region to the outskirts of Dublin. At the same time Murchad fell out with Muiris Mac Murchada.

This period heralded an unrivalled period of Ua Broin expansion, for they now raided the Mac Murchada territories in north Carlow and north Wexford. In addition, Murchad ejected the O'Tooles from Glenmalure about this time, settling his Gabhal tSiomoin followers there. On 29 June 1311 Murchad and the O'Tooles of Imaal burnt Saggart and Rathcoole, forcing Wogan and Muiris Mac Murchada to lead great army into the mountains. But at Glenmalure, Murchad along with David son of Fáelán Ua Tuathail fought them to a standstill, forcing the army to retreat.[88] Murchad also sought to

85 *Chartul. St Mary's, Dublin*, ii, pp 336; 'Book of Howth', p. 169.   **86** *Chartul. St Mary's, Dublin*, ii, pp 336–7; 'Book of Howth', p. 169. Glenmalure is spelt as Glendelorragh in the Book of Howth, while the burning of Tobber and Dunlavin is given as 6 July 1308. **87** Frame, 'The Dublin government and Gaelic Ireland', p. 179; Connolly (ed.), *Irish exchequer payments, 1270–1446*, p. 207; *Chartul. St Mary's, Dublin*, ii, p. 338; *DKR*, 45 (1913), p. 24.   **88** *Chartul. St Mary's, Dublin*, ii, p. 339.

strengthen his regional position by wooing Mac Murchada vassals such as the O'Nolans. At the same time he charmed and bullied the Wicklow Ostmen into his camp. In 1313 John Mac Turcaill found himself sharing a cell in Dublin Castle with one of Murchad's hostages, Walter Ua Broin. The pair plotted to escape, but their attempt was foiled by warders, resulting in their subsequent executions.[89]

Hugh Lawless and his fellow settlers gained relief from the marauding Ua Broin in Lent (March and April) 1313. According to the Dublin annalist, Deputy-Justiciar Edmund Butler, patron of the Lawlesses, brought a massive force into the mountains and cornered Murchad in his Glenmalure redoubt. After blockading the valley, Butler forced Murchad's submission, threatening the Ua Broin leader with destruction unless he returned to the king's peace.[90] Murchad took his time to plot his revenge on the Lawlesses. The Lawlesses, though, prepared themselves for the onslaught. In July 1314 Hugh Lawless was appointed constable of the Butler manor of Bray, while kinsmen made alliances with others threatened by the Irish advance. On 21 April Walter Lawless managed to get William Swift, the outlaw and former ally of the O'Tooles, admitted to fine.[91] Furthermore, Hugh Lawless now competed with Murchad for the support of the local Ostman lineages. By posing as a patron of the Archbolds, Hugh Lawless attempted to turn the tables on the O'Byrnes. Along with Maurice Tyrell and David Archbold, Hugh Lawless, on 28 April 1314, petitioned Edmund Butler for the pardon of Reginald Archbold and his men, arguing successfully that they were invaluable in the struggle against the Irish.[92]

The landing of Edward Bruce at Larne in May 1315 was to bring the storm of war to the doorsteps of the Wicklow settlers. Along with David son of Fáelán Ua Tuathail, Murchad was also allied to Laoiseach Ua Mórda of Laois. Now he seized the chance to even the scores with Edmund Butler and Hugh Lawless, directing deadly body blows at the settlers, burning the towns and castles of Arklow, Wicklow, Newcastle McKynegan and Bray before linking up with the O'Mores to sack Athy in late 1315.[93] Shortly afterwards, Edmund Butler braked the momentum of the Irish by beating the O'Mores in a pitched battle. The year 1316 was to be the apex of Murchad's career. But it began ingloriously. Early in the year Edmund Butler administered a double dose of defeat to the O'Mores at Castledermot, Co. Kildare and at Ballylehane

89 *Cal. justic. rolls*, iii, p. 285.   90 *Chartul. St Mary's, Dublin*, ii, 341.   91 J.T. Gilbert (ed.), *Historic and municipal documents of Ireland, 1172–1320* (London, 1870), pp 456–7; *Cal. justic. rolls*, iii, p. 318; for the continuing Butler acquisition of lands in Wicklow, see Fromund le Brun's grant of his lands at Glencap to Edmund Butler in March 1314, in *Ormond deeds*, i, no. 426, p. 168, no. 487, p. 195, no. 488, pp 195–6.   92 *Cal. justic. rolls*, iii, p. 314. These Archbolds owed 40s. for trepass in 1318: see the records of the county of Kildare in *DKR*, no. 39 (1907), p. 66.   93 'Book of Howth', p. 134; *Chartul. St Mary's, Dublin*, ii, p. 148.

on the borders of Laois and Carlow. In response to the defeats of the O'Mores, Murchad with a force of Scots exacted a terrible revenge upon the English and Welsh of Wicklow. Simultaneously, he checked the Lawless patronage of the Ostmen, making overtures to the Harolds and the Archbolds. On 8 February Hugh Lawless pleaded before Edmund Butler at Dublin for protection from the O'Byrnes, describing the plight of the Wicklow settlers, caught in 'a confined and narrow part of the country, namely between Newcastle McKynegan and Wicklow, where they have the sea between Wales and Ireland for a wall on one side, and the mountains of Leinster on the other where the said Irish felons are'. Lawless did not spare the ears of Butler, informing him: 'by the malice and wantonness of the Irish of the mountains of Leinster, felons of the king, they [the English] have been expelled and removed from their fortresses, manors and houses up to the present, and many of the said faithful subjects of the king have been slain by the Irish felons'.

Realising the importance of Ostman support for the Lawlesses, on 21 February Butler, with the approval of the council, assigned David Archbold and his men to defend Newcastle McKynegan from the Scots and the Irish threatening to besiege it.[94] This attempt to attach the Ostmen more firmly to the Lawlesses can be construed as a desperate effort to dissuade the rest of the Archbolds from revolt. In the days before 24 February, the Archbolds and the Harolds joined Murchad and the O'Tooles in an all-out assault upon the fitz Gerald barony of Wicklow, sacking Wicklow town.[95] And such was the their devastation of that barony that the sergeant could not execute his office, resulting in no rents being collected there for the entirety of 1316.[96] As he had earlier done in Shillelagh during 1295–6, Murchad was eradicating the English presence in east Wicklow by forcing the settlers to flee their lands and farms.

As mid-year approached, Murchad's luck changed. On 22 May his brother Dúnlaing was killed near Dublin.[97] Worse was to follow: in June David son of Fáelán Ua Tuathail's attack on Tullow was annihilated by the English with probable Mac Murchada connivance; this was followed up by another English victory over the Wicklow Irish at Baltinglass. On 8 September, Ua Tuathail narrowly avoided the fate of Dúnlaing when the Dublin citizens led by John Comyn attacked the encampment of his raiding party at Cullenswood. These reverses slowed the pace of Murchad's offensive, leading to a gradual improvement in colonist fortunes in east Wicklow.[98] There the Lawlesses managed to maintain their alliance with at least one of the Archbold lineages. On 29 September a Rithnius Archbold and Thomas fitz Simon Lawless took over from David Archbold the defence of Newcastle McKynegan until 2 November.[99] Further help for the Lawlesses was forthcoming from the

94 Connolly (ed.), *Irish exchequer payments, 1270–1446*, p. 236.   95 *Chartul. St Mary's, Dublin*, ii, p. 349.   96 *DKR*, no. 39 (1907), p. 67.   97 'Book of Howth', p. 135. 98 O'Byrne, *War, politics and the Irish of Leinster*, pp 68–9.   99 Connolly (ed.), *Irish*

marcher families of the Vale of Dublin, as evidenced by the presence of Maurice Howel of Carrickmines at Newcastle McKynegan from November 1316 to January 1317. The continued importance of Newcastle McKynegan as a government bastion was illustrated further by the appointment of Duncan McGoffrey, the former custodian of the Isle of Man, as its constable.[100]

Combined with the improvement of settler fortunes, Bruce's threat also began to recede in the winter of 1316–17, allowing the English to take the offensive in Leinster. In September 1317, Lord Lieutenant Roger Mortimer waged a successful campaign against David son of Fáelán Ua Tuathail in Imaal before defeating another Irish force on the borders of Uí Chennselaig. On his way back to Dublin, Mortimer invaded Murchad's lordship, forcing battle in Glenealy in east Wicklow, where Mortimer inflicted a heavy defeat upon the O'Byrnes and their Archbold allies; this forced Murchad to come to peace at Dublin Castle.[101] Moreover, Thomas fitz John FitzGerald, 2nd earl of Kildare, now attempted to recover the lost Geraldine influence in Wicklow at the expense of a weakened Murchad. After the submission of Murchad, Kildare gave security for his family's Archbold tenants on 28 October 1317. Later, on 2 September 1318, Kildare continued to exploit existent fissures among the Wicklow Irish, driving a wedge between Murchad's Ua Tuathail allies by giving Áed Óg Ua Tuathail land for service against his kinsmen of Imaal.[102] In return for this peace, Hugh Lawless suffered a considerable fiscal cost. In 1319 he resigned his commission as constable of Bray, complaining of crippling debts, pointing out that he could only get the profit of two salmon from the war-ravaged manor of Bray.[103]

It was not to be long before Murchad Ua Broin and Hugh Lawless locked horns again. In this struggle, local knowledge proved to be the key to the continued survival of the Wicklow colony. For between Michaelmas 1324 and Trinity 1325 John de Crescy and five esquires were in receipt of £10 for reconnoitring mountain passes used by the Leinster Irish.[104] Indeed, the government allowed the Lawlesses to be flexible in their dealings with the O'Byrnes. In an encounter during early May 1325 Murchad clashed with Hugh Lawless, capturing several of the latter's kinsmen. Aware of the predicament of the Lawlesses, the justiciar, John Darcy, agreed provisionally to release Magnus Ua Broin, Murchad's son, to Hugh Lawless, enabling him to arrange a prisoner exchange with the O'Byrnes. As part of these negotiations, Murchad met Kildare at Baltinglass Abbey, where the Irishman issued his letters patent of agreement, undertaking to deliver another son in exchange for the captive. This concluded, on 25 May Darcy wrote to the treasurer

exchequer payments, 1270–1446, p. 239.   **100** Ibid., pp 228, 243, 273, 315.   **101** *Chartul. St Mary's, Dublin*, ii, 356–7.   **102** Ibid., pp 356,7; 'Book of Howth', p. 142.   **103** Ball, *History of the County Dublin*, iii, p. 101; Gilbert (ed.), *Historic and municipal documents of Ireland*, pp 457–62.   **104** Connolly (ed.), *Irish exchequer payments, 1270–1446*, p. 303.

authorising him to allow Hugh Lawless to collect Magnus Ua Broin for the exchange.[105] But such was the nature of frontier warfare that Hugh Lawless did not have to wait long before the boot was on the other foot. In 1326–7 Hugh and his brother Walter Lawless captured Murchad's nephews, Gerald and Thomas, sons of Dúnlaing Ua Broin.[106]

As the 1320s wore on, the Lawlesses recovered from the O'Byrnes' depredations during the Bruce Wars. The recovering strength of the colony was further boosted by a major shift in the attitudes of the Ostman lineages of Harold and Archbold. Although during 1325 John son of Maurice Harold was among Ua Tuathail hostages in Dublin Castle, it was clear that the Ostmen regretted their alliance with the O'Byrnes, preferring now closer relations with the Lawlesses.[107] Moreover, the Archbolds and the Harolds had fought among themselves. Through the vouch-safe of Duncan McGoffrey, royal constable of Newcastle McKynegan, Maurice Harold, Henry Harold and John Miles, Alexander fitz Gilbert Harold accounted 10*l.* for killing William son of Reginald Archbold[108] Furthermore, the government and the archbishops of Dublin also sought to stabilise the marches, cultivating the remaining loyalist elements among the O'Tooles. To check David son of Fáelán Ua Tuathail of Imaal, the prominent Murchad son of Nicholas Ua Tuathail entered government service, while Malmorth (Máel Mórda) Ua Tuathail was appointed constable of the archbishopric's castle at Tallaght during 1326.[109]

On the other hand, some Irish loyalists and settler families had little stomach for continuing the struggle against the Wicklow Irish. John son of Ralph fitz Dermot of Rathdown entered the service of the archbishop of Dublin and took up the more secure post of bailiff on the archiepiscopal manor of Shankill, while the fitz Rhyses quit Imaal entirely for the safety of the Butler manor of Corduff near Dublin.[110] An unexpected boost for the settlers was the capture of David son of Fáelán Ua Tuathail by Sir John de Wellesley in 1328. At his trial before Justices Nicholas Hastocke and Elias Asborne in Dublin, David, described as 'the strong thief, the king's enemy, the burner of the churches, the destroyer of the people' was sentenced to be hanged, drawn and quartered.[111] The execution of the Ua Tuathail leader brought relief for the Lawlesses and the Ostmen. On 21 January 1329 John Lawless was recorded as holding the cantred of Wicklow for half a knight's

---

105 Frame, 'The Dublin government and Gaelic Ireland', p. 249; Gilbert (ed.), *Facsimiles of the national manuscripts of Ireland*, iii (1879), plate xiv. The hostages held by Murchad Ua Broin were Simon fitz Simon Lawless and his brother William, along with Alexander Bernagh. 106 Connolly (ed.), *Irish exchequer payments, 1270–1446*, p. 320. 107 Ibid., p. 311. 108 *DKR*, no. 42 (1911), p. 53; Connolly (ed.), *Irish exchequer payments, 1270–1446*, pp 303, 315; William son of Reginald Archbold may have been son of Reginald Archbold mentioned in 1314. 109 Frame, 'The Dublin government and Gaelic Ireland', p. 488. 110 M.J. McEnery and Raymond Refauseé (eds), *Christ Church deeds* (Dublin, 2001), no. 557, p. 141. 111 'Book of Howth', pp 149–50; *Chartul. St Mary's, Dublin*, ii, p. 366.

fee from Richard, 3rd earl of Kildare, while at the same time William fitz Hugh Lawless occupied the office of the royal constable of Newcastle McKynegan.[112] A real blow for the colony in east Wicklow was the death of Hugh Lawless probably sometime in 1329. The death of Lawless may have prompted Murchad Ua Broin to exploit the situation. Although Domnall son of Art Mac Murchada was a captive and David son of Fáelán Ua Tuathail executed, Murchad moved alone against the alliance of the Ostmen, Irish loyalists and the Lawlesses. The justiciar, John Darcy, keenly aware of the danger, listened to the pleas for help coming from Wicklow. Accordingly, Darcy based his troops around Newcastle McKynegan and Wicklow, but that the justiciar was supplied by sea indicates that Murchad had cut the overland route. On 15 August 1329 the colonist levies under Robert Lawless, Maurice Howel, Thomas Archbold and Thomas Harold, with the support of Darcy's troops, brought Murchad to heel after a bloody encounter. To prevent his defeated forces being hunted down, Murchad surrendered himself and was imprisoned in Dublin Castle, but he was shortly released in return for other hostages and was soon back terrorising the settlers.[113]

The escape of Domnall son of Art Mac Murchada from Dublin Castle in January 1331 signalled the outbreak of the Leinster War of 1331–2.[114] The war began with an English victory over the Irish on 9 April in Uí Chennselaig. In a coordinated attack, the MacMurroughs and the O'Byrnes seized Arklow on 21 April, while the O'Tooles ravaged Tallaght.[115] However, the conduct of this war was characterised by the intense bitterness that emerged between the Irish and the settlers. In mid-1331, the Irish 'plundered the English and burned churches', including the church at Freynstown in west Wicklow, having reportedly forced eighty people inside it. The Dublin annalist graphically described how 'a certain chaplain of the said church, clothed in sacred vestments' wished to leave the burning church with 'the body of the Lord'. As the priest attempted to leave, the Irish drove him back inside and burned him with the rest. In response to this atrocity, the pope ordered the archbishop of Dublin to excommunicate the O'Tooles. During Easter 1332 (between 19 April and 25 April) the exchequer paid the Dominican Richard McCormegan 6s. 8d. for pronouncing a sentence of excommunication upon the O'Tooles.[116] The Irish went on to take the castles of Newcastle Lyons, Ferns and Cowlaugh (Coillache, west Wicklow) that summer before attacking the liberty of

---

112 G. Mac Niocaill (ed.), *The Red Book of the earls of Kildare* (Dublin, 1964), no. 125, p. 106; Connolly (ed.), *Irish exchequer payments, 1270–1446*, p. 333.   113 Frame, 'The Dublin government and Gaelic Ireland', p. 255; *DKR*, no. 43 (1912), p. 28. Robert Lawless was killed fighting against the O'Byrnes on 15 August: see *Chartul. St Mary's, Dublin*, ii, p. 371. Raymond Lawless was killed through treachery at Wicklow in 1330: see *Chartul. St Mary's, Dublin*, ii, p. 373; 'Book of Howth', pp 155–6.   114 'Book of Howth', p. 156.   115 *Chartul. St Mary's, Dublin*, ii, p. 374; 'Book of Howth', p. 157.   116 Connolly (ed.), *Irish exchequer payments, 1270–1446*, p. 347; *Chartul. St Mary's, Dublin*, ii, p. 376.

Wexford. Described as 'full of malice, neglecting and small esteeming their duty to God and to the Church, persevering in their folly', the Irish were turned back by the English of Wexford on the banks of Slaney.[117] However, the gradual collapse of Murchad Ua Broin's alliance with Domnall son of Art Mac Murchada throughout autumn 1331 turned the tide in favour of the government. Late in 1331 Domnall mac Airt confirmed his rift with Murchad Ua Broin, entering government service for an annual fee of 40 marks, marking a decisive point in the war.

By 3 May 1332 Justiciar Anthony Lucy was ready to move against the Irish, retaking Clonmore castle, Co. Carlow on 15 June. Yet Murchad still remained dangerous. Indeed, he was boosted by the mysterious assassination of Murchad son of Nicholas Ua Tuathail on 11 June during a parliament in Dublin.[118] Lucy with James Lawless and Richard fitz William Lawless did not allow the O'Byrnes rest on their laurels for long, taking Arklow from them between 5 and 24 August.[119] While the Lawlesses had been aided by Murchad son of Nicholas Ua Tuathail in 1329 and 1331, they now cultivated Murchad Ua Broin's nephew Gerald son of Dúnlaing Ua Broin, their hostage of 1327. And as the noose tightened around the O'Byrnes, Gerald mac Dúnlainge with James fitz William Lawless and his brother Richard proved capable of catching Murchad off guard, capturing him during the latter half of 1331.[120] As in 1329, Murchad promised he would repent his ways. But upon his release, he unfurled his true colours once more. Throughout 1334 Gerald mac Dúnlainge opposed his uncle, while on 13 November 1334 Domnall son of Art Mac Murchada received £40 for the capture of one of Murchad's sons, Philip Ua Broin.[121] On 1 March 1335, Murchad dispatched a delegation, including Gerald mac Dúnlainge and Robert Lawless, to the justiciar John Darcy at Newcastle McKynegan. There they informed the justiciar that the now aged Murchad had agreed to a negotiated peace and that he would live with his wife live under English protection at Wicklow or Kilmartin. Typically, Murchad did not stay long in protective custody. He is last mentioned sometime between June 1335 and October 1337, negotiating at Fotherd in the O'Nolan lordship on behalf of many of the Leinster Irish with Prior Roger Outlaw, deputy to Justiciar John Darcy.

After Murchad's death sometime in 1338, several competitors emerged to contest for the Ua Broin leadership. One of these seems to have been Gerald mac Dúnlainge, but he appears to have ultimately lost out to Murchad's son, Tadc Ua Broin. Gerald mac Dúnlainge's defeat condemned him to a life of

---

117 'Book of Howth', p. 158.   118 *Chartul. St Mary's, Dublin*, ii, p. 379; 'Book of Howth', p. 160; R. Butler (ed.), *The annals of Ireland by Friar John Clyn* (Dublin, 1849), p. 25. 119 Connolly (ed.), *Irish exchequer payments, 1270–1446*, p. 353; *DKR*, no. 43 (1912), p. 54. 120 Frame, 'The Dublin government and Gaelic Ireland', p. 275. See Connolly (ed.), *Irish exchequer payments, 1270–1446*, p. 335.   121 Ibid., pp 275, 286, 290, 490–1.

service with English forces to maintain his power. He was not the only Irish noble in the pay of the government: witness the service of Fynnok and Cathal Ua Tuathail against the O'Byrnes in 1338–40 and 1342 respectively.[122] Indeed, the successful exploitation of the Irish dynastic splits often ensured the survival of the settlers. Moreover, Brother Alexander Lawless and Brother Gerald Lawless, both Dominicans, received expenses for going to parts of Wicklow and Arklow to treat for peace with the O'Byrnes between 1337 and 1339.[123] These friars were obviously keen for the restoration of peace near Arklow, for their kinsman Thomas fitz Michael Lawless was constable of Arklow castle in 1338–9.[124] The Lawlesses, though, must have drawn comfort from the continuance of their anti-Ua Broin alliance with the Harolds. For we find Peter Harold serving as constable of Ballytenneth (Powerscourt) from 6 August to 6 November 1338, while Elias Harold received a payment of £2 for his expenses in defending the marches of Leinster in 1337–8.[125]

This pattern of merry-go-round politics between the settlers and the Irish continued into the 1340s. However, the Irish, particularly the O'Tooles, were to concentrate increasingly upon the physical destruction of settler castles in north and east Wicklow, focusing upon Castlekevin and Ballytenneth (Powerscourt) in particular. At Ballytenneth during 1339–41, John Butler and Stephen de Crophull fought off the besieging Irish (probably the O'Tooles), but could not prevent the partial destruction of the castle.[126] As for Tadc Ua Broin, he seemed a less confident leader than his father Murchad, joining his cousin Gerald mac Dúnlainge for most of the early 1340s on government campaigns against the O'Tooles and the MacMurroughs. Indeed, the government was so pleased with Tadc Ua Broin's service on the 1339 campaign by the justiciar, Bishop Thomas Charlton, against the MacMurroughs, that they granted him a bonus of 13s. 4d. towards the cost of a robe.[127] During the summer of 1342 Tadc felt confident enough to throw off his allegiance to the government and resume the conquest of east Wicklow.

Although Domnall Óg Mac Murchada had fought the expedition of Justiciar John Morice from August to October 1341, he with the O'Tooles now saw the chance to get revenge on the O'Byrnes. Accordingly, Domnall Óg and the O'Tooles served on a government campaign against Tadc Ua Broin throughout July 1342.[128] Even though the MacMurroughs, O'Byrnes and

---

122 Ibid., pp 296, 306; J. Mills (ed.) *Account roll of the priory of Holy Trinity, Dublin, 1337–46* (Dublin, 1897; repr. 1996), p. 157. Before his service, Fynnok O'Toole had been captured by the English in 1337–9, see Connolly (ed.), *Irish exchequer payments, 1270–1446*, p. 392. 123 Connolly (ed.), *Irish exchequer payments 1270–1446*, p. 392; Frame, 'The Dublin government and Gaelic Ireland', p. 294. 124 Ibid., p. 390. 125 Ibid., pp 390–1. 126 To illustrate this point, in 1339–41 Stephen de Crophull was granted £5 for defending the castle of Ballytenneth (Powerscourt), while John Butler, constable of Ballytenneth, received expenses of £10:see Connolly (ed.), *Irish exchequer payments 1270–1446*, p. 402. 127 Connolly (ed.), *Irish exchequer payments, 1270–1446*, pp 396, 398, 405. 128 Frame,

O'Tooles had fought each other bitterly during these years, the fluid nature of Leinster politics ensured that reconciliation was soon on the cards. In 1343 these dynasties patched up their differences to threaten the settlers along the Leinster coast. Another major blow for the settlers was the fall of Castlekevin during 1343, prompting the justiciar Ralph de Ufford, on 24 November 1343, to dispatch John Butler of Ballytenneth and 42 footmen to defend Newcastle McKynegan from a combined force of MacMurroughs, O'Byrnes and O'Tooles.[129] Their fences mended now, the MacMurroughs, O'Nolans, O'Byrnes and the O'Tooles hatched another plan to wreak havoc throughout East Leinster.[130] This ended in disaster, de Ufford and the royal army wreaked devastation throughout Uí Chennselaig in autumn 1344, forcing the Irish to sue for peace. Even though government forces apparently never reoccupied Castlekevin, de Ufford's victory bought breathing space for the settlers of Imaal and east Wicklow.

With peace restored for the moment, the government implemented a longer-term strategy to pacify the Irish. The architect of this strategy was Justiciar Thomas Rokeby. The first step of Rokeby's policy was based upon the establishment of friendly lords in the Ostman and Welsh lordships in the marches of Dublin and Wicklow. Clearly, the Welsh and the Ostmen had persisted with their united front against the O'Byrnes, resulting in the gradual emergence of an overall captaincy of the borderlands of south Dublin and north Wicklow. The alliance of the Ostmen and the Welsh agreed with Rokeby as it dovetailed perfectly with his own strategy. On 23 April 1350 Rokeby put his stamp of approval on the Ostman/Welsh alliance, presiding over a college of Archbolds, Howels, Lawlesses and Walshes that elected Walter Harold as leader of his lineage.[131] On 29 August Rokeby put the second step of his plans into action, leading an expedition against the O'Byrnes, forcing them to sue for peace.[132] Rokeby then presided over the election, sometime in autumn 1350, of his protégé, John Ua Broin, the son of Tadc Ua Broin. Not content with settling the O'Byrnes, Rokeby, about Michaelmas 1350, reached an accommodation with Áed son of David Ua Tuathail, leader of the

---

'The Dublin government and Gaelic Ireland', p. 306.   **129** Connolly (ed.), *Irish exchequer payments, 1270–1446*, pp 317, 413; Butler (ed.), *Annals of Clyn*, p. 30; Frame, 'The Dublin government and Gaelic Ireland', p. 9. In the royal manor of Newcastle McKynegan during 1346, Walter fitz Thomas Lawless owed 1*l*. 2*s*. 8*d*. on the 34 acres just to the north of the castle , see *DKR*, no. 54 (1927), p. 22. In 1347 Robert Lawless and others were appointed guardians of the peace in the marches with the power to raise military force.   **130** H.F. Berry (ed.), *Statutes and ordinances and acts of the parliament of Ireland, King John to Henry V* (Dublin, 1907), p. 365.   **131** Walter Harold's electoral college consisted of electors drawn from the Archbold, Howel, Walsh and Lawless families, including Peter Howel, Richard fitz Michael Howel, Elias fitz Robert Walsh and Hugh fitz Robert Lawless, later constable of Newcastle McKynegan in 1353: see Curtis, 'The clan system among the English settlers in Ireland', pp 116–17.   **132** Curtis, 'The clan system among the English settlers in Ireland', p. 117; Connolly (ed.), *Irish exchequer payments, 1270–1446*, p. 442.

O'Tooles. That Aed Ua Tuathail was later lauded as 'defender of the faithful' contrasted starkly with the career of his own father David mac Fáeláin 'the strong thief, the king's enemy, the burner of the churches, the destroyer of the people'. In 1350–51, Rokeby also enticed others like Gilla Pátraic Ua Broin, Muirchertach Mac Murchada and Ruaidrí Ua Mórda into government service with the promises of fees.[133]

The relative peace that subsequently descended upon the Dublin marches lasted as long as the goodwill of the O'Byrnes. John Ua Broin stayed in English service until the summer of 1353, but was determined to assert his independence. Like his grandfather Murchad, John Ua Broin was intent upon conquering the remaining Lawless and Ostman lands in east Wicklow, and subjected their farms to a regular nightly regime of terror and burnings. As the leading marcher lineage in the region, the Lawlesses were vital to the continued survival of the Welsh and Ostman communities in east Wicklow. There was little room for the Lawlesses and the Ostmen in the plans of the O'Byrnes, leaving them with their backs to the sea and with everything to fight for. Indeed, Rokeby lent the Lawlesses every help to stem the tide, allowing them to become the principal agents of his government in the region. In 1353–4 Edmund Lawless, constable of Wicklow, was in receipt of £25 from the Dublin council for the defence of the town and adjacent parts against hostile Ua Broin attacks, while Hugh fitz Robert Lawless held the office of constable of Newcastle McKynegan in 1353.[134]

John Ua Broin's assertion of his power frightened other Irish leaders such as Muirchertach Mac Murchada, king of Leinster, and Áed Ua Tuathail. It is more than likely that the appointment of Áed Ua Tuathail as 'keeper of parts of the marches of Dublin and Kildare' was in response to the re-emergence of the Ua Broin threat in 1353.[135] In 1353–4 Muirchertach Mac Murchada, Ruaidrí Ua Mórda and Áed Ua Tuathail all supported the government, contributing forces to a major expedition into John's country. These efforts proved successful as John came to peace on 22 March 1354, surrendering 92 cows.[136] Within a month of the Ua Broin submission, Muirchertach Mac Murchada drew the Ua Broin leader into a wider plot against the government. This plot centred on a simultaneous rising of a confederation of Irish lords, involving the invasion of the English marches and the destruction of the king's 'faithful people'.[137] Rokeby, at great personal expense, made overtures to various Irish lords to foil the plot, lavishing clothing, money and precious items amounting to £200 on them.[138] Meanwhile Patrick de la Freigne hunted

---

133 Frame, 'The Dublin government and Gaelic Ireland', p. 342; Connolly (ed.), *Irish exchequer payments 1270–1446*, p. 444.   134 Connolly (ed.), *Irish exchequer payments, 1270–1446*, pp 453–6.   135 Ibid., p. 455. In 1353–4, Áed earned a fee of £8 3s. 4d. 136 Frame, 'The Dublin government and Gaelic Ireland', pp 350–2. Áed contributed 15 hobelars and 4 footmen to this expedition.   137 Ibid., p. 353.   138 Connolly (ed.), *Irish*

the king of Leinster down in late April and conveyed him to Dublin. There Muirchertach Mac Murchada and a Walter de Burgh were charged with treason on 28 April.[139] Regardless of Muirchertach Mac Murchada's capture, John Ua Broin broke his peace with the government and attacked the Lawlesses. As Gerald son of Dúnlaing Ua Broin had earlier tried to court government favour during the 1330s, Murchad son of Magnus Ua Broin, John's first cousin, supported the Lawlesses and the government to further his own ambitions. On a wider scale, the emerging war in Leinster displayed classic signs of extensive coordination among the Leinster dynasties. Indeed, John inflicted a heavy defeat upon Rokeby's army somewhere in east Wicklow, besieging the justiciar in Wicklow castle during October 1354. During negotiations John demanded the release of Muirchertach Mac Murchada. Rokeby apparently agreed. Between 21 and 26 October 1354, Rokeby had the captive Leinster king brought by sea to Wicklow and taught John a lesson by having Mac Murchada torn apart on the walls of Wicklow as a warning to the O'Byrnes, an act that shocked not only the Leinstermen but Irish lords countrywide.[140]

In response to the endemic violence in the marches, Rokeby launched a new strategy to slow the Irish advance, developing a series of defensive wards to protect the settlers, including Newcastle McKynegan, Kilmartin, Killoughter, Saggart, Ballytenneth (Powerscourt), Bray, Glenmore (Devil's Glen), Killiney, Ballycorus, Jamestown and Carrickmines.[141] Central to Rokeby's efforts to contain the O'Byrnes was Áed Ua Tuathail. For Rokeby, Áed Ua Tuathail's ability to resist John Ua Broin's forces and his skill in negotiating with the Ua Broin leader was invaluable. The importance of Áed Ua Tuathail's support for the government was further illustrated by the fact that John le Prestescone was engaged to equip and train his men. However, the O'Byrnes put the O'Tooles under intolerable pressure for defending the English. On 16 June 1355 Áed agreed with Rokeby to defend the English of Tallaght for 40 days, policing the western foothills of the Wicklow mountains with 20 hobelars and 40 footmen. Furthermore, Áed Ua Tuathail's brother, John Ruad Ua Tuathail, was also engaged to protect the settlers of Imaal from the O'Byrnes.[142] In the end, the pressure from the O'Byrnes proved too much for the O'Tooles. That summer John Ua Broin unwound Rokeby's alliances among the Leinster Irish, prompting Áed Ua Tuathail and his brother John Ruad to desert the English and join him shortly after 9 August 1355. The defection of the O'Tooles was a significant blow to Rokeby's overall strategy, exposing the vulnerability of the settlers and Ostmen of Wicklow to combined attacks from the O'Byrnes and O'Tooles. Indeed, the government quickly repaid the O'Tooles in their own

exchequer payments, 1270–1446, pp 461–2. **139** Ibid., pp 462, 464. **140** Frame, 'The Dublin government and Gaelic Ireland', p. 353; A.M. Freeman (ed.) *The annals of Connacht* (Dublin, 1944), s.a. 1354. **141** Frame, 'The Dublin government and Gaelic Ireland', p. 359. **142** R. Frame, 'English officials and Irish chiefs in the fourteenth century', *E.H.R.*, 90 (October, 1975), pp 773–4.

coin, invading Imaal to burn Aed Ua Tuathail's fortified residence and other settlements there.

At the close of 1355 Muirchertach Mac Murchada's son, Art Mac Murchada the elder (father of the famous Art Mór Mac Murchada), had submitted, but the O'Tooles and the O'Byrnes refused to. Throughout 1356 the O'Byrnes and the O'Tooles concentrated their energies on destroying the system of defensive wards instituted by Rokeby, particularly those at Killoughter, Kilmartin and Newcastle McKynegan. All of these wards, held by the Lawlesses, underpinned the continuing survival of the colony in east Wicklow.[143] Plainly, the O'Byrnes were now forcing the Lawlesses and their allies out of east Wicklow, compelling them to begin a retreat northward towards Bray. The Lawlesses, fighting for their lives, ensured that struggle with the O'Byrnes would be a fight to the death. The savagery of this local struggle can be shown from records dating from 1356–8. At this stage, the colony in east Wicklow entered its death throes, but its defenders employed every stratagem against the O'Byrnes in a desperate bid to turn them back. Spies and assassins now became a regular feature of this warfare, while forces led by Adam Beg, Adam Barry, Murchad son of Magnus Ua Broin, David Lawless, Thomas de Blakebourn and William fitz Richard Lawless went on nighttime expeditions to burn the settlements of the O'Byrnes and the O'Tooles, forcing them to resort to dwellings far from the king's faithful people.[144] Luck was with the Lawlesses, as Art Mac Murchada the elder's support for the government finally forced the O'Byrnes and the O'Tooles to submit in 1357. As a sign of repentance, John Ua Broin and Áed Ua Tuathail joined a summertime hosting against the troublesome Uí Broin of the Duffry in Wexford, but they were only biding their time.

About May 1358 the O'Byrnes and O'Tooles broke their truce with the government. With the O'Tooles, John Ua Broin attacked English vills such as Saggart nestled amid the foothills of the western Wicklow mountains. There the Harolds had replaced the O'Tooles as defenders of the colony, for in 1358–9 William fitz Richard Harold and Walter Harold earned £5 for defending Saggart and for recovering booty from the O'Byrnes and the O'Tooles.[145] In July Áed Ua Tuathail and John Ua Broin unleashed their forces again in east Wicklow, besieging the principal Lawless fort at Killoughter. Although in August John Ua Broin, captured by James Butler, 3rd earl of Ormond, promised fealty and repentance, we soon find him cutting northward into the Dublin marches and aiding the MacMurroughs and the O'Mores to sever the royal highway

---

143 William fitz Richard Lawless defended Killoughter between 2 August and 30 September 1356: see Connolly (ed.), *Irish exchequer payments, 1270–1446*, p. 471. Donald fitz Paul Lawless and a company of 16 footmen guarded Kilmartin between 2 August to November 1356 (ibid.). David Lawless was constable of Newcastle McKynegan between 17 August to 30 September 1356 (ibid.). 144 Connolly (ed.), *Irish exchequer payments, 1270–1446*, pp 483, 505. 145 Ibid., p. 494.

through the Barrow valley.[146] During July 1359 a combined Ua Tuathail/Ua Broin force laid siege to Carrickmines in the Vale of Dublin, forcing Ormond, now justiciar, to march to its relief. After bitter fighting lasting some days, Ormond lifted the siege, forcing the Irish to withdraw. Peace eventually came with Ormond's victory in early August over the O'Mores and Art Mac Murchada the elder. A general peace was made on 12 August 1359, and John Ua Broin voluntarily submitted at Carlow where he seems to have been knighted.[147] Although the O'Byrnes and the O'Tooles were now at peace, the colony in Wicklow had been fatally wounded. After the late 1350s, it was clear that the O'Tooles had won full control of Imaal as nothing further is said of the settlers of Imaal, the O'Tooles having already conquered the Glendalough region after the fall of Castlekevin in 1343. As for the Lawlesses, John Ua Broin had effectively broken their power, as the events of the 1360s would prove.[148]

   The pressure on the English of Leinster brought Lionel of Clarence to Ireland on 15 September 1361. Alarmed by the desperate plight of the settlers in east Wicklow, Lionel marched his army into Wicklow.[149] There the (recently knighted) Sir John Ua Broin attacked Lionel's army, killing 100 English soldiers, compelling the lord lieutenant to seek the sanctuary of Wicklow town. In spite of this defeat, Lionel learned from it, combining his forces with those of the marchers to successfully stabilise the region between October 1361 and May 1362. Indeed, Lionel shored up the English position along the Barrow valley by refortifying Carlow and defeating Art Mac Murchada the elder. Later, at a parley, he treacherously captured Art and his tánaiste, Domnall Riabach Mac Murchada, confining them in Trim, where they were either murdered or died naturally in July 1362. Lionel sealed the English commitment to Carlow by relocating the exchequer and the common bench there, before campaigning separately against the O'Mores and the O'Byrnes. But the slide in Lawless stock continued remorselessly, as evidenced by the removal, for uncertain reasons, of Maurice Lawless from his constableship of Newcastle McKynegan on 18 June 1364.[150] At the same time, Sir John Ua Broin continued to strengthen his hand by playing both sides, currying favour with the English by serving against Diarmait Láimderg Mac Murchada. For Sir John's services against Diarmait Láimderg in 1365–6, he received a fee, while his son Tadc and a John Ua Tuathail (probably John Ruad, the brother of Áed Ua Tuathail) were knighted. By 1367 relations had improved between the government and the MacMurroughs, as evidenced by Edward III's

---

146 Frame, 'The Dublin government and Gaelic Ireland', pp 373–4.   **147** O'Byrne, *War, politics and the Irish of Leinster*, p. 102.   **148** Connolly (ed.), *Irish exchequer payments 1270–1446*, p. 516. There were Ua Broin hostages in Dublin Castle from 10 September 1360 to April 1361.   **149** Ibid. William fitz Richard Lawless retained by the council at £1 per week because of his warlike incursions in repelling the Irish enemies of Leinster, who were attacking the king's faithful people by night and day.   **150** Ibid.

recognition of Diarmait Láimderg in July as leader of the Leinster Irish. Peace was short-lived, for the threat to the Barrow corridor re-emerged. Separate campaigns were launched against the O'Tooles and the MacGillapatricks throughout 1367–8.[151] The potency of the Mac Murchada threat to the Barrow region required drastic action. After his arrival in Ireland on 20 June 1369, the lord lieutenant, Sir William of Windsor, a veteran of Lionel's campaigns of 1361–2, captured Diarmait Láimderg and his *tánaiste* Gerald Mac Murchada, executing them later that year.[152]

Windsor also set about settling the borders of the Pale, marching against the O'Tooles in the early summer of 1370. His attention was soon to be distracted from the Wicklow campaign by news from Munster that Gerald, 2nd earl of Desmond, had been defeated by the O'Briens at Monasternagh (Limerick) on 10 July. The death of Sir John Ua Broin in the late 1360s led to a dynastic civil war among the O'Byrnes, but this discord did not prevent them from exploiting Windsor's preoccupation with the O'Briens in the 1370s. Bereft of government service, the Lawlesses were powerless to prevent the O'Byrnes from seizing Wicklow and Newcastle McKynegan in the summer of 1370 and, although these fortresses were quickly retaken, it was not before the O'Byrnes razed Wicklow.[153] On 27 March 1371, Windsor brought the O'Byrnes to peace, signing a treaty with their next recorded overlord Braen son of Philip Ua Broin (Sir John's first cousin) in Christ Church cathedral, Dublin. In coming to this peace, it was clear that Braen mac Philip was motivated by a need to deal with his rebellious cousins. But the terms of the peace illustrate the complete collapse of the Lawlesses as a counterpoise to the O'Byrnes in the region. Braen mac Philip agreed to rebuild the church of Wicklow, to acknowledge the rights of the archbishops of Dublin, and never to obey any Mac Murchada.[154] This peace was to last three years, allowing the remaining Lawlesses a breathing space. On 16 June 1372 Hugh fitz Richard Lawless was appointed as constable of Newcastle McKynegan until 19 February 1373. Significantly, Hugh fitz Richard was the last Lawless constable of Newcastle McKynegan. Importantly, his appointment was to be in times of peace, indicating that the government placed little faith in his ability and that of his lineage to resist any future Ua Broin attack.[155] The Harolds must have been marginally stronger, for Thomas Harold was granted the constableship of Newcastle McKynegan from 30 September 1373 to 18 February 1375, a period that saw considerable warfare in east Wicklow.[156]

Unsurprisingly, once Braen mac Philip had dealt with his rivals and renewed his alliance with Áed Ua Tuathail, he soon turned his back on his

151 O'Byrne, *War, politics and the Irish of Leinster*, p. 102. **152** *Annals of Connacht*, s.a. 1369; *Annals of Ulster*, s.a. 1369. **153** *Chartul. St Mary's, Dublin*, ii, p. 397; Price, *Placenames*, p. lxvii. **154** TCD, Ms E.3.25 (588), ff 202v–204. **155** Connolly (ed.), *Irish exchequer payments, 1270–1446*, p. 529. **156** Ibid. Thomas Harold earned a salary of £96

agreement with Windsor and embarked on the conquest of north Wicklow. In 1374 the O'Byrnes abandoned their treaty with Windsor by taking and demolishing Newcastle McKynegan, forcing him to send aid to Wicklow. But this was futile as the O'Byrnes burnt Wicklow to the ground, angering Windsor so much that the council at Naas had to order him not to march against the O'Byrnes lest Ulster became unstable. In any case, Windsor's government had by September managed to reestablish a semblance of control over the Leinster coast, retaking Wicklow and Newcastle McKynegan.[157] Braen mac Philip maintained his pressure, seizing Wicklow and Newcastle McKynegan during 1376, and he briefly grabbed Kindlestown castle in 1377. The only notable reverse suffered by the Wicklow Irish in these years was the killing of Áed Ua Tuathail by the English in 1376. Despite this, the seemingly smooth transition of the Ua Tuathail leadership to Sir John Ruad Ua Tuathail, Áed's brother, further underlines the strength of the Irish ruling families of East Leinster. And by the time of Braen mac Philip's death in 1378, his power extended from Bray to Tullow.[158] About this time the Lawlesses finally extracted themselves from east Wicklow, moving to their more secure lands at Old Connaught and Shanganagh near Bray, holding other lands later at Carrickmines and Saggart in 1389.[159] But they were to remain bitter enemies of the O'Byrnes, contributing troops regularly to government hostings into Wicklow.[160] A similar fate befell the Ostman lineages of Harold and Archbold. After Ua Broin had forced them northward, in the 1390s the Archbolds eventually occupied the lands around Kindlestown, a territory later known as Archbolds' Country.[161]

By 1400 the Irish had largely driven the settlers out, pushing them north or into enclaves such as Wicklow town. The erosion of Henry II's 'community of outlook' meant that distinction and diversity, rather than accommodation and integration, were the dominant themes of the relationships between the English crown and the Irish nobility of Leinster. Yet this 'community of outlook' left a considerable imprint upon the polities of Leinster, as the marriages between the settler and Irish elites show. During the early fourteenth century, Diarmait Ua Dímmusaig (O'Dempsey) of Clanmaliere had been the husband of Isabella de Cadel, daughter of William de Cadel, former royal seneschal of the liberties of Kildare and Carlow. Indeed, Art Mór Mac Murchada of Leinster and his son Donnchad were married to Elizabeth de Veel and Aveline Butler respectively.

8*d*. for his service as constable of Newcastle McKynegan in 1373–5.   **157** *Chartul. St Mary's, Dublin*, ii, pp 283,4; O'Byrne, *War, politics and the Irish of Leinster*, p. 106. **158** O'Byrne, *War, politics and the Irish of Leinster*, p. 106.   **159** Curtis, 'The clan system among the English settlers in Ireland', p. 119. They also held lands at Kilruddery near Dalkey in the fifteenth century.   **160** Ball, *History of the County Dublin*, ii, p. 102. About 1394 William Lawless was killed defending the frontiers of the Pale from the Irish.   **161** In 1368 Hugh Lawless was tried for unjustly ejecting William fitz Thomas Lawless from the

Even the O'Byrnes and the O'Tooles who had worked so hard to uproot the Welsh and Ostman lordships in Wicklow, were considerably affected by the hybrid nature of the marches. One of their major areas of communication and cooperation with the settlers was in trade, particularly in wine, wool, weapons, butter, timber, and livestock. The close relationship between the Irish lords of Wicklow and the merchant classes of Dublin was demonstrated in 1392. Then Gerald son of Tadc Ua Broin, lord of the O'Byrnes, offered a sea-going barge to Esmond Berle of Dublin in payment for his debts.[162] In 1395, Feidlim Ua Tuathail of Uí Muiredaig also attested to the importance of this trade, saying: 'for without buying and selling I can in no way live', while in 1425 Donnchad son of Braen Ua Broin promised to protect merchants travelling across his lordship.[163] In particular, the O'Byrnes had a quick eye for a profit. Instead of seeking to burn the port town of Wicklow on a regular basis, they now placed this commercial hub under their protection. For this protection, the townsmen of Wicklow paid a 'black rent' to the Ua Broin lords and were then left to trade in peace, while the O'Tooles were to supply three sheriffs of Dublin during the sixteenth century.[164] On the other hand, the settlers were also influenced by the hybrid culture prevailing in the marches. According to a complaint levied against Henry fitz William Walsh of Carrickmines in 1468, he spoke Irish, wore Irish dress and was reputed to use Irish law whenever it suited his purpose.[165] Evidently, where once royal government had dictated these communities' terms of interaction, its decline ensured that decisions taken in the halls of the Irish now were the new rules of engagement.

lands of Old Connaught near Bray: see Ball, *History of the County Dublin*, iii, p. 102. In 1394. the lands of John fitz James Archbold and Hugh Lawless at Kindlestown were confiscated and granted to Janico Dartas. At the end of the fifteenth century the Archbolds held the manor and lands of Much Bray and Little Bray in the south of Dublin, which they retained in 1536–7: see Curtis, 'The clan system among the English settlers in Ireland', p. 119. For the Archbolds at Kindlestown, see L. Simpson, 'Dublin's southern frontier under siege: Kindlestown Castle, Delgany, County Wicklow', in S. Duffy (ed.), *Medieval Dublin IV* (Dublin, 2003), p. 298.   **162** J. Graves (ed.), *A roll of the proceedings of the king's council in Ireland, 1392–93* (London, 1877), pp 180,1.   **163** Ibid., p. 207; E. Matthew, 'The governing of the Lancastrian lordship of Ireland in the time of James Butler, fourth earl of Ormond *c.*1420–52', Ph.D. thesis, University of Durham 1994, pp 191–2, appendix III, no. i, pp 574–6.   **164** Brewer and Bullen (eds), *Cal. Carew MSS, 1515–74*, no. 170, pp 193–4; Nicholls, 'Críoch Branach', pp 8 and 16.   **165** H.F. Berry (ed.), *Statute rolls of the parliament of Ireland, 1–12 Edward IV* (Dublin, 1914), pp 461–3.

Outline Genealogy

The Lawlesses, 1250–1380

Keys
viv. = alive
d. = died
sl. = killed
cons N = constable of Newcastle

Walter ?

Hugh

Sir Hugh Lawless m Isabella de Sauntref   Walter   Simon?
*d.c.*1329   *viv.*1327

Robert   William   John ?   Raymond ?   Walter   Simon   William   Richard
*viv.*1335   *cons N*   *viv.*1329   *sl.*1330   *viv.*1346   *viv.*1325   *viv.*1325
         *sl.*1330

Hugh
cons N
*viv.*1353   James   Richard
         *viv.*1332   *viv.*1332

            William   Hugh
            *viv.*1360   *cons N*
                   *viv.*1373

Outline Genealogy

The Fitzrhys of Imaal 1150–1300

> **Key**
> *viv.* = alive

Philip
|
Rhys
viv. 1207
|
Philip
viv. 1229
|
Geoffrey   m Annabel de Offynton
viv. 1293
|
Simon
viv. 1293

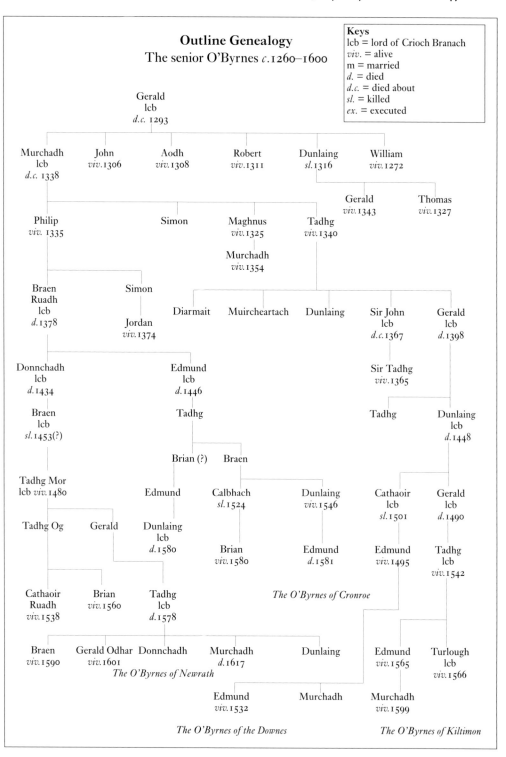

Outline Genealogy
The senior O'Byrnes *c.*1260–1600

Keys
lcb = lord of Crioch Branach
viv. = alive
m = married
d. = died
d.c. = died about
sl. = killed
ex. = executed

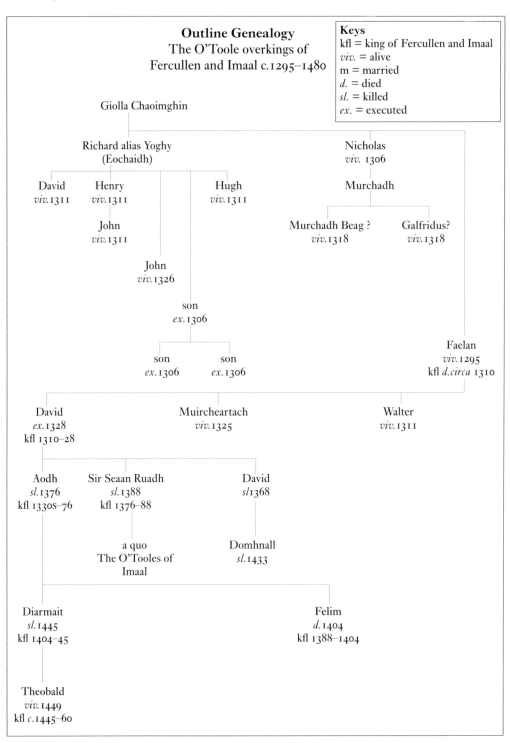

Outline Genealogy
The O'Toole overkings of
Fercullen and Imaal c.1295–1480

Keys
kfl = king of Fercullen and Imaal
viv. = alive
m = married
d. = died
sl. = killed
ex. = executed

Giolla Chaoimghin

Richard alias Yoghy   Nicholas
(Eochaidh)   *viv.* 1306

David   Henry   Hugh   Murchadh
*viv.*1311   *viv.*1311   *viv.*1311

John   Murchadh Beag ?   Galfridus?
*viv.*1311   *viv.*1318   *viv.*1318

John
*viv.*1326

son
*ex.*1306

son   son   Faelan
*ex.*1306   *ex.*1306   *viv.*1295
                                          kfl *d.circa* 1310

David   Muircheartach   Walter
*ex.*1328   *viv.*1325   *viv.*1311
kfl 1310–28

Aodh   Sir Seaan Ruadh   David
*sl.*1376   *sl.*1388   *sl*1368
kfl 1330s–76 kfl 1376–88

              a quo   Domhnall
              The O'Tooles of   *sl.*1433
              Imaal

Diarmait   Felim
*sl.*1445   *d.*1404
kfl 1404–45   kfl 1388–1404

Theobald
*viv.*1449
kfl *c.*1445–60

Excavation of the medieval river frontage at Arran Quay, Dublin

ALAN HAYDEN*

ABSTRACT

This report describes the results of limited archaeological excavation under-taken in advance of development, at Nos 9–14, Arran Quay, Dublin, in the summer of 1990. The earliest features uncovered were two front-braced tim-ber revetments, the first dating to *c*.1305 AD and the second to slightly later. There may also have been a third revetment but none of its timbers survived. The first stone quay wall replaced the revetments in the mid- to later fourteenth century. A later stone wall, which further extended the quay into the river, survived only intermittently. This wall would appear to date to the late fifteenth or early sixteenth century. In excess of 5,500 sherds of pottery, a large assem-blage of medieval ceramic roof and floor tiles, bronze pins, wood and leather objects, a few scraps of fabric and an inscribed gold finger ring were found. An interesting sample of animal, fish and bird bones was also uncovered.

INTRODUCTION

The area of the proposed development consisted of the river frontage of the block defined by Arran Quay on the south, church Street on the east, Hammond Lane on the north and Lincoln Lane on the east (fig. 1). An archaeological assessment of the area undertaken in 1990 indicated that archaeological deposits, up to 1.3m in depth, survived only in a limited area at the southwest corner of the site (Gowen 1990). The excavation was located in this area of the site and was undertaken in a six-week period in July and August 1990.

HISTORICAL BACKGROUND

The site is located in the medieval suburb of Oxmantown and lies in the inter-tidal zone on the northern side of the medieval course of the river Liffey,

* With contributions by Finbar McCormick, Sheila Hamilton-Dyer, Tanya O'Sullivan, Dáire O'Rourke, Joanna Wren, Joe Norton, Libby Heckett, Aoife Daly, David Brown, and Michael Kenny.

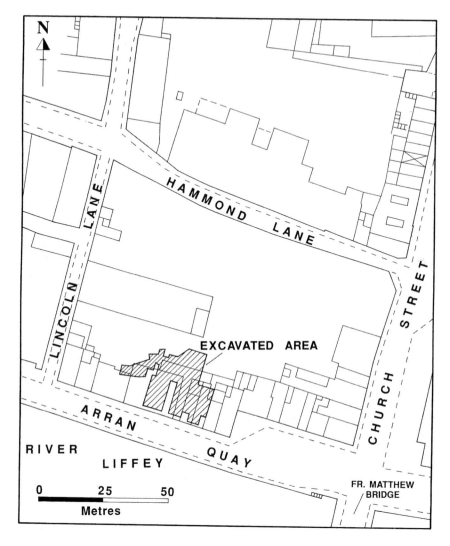

1 Location of site and excavated area

between the two earliest crossing points on the river. To the west lies the
supposed site of the *Áth Cliath* ('the ford of hurdles') that gave the city its
name and to the east lies the site of the only medieval bridge that crossed the
river in the vicinity of the city. Little archaeological excavation had taken
place on the northern side of the Liffey before the site under discussion was
excavated. An excavation at the Four Courts revealed a possible part of
St Saviour's Dominican priory and the sluice-gate at the end of a watercourse (MacMahon 1988). Other excavations were undertaken in 1993 near

St Michan's church by Beth Cassidy, and on Church Street by Linzi Simpson. The latter uncovered a mid thirteenth-century timber-lined watercourse extending on an east-west line across the north side of the block where the site under discussion was located.

The medieval Liffey was substantially wider and shallower than its modern counterpart. In the area of Arran Quay it may originally have been *c.*300 metres in width (Clarke 1978), corresponding roughly to the 5m OD (Poolbeg) contour or slightly lower, which marked the level of high tide (de Courcy 1984, 164). Mitchell (1987, 7) suggested a level of *c.*4m OD for the spring high with neap high being at *c.*3m OD. More recent work by de Courcy suggests a maximum height of 5.3m OD for maximum high tide in time of spate (pers. comm). The tidal reach of the river may originally have extended as far upstream as Chapelizod. It was reduced in 1220 when the prior and brethren of Kilmainham constructed a weir at Islandbridge, which controlled, and still does, the effect of the incoming tide on the river (de Courcy 1990, 244). The river as a result of the nature of its catchment area was prone to sudden floods and silting, and was originally known as *Ruirtech*, meaning 'swiftly running or furious', even back to the eighth century (de Courcy 1990, 224). Sudden floods were common and even as late as the eighteenth century Edmund Burke, who was born in No. 12, Arran Quay, complained of being trapped in the first floor of a house there in 1746, by floods (ibid.). The sudden floods probably frequently washed away structures on the edges of the river. They would also appear to have deposited large amounts of silts and sand in the river. There are frequent references to the choking of the river with silt and the inability of large ships to dock in the town from the fourteenth to the eighteenth centuries. The silting up of the river may have been, in part, the reason for the constant encroachment of the quaysides during the medieval period. This encroachment also may in itself have served to increase the very silting it was trying to overcome. The excavations carried out at Wood Quay (Wallace 1981) and more recently at Usher's Quay (L. Swan†, pers. comm) and at Arran Quay itself, uncovered huge deposits of river silt that appeared to have built up very rapidly at many levels.

John, as lord of Ireland, in a charter dated 15 May 1192, stated that 'Every citizen may, for his own advantage, build wherever he wishes on the bank [of the river], but without damage to the city or citizens' (Gilbert 1889–1944, i, 5). Excavations on the southern side of the river at Wood Quay, downstream from Arran Quay, illustrated the pattern of this encroachment. A series of wooden revetments dating from the later twelfth to the thirteenth century, followed by an early fourteenth-century stone wall, narrowed the river, and finally quay walls of early eighteenth-century date brought it to its present width (Wallace, 1981). The reclamation of the northern side of the Liffey does not, unfortunately figure in the surviving historical records until the late seventeenth century. Some form of reclamation, on the west side of Oxmantown, at the end of Hangman [Hammond] Lane, may be referred to in 1468 when it was ordered in that dung should not be cast elsewhere in the city but only 'Without Hankman ys lane, in the holles and pittes there' (Gilbert 1889–1944, i, 328–9). In 1486 a similar order was made (ibid., 370). The area lay outside the walled medieval city, although within its suburbs, and little archaeological excavation has taken place there. In the area of Arran Quay the river is presently about forty metres in width, and hence it appears to have been narrowed by about 250m since the medieval period.

Medieval quays are however known further downstream at St Mary's abbey (see below). From the eleventh century, when it is mentioned in connection with the battle of Clontarf (Gilbert 1854–9, i, 319), a bridge has been in existence across the Liffey in the vicinity of the present Fr Mathew Bridge. The excavated area lay some 150m west of the present bridge. The bridge and its replacements remained the only structure spanning the river in the vicinity of the town until the late seventeenth century. The bridge was built on what was probably the narrowest part of the river close to the town; Speed's map of 1610 shows a small area of land jutting out into the river beside the bridge (fig. 2). A detailed history of the bridge is given by de Courcy (1990). The construction of the bridge with its abutments at either end would have changed the flow of the river somewhat. One would expect that silting would have taken place upstream behind the abutments and that the channel under the arches of the bridge may have been scoured out due to the narrowing of the river channel in the area.

The excavated site lies in the suburb of Oxmantown, on the north bank of the Liffey and without the city walls. The suburb supposedly got its name ('Austmannaby', 'Ostmanby', 'Ostmantown', 'Oestmantown', 'Oxtmanton', etc.) as a result of being the area to which the native population of Ostmen moved after the Anglo-Norman takeover (Wallace 1985, 381–2). Whether this was a voluntary exodus or not is unclear as is the date of its happening (Simms 1990, 49). Suburbs certainly existed from an early date on the northern side of the Liffey. A confirmation of lands to the priory of Holy Trinity by King John, dated to 1202, includes 'all these with their appur-tenances in churches and chapels, with ports and vills, within the burg and without, and on each side of the watercourse of the Amliffi' (McNeill 1950, 29) and the charter of John dated to 1192 includes Oxmantown as part of the city (Gilbert 1889–1944, i, 2–3). A settlement may have existed in the area at an even earlier stage as St Michan's church appears to have been established there by the early twelfth century. Speed's map of 1610 (fig. 2) shows the suburb on the north side of the river as a thriving area with regularly laid out streets and properties, mills and ecclesiastical centres. Sixteenth-century extents of ecclesiastical property in the area also suggest a similar density of

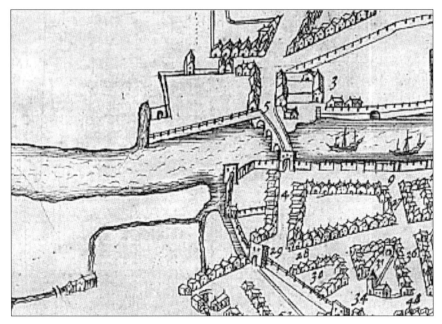

2 Speed's map (1610) showing the area of the site

population. There are numerous examples of grants of lands and mentions of 'Meses' or 'Messuages' in Oxmantown in the corporation records dating from the thirteenth and fifteenth centuries (Gilbert 1889–1944, i, passim). Orchards and gardens are also mentioned in the early seventeenth-century account of the 'Riding of the Franchises'. Some of the streets shown on Speed's map are mentioned in earlier documents, for example: 'Hongemon Lane', 'Hangmaes Lane', etc. in 1454 (ibid., 281–2), 1466 (ibid., 322), 1468 (ibid., 328–9) and 1486 (ibid., 370), 'Brode Street' in 1262 (ibid. 94), Comynes Lane in 1470 (ibid. 341) and Mary Lane in 1501 (perhaps identical with Brode Street, ibid., 387). Houses are mentioned on these streets in many references, for example, a stone messuage in Oxmantown near the bridge and opposite the chapel of St Mary is referred to in the Christ Church deeds (McEnery and Refaussé 2001, no.417).[1] This house is shown on Clarke's 1978 map at the west side of the north end of the bridge. In a reference dated 5 April 1526 it is described as bordered by the Liffey on the south and by the road on the east. There was a garden to the west belonging to Thomas Tyre. The property belonged to the priory of the Holy Trinity at Christ Church and was at that time being let to the lord of Howth (ibid.).

The suburb does not appear to have been walled but gates were ordered to be built at the end of Comynes Lane in 1470 (Gilbert 1889–1944, i, 341) and

1 I am grateful to Dr Howard Clarke for bringing this reference to my attention.

at the end of Hangman Lane in 1466 (ibid., 322). The latter is described as a 'Yate of lyme and stone'. A large open area, Oxmantown Green, lay to the west of the suburb. This was not developed until the late seventeenth century, although intrusions into it are mentioned from earlier periods. Another smaller open are lay outside St Mary' abbey and was maintained as 'common pasture according to the crosses placed there' (ibid., 170). While St Mary's abbey possessed a harbour, no description of it survives. A 'slypp fro the chapell of the Mary Grace besyde the key of the said cite unto the yate of the said house' was granted to the Dominican priory of St Saviour's in 1480 (ibid., 389). Another 'slyppe at the North end of the Bridge' was let for 'a terme of fyftie and one years' to John Burnell in 1557 (ibid., 465). As noted below the north side of the river appears to have been reserved for the landing of fish while the south side was used for the docking of merchant ships.

Three ecclesiastical centres were located in Oxmantown, and are illustrated on Speed's map: St Mary's (Cistercian), St Saviour's (Dominican) and the parish church of St Michan's. All are medieval foundations. St Mary's dominated Oxmantown. Along with St Thomas's abbey, it was the most important and most powerful abbey in the city. It was founded in *c*.1139 as a Savignac house but soon submitted to the Cistercian order (Gwynn and Hadcock 1988, 131). Little of its building history survives. All that remains today is the Chapter House, which dates to *c*.1200 (Stalley 1987, 244). The abbey appears to have been at least damaged by a fire in 1304 (Lydon 1988, 34). It was evidently a large and powerful centre and owned huge tracts of land on the eastern side of Oxmantown but also owned many messuages and plots in all areas of the suburb. There are frequent records of grants of moneys and land from the mayor and commonalty, and from private citizens to the abbot and monks of St Mary's, contained within various sources (e.g., Gilbert 1889–1944, i, 83, 93, 104 and 170). It also possessed mills. It was the richest of the Irish Cistercian houses (Stalley 1987, 24 and 244) and an extent of 1540 lists fifty houses, thirty-two tenements, one shop, two empty plots and at least thirteen gardens in St Michan's parish alone (White 1943, 6–9). It possessed ships and traded with England and the continent. Access for ships and boats was agreed by the commonalty of Dublin and they were harboured in the mouth of the river Bradogue (Carville 1972, 41). They also had 'a little bote to fishe on the Liffe' (Gilbert 1889–1944, i, 175) and possessed fishing rights on the river granted by Lord John during his expedition to Ireland in 1185 and confirmed by charter from John as king in 1200 (Went 1990, 183), a privilege usually jealously guarded by the town and which led to disputes between the abbey and the town over the succeeding centuries (ibid., 185–7, 189). The abbey was surrendered on 28 October 1539 (Gwynn and Hadcock 1988, 131).

The Dominican friars arrived in Dublin in 1224 and are supposed to have settled on land granted to them by St Mary's abbey (ibid., 224). This has been disputed. It is suggested instead that Audeon Brun and Richard de Bedeford originally granted a piece of ground to the canons of Christ Church, on which to build a chapel in honour of the Holy Saviour, and that this was later given to the Dominicans (O'Sullivan 1990, 83–5). The area in which they settled appears to have been on the eastern side of the north end of the medieval bridge over the river, close to the excavated site. No remains of the priory survive above ground today. Excavations on this site, at the Four Courts, revealed no surviving part of the priory, although the finding of architectural fragments, human remains, medieval floor tiles, a sluice-gate and channel – and the discovery of about thirty human skeletons in the 1960s – suggest that the priory lay in this area (MacMahon 1988, 276). The new church of the priory was dedicated in 1238 (Gwynn and Hadcock 1988, 224). A general conflagration appears to have razed this part of the northern side of the river in 1304, the priory and St Mary's being amongst the casualties (Lydon 1988, 34). However, rebuilding began soon after with Lord Eustace le Poer laying the foundation of the new priory church (Warburton et al. 1818, 358). The friars received 35 marks annually from king's alms and continued to receive similar sums intermittently until 1356 (O'Sullivan 1990, 87–8). John le Decer, then provost of the city, erected a large 'stone pillar' within the church and 'laid a great stone upon the High altar' in 1308 (Warburton et al.1818, 359). With the approach of the Bruces on Dublin in 1316, the priory was partly demolished on the orders of the mayor, Robert de Nottingham, in order to stop the invaders occupying it and to provide stone for strengthening the defences of the western part of the town (ibid., 360). Once again it was not long before the priory was reconstructed, this time by the citizens of the town, on the orders of Edward II (Gwynn and Hadcock 1988, 225). The new bridge, which was built across the river in 1428 linked the priory to a 'House for philosophy and divinity' which it possessed on Usher's Island on the south side of the river (ibid., 209). In the fifteenth century the priory apparently acquired the land called the Gibbet Mede (O'Sullivan 1990, 91) which lay immediately to the northwest of the site of the excavated area. The priory was surrendered on 8 July 1539 and in 1541 permission was given to demolish the church. The other buildings on the approximately three-acre site were reportedly worth nothing above repairs (Gwynn and Hadcock, ibid.). The possessions of the friary included c.93 acres, two messuages, twenty-one tenements or cottages valued at £21 17s. 10d., excluding two tenements then waste (ibid.). In 1542 the priory passed into private ownership and in 1582 the King's Inns were established there (ibid.) and they are shown occupying the site on Speed's map of 1610.

St Michan's church was the parish church of the area and was probably founded in the early twelfth century by Bishop Samuel who ordained that he be buried there (Gwynn 1990, 55). Today little remains of the medieval fabric of the church, which was rebuilt in 1585–6 by Dr John Pooley (Craig 1980, 41).

In 1662, James, duke of Ormonde, returned to Ireland as viceroy. His return marked the beginning of a new phase of development in Dublin. Perhaps his

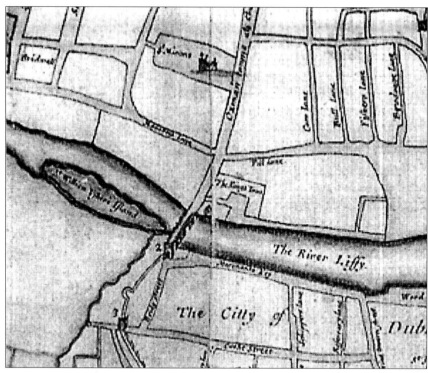

3 1673 map of Dublin showing area of site

most memorable contribution to the city was the encouragement of the building of open quays along the river. The Corporation leased out much of the river frontage for development by private speculators in the seventeenth century, although they themselves built Aston Quay (McCullough 1989, 33). On the north side of the river Sir Humphrey Jervis purchased some twenty acres of the former lands of St Mary's abbey in 1674. The proposed development included a new bridge (Essex Bridge) across the Liffey. When Ormonde returned he suggested a modification of the proposed development that included a wide stone quay (Craig 1980, 25–6). This proved to be the prototype for the ensuing development of the Liffey quays. The most important leases in the history of the development of quays on the northern side of the river proved to be the grants to Amory in 1674 and Ellis in 1682. These two leases covered most of the northern shore of the Liffey then within the compos of the city. Johnathon Amory was granted a large area of the northern side of the Liffey, south of the Jervis estate, which included the modern Ormonde Quay, Batchelor's Walk and Eden Quay (Craig, 1980, 46), on the proviso that any development must include the provision of an open quay 'sixtie foot for a highway' adjacent to the river (Gilbert 1889–1944, v, 58–9). William Ellis had spent 'Considerable summes' acquiring land in Oxmantown and was granted

4 'View of Dublin from the Wooden Bridge, 1698' by Francis Place

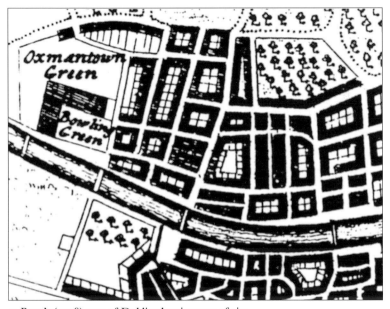

5 Pratt's (1708) map of Dublin showing area of site.

a lease in 1682 of the area of the modern Ellis and Arran Quays, 'With designe to make a quay along the river to the Parke wall ... to the honour, beauty and profitt of the citty' (Gilbert 1889–1944, v, 237). The lease stipulated that an open area 'Six and thirty foot wide' be left adjacent to the quay (ibid.). This clearly reflects Ormonde's thinking, the quays being for the beautification of the river frontage rather than for commercial traffic. The map of Dublin dated 1673 (fig. 3) depicts the Arran Quay area not long before the erection of the new quays, while Brooking's map of 1728 shows the new quay in place.

A drawing by Francis Place, dated 1698 (fig. 4), also illustrates the area to the west of Arran Quay before the completion of the Ellis Quay and shows a sloping foreshore leading to an older quay wall. It also shows Ormonde's early seventeenth-century pavilion (bowling green), and a four-arched bridge span-

ning the river. The drawing (which was made from the area of the present Queen
Medb Bridge) appears to suggest (although the perspective renders details
unclear and the Arran Quay area is hidden behind buildings) that Arran Quay at
this time stood further out into the river than Ellis Quay, and lay on a line with
the northern end of the bridge. This could suggest that the Arran Quay area had
some form of quay wall, which extended westwards from the bridge before
turning northwest towards the older river shore by this time. Pratt's highly
stylised and undetailed plan of Dublin made in 1708 (fig. 5) shows the area after
the new quays had been completed. In the Francis Place drawing the bridge is
also shown as being higher than the surrounding land. This fact is echoed on
Brooking's map of 1728, which shows a group of buildings on either side of the
bridge where it intersects with the north shore of the Liffey. They were built on
either side of the bridge against the sides of the northern abutment, which rose
above the ground level in the area. The top of the abutment was higher than the
surrounding land in order to bring the deck of the bridge above the level of the
river. The link between the bridge and the north shore of the Liffey lay some
twenty metres back from the river (de Courcy 1990, 253). Although these houses
are long gone, their existence has been fossilised by the unusual step back of the
present houses at the eastern end of Arran Quay.

The large houses that until recently stood at Arran Quay date from the
Georgian period. Edmund Burke was born in 1728 in No. 12 Arran Quay,
which was demolished in 1950 (Craig 1980, 326).

THE EXCAVATION

The excavated area occupied the street frontage on the north side of Arran
Quay and lay 14m back from the present north bank of the river Liffey. The
substantial houses that had occupied the area were demolished in 1990. An
area of 265 square metres was excavated. Modern ground level lay at 6.2m
OD (Poolbeg). The cellars of the demolished Georgian houses were on average
2.2m in depth. Stratified archaeological deposits, varying from 0.80m to
1.30m in thickness, survived beneath them.

Natural Deposits Archaeologically sterile river-deposited gravel was reached
at between 3m and 3.2m OD, at the northeast corner of the site. It sloped
gently downwards to the south and west and at the southwest corner of the
site lay at between 2.45m and 2.6m OD. The top of the naturally formed
deposits at nearby Inns Quay lay at similar levels (MacMahon 1988). Further
downstream at Winetavern Street on the other side of the river natural
deposits were reached at around 2m OD (Walsh 1997, 147; Mitchell 1987, 12).

Sandbank (13/80) (fig. 6) A succession of layers of sand and silt built up to
form a bank up to 1.3m in height and with its long axis on a north–south line,

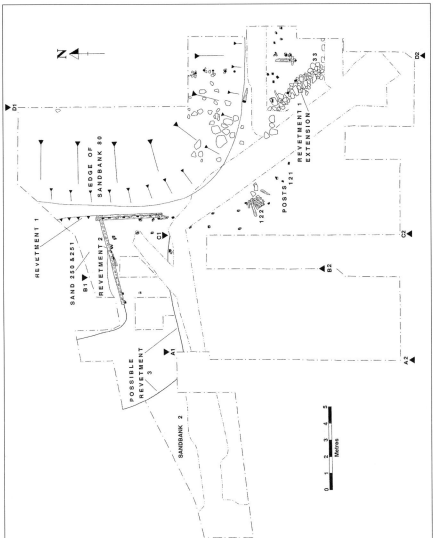

6 Plan of excavated area showing sandbanks and revetments

at the north-eastern area of the site. The earliest layers (30 and 39) in the bank were at its eastern side, while the succeeding layers (80/13) extended further to the west (upstream). All the layers in the bank consisted of numerous 3mm to 5mm-thick lenses of sand and silt which, although they undulated some-what, followed a horizontal line. The bank appears to have been naturally deposited by the river. A Dundry-stone door or window jamb fragment (13:1) was found embedded in the upper layers of the sandbank.

Discussion The layers in the sandbank indicate that it built up from east to west. It probably developed behind an obstacle downstream, which trapped silt being carried by the river. Speed's map of 1610 shows a small peninsula jutting out into the river from its north bank immediately east of the bridge that, in medieval times, lay *c.*150m east of the excavated area. This feature would have provided such a trap for river-borne silt. The bridge itself probably had abutments projecting into the river at both its ends, as appears to be common in medieval bridge construction (e.g., Exeter (Henderson 1981) and Kingston-upon-Thames (Potter 1991)) and these would have provided further traps for silt. How long the sandbank took to develop is unclear, as its initial east side lay outside the area of the excavation. Banks of sand appear to have developed very rapidly at times in the river, as evidenced at Usher's Quay (L. Swan†, pers. comm) and in later levels at Arran Quay itself. Its existence and shape greatly influenced the subsequent land reclamation of this area.

Level 1

Revetment 1 (figs 6–9) An L-shaped (in plan) timber base-plated and front-braced revetment was constructed just outside the western and southern edge of the sand bank (80). The northern part of the revetment, on the west side of the earlier sandbank, survived up to 0.45m in height. (Fig. 7) At the south-western and southern sides of the sandbank, however, only timbers driven into the riverbed survived *in situ* as this area was later re-exposed to river erosion. Where it survived most fully the revetment took the form of large oak base plates – three of which (52, 53 and 54) survived – laid horizontally on the riverbed and joined end to end by double pegged through-splayed scarf joints. The northernmost base plate (54) was robbed out and reused in Revetment 2 (see below). On the riverward side of the base plates, oak retaining-posts were driven into the ground to stop the structure slipping due to the pressure of deposits on its landward side. The base plates held oak and ash uprights in pegged mortises. These in turn retained horizontally laid oak plank shuttering on their landward side. There were 'composite' posts opposite almost every second upright, about 1m to the riverward side of the revetment. They probably secured the bases of raking front-braces that were jointed into every second upright in the revetment. Only one base plate (53) survived to its full extent. It measured 4.02m in length and was of rectangular section, 0.26m in width by 0.11m in thickness. It was joined to the other base plates by through-splayed scarf joints, secured by two face pegs measuring between 25 and 28mm in diameter. The base plate held nine mortises, aver-aging 40–60mm in width by 120mm in length, regularly spaced 280–320mm apart. The stumps of five uprights survived in their respective mortises to a maximum height of 0.30m. The most northerly was of ash and the remainder were of oak. Three were simple squared posts and the other two were split half-round section timbers. None of the uprights were tennoned or shoul-dered and all but the ash example (which was smaller) appear to have fitted tightly into their mortises. Eight of the mortises retained either the dowel

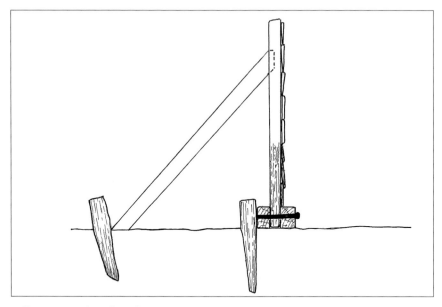

7 Reconstructed section of revetment 1

used to secure the upright in position or the hole bored to accept the now decayed dowel. All the surviving dowels were hammered into the base plate from the east side. These and the holes were of similar dimensions to the face pegs described above.

The uprights retained horizontally laid radially split oak planks (48) on their landward side. The planks varied from 20 to 50mm in thickness and were up to 200mm in width and up to 2.5m in length. Two courses of planking (300mm high in total) survived over most of the surviving length of base plate 53, but in the area of the join between base plates 53 and 52 higher courses of planking survived, though they had collapsed westwards. No nails were utilised and the planks were held in place by the pressure of material dumped behind them. In places the planks overlapped the one below but were in general set on the edge of the underlying one. There were five large posts or 'composite' posts (47.1–5), driven up to 0.60m into the riverbed, against the riverward side of the base plates. They varied in size from single timbers 135mm by 102mm across to a group of three timbers each measuring *c.*30mm by 70mm across, hammered into the ground close together. None of the timbers survived to a height greater than 200mm above ground level. They may in fact have stood no higher originally. These posts stopped the base plates being pushed into the river by the pressure of deposits behind them. There was a further row of posts set *c.*0.80m away on the riverward side of the base plates. Each post in the row lay opposite every second mortise in the base plates and was either vertical or leaned to the west. These were anchors for diagonal front braces, which did not survive.

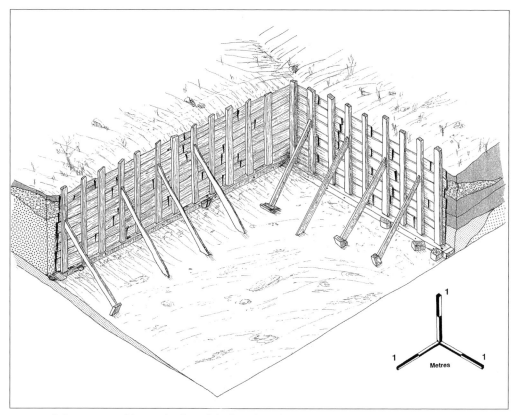

8 Reconstructed isometric view of the junction of revetment 1 (right) and 2 (left)

No base plate survived to the north of 53. The infill behind the revetment
north of base plate 53 was cut away on its western side and replaced by
material (250 and 251) dumped behind Revetment 2. The cut (49) extended in
a straight line as far as the northern limit of the site. One of the base plates
(54) used in the later Revetment 2 would appear to have originally been lain
here. The east end of 54 matched exactly both in size, slope of the joint, and
the placement of the face pegs, the north scarfed end of 53. Part of a mortise
survived at the end of the 54 base plate. This had no function in the later
revetment but matched in size and position the northernmost upright in
Revetment 1 which was set in a mortise that cut partly through the area of the
scarf joint at the north end of 53. There was also a notch on the side of the
reused base plate. This matched the position of one of the retaining posts of
the earlier revetment. This suggests that the 54 timber originally functioned
as the base plate attached to the north end of 53 in the Level 1 revetment and
had been later removed for reuse when this part of the revetment became
obsolete. Only the northern end of the base plate 52 attached to the south end

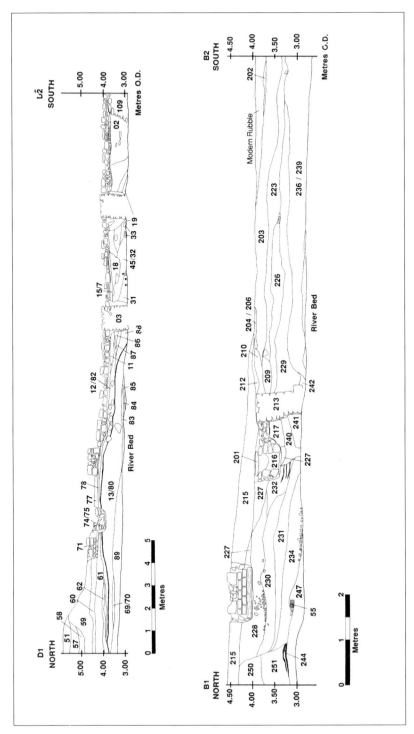

9 Sections D1–D2 and B1–B2 (see figs. 6 and 11 for locations)

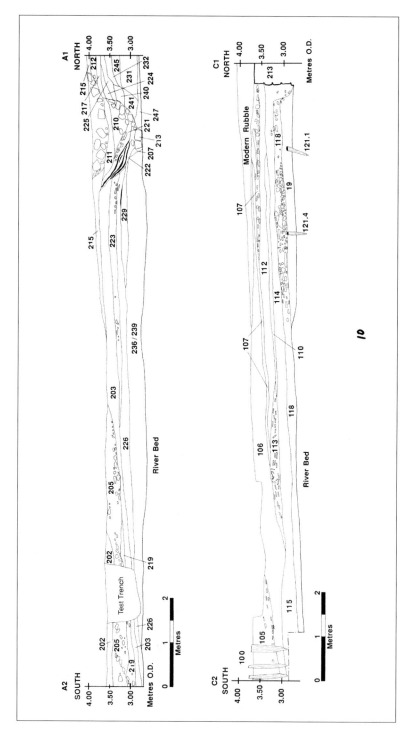

10 Sections A1–A2 and C1–C2 (see figs. 6 and 11 for locations)

Plate 1 Natural sandbank from west.

Plate 2 Revetments 1 (top) and 2 (bottom) looking southeast.

Plate 3 Revetment 1
(right) and Revetment 2
(top) from south.

of 53 survived. It was scarfted and formed the lower element of the joint. It was of similar dimensions to base plate 53. Samples from base plates 53 and 54 were submitted for dendrochronological dating and yielded the following dates: 53: AD 1305 or slightly later: 54: AD 1304 +/− 9 years.

South of where the base plates survived, the former existence of the revetment is evidenced only by the stumps of the timbers driven into the riverbed. This area of the site was eroded by the river at a later period, when it was exposed again outside the quay walls. Two lines of posts and 'composite' posts (121), corresponding in their alignment and spacing to the retaining posts and front-brace anchors of the surviving portion of the revetment, were all that survived south of the base plates. A group of twelve small timbers (122) were the only remains of the upper part of the revetment to survive in this area. This group consisted of small oak planks and a re-used ash barrel-stave (122.2) nailed to and lying on two ash timbers (122.13 and 122.14) which ran

Plate 4 Composite brace support at south end of Revetment 1.

at right angles to them. The timbers had been badly attacked by woodworm. They were probably originally part of the shuttering of the revetment as the two timbers at right angles to the rest lay 0.34m apart (similar to the spacing of uprights in the surviving part of the revetment). They were also of similar size to the surviving uprights. At the south end of this line a lesser number of posts survived. The line swung around to the east at its southern end. This area was heavily disturbed by the insertion of the later river wall (109). To the east of the later wall a greater number of posts (36 and 37) survived to show that the revetment extended eastwards, beyond the eastern limit of the excavation. Two rough lines can be discerned amongst extra posts. The latter possibly represent repair or reinforcement to this area of the revetment that extended furthest out into the river.

A composite base (38) for a raking brace survived close to the eastern limit of the site. This consisted of a squared rectangular oak baulk (38.1) that

Plate 5 Revetment 2
from east.

measured 1.07m in length, 0.95m in width and 0.70m in thickness. It had a
long central mortise. The timber was laid at right angles to the lines of the
posts. An ash plank (38.4) was lapped over its south end and the joint secured
with two face pegs. A post (38.3) driven into the ground stood in the south
end of the mortise while another (38.2) was stood at the south end of the
timber. This form of base has close parallels in the revetments uncovered at
Church Street in 1993 and dated to the mid-thirteenth century (L. Simpson,
pers. comm) and would have anchored the base of a raking brace at the front
of the revetment. The stumps of other posts driven vertically into the ground
also survived in the area.

Reclamation behind Revetment 1 Organic refuse, river silt, sand, gravel,
and stones were dumped behind the revetment to raise the ground level. The
individual dumps varied from small spreads a few centimetres in thickness to

large layers of silt and organic material up to 0.40m in thickness. The layers collapsed in places out over the stump of the revetment after it had been removed. In places subsequent river action eroded much of these deposits. The building of the later stone quay wall (109) also removed a large amount of these deposits and the deep foundations of some of the later cellar walls also divided them into isolated 'islands' of stratigraphy. The bases of a line of wooden stakes (16) extended in a north-south direction in the top of the surviving deposits behind the revetment. The stakes were hammered in from above the highest surviving layer (12) in the area. All were pointed and driven into the ground for between 10mm and 200mm The ground level from which the stakes had been driven was probably not much higher than the surface of deposit 12, as the packing stones hammered in around the posts survived. This suggests that the ground in this area was raised to *c.*1.3m above the level of the riverbed and that Revetment 1 originally stood to at least this height.

River silt During the life of Revetment 1 river silts were deposited to a thickness of 100mm to 450mm against its outer face. The later Revetment 2 was constructed on the surface of a layer of silt measuring up to 250mm in thickness that had built up against the riverward side of Revetment 1. This indicates the height to which the silts had built up in Level 1. A similar depth of silt appears to have built up in Level 2 (see below).

Discussion The base plates of the revetment yielded a dendrochronological date of *c.*1305 AD. Both the samples retained substantial amounts of sapwood and appear to be in a primary position. The pottery in the deposits dumped behind the revetment, though not capable of such a precise dating, fits comfortably into this period. The revetment itself, although only surviving to less than 0.5m. in height, is easily reconstructed when other excavated examples are taken into account (e.g., Wood Quay, Revetment 1210 AD, section B (Wallace 1981)). This latter example is its closest parallel and is a near identical structure. The revetment consisted of horizontally laid base plates joined end to end by pegged-through splayed scarf joints. Regularly spaced mortises in the base plates held pegged upright timbers, which in turn retained horizontally laid radially split oak planks on their landward side. The planks were held in place by the pressure of deposits dumped behind them; no nails were used. The whole structure was held in place by two elements. The first consisted of large posts hammered into the ground in front of the base plates. Where large timbers were not available a number of smaller ones were hammered into the ground close together ('composite posts'). The second element supported the upper part of the revetment and consisted of timbers hammered into the ground opposite every second upright *c.*1m away from the front of the revetment. These sloped away from the revetment. By analogy with the Wood Quay and other examples, each would have butted against the base of a timber

Plate 6 Quay walls
from above
(north at left)

diagonal brace, the other end of which would have been jointed into the upper face of the upright. There was no evidence for a joint on the base of the anchoring timber. It therefore appears that the brace must have simply rested on the riverbed. The braces would probably have sloped at *c.*45 degrees.

The single surviving base (38) for a raking brace at the north end of the revetment suggests that this end may have been more stoutly built. The upper levels of the material dumped behind the revetment were truncated by later cellars and survived up to 1.3m in thickness. This suggests that the revetment stood to at least this height. The material dumped behind the revetment probably derived from elsewhere in the city or its environs and consisted of household and industrial refuse as well as layers of stones and clay. Due to the construction of deep cellars beneath later buildings the uppermost layers of these deposits, and hence the newly formed ground level behind the revetments, did not survive.

Plate 7 Drain opening through quay wall.

Level II

A second wooden revetment was erected on the western side of Revetment 1 towards its northern end. It extended the reclaimed area by up to 8m westwards. At its western end the revetment appears to have turned northwards. No timbers on this side survived, however. The area behind the revetment was infilled with sand and gravel.

Revetment 2 (figs 6 and 8) The surviving elements of Revetment 2 consisted of two base plates with retaining posts, stumps of uprights, a short length of planking and a single anchor for a diagonal front brace. The eastern base plate (54), as noted above, appears to have originally formed the northern end of Revetment 1. It was lifted from its original position, turned through ninety degrees, and relaid. Its east end was notched and slotted behind the northernmost upright of Revetment 1. The base of 54 sat some 50mm higher than the top of the base plates of Revetment 1. The removal of the 54 base plate, planking, etc. above it left a vertical edge (49) on the deposits originally dumped behind it. This was fossilised when the area behind Revetment 2 was infilled. The base plate 54 was a squared rectangular section oak baulk and measured 2.44m in length, 190mm in width and 90mm in thickness. It had the upper element of a scarf joint, with two holes for face pegs, at its east end. Its west end was scarfed (being the lower element of the joint) but was also diagonally trimmed, and held a single hole for a face peg. Base plate 54 held 6 mortises. The easternmost (54.1) derived from its original function in Revetment 1 and was no more than a notch in the end of the base plate. The remaining 5 mortises were regularly spaced *c.*300mm apart and varied in size from 110 x 48mm to 126 x 44mm, except in the case of the mortise cut in the area of the western scarf (54.6) which measured 75mm by 25mm Some of the mortises (notably 54.2 and 54.3) showed clearly from the rounded extensions at their ends that they had been drilled out with a bit of *c.*40mm diameter.

The western base plate (55/235) measured up to 3.4m in length and varied in section from rectangular (180mm wide by 80mm thick) at its east end to semi-circular at its west end (135mm wide x 110mm thick). It had irregular sides and was only roughly dressed to shape. Its west end was trimmed square with an axe while its east end was scarfed. It was of ash and was also a reused timber. Three shallow stopped sloping mortises were cut in its upper face. These had no function in Revetment 2. One of the mortises associated with its reuse in Revetment 2 was cut partly through one of the earlier mortises. The timber in its primary form is similar to timbers reused as base plates in the river Poddle revetments in Patrick Street/Nicholas Street, Dublin (Walsh 1997). It may originally have functioned as a wall plate, the sloping mortises holding angled tenons at the lower ends of rafters. The eight secondary mortises in base plate 55/235 varied from 33mm to 58mm in width and from 90mm to 120mm in length. They were, however, regularly spaced also *c.*300mm apart. Dowel holes or dowels, to secure uprights, survived in all but the two western mortises. Where it was possible to judge, the dowels appear to have been hammered in from the northern side. The dowels and holes are of the same diameter as those in Revetment 1.

The two base plates, were joined together by an ill-fitting scarf joint secured by a single face peg. The joint was further secured by an upright set in a mortise cut through both timbers. The upright that survived in the area of the scarf joint was secured in an unusual manner. A dowel was set in a hole that ran at a 45-degree angle from the top of base plate 55/235 down into the upright and out into the river silts below. Uprights survived above the level of the base plate in only two mortises, 54.6/55.1 and 55.3. These two were simple unshouldered rectangular section oak timbers and stood to a maximum height of 0.45m and leaned substantially to the south. Both fitted tightly into their mortises. Stumps of uprights survived in three other mortises. The radially split oak planking (90) laid behind the uprights survived only in the area of the two surviving uprights. It leaned markedly outwards. Up to 3 courses of planks remained (total height, 0.48m). Other plank fragments (92) survived in the river silt outside the revetment. Four retaining posts, along with the placing of the east end of 54 behind Revetment 1, prevented the base plate moving riverwards. The posts varied from 65 x 135mm to 30 x 96mm in section. All were squared oak posts and varied from 450–553mm in length. They were driven up to 400mm into the underlying silt and river gravel. All leaned substantially outwards. A single anchor (91) for a diagonal front brace survived near the west end of 55. It was a squared rectangular oak post measuring 21 x 8mm in section and up to 305mm in length. It also leaned markedly to the south.

Land reclamation behind Revetment 2 After the erection of Revetment 2 the ground level behind it was raised by the deposition of sand and gravel. This material survived to a maximum of 1.05m in height. The landfill behind Revetment 2 sealed a 100mm to 150mm-thick layer of river silt (247/51) that had built up outside Revetment 1. The initial dump (of material 244) consisted of lenses of organic matter totaling 20mm to 50mm in thickness. Fragments of a Stonge polychrome jug were recovered from this layer, suggesting that the revetment dates from the first half of the fourteenth century. Above this there were larger deposits of gravel and sand (250 and 251). These survived up to a thickness of *c.*1m. No further deposits survived above them. The sand and gravel (250 and 251) had a near vertical edge (238) on its south side where it extended to between 0.2m and 0.8m from the north side of Revetment 2. The west side of the sand and gravel layers (250 and 251) was also near vertical and extended in a line northwards from the west end of base plate 55. This suggests that the revetment had turned northwards at this point. No timbers survived in this area. At the southern side of the gravel and sand a layer layer of gravel, sands and organic material (234, 248, 249), up to 350mm thick, spread southwards for up to 3m from the edge (238) of the 250/251 material. It covered base plate 55/235 in places and gradually thinned as it extended southwards. This, due to its similarity, would appear to have been later than the collapse of the material dumped behind the revetment. It overlay silt (247, 51) that built up against the outside of Revetment 2.

Extension to south end of Revetment 1 (fig. 6) The southern end of Revetment 1 appears to have been replaced by a stone wall or stone-footed timber structure that extended the reclaimed area further out into the river. Evidence for this extension survived only in a small stratigraphically isolated area. Two rough courses of large limestone blocks (33) formed a rough wall or footing up to 0.7m in width that extended in a southeast-northwest direction.

The footing was set on and into the tail end of the deposits that collapsed southwards when Revetment 1 was removed. The stones also overlay the stumps of some of the posts of Revetment 1. Silt and organic refuse (19, 27, 32 and 123) was dumped behind the footing but survived to a very limited extent due to later disturbance.

Discussion Although even less survived of Revetment 2, it is clear from its remains that it took the same form as the earlier revetment. The revetment was butted up against the north end of Revetment 1, which would have made part of the latter structure obsolete when sand and gravel was dumped behind the new revetment. To avoid wasting the large timbers of Revetment 1 that lay in this area, one of the base plates was removed and reused in the new revetment. This new revetment was constructed not on the riverbed but on a layer of silt that had built up against the outer face of Revetment 1. The pottery from this level also appears to indicate a date in the early part of the fourteenth century for the structure. No dendrochronological dates were obtained from the revetment, as the only substantial oak timber in it was a reused element of Revetment 1. The presence of Stonge polychrome in the deposits dumped behind the revetment suggests that it dates to *c.*1280–1310 AD, as the production of this pottery is quite securely dated to this period (Dunning 1968). However, as much of the pottery included in these deposits may have been discarded a considerable time before the layers were removed and dumped behind the revetment, a later date is possible. But the small amount of river silt that had been deposited against the outside of Revetment 1 would suggest that the later revetment dates to only very slightly later than the earlier structure. Again the revetment seems to have expanded the area of reclaimed ground by very little.

The extension to the south end of Revetment 1 that appears to have been put in place at this time is less easy to reconstruct. The low unmortared stone footing ran on a roughly diagonal line from the elbow of Revetment 1 out into the river. What form of superstructure it held and its detailed construction is unknown. It was, however, most probably wooden. Combinations of stone footings and wooden revetments are known, for example, from Winetavern Street, Dublin (Walsh 1997). In another way this extension represents an important advance on the earlier wooden revetment, in that it did not extend at right angles to the flow of the river. Its diagonal line would have rendered it more resistant to the force of the water flowing down the river. The earlier structure had probably to be replaced in this area as it projected farthest out into the river and it was most susceptible to damage. This lesson was quickly learned and the later stone quay wall in this area followed the line established by the extension to the revetment.

Level III (fig. 6)

After Revetment 2 and the extension to Revetment 1 had collapsed or been removed organic material, silts and clays were deposited over their remains. Outside and over the extension to Revetment 1, layers of silt (44 and 45) were probably water-deposited. They were succeeded by layers of organic material (50, 18 and 42) and layers of silt mixed with organic material (15 and 17/25). These deposits extended at least as far as the southern side of the site and totaled *c.*0.80m in thickness. After Revetment 2 was removed the deposits behind it were left with a steep edge where the revetment had once stood. A series of layers of dumped material built up against this edge and over the remains of Revetment 2. The first dumps consisted of organic material containing small amounts of silt (231/245 and 230). An early fourteenth-century English Jeton was recovered from the 245 deposit. These were succeeded by small dumps of gravel, sand and silt (232/228), a thick deposit of stiff boulder clay (227/224) and finally by layers of organic material (224, 225 and 217). In all, some 0.90m in thickness of these deposits survived. All these layers extended out beyond the line of revetment by some 4.6m on its western side and by 1.6m on its southern side. These layers all ended abruptly in a near vertical face (256) some 0.90m in height. On the riverward side of this edge a massive sandbank built up. It measured up to 0.90m in thickness and was composed of lenses and thick layers of sand and fine silt containing patches of organic material (241, 240, 236, 239, 243, 119, 120 and 252). In appearance the sandbank was virtually identical to that which had built up further east before any reclamation had taken place in the area. The sandbank extended as far as the westernmost limit of the excavated area and was of similar thickness over its whole extent. Its top sloped downwards to the south, however. It is difficult to determine it exact southern edge as it was later eroded away and later river deposits in the area had become mixed with it. Also the later quay walls (see level IV) were set in trenches cut through its edge.

Discussion The 1.1m in thickness of organic deposits that lay over and outside Revetment 2 would have been liable to erosion by the river unless protected in some way. They obviously survived for some time as the later quay wall was set in a trench cut partly through them. This suggests that another revetment must have existed in the area. No remains of a revetment survived. It is possible that some form of back-braced revetment anchored into the organic layers themselves could have existed. If removed, if would have left no visible remains as it need not have included elements hammered into the riverbed. The poorer surviving part of Revetment 1 clearly showed how little evidence of the presence of a revetment would remain if the timbers were later removed. The vertical edge of the organic deposits and the existence of the large sandbank against that edge suggest that river action may

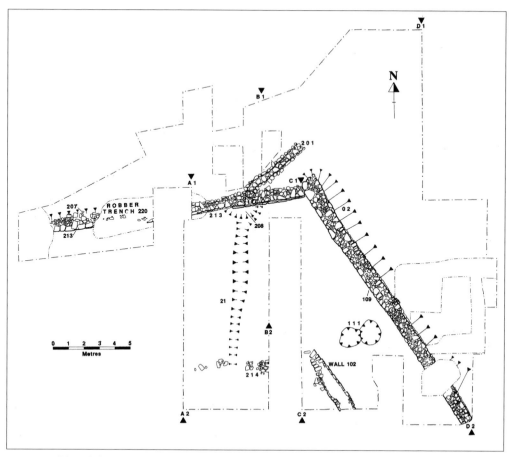

11 Plan of river walls, medieval (109/213) and post-medieval (102/214)

have been responsible for the removal of the putative revetment. Such
sandbanks could accumulate rapidly in times of heavy flooding. This would
also be a time when the river was at its most powerful and destructive and
could easily have washed away a revetment. The pottery from these deposits is
indicative of a date in the first half of the fourteenth century. An English
Jeton (245:13) from these layers was of similar date. This suggests that this
possible third revetment was not greatly later in date than Revetments 1 and 2
and shows the rapidity of encroachment into the river. This may also explain
the poor construction of the revetments, in that they were not expected nor
required to survive for more than a short period.

Level IV
Stone quay walls (figs 11 and 12) A stone quay wall was built in two phases,
109 and 231, to replace the earlier wooden revetments. The earlier part of the

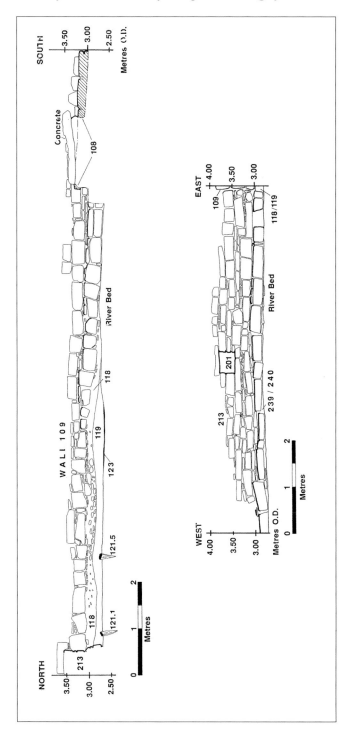

12 Elevations of medieval river wall. Top (109), bottom (213)

wall (109) extended northwestwards from beyond the southeast corner of the site and terminated on the line of the putative Revetment 3. The second part of the wall (213) extended westwards from the end of wall 109 to beyond the western edge of the site. The east end of wall 213 butted against the face of 109; no attempt was made to key the two together. The southeast to northwest aligned stone wall (109) was built in a foundation trench (02) cut through the organic and silt layers originally laid down behind Revetment 1, behind the extension to Revetment 1 and behind the putative Revetment 3. The base of the trench was cut into the accumulated river silts, etc. (118, 119) at the south end of Area 1 and has a maximum depth of 1.05m. However, as the wall extended northwards the trench became shallower and the wall rested on the surface of the 118 deposit. There were many limestone chippings on the surface of the 118 layer closest to the wall. Similar chippings were used as spall stones in the wall. The line of the wall indicates that it was not the intent of its builders to reclaim more land from the river but to protect that which had already been reclaimed and which to a certain extend had begun to be eroded by the river.

Wall 109 was built as a free-standing structure 0.85–1m in width and up to 0.9m in height (including plinth). The southern half of the west (front) face of the wall had a generally single course plinth projecting irregularly up to 0.1m beyond face of wall. There the base of the wall rested on the underlying natural gravel. Over its northern half where the wall sat on river silts (51, 119, and 118) it lacked a projecting plinth. The front face was composed of large rectangular squared blocks of limestone (up to 1.0m x 0.6m x 0.3m), laid in rough courses, with smaller stones and stone chippings used to level the stones. No traces of rendering survived on the face of the wall. The rear face of the wall was battered, most noticeably where it survived to a greater height at its southern half, where it was composed of much smaller and less regular stones, often water-rolled. The rear face of the northern half of the wall was of similar build to its front face. The two faces revetted a heavily mortared rubble core. The mortar utilized was yellow-white in colour and sandy in texture and contained small flecks of charcoal, slate, lime and stone. A total length of 18.8m of wall 109 survived within the excavated area. The trench (02) on the west side of the wall was backfilled with yellow sand that contained stones and gravel (22).

The second part of the wall (213) was built on a line westwards from the northwest end of wall 109. It extended for a length of at least 16.2m. The wall, in contrast to the other quay wall (109), was not built as a free-standing structure. A cut (207) was made through the deposits that lay in front of Revetment 3, and through the sandbank (252) that built up against its west side. The wall was then built up as heavily mortared rubble rear, retained on its south side by a well-built face. The base of the trench was cut into the underlying river silts so that the base of the wall rested on the underlying natural river gravel. In places, however, a thin layer of silt (243) survived beneath the wall. The trench was up to 0.3m wider than the wall on its south side. There it survived intermittently as an edge in the underlying silts 236/239, 118 and 119. The latter appeared to have been washed back into the trench in places. The south face of the wall had a single coursed footing that projected intermittently up to 0.15m beyond the wall face. Footing and the wall were composed of squared rectangular limestone blocks (up to 0.8m x 0.5m x 0.3m) laid in rough courses. There was a batter of *c*.150 to 200mm over its height on the face. The mortar used in the face and in the rear of the wall was similar to that used in the other wall. No traces of rendering survived on the wall face and the mortar between the stones of the face had been eroded away. The east end of the wall abutted the west face of wall 109. No attempt was made to key the two walls together. Small stones had in places been fitted between the end stones of wall 213 and the west face of wall 109. The westernmost 10m of the wall had been robbed out entirely in places and survived to a maximum of 1 course high on the south face. In places, however, rubble from the rear face survived to a maximum height of 0.5m.

A stone lintelled drain (201) was built as one with the wall. It extended in a curve from northeast to southwest and exited out through the wall three courses above the plinth. Only a length of 3m of the southern end of the drain survived later disturbance. The drain consisted of a floor of flat slate slabs, with side walls composed of small uncoursed and unmortared, unshaped stones. The side walls in places rested on the floor slabs, a weak form of construction which led to the cracking of the floor stones. Flat slate and limestone capstones survived only at the southern end of the drain. The internal channel measured 0.32–0.45m wide and was up to 0.35m in height. The exit of the drain through the wall face was of similar size. The southernmost capstone of the drain was thicker than the others and formed part of the wall face. The southern end of the drain was completely filled by silty organic material (216). Over the rest of its length it was only about two thirds full.

Channel 218 and pool 208 (fig. 11) The water issuing through the wall from the drain formed a channel (218) in the deposits that lay outside the wall. The channel measured up to 0.5m in width and up to 0.3m in depth. It got gradually shallower as it extended southwards and merged with the underlying deposits, about 11m south of the wall. The channel appears to have silted up and been naturally recut numerous times, the whole feature rising as the deposits rose outside the wall. As it rose the channel became shallower and narrower and less easy to distinguish from the surrounding deposits. At the head of the channel immediately outside the wall a deeper 'pool' (208) was formed by the water cascading down from the wall. This was up to 0.70m in depth and removed earlier deposits down to the level of natural gravel. Like the channel (218) it appears to have silted up gradually, finally being blocked by the later 203 material (see below). The fill of the pool consisted of silts at its base but the uppermost 0.20m held organic material (209) and was similar to fill 216 of the stone lined drain 201.

Deposits outside the quay walls After the construction of the quay wall layers of silt, stones and organic material accumulated on its riverward side. These built up to a thickness of *c.*0.8m before the walls appear to have gone out of use. The deposits took the form of dumped material – organic and inorganic – which was periodically eroded and mixed by river action, and river-deposited silt, sand and fine gravel. All the layers consisted of numerous small lenses and pockets of different material. The layers do not represent individual dumps but phases in the general dumping and river deposition. In general, the material deposited outside the wall was all very similar and layers merged into each other and were often difficult to follow precisely, except in section. All the layers sloped downwards as they extended southwards away from the walls.

Discussion The deposits, which built up against the riverward side of the wall contained substantial amounts of pottery and roof and floor tiles. There were sherds of line-impressed floor tiles in the earliest deposits. These are generally dated to the fourteenth and fifteenth centuries. The pottery present in these layers consisted mainly of Dublin temper-free wares with lesser amounts of Dublin wheel-thrown and Leinster cooking wares. Layer 229 contained a large number of small (less than 200mm high) squat Stonge jugs glazed only on the handle and on a small area under the spout. The concentration of this type of pottery in a discrete area suggests the dumping of a small group of jugs together at one time. Two sherds of Siegberg and a sherd of Langerwehe stoneware were also uncovered from these earliest layers. These date to the early part of the fifteenth century and suggest a date for the construction of the walls. The deposits outside the walls continued to accumulate through the fifteenth and sixteenth centuries as is shown by the presence of Late Stonge, Beauvais and Spanish wares; some of the latter having close parallels from Armada wrecks. The locally produced temper-free and wheel-thrown wares were also present throughout these deposits. Other local wares also make their appearance in these deposits. They do not appear to have exact parallels elsewhere but some of the fabrics and forms are not unlike those noted from sixteenth-century levels of the moat at Dublin Castle.

The final gravel layers (106 and 203) and the final organic deposits (105 and 205) that were deposited outside the river walls contained pottery dating to the late sixteenth and early seventeenth centuries. This suggests that the quay walls existed until the later sixteenth or early seventeenth century and hence had a life of *c.*200 years.

Level V (figs 11 and 13)

The quay wall (213) was partly robbed out and replaced by a wall that survived only to a limited extent further south. As noted above the deposits outside the wall all sloped down to the south. When the later cellars were inserted in this area the uppermost of these layers were removed over the northern half of the site while those at the southern end still survived. There was a large robber trench over all but the eastern metre or so of the old quay wall (213). It survived to a depth of up to 1.1m and measured up to 2.2m in width. After the removal of the stones of wall 213 the trench was backfilled. Its base was filled with grey silt containing lenses of loam and slate fragments (221/222). The upper part consisted of soft dark brown organic material (210) that contained spreads of charcoal flecks and shells (211).

Wall 102/214 On top of organic deposits 105, 205 and 219, that post-date the destruction of the quay wall 213 a new wall (102) was built. Only a length of 4.1m intruded into the excavated area. The wall ran parallel to the old quay wall 5 to its west. The new wall was up to 1.15m in width and survived as a single course of large rectangular blocks bonded with a very hard pinkish white mortar.

Discussion The pottery recovered from the fills of the robber trench over the earlier quay wall (213) consisted of a mixture of medieval types and of late sixteenth-/early seventeenth-century types. The medieval sherds are residual and are presumably derived from the deposits into which the robber trench was cut. The 102 and 202 layers that were deposited against the sides of the later 102 wall also contained late sixteenth-/early seventeenth-century pottery. This date suggests that the river walls built in this phase of activity may be those shown on Francis Place's drawing of the area. This sketch is dated 1698 and shows the site before the erection of Ellis's new quays in the early eighteenth century. A wall is shown on the river frontage at the east end of the area. It extends westwards before turning diagonally northwestwards. This suggests that the wall stood for around a century before it was demolished to make way for the new Arran Quay.

Level VI (fig. 13)

Only a small group of features survived from this late date at the south side of the site. They consisted of a dense cluster of oak piles (100) that covered an area at least 9m in length (east-west) by 0.8m in width (north-south). They extended in rough lines in a north/northeast to south/southeast direction. Most of the piles were of rectangular section averaging 100 x 60mm They varied in length from 0.4m to 1.15m but the tops of all had been truncated by later cellar building. They had pointed bases generally sawn from four sides. One contained a dowel hole suggesting re-use. None were large enough to

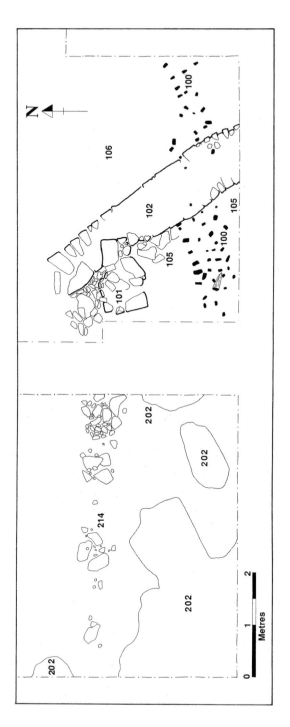

13 Plan of post medieval river wall (102/214) and later piles (100)

allow dating by dendrochronology. The piles did not correspond to any of the walls of the later buildings on the site and their alignment is also different. The corner of the earlier quay wall (102) was cut into and a rectangular stone pier (101) was built 0.9m north of the lines of piles (100). The pier was constructed of stones and some red brick bonded by hard, almost cement-like, mortar. A few sherds of gravel-tempered pottery were found in the disturbed soil (103) around the pier.

Discussion The line of the piles does not correspond to any of the walls of the large demolished houses and may suggest that they lay beneath structures that predate those buildings. They evidently date to the late seventeenth or early eighteenth century and may be part of the earliest buildings erected on the new Arran Quay.

Level VII
The large eighteenth-century houses which stood on the site and which were demolished in recent times belong to this level. The houses had cellars averaging 2.2m in depth. The rear (north) walls of the buildings rested on a foundation of wood and red brick (237). The other walls of the buildings rested on stone or red-brick footings. The foundations were generally little deeper than the floor of the cellars but a small number of internal walls (01, 03, 08) in the southern half of the site were set on footings which were set in trenches cut down to the level of the natural river gravel. During construction of these buildings all underlying layers were removed to a depth of 2.2m below modern ground level. A thick layer of redeposited yellow boulder clay (215) appears to have been laid down beneath the floors of the cellars. A large drain (108) was built using the old quay wall (109) as its base. It began beyond the northeast corner of the site and ran in a south-westerly direction to the northern end of wall 109, which it then followed southeastwards to beyond the southern edge of the site. It was built of limestone flags and concrete, and was partly filled with organic material that contained nineteenth-century pottery and glass.

CONCLUSIONS

The wooden revetments and stone walls uncovered at Arran Quay were the first excavated features relating to medieval land reclamation to be unearthed on the north bank of the river Liffey. Wooden revetments, stone walls and docks have been uncovered on the southern shore of the river (Wallace 1981; Swan 1991; Walsh 1997) where the sequence of encroachment is much better known.

Timber revetments Although the wooden revetments at Arran Quay survive to a much lesser extent than those uncovered in other Dublin sites their original shape and structure can be readily reconstructed with reference to these other sites. The two earlier Arran Quay revetments belong to the general group of front braced vertical revetments that are found in north-western Europe and find general parallels in England at sites such as Seal House (Scholfield 1975), Custom House (Tatton Brown 1974), Trig Lane (Milne 1981, and Milne & Milne 1978 and 1982), and Swan Lane, London (Egan and Pritchard, 1991, 9–10), and Hull (Ayers, 1979) and King's Lynn (Clarke and Carter 1977). In Ireland front braced revetments have been uncovered in Dublin at Wood Quay (Wallace 1981), Patrick Street (Walsh 1997) and Usher's Quay (Swan 1991) and a more fragmentary example is recorded from Drogheda (Sweetman 1984). These and other examples show differences in the way the raking front brace is anchored at its outer end and in whether or not it is attached to the main base plates of the revetment. In the case of Wood Quay and some of the London sites, a number of different types occur on the one site.

There was no evidence of subsidiary base plates at Arran Quay, with the exception of the single composite base (38.1) for a raking brace at the south side of Revetment 1. The latter does not appear to have been linked to the main base plate of the revetment. It simply anchored the base of the raking brace more firmly. There were similar composite structures in the mid thirteenth-century revetment excavated at Church Street (Linzi Simpson, pers. comm). Instead of subsidiary base plates the rest of Revetments 1 and 2 utilised anchors consisting of a post or group of posts, hammered into the ground at an angle leaning away from the revetment. These lay about 1–1.50m away from the revetment. Large posts were also hammered deeply into the ground in front of the main base plates to stop them slipping outwards. These details are closely paralleled in Section B of the 1210 AD revetment at Wood Quay (Wallace 1982, 284–5) and suggest that the Arran Quay revetment took the same form. The bases of the braces may have simply butted onto the ground against their anchors (as evidenced at Wood Quay) as there were no joints or dowels in the seemingly complete anchors. The way in which the braces were attached to the upper part of the uprights could not be discerned, as they did not survive, but they were probably jointed in the manner of the Wood Quay examples. In the case of the revetments from Arran Quay and Section B from Wood Quay, the retaining posts on the riverward side of the main base plates were required as there was nothing else to stop the base of the revetment sliding forwards, as the braces only held its upper part in place. The revetments would have originally stood to a height of about 2.5 metres. This is estimated by subtracting their basal level, 2.75m OD, from the maximum spring tide level (4.8m OD), and allowing about half of a metre of freeboard to cope with the occasional storm driven high tides (de Courcy, pers. comm).

The Arran Quay revetments display marked similarity to the other Dublin revetments in the range of carpentry used. The base plates are joined by simple through-splayed scarf joints held in place by face pegs. This form of joint was the most utilised at Wood Quay and Patrick Street (where some joints had up to four pegs) and was also utilised at Usher's Quay. There were mortises for uprights in the area of the scarf joints at Arran Quay. This also was the case at Patrick Street and Wood Quay and would have greatly weakened the joint (Wallace 1982, 279). The uprights appeared in some cases to have been too small for the mortises in which they were set. This ill-matching of mortise and upright was also noted at Wood Quay (ibid., 283). None of the bottoms of the uprights in the Arran Quay revetments appear to have been shouldered or tennoned. This is unusual and is not the rule at the other Dublin sites and suggests a more sloppy approach on the part of the carpenters at Arran Quay. Virtually all the uprights were further secured in place by dowels. This again appears to be the general rule elsewhere except in the case of Section D of the Wood Quay revetment where the very fine fitting of mortise and tennon rendered dowels unnecessary in some cases (ibid., 283). As appears usual from the Dublin revetments – except that uncovered at Cornmarket (Hayden 1993) – the planks placed behind the uprights were not nailed, but held in place solely by the pressure of the material dumped behind the revetment. At Arran Quay the only nails in the whole structure were those used to attach the barrel staves (122) to the uprights in Area 1. The horizontal planks were radially split and of similar dimensions to those previously recorded from the city. As in the case of the Wood Quay and Patrick Street revetments all finishing of the timbers was done with axe, adze, chisel and auger, no use of a saw was attested.

The earlier revetment at Patrick Street was dated to *c.*1204 AD (Walsh 1997, 170), while those from Wood Quay belong to the thirteenth century, the earliest being erected in *c.*1210 AD (Wallace 1981, 115) and no date is yet given for that found at Usher's Quay. The earlier revetment at Arran Quay is dated to *c.*1305 AD and the second to shortly after. The similarity of the structures in this group of revetments, whose construction spans over a century, appears to show a marked degree of continuity and conservatism. Wallace (1982, 228) commented on the persistence of the through splayed scarf joint in the thirteenth-century revetments at Wood Quay, despite the existence in Ireland and elsewhere of stronger and more sophisticated joints. He also noted that the generally poor quality of the carpentry of the revetment contrasted to that found on, for example, mills and other structures. Some of the work on the timbers that were later reused in the revetments also showed more sophisticated carpentry. This is reflected in Patrick Street where the most sophisticated joint was on a large rafter that was later reused in the revetment (Walsh 1997). Wallace (1991, 288) noted that this probably reflected the presence in Dublin of 'professional quay builders, the conservative nature of whose carpentry had long been tried and trusted'. The poor construction of the Arran Quay revetments, notably the second, with its flimsy ash base plate (55) and the persistence of outdated joints and weak points, like cutting a mortise in the area of the joint between base plates, also shows the same conservatism but may also reflect the fact that the structures were not regarded as being important in themselves. They would, in any case, have been largely hidden from view after completion. Also it is possible they were never expected to, nor did they appear to, survive for any great length of time. The very short life of individual revetments is shown at Arran Quay where all three successive examples dated to the early fourteenth century

The form of the possible third revetment evidenced only by a fossilised edge in organic deposits and dating probably to roughly the middle of the fourteenth century is unclear. It was possibly back braced, as no timbers hammered into the riverbed were uncovered. A back braced revetments, dating to the thirteenth century have been excavated in Dublin at Wood Quay (Wallace 1981) and some of the revetments along the river Poddle in the early thirteenth century may also have been back braced (Walsh 1997, 107). The first revetment at Arran Quay dated to *c.*1305. A fire devastated Oxmantown in 1305 including among its casualties St Mary's and St Saviour's (Lydon 1988, 34). The subsequent rebuilding of the suburb may possibly have provided the impetus for the reinforcement of the riverbank and renewed reclamation of the land along its edge.

Stone Walls The erection of the walls in the mid- to later fourteenth century was a much larger-scale project than the building of the earlier wooden revetments. Walls would also have been much more expensive to construct. Eagan (1991, 12) notes a price £20, in 1347, for a wooden revetment, at Broken Wharf, London, while a quay wall cost £9 13s. 4d. for every 16.5 square feet in 1389 at the Tower of London. While the revetments could be interpreted as riverward advances of individual properties (though there is no evidence to suggest this unless the narrowness of the area reclaimed by Revetment 2 can be suggested to represent an individual landholding), the building of the walls was clearly the work of a larger group. Medieval stone quay walls have been uncovered at a number of sites in Ireland, for example, Charlotte's Quay, Limerick (Lynch 1984), Wood Quay, Dublin (Wallace 1981) and Kyrls Quay, Cork (Hurley 1993, 8–9), and in Britain at, for example, Perth (Bowler 1991, 54–59), Hartlepool (Daniels 1991, 43–53), Bristol (Jones 1991, 19–35) and London (Hobley 1981, 1–9). A variety of features such as slipways, watergates and stairs have been uncovered at these and other sites. Drains emptying through the wall like the Arran Quay example are also recorded at Charlotte's Quay Limerick and Kyrls Quay, Cork.

Revetment 1 presented a flat face to the river flowing eastwards. This would be particularly vulnerable to attack by floodwaters. This lesson was apparently soon learned by the builders of the extensions/repairs to the south end of this revetment. They changed the line of the south end of the structure so it ran diagonally to the line of the river and not at right angles to it. The gentle angle of the first quay wall (109) followed this line and would have made it more resistant to water flowing from the west. The line of the wall 109 would also have lessened somewhat the build-up of silt in the angle between it and wall 213 as it would have encouraged a flow of water back into the river carrying the silt with it, rather than a straight face against which silt could be deposited.

The first quay wall at Arran Quay appears to be of later fourteenth- or early fifteenth-century date and was therefore about a hundred years later than the first stone quays uncovered at Wood Quay on the south side of the river (Wallace 1981). This reflects the different status of the two areas. There may be a similar time lag in the construction of the revetments. Encroachment on the southern bank of the Liffey at Wood Quay began in earnest in the early thirteenth century while at Arran Quay the earliest revetment appears a century later. It is not however clear whether the Arran Quay revetments are the first built in this area or whether others exist further east or north closer to the original edges of the river. It should also be remembered of course that the riverside in the vicinity of St Mary's abbey may have been revetted or walled at an earlier date than happened further north at Arran Quay. The stone quay walls appear to have stood for around two hundred years before their replacement in the late sixteenth or early seventeenth century. This wall survived very poorly on the site but appeared to echo the line of the medieval quay wall in that it turned diagonally into the river at its east end. It did not advance the line of the river frontage by more than a few metres. It stood for around a century and is probably the wall shown on Francis Place's drawing (1698) of the area. This wall was replaced by Ellis's new Arran Quay, which was built before 1728 as it is shown on Brooking's map of that year. This river wall lay outside the south limit of the excavated area.

What was the primary reason for the erection of the Arran Quay structures and the reclamation of the land behind them? Milne (1981, 330) listed four reasons for revetment building: first, to win more land; second, to provide a deeper berth for shipping; third, to overcome the ever-present problem of silting, and fourth, to create a sounder water frontage. In the case of Wood Quay, Wallace suggested the main reasons for the erection of revetments there was the increased size of shipping and the problem of silting in the Liffey (Wallace 1981, 109). Wood Quay lay on the southern bank of the river, in the part of the city where trading was concentrated. The northern side of the river was not within the medieval town proper and as a result was probably less heavily populated and only began to see settlement of any consequence in the later twelfth and early thirteenth century. Also much of the area belonged to the abbey of St Mary's and the priory of St Saviour's. St Mary's was involved in fishing and trade and had its own ships and harbour (Carville 1972, 35–48). The relative importance for trade of the two sides of the river is clear from an agreement made in 1261 where 'the nets of the mayor and commonalty, as well as those of the Prior [of the hospital of St John of Jerusalem] and his successors, are to be emptied solely on the lands of the north side [of the Liffey] between the bridge of Kylmanynam and the sea' (Gilbert 1889–1944, i, 162). The southern bank of the river was then free to act solely as docking for merchant shipping. The north bank of the Liffey downstream of the bridge is shown on Speed's 1610 map as being, with the exception of one small area, unrevetted and possessing an irregular outline, suggesting no riverside development had taken place there even by this late stage. Some of the lands of St Mary's are shown walled on Speed's map, the wall on part of the southern side of the lands is shown running along the riverbank, and it is possible that some form of quay may have existed there at that time. The map also shows a regular riverside in the area of the future Arran Quay. This is probably the later quay wall (102/214) discovered in the excavation.

The Arran Quay area lay not only on the north side of the river but was also upstream of the medieval bridge (de Courcy 1990). The bridge would have obstructed river traffic to some extent. There is, for example, mention of a fixed net on the bridge in 1261 (Went 1990, 186). The presence of a small medieval dock at Usher's Quay (Swan 1991), also upstream of the bridge, suggests that at least smaller ships could navigate it. There are also several medieval references to the rights of citizens' boats to pass between areas that lay on either side of the bridge (Went 1990, 186). The use of front braced revetments in the Usher's Quay dock also shows that ships were able to berth close to them. In medieval Dublin spring high tide appears to have been between 4 and 5 metres OD (de Courcy 1984, 164). De Courcy (pers comm) has more recently suggested a level of 4.80m OD for maximum spring tide in calm conditions. At Arran Quay, Revetment 1 was built when the riverbed outside them lay at a level of between 2.5m and 3m OD and the stone quay walls when the riverbed had risen by a further 0.3–0.4m. This would have given a draught of only two metres at spring high and probably less than a metre at neap high. The excavated channel (218) snaking its way across the silt outside the river walls (109/213) at Arran Quay shows that the water level must have receded far away from the walls at low tide. This would suggest that only the smaller ships could have berthed against the revetments and the walls and only for very short periods when spring high tides and to a lesser extent when neap high tides allowed. It is, however, unclear where the north end of the extensions to Revetment 1 and wall 109 lay and it is possible that they may have provided berthing facilities for larger ships, as they lay further out into the river. It should however be remembered that ships often docked stern or prow on to land (Marsden 1981, 23). The prevalent type of medieval ship at this time was the cog which was generally less than 30m in length and had a very shallow draught and could settle on the river bed after the tide had receded, being refloated when it returned (McGrail 1981, 19; Marsden 1981, 22). It is however probable that ships of this size could not have berthed at Arran Quay.

Fish processing was certainly taking place in the area. This is evidenced by the presence of a number of small wooden pins which on other sites were used in the production of stock fish (Lindt 1991, 74–5) and by the disproportionate number of cod and ling heads uncovered. The Chain Book mentions a rule that 'fish are not to be eviscerated in the fish markets but only on the bank of the waterside' (Gilbert 1889–1944, i, 219). It would seem unlikely that the revetments and stone wall would have been built to have berthed small lighters and the odd fishing boat, which could only have tied up for short periods at specific times. The naturally sloping shore could easily have accommodated such small boats and their small cargoes unloaded there. Silting was an ever-present nuisance in the Liffey and from medieval times to the seventeenth century complaints are recorded about the inaccessibility of Dublin to large ships (Wallace 1981, 117). During the medieval period larger ships had to offload at least part of their cargo at Dalkey. Added to this problem was a dam built across the river in the vicinity of the present O'Connell bridge, before 1220, by the friars of Kilmainham (Went 1990, 184–5). Though this structure was no doubt soon removed traces of it were found when the modern bridge was being built (ibid.).

The excavated area lies only about sixty-five metres to the north of the site of the medieval bridge across the Liffey. Speed's map of 1610 shows that the abutment at the northern end of the bridge projected well out into the river. This was probably also the case on the earlier bridge, which was built in the same place by at least 1307, permission having been granted by King John in 1214. The construction of this abutment would have caused silt to be deposited upstream of it by the river, as happened against the upstream side of the recently excavated medieval bridge at Kingston-upon-Thames (Potter 1991, 141–4). This may have been at least partly the cause for the development of the large sandbank uncovered in the lowest levels of the Arran Quay excavation. Speed's map also shows that a small peninsula jutted out into the river from the north bank in the vicinity of the bridge. This may also have contributed to silting in the excavated area of the medieval river. The rate of build-up of silt at Trig Lane, London has been estimated at *c.*1–2cm *per annum* (Milne 1981, 36) and such a rate is easily supportable at Arran Quay where *c.*15cm of silt had been deposited between the erection of Revetments 1 and 2. The Liffey was also prone to sudden floods, which could have deposited large amounts of silt in a very short time, as appears to be evidenced by the large sandbank against the west side of Revetment 3 at Arran Quay. Similar large build-ups over short periods were noted directly across the river at Usher's Quay (Swan, 1991). The continued encroachment of quays on the river has been shown in the case of Bristol to have accelerated the degree of sedimentation by as much as 800–1200 percent (Jones 1991, 19).

Although the exact southern limit of the revetments and quay walls was not discovered, the amount of land reclaimed from the river at Arran Quay is very small compared to that at Wood Quay. This advance had been made largely by Revetment 1 and its extensions at the east side of the site. The area of the rest of the site did not advance this much until the sixteenth/early seventeenth century. Earlier encroachment may have happened further east and north of the excavated area but the virgin appearance of the early sandbank (13/80) and the lack of any earlier archaeological deposits may militate against this. The advance westwards was much more substantial. Between the fourteenth and late sixteenth centuries the previously unrevetted riverbank had been gradually given a firmer and more defined edge, which stretched westwards beyond the limits of the excavation. The builders of the first stone river wall were responsible for the vast majority of this develop-ment, although again the walls only enclosed banks of silt and sand that had naturally built up, they did not further advance the river bank any more than it had naturally moved. Even the later quay wall (102/214) only advanced the river by a few metres in the post-medieval period.

One is then left with the suggestion that the main reason for the erection of the revetments was to provide a sounder and better frontage along the riverbank. Revetment 1 was constructed taking advantage of a sandbank that had built up in the river, and the next major advance – the later fourteenth-century stone quay wall – was again built around river-deposited material. The land was therefore reclaimed in a series of opportunistic advances when natural build-ups of silt provided an occasion to win it and provide the river with a more secure bank. Only Revetments 2 and 3 made any attempt to actually win land from the river itself and the amount reclaimed could hardly be called extensive. The reasoning behind the construction of the revetments may have been to allow the land behind the revetments to be put to greater use once its periodic inundation and erosion by floodwaters had been controlled by the new river frontage.

ACKNOWLEDGEMENTS

A special thanks to all those who worked on the site: site supervisors: Kieran Campbell, Finn O'Carroll and Edward Bourke; Finds Assistants: Cathy Johnson, Eileen Whyte and Hilary Opie; draughtspersons: Andy Shelley and Helen Kehoe; and the excavators: Jodie Barrett, Don Brophy, Paddy Byrne, Fran Curran, the two Johns, 'Eliot', Murrough O'Brien, Dervla Cotter, Maeve O'Callaghan, Annabel Konig, Eddie McGinley, and David Jennings.

Thanks also to Jeanette d'Arcy who did the wages. The plans were drawn by Georgina Scally and the finds by the writer.

APPENDICES: FINDS AND OTHER REPORTS

The finds were numbered in the following way: excavation number (omitted in descriptions): context number: 1-infinity (by context).

POTTERY*

Later medieval pottery from Level IV
The usual assemblage of late thirteenth- to early fourteenth-century pottery was uncovered from the deposits associated with Revetments 1 to 3 (Levels I–III). The types represented include Stonge Polychrome and green glazed jugs, North French jugs, Redcliffe, Ham Green, and Minety wares, but the majority consist of local Dublin and North Leinster wares (fabric types 001–004). An unremarkable assemblage of seventeenth- to nineteenth-century pottery was also uncovered from deposits from levels V to VII. However the pottery included in the silt that built up outside the first quay walls from the early fifteenth to late sixteenth century (Level IV) is of interest as deposits of this date have rarely survived to be excavated in Ireland. Several of the types uncovered are rare in Ireland and are listed below. The typical Irish medieval pottery types as well as sherds of Saintonge glazed and unglazed wares were also present.

Rhenish stonewares Two sherds of fifteenth- to sixteenth-century Siegberg stoneware and a sherd of early fifteenth-century Langerwehe stoneware were recovered. The presence of both Siegburg and Langerwehe stonewares is unusual as both of these wares occur very rarely in Ireland. The Langerwehe wares tend to date to the first half of the fifteenth century (Gaimster 1987, 343) while Siegburg has a longer span over the fifteenth and sixteenth centuries (Hurst et al. 1986, 176–184). There are a few instances of stonewares occurring in medieval contexts in Ireland but on the whole, they do not come in bulk until the sixteenth century with the Cologne, Raeren and Frechen products.

Iberian A single sherd which was part of a shallow bowl made of fine light grey-buff fabric was found. It is tin-glazed on the inner surface (now discoloured black). This ware is similar to material from Dublin Castle, which Hurst felt was probably Mediterranean but could not be more definitive. At Dublin Castle, it came from sixteenth-century moat-fill.

Spanish: early Valencian lustreware A single body sherd from a straight-sided, flanged bowl (see Hurse 1977, nos 24, 25, 87–8 for parallels) was uncovered. The decoration comprises parallel diagonal lines, painted in lustre, on the outside and

_____

* This is a summary of a report compiled by Rosanne Meenan who identified the pottery and its background.

intersecting arcs on the inside. Hurst dates this form to late fourteenth/early fifteenth century (ibid., 84). This sherd of early Valencian lustreware is the only known example of that ware in Ireland. Again, the lustrewares do not occur at all frequently in Ireland–a very small number of sherds of mature Valencian lustreware were found in Waterford city and Dublin Castle. Late Valencian lustrewares are the most commonly found.

Spanish: Merida-type wares Ninety-two sherds of Merida-type wares were uncovered. The vessel types represented consisted of jar, bowl, jug, small bottle, costrel and amphora. These included fifty-three sherds of a large undecorated jar. The closest parallel for this form is a holemouth jar from the *Trinidad Valencera* illustrated by Hurst (1986, 70–1, fig. 31.88) and dated to 1588. The base of an unidentified vessel, possibly a bowl from Seville, was also uncovered. If it was a bowl, a footring would be expected; however, it may have originated in a vessel such as the curved-sided bowl illustrated by Hurst which was found in the *Girona* (Hurse 1986, no. 85, 70–1). A number of different vessel types were produced in the Merida area in the unglazed fabric and so, unless diagnostic sherds were present, it was not always possible to indicate the vessel forms found at Arran Quay. Merida-type wares were being imported from the thirteenth century onwards (Hurst 1986, 69). Some of the remaining sherds would fit in with a fifteenth-century date, but the majority of the vessel types identified tended to date to the late sixteenth century, having parallels on Armada ships.

French Twenty-one sherds of general French type wares were uncovered. The forms represented included bowls, a small cup, a chafing dish, a large pitcher and jugs. A body sherd decorated with polychrome paintwork dating to the sixteenth century is also included.

Northern French A body sherd and handle probably of North French origin were uncovered.

Beauvais A rim sherd from an unidentified vessel and a handle and two body sherds from a Beauvias chafing dish were uncovered. The handle springs from the rim and would presumably have met the body at the base of the dish. Glazed in dark apple green glaze all over. The closest parallel is a Beauvais vessel illustrated by Hurst (1974, 238) and dated to the late fifteenth and early sixteenth centuries.

English Two sherds from round bellied vessels such as cups or drinking jugs. Cistercian ware – this dates to the second half of the fifteenth century into the sixteenth century. Probably made in the north of England. A base and body sherd, similar in style of glazing and the grooving to the early brown-glazed wares from Dublin Castle which would have dated to the sixteenth century. This sherd is probably an import from the Lancashire/North Wales area.

Dutch: South Netherlands maiolica A sherd possibly of a South Netherlands maiolica flower vase was included among the Dutch pottery uncovered. It has blue painted decoration on outer surface in the form of concentric lines with blue blob underneath. They have not been found in archaeological contexts dating to before 1500 and seem to have lasted well into the sixteenth century (Hurst 1986, 119) The neck of Dutch tin-glazed drinking jug, decorated with a blue flower which is brought

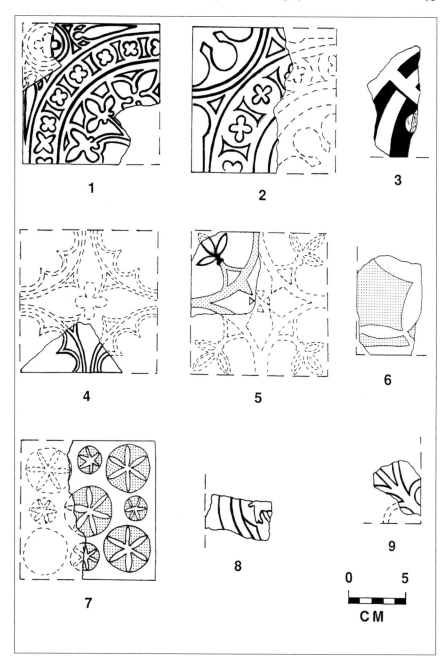

14 Ceramic floor tiles

up to the rim, was also uncovered. The fabric and the pinkish internal glaze is very similar to the sherd of South Netherlands maiolica. This sherd is from a drinking mug and as such dates to the sixteenth century.

Irish In addition to a large number of sherds of the typical Dublin medieval glazed and cooking wares, a large number of sherds of other locally produced glazed and unglazed vessels were also uncovered. These were made from several different fabric types. One type was a green glazed, quartz-tempered ware. It is not dissimilar to the previously identified Dublin medieval ware but is coarser and fired to a different colour, which also resulted in a browner glaze. However, it is not similar to the English or French wares imported at that period. The vessels appear to have been very large – although no rim survived, a couple of curved sherds indicate the neck of a jug. The decorative motifs and the absence of glaze on the interior suggest a continuation of the medieval tradition and it is possible that this is a ware which came into production in the fifteenth century. Different kilns were probably supplying the Dublin market at any one time, some of which may have lasted longer than others. The sherds of Irish medieval types from this level showed no marked difference to those from the medieval levels. While it is possible that some are residual the sheer number of sherds uncovered and the presence of definitely fifteenth- and sixteenth-century imports, suggests that these local wares continued in production throughout much of this period in forms largely unchanged since the later thirteenth/early fourteenth century.

MEDIEVAL FLOOR TILES (fig. 14)

Introduction A total of 324 fragments of medieval ceramic floor tiles were recovered. Of these, 23 fragments were two abraded to allow classification. Of the remaining 301 fragments, 267 were of line-impressed type, 12 were of relief or false relief type, 3 were of two-colour type and 19 were plain tiles. The tiles were uncovered from the deposits dumped on the riverward side of the wooden revetments and the stone quay wall. None were found in a primary position. The tiles are described following Eames and Fanning (1988) classification where the initial letter indicates the type of tile (T= two colour, L=line-impressed and R=relief). Plain tiles are recorded as 'P'. The subsequent number indicates the decorative motif. 'LN', 'TN' and 'RN' are used to indicate line-impressed, two-colour and relief tiles with previously unrecorded decorative motifs.

Two-colour tiles Three fragments were recovered. Fragment 301:17 was to abraded to discern its decoration. The second (106:176) was incomplete and was of either T212 or T213 type. The third fragment (219:8) (fig. 14.3) was of a previously unrecorded type. Its decoration consisted of a number of curving diagonal bands crossed by a straight line. Too little of the tile survived to reconstruct its decoration completely but it would appear to have been part of a four-tile pattern.

Line-impressed tiles The vast majority of tiles recovered were of this type, 267 fragments are recorded. Of these 50 were not identifiable to type due to their eroded state or small size. Of the remaining 217 fragments, 200 were of 17 to 19 previously recorded types. The types are listed below, with the number of fragments recovered in brackets.

L4	(12)	L59	(3)
L6	(7)	L65	(11)
L8	(1)	L72	(26)
L10	(2)	L73	(12)
L14	(13)	L76	(6)
L19 or L20	(3)	L76 or L77	(6)
L20	(30)	L78	(11)
L38	(31)	L81	(13)
L46	(1)		
L49	(11)		
L55	(1)		

The remaining seventeen fragments were of 5 previously unrecorded types. **Type A** Six fragments were recovered (223:107, 301:8, 203:108/184, 229:8, 106:285 and 229:143). A further 13 fragments were either of this type or of L78 type. This type is a variant of L78. It differs in the orientation of the quatrefoils and the shape of the two end quatrefoils, in the curving diagonal band. It also differs in having a double line enclosing the motif in the top left-hand corner of the tile. The motif in the lower right corner of the tile is identical to that on the L78 type. It is therefore unclear, in the case of the thirteen fragments of this area of the tile, whether they are of L78 type or of the variant type. **Type B** (fig. 14.4) Two fragments were recovered (226:98 and 226:104). This type is a variant off the L74 type. It differs in having double, rather than single, lines defining the decoration. **Type C** (fig. 14.8) One incomplete fragment was recovered (203:182). The decoration consists of a four-legged animal, probably a boar, as it is similar to the boars depicted on types L1 and LM1 (Eames and Fanning 1988), within a triple lined circular border. The innermost line has small inwardly pointing triangles on its inner side. Only the hind legs and rump of the animal survived on the fragment. This pattern is known from tiles in England (Eames 1980, no. 164) and a fragment of a similar tile was recently uncovered from the town fosse at Nicholas Street, Dublin (Hayden 1997). **Type D** (fig. 14.9) One incomplete fragment was recovered (219:3). Only the lower right corner of the tile is represented. The decoration consists of a five-stemmed plant, running diagonally across the tile. The two outer stems curl back on themselves. This is probably a variant of the L77 type, which has a similar motif in its lower right corner. It differs from the L77 type however in having the outer stems defined by double rather than single lines. **Type E** (fig. 14.1) Seven incomplete fragments were recovered (112:109, 203:61, 106:31, 106:175, 301:113 and 106:13). These tiles appear to be a variant of the L76/L77 types. The differences are however only very slight. They differ in the amount and placement of the curvaceous infills between the plants and in having the two triangles, that lie on either side of the roundel in the upper left corner, joined together.

It was possible to discern in the case of only 71 fragments whether they were derived from full or half tiles (full tiles scored and split for use at edges of panels). Of the 71, 50 were full tiles and 20 were half tiles and a further one example had been scored for halving but not broken. The line-impressed tiles vary from 19mm to 28mm in thickness, with the majority being between 19 and 22mm thick. Where it was possible to tell the original size of the tile this varied from 117mm to 125mm across, except in the case of the L72 example which measured only 110mm across. This variation in size occurred within individual types, e.g., the L20 type varied in size from 117mm to 124mm across. The size of the decoration is the same on all the tiles of a particular type showing the same stamp was used for each. The variation in size of the tile appears to be only a result of utilizing slightly different sizes of moulds to produce tiles of one type. Not all the tiles are exactly square; in many cases, adjacent sides of the one tile, vary in size by up to 4mm The colour of the glaze utilised varies from various shades of green to brown. Some of this variation may be due to soil conditions. A lighter green colour was achieved by applying a white slip beneath the green glaze. The presence of a number of wasters may be an indication that the tiles were made locally. Their fabric, which contains mica flecks in abundance, would imply local manufacture. It is similar to that which is use to manufacture local pottery dating from the thirteenth to fifteenth centuries.

Relief tiles Twelve fragments of relief tiles were recovered. Types R1 and R3 are represented and also two previously unrecorded types. **Type R1** (fig. 14.7) Counter relief tile. Six fragments were recovered (106:2, 112:110, 210:1, 226:1, 239:9 and 246:2). This type is only known previously from a single fragment from Inns Court, Dublin (MacMahon 1988, 30). This fragment represented about a quarter of a full tile. The fragments uncovered from Arran Quay allow reconstruction of all but one corner of the tile. The decoration consists of small and large false relief sexfoils (there is a similar stamp on a medieval ceramic Nuneaton Ware mortar from Coventry (McCarthy and Brooks 1988, 367). MacMahon (ibid., 303) states that two stamps would have been used to create the decoration, repeatedly stamping the tile with each. However the shape of each of the sexfoils is slightly different. Also, their orientations on different areas of the tile are slightly different, and this is repeated on other fragments. This shows that a single large stamp with all the sexfoils carved on it must have been used to create the decoration. This would be more appropriate to the rapid and repeated production of tiles. The reconstructed tile measures 118mm square. One example (245:2) is only lightly stamped and green glazed while the remainder possess a purple-black glaze. Two of the fragments (112:110 and 239:9) may be wasters. **Type R3** Counter relief tile. Two incomplete fragments were recovered (239:4 and 301:10). The former example is stamped very lightly and green glazed while the other possesses a purple-black glaze.

Previously unrecorded types: Type A (fig. 14.5) Counter relief tile. Two corner fragments were recovered (106:162 and 229:7). The decoration consists of a central cross(?), with diamond-shaped arms and outward pointing split stemmed trilobate 'flowers' at the corners. Fragment 106:162 is green glazed while the other possesses a purple-black glaze. The pattern appears to be a variation of that used on the line-impressed tiles type L66. **Type B** (fig. 14.6) The only true relief tile represented. One corner fragment was recovered (239:3). It appears to have been a waster as the glaze is bubbled and burnt. The decoration, though partly obscured, appears to take the form of a four-lobed flower/cross set saltire-wise with small motifs between the arms and a large petal-like motif attached to one of the ends of the cross/flower. At least one edge of the tile appears to be outlined by a ridge. The relief tiles vary from 22mm to 26mm in thickness.

Plain tiles Twenty-two fragments of plain undecorated tiles were recovered. Where it was possible to discern their original size – in only two cases – they measured 116mm and 117mm across. The tiles varied from 15mm to 34mm in thickness with the majority being between 19 and 24mm thick. They were glazed either green or brown, a white slip being used to achieve a lighter green colouring.

Discussion None of the tiles were discovered *in situ*, the majority were recovered from material dumped into the river after the construction of the stone quay walls in the mid- to later fourteenth century. With the exception of two tile types (L55 and R3) all the previously recorded types represented at Arran Quay are known from other Dublin sites. The only previously recorded example of the L55 type tile is unprovenenced (Eames and Fanning 1988, 90). This type however is a variant of the L52–54 types, which are known from sites in Dublin (ibid., 89–90). The R3 type is only known previously from St Canice's, Kilkenny and from Mellifont, County Louth (ibid.). In Dublin, 11 of the types from Arran Quay are known from St Patrick's, 10 from Christ Church, 9 from St Saviour's, 8 from St Mary's and Dublin Castle, and smaller numbers from other sites. If one lists the types that are recorded from Arran Quay but least frequently at other Dublin sites interesting facts emerge. The L81 and R1 types are previously recorded in Ireland only at St Saviour's, Dublin, the T212/213 and L65 types at Christ Church, Dublin. In Dublin the L19 type is previously recorded only from St Patrick's and St Mary's, the L49 and L72 types from St Saviour's and St Mary's and the L73 type from St Saviour's, St Mary's and St Patrick's.

  If one discounts the tiles from St Patrick's and Christ Church, as these are the two cathedrals of Dublin, the tile assemblage from Arran Quay displays marked similarities to those from St Saviour's and St Mary's. These two sites are also linked by their close proximity to each other and the fact that St Saviour's may have been founded on land given by St Mary's (Gwynn and Hadcock 1988, 224). The excavated area at Arran Quay lies less than 150m from the site of St Saviour's and it seems probable that the Arran Quay tiles derive from that site especially as two of the types recovered (L81 and R1) are only known previously in Ireland from St Saviour's. The presence of a number of wasters suggests that the tiles may have been manufactured on the site of the priory. Not enough of the detailed building history of the priory survives to suggest exact dates for all phases of building or renovation work carried out there. However, given the accepted dating for the different types of tiles (Eames and Fanning 1988) they can be broadly linked with different phases of rebuilding and repair carried out on the priory church. It is most likely that the two colour tiles recovered formed part of the original floor of their first church, which was dedicated in 1238. The priory burnt down in 1304 and was soon rebuilt (Warburton et al. 1818, 358). In 1316 it was partly demolished to provide materials to strengthen the town defences on the approach of the Bruces (Gwynn and Hadcock 1988, 225). It was however soon rebuilt with the east window and bell tower being rebuilt before 1351 (ibid.). The new church was consecrated in 1402 (ibid.). It is probable that the line-impressed tiles and counter-relief tiles derive from this phase of rebuilding. All the tiles were recovered from late fourteenth-/early fifteenth-century dumps outside the stone quay walls (109 and 213).

THE ROOF TILES
by Joanna Wren

Medieval crested ridge tiles Eighty-eight sherds of crested ridge tiles were uncovered, of which only fifteen were complete enough to classify. Four types were identified: tiles with high cockscomb crests, with low cockscomb crests, with flat-topped crests, and with boxed crests. Two of the tiles were decorated with applied thumbed strips, one had thumbed decoration on its crest and one on its exterior face. They were made in two fabrics (see below).

High cockscomb crested ridge tiles Three sherds are from tiles of this type and all were made in the same fabric type. One tile came from an early fourteenth-century context and the other two from contexts dating to later in the fourteenth century. Tiles with this type of cresting were introduced into Ireland by the Anglo-Normans at the beginning of the thirteenth century (Wren 1987, 32) and they continued to be made until the late fourteenth century.

Low cockscomb crested ridge tiles One sherd (203:139) of this type was recovered from a fifteenth-century context and was made in type 2 fabric. Tiles of this type replaced the high cockscomb variety in Ireland and England in the late fourteenth century and early fifteenth centuries (Wren forthcoming (a)). This style of tile continued in production until the eighteenth century.

Flat topped crested ridge tiles Five sherds of this type were recovered. One (230:29) was made in type 1 fabric and came from an early to mid-fourteenth-century context, while the other four sherds were made in type 2 fabric and came from contexts dating from the mid-fourteenth to early fifteenth centuries. This type of tile began to be produced in both mid- and north Leinster in the thirteenth century and continued to be made until the late fourteenth century (Wren 1987, 36). Four of the tiles have stabmarks in their crests; ridge tiles' crests were often stabbed to aid firing (ibid., 28). On one sherd (112:1) from a late fourteenth-century context the marks are particularly regular and shallow and they appear to have a decorative function similar to that of the incised lines found on the crests of some of the later boxed crested ridge tiles (see below).

Boxed crested ridge tiles Six sherds of this type were recovered and all have double incised line decoration and were made in type 2 fabric. Two were decorated with double incised curving lines on their exterior faces and three with double incised vertical lines on each side of their crests. In one case (226:95) the vertical lines continued down the body of the tile. Boxed crested ridge tiles are a modification of the earlier flat-topped crested tiles (ibid.). In the same way as the high crested cockscomb type was replaced by the simplified low cockscomb variety, the more elaborated flat-topped crests gave way to the more standardised and simpler boxed crests. These crests have a straight back and front and a sub-rectangular profile. The valleys between each crest are usually flat, and when these tiles are seen from the side it appears that a series of rectangular box shapes have been applied along the ridge. The vertical incised lines decorating the tiles are a development of the stab marks in the earlier flat topped crests. Due to improved firing techniques the marks were no longer functional and were retained as decoration. The curving lines probably developed as a combination of the double vertical lines with curved line motifs found on earlier tiles (ibid., 39).

Three of the sherds came from later fourteenth- to fifteenth-century contexts and one came from a sixteenth- to seventeenth-century context. Boxed crested ridge tiles usually date to the late fourteenth and fifteenth centuries (Wren forthcoming (b)) and their distribution is mainly confined to mid- and north Leinster. One example is known from Cork (S. McCutcheon, pers. comm) but this may be an import. In particular, seven tiles of this type, including one kiln waster, were found with late fourteenth- to fifteenth-century floor tiles at the Magdalene Street kiln in Drogheda (Campbell 1985, 48). In Dublin tiles of this type have been found at many sites, for example: Wood Quay (P.F. Wallace, pers. comm); Winetavern Street (B. Ó Ríordáin, pers comm); Dublin Castle (Wren forthcoming (b)); St Mary's abbey (M. McMahon, pers. comm); High Street (D. Murtagh, pers. comm) and Patrick Street (Wren 1997).

Louvres Two of the ridge tiles (234:1 and 203:212) had the remains of louvres attached to their crests. Both were made in type 1 fabric. One (203:12) was decorated with applied strips around its base and across the body of the tile. Louvres were smoke-ventilators functioning with the central open hearths found in many medieval buildings. Ceramic louvres were rounded, wider at the base than at the top, with holes cut in their sides. The wind traveled through the holes creating a decrease in pressure inside the louvre, which caused the air to be drawn up from the room below, and out through the louvre. One of the sherds (234:1) came from an early to mid-fourteenth-century context and the other (203:12) from a fifteenth-century context. An example of this type found in Southampton was dated to the late thirteenth century (Dunning 1975, 186–96).

Pantiles Three sherds of pantiles were recovered. This type is seen as a development of the oldest form of clay roofing (Davey 1961, 53) where curved roof tiles or *imbrices* were used in conjunction with flat flanged tiles or *tegulae*. In the pantile the two are combined into one. Pantiles appear to have been first introduced into Ireland in the late seventeenth century. The three sherds recovered were from unstratified and disturbed deposits.

Fabric There are two types of fabric in this group of tiles. Type 1, coarse and hard, incompletely oxidised, with bright red or orange margins and a strong grey core. Inclusions: o calcite up to 1mm, common; quartzite *c.*1mm, sparse; mica below 1mm, common: unidentified grey stones *c.*1mm, common. Suggested date: thirteenth-fourteenth century. Type 2, rough/coarse and very hard, incompletely oxidised, red or orange margins and a patchy light grey core. Inclusions: calcite 1mm, sparse; quartzite 1mm, sparse; mica below 1mm, sparse; unidentified grey stones 1mm, sparse. Suggested date: late fourteenth to fifteenth century.

TOKEN
by Michael Kenny

245:13 Obv. no legend, lions head facing. Rev. Cross Moline Reverse. Partially cracked. 19.1mm max. dia., 8mm thick. English jeton. *c.*1300–1350. Similar to Mitchener (1988) 217 and 243, but with border of 209. Latten. See also Barnard (1981) Plate 1, No. 32.

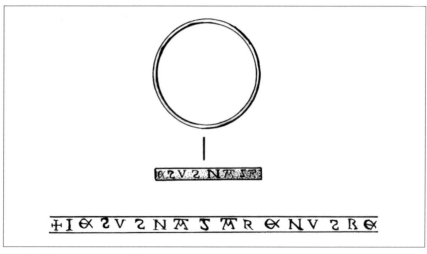

15 Gold finger ring (119:17) (Scale 2:1)

GOLD

Finger ring (fig. 15) 119:17 Gold finger ring 21mm diameter, 2.7mm wide, 0.8mm thick. Engraved in Lombardic script on outer side '+ IEXSUS NASAREXNVS REX'. With the exception of the first 'S' in 'Nasarenus' all the 'S' letters are back to front and the letters 'EX' are conjoined in both cases. The initial cross is seraphed and there are no symbols or spaces to divide the inscription into individual words. A stain after the 'R' in 'Nasarenus' may indicate the position of the joint in the ring. Inscribed finger rings were popular during the medieval period. The religious nature of the inscriptions need not necessarily indicate that the owner was an ecclesiastic (Hinton 1982, 15). The inscription used is talismatic (Evans 1922, 128–9) and is also known from other objects of medieval date. A thirteenth- or fourteenth-century gold ring brooch from Islay in Scotland, was inscribed with exactly the same inscription in the identical type of lettering used on the Arran Quay ring. A number of other fourteenth-century Scottish brooches have inscriptions reading IESUS NAZARENUS REX IUDEORUM (Callender 1924, 165). A silver brooch from London was inscribed IESUS NASARENUS in Lombardic lettering (Egan and Pritchard 1991, 254–5). A leather chalice case from Cawston in Norfolk, dated to *c.*1373–82 AD was inscribed on the lid with '+IHESUS NAZARENUS REX IUDEORUM +' (Alexander and Binski 1987, 238). A bell from the Lynn foundry, also in Norfolk, and dated to *c.*1320 AD was inscribed in Lombardic capitals '+IHC:NAZARENUS: IUDEORUM'. Another bell from Woodrising had the same inscription and lettering but also had the name of the founder and is datable to *c.*1333 AD (ibid., 244). The use of Lombardic script indicates that the ring dates to the later thirteenth or early fourteenth century. This script gradually went out of use in the fourteenth century being replaced by the Gothic Black Letter script. The ring shows little signs of wear and therefore may not have been very old when lost. The 119 deposit, from which it was recovered, dates probably to the mid- to later fourteenth

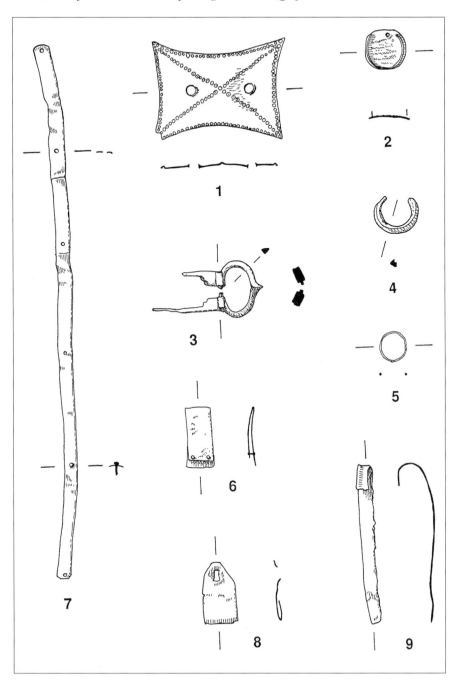

16 Copper alloy objects (scale 1:1)

century. The reversal of the letter 'S' on the Arran Quay ring is not unusual: the silver brooch from London also has reversed 'S's' (Egan and Pritchard). Letters were sometimes stamped upside down or back to front on medieval jewellry (Callender).

Copper alloy (figs 16 and 17)

Plaque (fig. 16.1) 111:22. Sheet copper alloy plaque, rectangular with concave sides. One corner broken. Decorated with border and saltire of 2mm dia. repoussé bosses. Two 5mm dia. perforations on either side of centre on long axis, 33.5mm apart. Length: 77mm Width: 57mm Thick: 0.5mm

Mirror (fig. 16.2) 118:15. Square copper alloy sheet with rounded corners, 2mm dia. perforation close to edge. 3.5mm wide copper alloy strip soldered on edge around three sides of square sheet. May originally have also been attached to fourth side but broken. Traces of wood in interior. Length: 23mm Width: 23mm Small cased mirrors have only recently been recognised from medieval sites in Ireland but appear to be quite common finds in England (Bayley *et al.* 1984, 399–402). They are made either of copper alloy like this example or of lead-tin. The glass rarely survives. A hinged lid would originally have been present.

Buckle (fig. 16.3) 106:1. Pronged 'Jew's Harp' belt buckle. Sub-triangular section copper alloy. Pin missing but square section pin-bar survives. Attached to pronged strap end, 40mm long, consisting of two rectangular arms with stepped terminals that grip buckle. Pointed pin-rest on bow. Length: 32mm Width: 22mm Buckles of the pronged 'Jew's Harp' type are known from English sculptures and examples generally dated to the fourteenth century (Ward- Perkins 1967, 267–62, and Egan and Pritchard 1991,22). They were probably used on civil costume (ibid.). The example from Arran Quay is identical to a buckle found at Fishbourne, England (Cunliffe 1971, 110 and 113) and to numerous examples from London (Egan and Pritchard 1991, 75). A similar example retaining its plate was recently uncovered from fourteenth-/fifteenth-century levels over the town ditch at Nicholas Street, Dublin (Hayden 1997).

Buckle (fig. 16.4) 103:3. Penannular ring, of sub-triangular section (4mm by 3mm). Tapers to blunt point at both ends. Ends broken. Probably bow of buckle. Diameter: 27mm

Ring (fig. 16.5) 2:8. Annular ring of 1mm dia. circular section copper alloy. Diameter: 27mm

Strap end (fig. 16.6) 229:2. Rectangular sheet of copper alloy, folded back on itself and fastened by two 1.5mm dia. round headed copper alloy rivets. Length: 39mm Width: 15mm

Book/casket mount (fig. 16.7) 236:2A and B. Convex section sheet copper alloy, in two fragments. Ends diagonally trimmed at corners. Six central regularly spaced (60mm) rivet holes (1.5mm dia.). A rivet, with 2mm dia. circular head survives in one hole. Length: 310mm Width: 8mm Thick: 0.4mm Book or casket mounts of this type have been found quite frequently on medieval excavations (several examples were found in Waterford (Hurley et al. 1997), and range in date from the twelfth to the fifteenth century. The Arran Quay example is probably fourteenth-century in date.

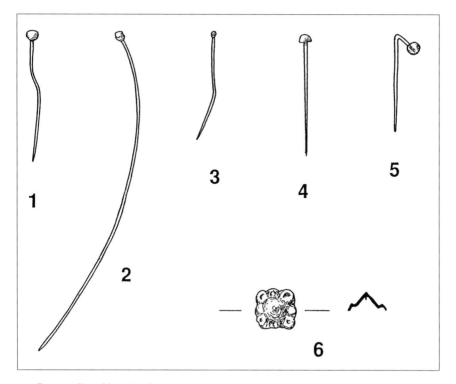

17 Copper alloy objects (scale 2:1)

Sheets and strips (figs 16.8 and 16.9) Six pieces of copper alloy sheet with straight or ragged cut edges were uncovered. Two examples are illustrated (245:3–fig. 31.8 and 266:188 fig. 31.9). The edges were either cut with a shears or a chisel. They are from the production of sheet copper alloy objects.

Decorated mount (fig. 17.6) 110:1. Square sheet copper alloy. Raised central boss surrounded by eight smaller bosses with alternately raised and hollowed centres. Central boss pierced by 1mm dia. copper alloy rivet. Length: 11mm Width: 11mm Not dissimilar to examples from Winchester (Biddle 1990, 1088), probably for attachment to cloth, leather or wood.

Copper alloy drawn wire pins (fig. 17.1–5) 48. Copper alloy drawn wire pins were uncovered. All consist of a length of circular section copper alloy wire 0.5–1.5mm in diameter with a simple head. Dimensions of individual pins are given in table below. The heads take four forms: (1) Coiled–a piece of the same wire as used in the shank is twisted around the top of the shank to form the head (Example 206:1–fig. 17.3); (2) As for (1) but the wire is hammered to form a rough sphere (Examples 106:123A and 112:42A–figs 17.1–2); (3) The head consists of a mushroom shaped piece of solid copper alloy either soldered to the shank or else the shank is passed through the head (Example 114:2A–fig. 17.4); (4) A single example (117:1A) with the head composed of a sphere of green glass (fig. 17.5). Pins with heads of types 1–2 are common finds from medieval excavations, e.g., Duiske abbey (Bradley and Manning 1981, 419–20), Patrick Street, Dublin (Hayden 1997), Waterford (Hurley et al. 1997), Limerick (Lynch 1984, 315–6), Narrow Quay, Bristol (Good 1987, 106), St Peter's Street, Northampton (Oakley1979, 260–62) and Bordesley abbey (Watt and Rahtz 1983, 129–206), etc. Pins with head type 3 are less common but are recorded from Northampton (ibid.). All were probably used in dressmaking (Ford 1987, 123) or for fastening clothing such as veils or shawls (Biddle 1990, 564). Their occurrence with burials, for example, the graveyard of St Peter's church, Waterford (Hayden 1989), St Stephen's leper hospital, Dublin (Hayden 1991), Duiske abbey (Bradley and Manning 1981) and Bordesley abbey (Watt and Rahtz 1983) shows they also saw use as shroud pins. The single glass-headed pin (117:1A) is unusual, although a pin from Greyfriars, Northampton had a glass inset (Oakley 1978, 151). Recently however a number of glass-headed pins have been uncovered in London (Egan and Pritchard 1991, 297–9). Pins of these types range in date from the thirteenth to nineteenth century (Biddle 1990, 131–3 and 560–71 and Hayden, 1993), the examples from Arran Quay being fourteenth- to sixteenth-century in date.

Wire drawn copper alloy pins: dimensions and head type

Number	Length (mm)	Head Type	Head Diameter (mm)
106:123 A	32.3	2	
B	61	2	2.5
C	41	2	4
D	55	2	2.5
E	44.5	2	2.5
F	40	missing	
G	38	missing	
H	60	missing	
I	40	missing	
J	40	missing	
K	42	missing	
L	39	1	2
M	36	2	3
N	25	2	2
114:2A	37	3	4
B	38	3	4
C	22	2	2.5
D	36	2	4
117:1A	29	4	4
B	31	1	3
C	36	1	2
D	15	1	2
E	38	missing	

→

F	38	missing	
G	24	missing	
206:1	33	1	1
229:1	55	2	3
112:42A	100	2	2
B	57	2	3
C	40	3	4
D	41.5	2	3.5
E	42	2	3
F	54	2	3
G	37	2	3.5
H	40	2	3
I	40	2	2
J	34	2	1.5
K	59	2	2
L	36	missing	
M	49	missing	
N	52	missing	
245:2	46	3	3
203:20	58	4	
120:1	36	1	2
236:1A	49	2	4
B	46	2	2
C	42	missing	
D	44	2	4

Iron

Blade? (fig. 18.1) 226:92. Corroded iron, convex rear face with raised rib along centre of upper face. Length: 48mm Width: 53mm Thick: 20mm.

Rivets 242:3A (fig. 18.2). Corroded iron rivet. Shank 6mm square in section, 45mm long. Rectangular rove head, 31 by 35mm, 5mm thick. Other head round 31mm dia., 5mm thick. Length: 72mm 242:3B. (Not ill.).Corroded iron rivet. Shank 7mm square section, 38mm long. Incomplete rectangular rove head, 31 by 18mm Other head round 22mm dia. End of shank protrudes above this head. Length: 60mm.

Unidentified object (fig. 18.4). 110:164. 58mm long, 7mm square section shank, tapering to point. Semicircular flange, 10mm by 7mm at blunt end, with notch and central depression.

Lead

Vessel leg/handle (fig. 18.3) 203:357. Curved leg with clubbed lower end and pointed and fluted upper end. Flat on rear, three faceted on face. Length: 116mm Width: 12mm Thick: 8mm Medieval ewers and cauldrons were often equipped with subtriangular section legs (e.g., Ward-Perkins, 1967, Plates LI, LII and LVI). They range in date from the twelfth to the fifteenth century, the Arran Quay example is likely to be later fourteenth- or fifteenth-century in date.

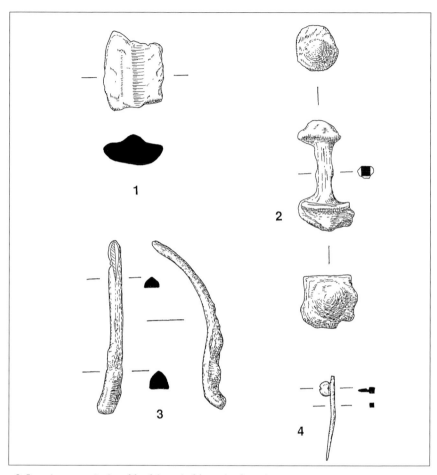

18 Iron (nos. 1, 2 & 4) and lead (no. 3) objects (scale 1:1)

Stone

Roofslates (fig. 19.1 and 19.2) Large numbers of fragments of red and grey slates were encountered on the excavation. Only ten of these retained a suspension hole. The red slates derive from eastern Leinster (Walsh 1997). Only one example (226:1) would appear to be complete and is of small size and triangular shape. One slate (106:24) appears to have been used as a base on which other objects were held while holes were drilled in them.

Nook shaft (fig. 19.4) 110:6. Incomplete carboniferous limestone colonette. Slightly oval in section, one side partly flat, possibly to aid setting against wall. Both ends broken. Length: 170mm Width: 73mm Thick: 65mm Thirteenth century.

Dundry-stone window or door jamb (fig. 19.5) 13:1. Fragment of Dundry-stone window/doorjamb. Axe dressed on three faces, rebate 23mm by 25mm on one arris. Length: 75mm Width: 75mm Thick: 51mm Thirteenth century.

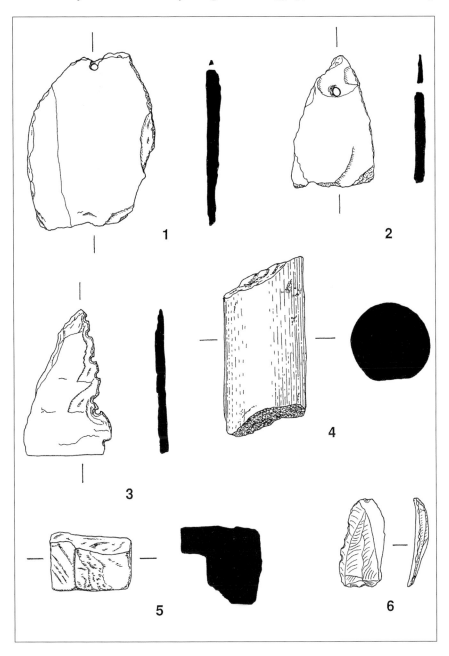

19 Stone objects (scale 1:1)

Flint blade (fig. 19.6) 114:74. Convex in profile, secondary retouch on long edges, point broken. Length: 52mm Width: 27mm Thick: 9mm

Bone, Antler and Ivory

Knife handle (fig. 20.1) 301:109. Antler. Flattened semicircular section, decorated on curved side with three longitudinal bands of incised lozenges separated by incised grooves. Three perforations down centre of curved face. Two perforations in lower end. Upper end has convex hollow on rear face to accept quillion of blade. Length: 86mm Width: 20mm Thick: 7mm Late medieval scale tang knife handle plate, from disturbed layers. One of two decorative plates that would have been attached to flat tang on end of blade. Examples of similar shape, but with different decoration are known from fourteenth- and fifteenth-century levels in London (MacGregor 1989, 116) and elsewhere in England from the twelfth to the sixteenth centuries (MacGregor 1985, 170).

Parchment prickers (fig. 20.2 and 3). 106:122. (fig. 35.2).Incomplete lathe turned polished circular section ivory stylus. Oval head, 6mm dia., 7mm long. Collar composed of single 1.5mm wide raised rib at top of shank. Lower portion of shank missing, but socket for metal point present. Length: 64mm Max. shank Dia: 4.5mm 114:1. (fig. 35.3).Head (shape and size as above) but collar composed of two 0.5mm wide raised ribs. Incomplete, lower portion of shank missing. Length: 36mm Max. shank dia.: 4mm A relatively common find on medieval excavations. This type of object is little changed from the Roman times to the late medieval period (MacGregor 1985, 124). They are characteristically lathe turned, have a rounded or ovoid head and raised ribs at the top of the shank and an iron or copper alloy point inserted in the lower end (ibid., 124). MacGregor believed these objects to be 'Punctoria' (parchment prickers) used to lay out lines in manuscripts. More recently Ramsey has argued that they may be styli due to their common occurrence on medieval sites, the presence of holes made by a blade as laying out lines in manuscripts, and the finding of a similarly shaped object with a set of wax tablets from Namur (Alexander and Binski 1987, 382–3). Biddle (1990) appears finally to have put the argument to rest in his description of these objects as prickers. They are recorded from many English sites, excavations at Battle abbey in particular producing a large number of these objects associated with wooden frames that would have held wax tablets (Hare 1985, 149–51). A number of examples are also known from Irish medieval sites, e.g., Waterford (Hurley et al. 1997) and from Patrick Street, Dublin (Hayden 1997).

Peg (fig. 20.4). 112:41. Small bone peg of circular section. Shank tapers to blunt point, head spheroid 6mm dia. Length: 44.5mm Max. shank Dia.: 4.5mm.

Bead (fig. 20.5) 301:283. Circular polished bone bead of biconical shape. Vertical sided central perforation 5.5mm dia. Dia.: 11.2mm Thick: 3.5mm.

Amber

Bead (fig. 20.6) 249:1. Cylindrical amber bead with central parallel sided 2mm dia. perforation. Length: 6mm Diameter: 8mm.

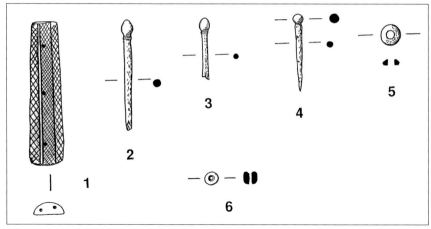

20 Bone, antler, ivory and amber objects (scale 1:1)

Moss Rope

225:1. Length of two-strand rope composed of stems of Polytrichum commune var.[1] Ropes composed of this moss, whose stems can measure in excess of 200mm in length have also been uncovered at Patrick Street and Winetavern Street, Dublin, (Hayden 1997) at Dublin Castle (B. Collins, pers. comm) and in Perth (Robinson 1987, 208).

Wood[2]

Pins (fig. 21.1–3) 245:203 A–C. A (fig. 21.1) is a sub-rectangular section tapering to sharp point; broader end cut square; slightly curved in profile. Length: 135mm Width: 5mm Thick: 4mm (Taxus–yew). B (not ill.) is a sub-rectangular section tapering to sharp point; broader end broken; slightly curved in profile. Length: 72mm Width: 7mm Thick: 5mm (Taxus–yew). C (fig. 21.2) is a sub-rectangular section tapering to sharp point; broader end cut square; double curved in profile. Length: 103m. Width: 6mm Thick: 6mm (Taxus–yew). 213:32 (fig. 21.3) has circular section tapering to sharp point; broader end cut square; slightly curved in profile. Length: 92mm Width: 6mm Thick 6mm (Taxus–yew). Similar objects were found in late fifteenth-century levels at Narrow Quay, Bristol (Good 1987, 198), in seventeenth-century contexts at Charlotte's Quay, Limerick (Lynch 1984, 317–8) and large numbers were recovered from waterfront excavations in Tønsberg, Norway (Lindh 1991, 74–5). In the latter case very few have been found away from the waterfront area of the town. The objects were apparently used to hold open gutted fish and to pin the tails of fish together, when they were being hung for drying. The pins are typically of flat or oval section and pointed at one or both ends (ibid.). A rule in the 'Chain Book of Dublin' states that 'Fish are not to be eviscerated in the fish markets, but on the bank at the water-side' (Gilbert 1889–1944, i, 219). The presence of these pins in riverside deposits at Arran Quay shows that fish processing did take place where the fish were landed in

---

1 Identified by Brenda Collins.   2 Species identification by Aoife Daly.

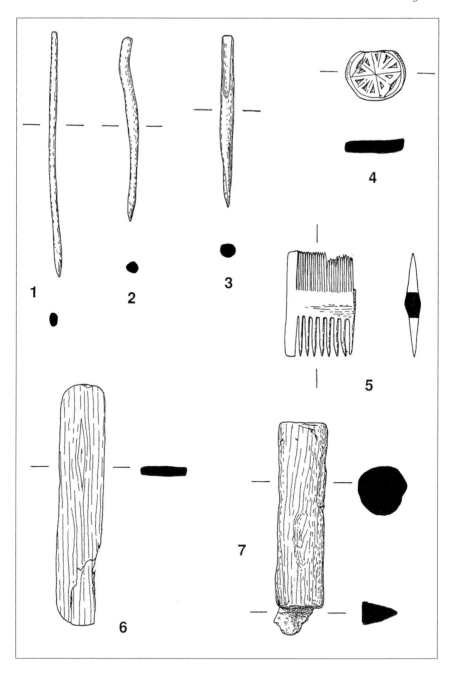

21 Wooden objects (scale 1:1)

medieval times, as quantities of cod and ling bones were also uncovered at Arran Quay, indicating the production of 'Stock Fish' on the site.

Gaming piece (fig. 21.4) 51:65. Oval gaming piece decorated on one face with incised circle divided by diagonal lines into four quarters. Two opposing quarters are divided into three triangular areas with recessed centres, the other two into two triangular areas again with sunken centres. Diameter: 27–32mm Thick: 5mm (Betula–birch). A not dissimilar example with six radially arranged triangles was recovered from a late fourteenth-/early fifteenth-century context at Threave Castle, Galloway (Good and Tabraham 1981, 119).

Comb (fig. 21.5) 210:25. Incomplete double sided single piece wooden comb, Class J (Dunleavy, 1988). The teeth on the opposing sides are different sizes. One side has 22mm long teeth with 7.5 teeth percm, while the other has 24mm long teeth with 2.5 teeth percm Flattened lentoid section. Bevelled end plate. Length: 39mm Width: 56mm Thick.: 7mm (Alnus–alder). Class J combs were made in a range of materials – bone, ivory, horn and wood. They are known from numerous English sites dating from the medieval period to the seventeenth century (MacGregor 1985, 77–81). From Ireland they are also mainly known from illustrations and examples in materials other than wood. Irish examples in wood were recovered from a seventeenth-century context at Emlagh, County Kerry (Dunleavy 1988, 372), and from medieval levels at Grand Parade, Cork (Hurley 1989), and Waterford (Hurley et al. 1997). The Irish examples of class J combs do not usually possess teeth of different size (Dunleavy 1988, 350) although both the examples from Cork and Arran Quay did. Another closely comparable wooden example was recovered from a later fifteenth-century context at Narrow Quay, Bristol (Good 1987,108). The example from Arran Quay dates to the later fourteenth to early fifteenth century.

Box lid? (fig. 21.6) 224:3. Rectangular in shape with rounded corners. Flat rectangular section. Length: 132mm Width: 26mm Thick: 5mm (Taxus–yew). This is possibly the sliding lid of a small box of a type known from earlier contexts from Wood Quay, Dublin (Lang 1988, 6).

Knife handle and blade (fig. 21.7) 51:67A and B. A is an undecorated wooden knife handle of circular section. Length: 102mm Max. Dia.: 28mm (Pinus–pine). B is a whittle tang and base of iron blade survives in handle. Tang of square section, 15mm long. Blade of triangular section. Length: 13mm Width: 20mm Thick: 11mm

LEATHER
by Dáire O'Rourke

There are 129 leather finds from the Arran Quay excavation. These were found in a wide number of contexts throughout the site, with no context that could be described as a leather-working layer or else as a dump from a leather worker in the vicinity. The leather finds would seem to represent normal loss or dumping of objects that were no longer required by the owner.

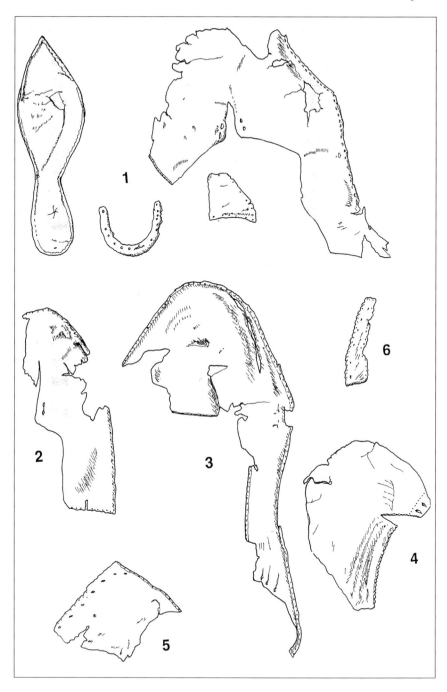

22 Leather shoes (scale 1:2)

Footwear-uppers There are twenty-six upper fragments. Of these three are in too bad a condition to be diagnostic. Of the extant classifiable upper pieces, a number of different styles are represented.

Class 1. There are two uppers, one almost complete, which form part of this class. 117:220 (fig.22.1) is from a later fourteenth-/early fifteenth-century deposit and is made of calf skin. The sole is also extant. The upper is of the wrap-around variety, though the toe has been partly torn away. The shoe is for the right foot. At the instep, the leather is slit, with two thong holes at either side of the instep. Here a leather thong or possibly a piece of ribbon would have been threaded through the thong holes for fastening. The heel is cut higher than the quarters and at the heel there is evidence for quite a high heel stiffener. The top edge of the quarters and heel is stitched with a shipped seam, either to facilitate a top band (an extra piece of leather stitched along the top edge to raise the height of the quarters, thereby converting the shoe into an ankle boot), or else to prevent the leather from splitting. Occasionally if the leather was insufficiently fanned or, in particular, if sheepskin was used in footwear manu-facture, after a while the leather would split into its grain and flesh layers. Thus a very common device used on medieval footwear to prevent this was to stitch the top edge of the leather. From a similar period, but a different context, is 223:214 (fig. 22.2); although in a very fragmentary state, it is of a similar style to that above.

Class 2. This class is also of the wrap-around type but differs from Class 1, in that the footwear is seamed at the side, by a number of thong hooks. The most complete upper of this class is 50:27 (fig. 22.3). It is from a mid fourteenth-century layer and is made from sheep or goatskin. It is of the wrap-around variety, the left-hand wing ending in a butt seam. The right hand wing extends to the quarter where the leather has been cut. There is evidence here for two thong holes for fastening. A small fragment of heel stiffener is also *in situ*. A quarter fragment similar to above is 119:51 from a mid fourteenth-century layer. It is made from goatskin. Although in a very fragmentary condition, two thong holes are clearly discernible. Similar to above, though with obvious differences, is 118:94 (fig. 22.4) from a mid- to late fourteenth-century layer. It is made from deerskin. Its similarity to the above lies in the fact that there are two thong holes at the right hand wing. The upper is not of the wrap-around variety as the left hand quarter ends in a butted seam, as does the right hand wing, where the two thong holes are situated. There is evidence that a lining would have been *in situ* at the thong fastenings and also at the instep, is seen by the presence of stitchmarks, visible only on the flesh side of the leather. A whipped seam runs along the top edge of the leather, for the reasons already cited above. Belonging to the same class, though with some slight differences, are three quarter fragments. 248:53 (fig. 22.5), from a mid-fourteenth-century level is a quarter fragment, made from sheep-skin. It is a boot quarter fragment, with six slits for fastening along one side. The lining, 248:54 (fig. 22.6), is still extant and is made from sheep or goat skin. This lining would have been stitched to the slit/thong holes at the edge of the quarter, to reinforce the leather and prevent it from tearing when fastened. A similar quarter fragment to the above is 245:216 from a mid-fourteen layer. There is a slight variation as the bottom edge is cut, possibly to facilitate an insert. This quarter fragment is made from goatskin.

Class 3. This class is different to the above, in that the vamp is completely detached from the rest of the upper. Two vamps are similar in style, though they come from chronologically different contexts. 12:113 (fig. 23.1) comes from a late thirteenth-century/early fourteenth-century level and is made from calf skin. It is a child's vamp, with the left-hand side quite badly torn. The right-hand side wing ends in a butted seam. The instep is rounded, with two thong holes for fastening, with a piece of thong *in situ*. Of a similar style to this vamp is 211:24, from a fifteenth-century layer. This vamp is also of calfskin, and though in a very fragile condition, two tie holes at the instep are clearly discernible. There are five vamp fragments that cannot be fitted into any class, as they are too fragmentary and the method of fastening is not in evidence. However, of those five, two are very similar in style of instep and both are from the same mid fourteenth-century context. 245:210 consists of a vamp of calfskin, which is very badly torn, though the instep clearly extends to a point. The same style of instep is seen on 245:209. Most of the vamp is torn away, with just the instep extant. In this instance, a vamp stripe runs along the centre of the instep. This is also of interest as it is the only upper fragment with any decoration on it from Arran Quay. Three other vamps are extant. 112:116 from late thirteenth-/early fourteenth-century context is made from goat skin. 119:50 from the mid fifteenth-century level is made of sheep or goat skin and 117:222 (fig. 23.2) from a late fourteenth-/early fifteenth-century level is made of calf skin. The sole, accompanying this upper is very pointed.

Inserts Associated with these upper pieces are two triangular shaped inserts, both from the same late thirteenth-/early fourteenth-century layer. 51:79 and 51:84 are both made from cattle. The former is butt seamed on one side, while a whipped seam runs along the other, while the latter is butt seamed on two sides being torn on the third side. Inserts are very common among medieval turn-shoe footwear. Odd pieces of leather were kept for re-use in general to finish the wrap-around pattern of most medieval shoes. It was a 'biologically friendly' method of shoe manufacture, where nothing was allowed to go to waste and the pattern of the shoe was completed by using up odds and ends of leather.

Stiffners Also incorporated into medieval uppers was the stiffner. Already mentioned above where they have been found in situ in an upper, these are primarily triangular or semi-circular in shape. Three stiffners were found detached from their uppers–two came from a late thirteenth-/early fourteenth-century layer. Both are triangular in shape, 51:78 being of calf skin and 51:83 being of goat skin. 12:118, from a similarly dated level, is also triangular in shape and made from calf skin.

Thongs Thongs are the final item to be associated with uppers. Two detached thongs, both from the same late fourteenth-/early fifteenth-century deposits, were uncovered. 110:238 is made from calf skin and consists of two pieces of thong knotted together. 110:240 (fig. 23.3) is made from cattle. It is in the form of a strip of leather, the ends taper into two long slits. The thong is stitched at the wider end.

Soles 27 of the soles uncovered are in too fragmentary a state to be diagnostic. Of the classifiable soles, six have a round toe. 234:4 (fig. 23.4) comes from the mid fourteenth-century dump fill. It is complete, with a very broad tread and measures 255mm in length. 51:73 (fig. 23.5) comes from a late thirteenth-/early fourteenth-century con-

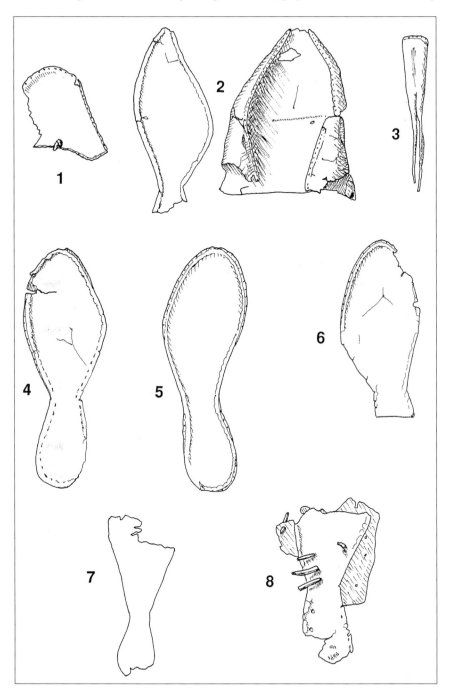

23 Leather shoes (scale 1:2)

text. It is a complete, measuring 260mm in length. It is unusual as the tread is quite extended. Seven of the soles have quite a pointed toe. Five soles are of the composite variety. Here a number of different pieces were used to make up the one sole. This is another example of the re-use of leather or of the using-up of scraps. 245:208 (fig. 23.6) from a mid fourteenth-century dump, consists of a sole, cut away just above the waist, with a line of stitch holes running along here. 231:34, also from a mid fourteenth-century context, is a half sole consisting of tread and waist, though the left hand side of the tread is partly torn away.

Cobbling and re-use of leather As has been noted above, the use and re-use of leather was not uncommon in the medieval contexts of Arran Quay. This is seen in the composite soles and the variety of composite uppers, incorporating inserts. It is a viable and cost-effective approach to leather-working and usage. There is evidence from the leather finds that such re-working and re-usage of leather was going on around the site. There are five soles, which have evidence of being cut up after use. These include 12:109 (fig. 23.7) from a late thirteenth-/early fourteenth-century layer; the lasting seam has been crudely cut away, and 120:3 from a mid fourteenth-century layer; the sole here has been cut away for re-use, with slashes cut along the length. The lasting seam of one upper (118:94, mentioned above) (fig. 22.4) has been cut away from the edge. Perhaps the upper was to be used for a smaller foot as the lasting seam and sole were too worn for the upper. Such leather being cut appears among eight other fragments of leather, all of which are undiagnostic and come from five different contexts. That repairs were made on footwear without going to the extravagant trouble of removing lasting seams, or stitching composite soles, is evident in the material remains of one crude patch detached from its object and of one patch still *in situ*. The latter 12:110 (fig. 23.8), from a late thirteenth-/early fourteenth-century level, is a sole in a very fragmentary condition, with a very large patch attached in a rather crude fashion. The patch is considerably larger than the sole. This crudity of repairs points to it being the work of an individual owner as opposed to a professional cobbler.

Post-medieval footwear The post medieval footwear was the easiest to identify. The method of footwear manufacture changed from the turn-shoe technique to a welted construction, *c.*1500 AD. The welted shoe allowed for a heavier type of shoe to be made which was more in keeping with the travel and warfare of the post-medieval period. The welt is a strip of leather stitched between the upper and the sole. The welt is broad, allowing for the upper to be stitched to the welt and an insole. The welt is left to protrude around the edges and then a heavier sole is stitched here. This new method of construction meant that the principal seam was at the back as opposed to the turn-shoe technique when it was at the side. There are four sole fragments and five insole fragments of post-medieval footwear from six different contexts. Two other post-medieval soles from F301 are square toed and appear to be eighteenth-century in date. One, 301:321 (fig. 24.1), is almost complete, measuring 259mm in length and has the remains of a stacked heel *in situ*, the jumps of which are held together by nails. There is one early post-medieval upper, 110:236. It consists of the heel and quarters in one piece and a long triangular insert. The right hand side extends upwards and ends in a point. The lasting seam is torn and tattered and the left-hand side ends in a closed seam.

Other worked leather While footwear invariable forms the largest amount of leather finds, other worked leather objects are also in evidence. **Harness** Six possible harness pieces came to light from five different contexts, all giving a mid- to late fourteenth-/early fifteenth-century date. All are made from cow hide. A typical example of the horse harness is 236:277 (fig. 24.2) from a mid- to late fourteenth-century context. It is 273mm long, 22mm wide and 5mm thick. It is cut at one end and has holes for mounting it into a buckle plate and is torn at the other end. Horse harness had been found on most medieval urban sites in the country. Belts or Straps Four straps or belt fragments were found. One belt, 225:7, consists of six different pieces. The overall length of this strap is 744mm and is made from calf skin. Two others, 210:26 and 224:213, are made from cattle. 223:212 (fig. 24.3) is so worn that the grain pattern is too hard to discern. There are 21 metal studs along the length, with evidence that these studs would have continued right along the length of 200m. The function of such a strap is hard to define and it may have been more decorative in nature. **Binding Strips** There are three binding strips, two from the initial clearance layer (F301) and the other from F110. 301:328 (fig. 24.4) is made from sheep skin. It is a rectangular piece of leather, with crude stitch holes along either side. It is cut at both ends. It is probable that all three binding strips are from clothing as opposed to footwear. **Sling** 110:235 (fig. 24.5) is an unusual piece of leather, from a layer dated to the later fourteenth early fifteenth century, made of cattle hide and is 174mm in length and at its mid point its widest is 77mm, then tapers to either end. There are four long slits along the length with one perforation at either end. Somewhat similar items were found during the Wood Quay excavations and have been thought to be either a shoe fastening or a hair tie. However, the length of this leather piece prohibits either of these two theories and so it is tentatively identified as a sling for either warfare or hunting. While none, to the author's knowledge, have been unearthed, among the contemporary histories the use of slings is considered mandatory for the fighting or hunting man. **Bag** 118:93 (fig. 24.6) comes from a mid- to late fourteenth-century layer. It consists of a piece of leather folded in two and stitched along three sides with a whipped seam. Along the fourth edge, the leather is folded at both ends, but in the centre, the leather is cut in a curve, where it is stitched with a whipped seam. To one side there are two slits which penetrate the leather. The bag measures 186mm by 179mm It is 2mm thick, though the grain has been so smoothed making identification of the leather impossible. How the bag would have been carried or attached is not evident, though this may belie its own particular function.

TEXTILES

by Elizabeth Wincott-Heckett

Three pieces of fabric were uncovered from the excavation. 28:6. Yarn, 80 by 5mm, animal hair (?goat). Single thread loose S-spun, then medium twisted Z-twisted into 2-ply. Individual thread diameter 1.37mm, plied yarn 2.77mm Colour: 10YR 2/2 very dark brown. Type of yarn used to weave coarse tabby cloth. Early fourteenth century. A short piece of yarn, perhaps goat hair. It is 2-ply yarn, with the single thread being loose S-spun, and then Z-twisted into a two-ply strand. This type of yarn and the

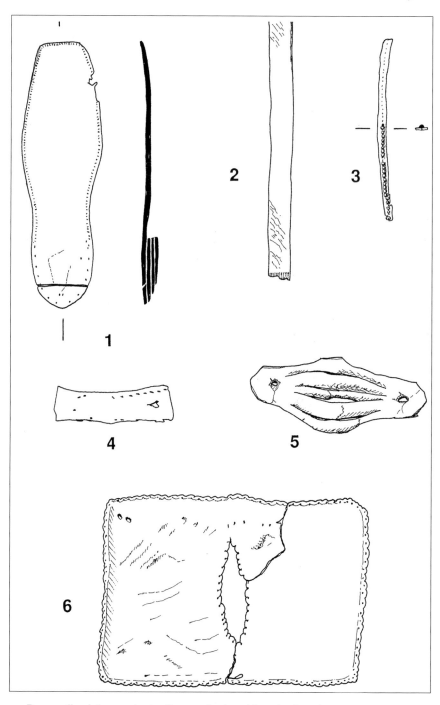

24 Post-medieval shoes and miscellaneous leather objects (scale 1:2)

cloth made from it is commonly found on medieval sites at least from the tenth century onwards. The cloth usually made from this type of yarn is a tabby (plain) weave of coarse quality with perhaps 3–4 threads to thecm in both warp and weft systems. It seems likely that the cloth was used for several purposes: cloaks, blankets and shrouds and as a backing material in an age which could not use paper or cardboard (Crowfoot 1990, 485; Walton 1988, 82; Wincott-Heckett 1990, 81–6 and forthcoming).

211:1. A piece of 2/2 twill wool cloth. a) 150 by 87mm (three layers). b) 50 by 30mm with remains of metal attachments. Wool fibres fragile, warp system medium S-Spun, 0.73mm diameter, 8–9 threads percm, weft system medium S-spun, 0.89–0.90mm diameter, 9 threads to thecm Cloth thickness, 1.35mm, combed yarn, regular close weave. Colour 10YR very dark brown. Wool woven in a 2/2 twill and has been stitched and shaped. There was a copper alloy ring, 7mm in diameter, consisting of a number of strands of wire twisted together adhering to the textile and is likely was originally attached to it. Several other small iron rivets and mounts were also pushed through the fabric. A further accretion has a small piece of copper alloy protruding from it. In the fourteenth/fifteenth centuries various dress accessories were worn. Belts and straps were often decorated with small metal shapes, some of which had small rings for suspending further decorative pieces. Recent analysis of a large number of dress accessories from London illustrates their wide range of forms and showed that 'Mounts usually have rivets for attachment to leather or textile. Although many mounts were used on leather some were used on cloth' (Egan and Pritchard 1991, 162). Also referred to is a Spanish tomb effigy of the thirteenth century, 'With a proliferation of mounts all over a surcoat worn with armour' (ibid.). Both in France and England and indeed in Europe generally there are accounts of metal ornaments for clothes. From Czechoslovakia there are examples in medieval paintings of plastically superimposed decorative motifs on textile which seem to represent cloth adorned with metallic decorations. One representation of an angel by the Master of Vyssi Brod (*c.*1350) shows studs down the trimming of a cloak (Sronkova 1954, 51). In France and England such ornaments were of precious metals (Newton 1980, 36–7 and 57). There were the customary inefficient interdictions throughout Europe generally against the lower orders attempting to dress themselves in similar extravagant styles (ibid. 131–2). It is not possible to discern exactly what the Arran Quay textile represents but it is likely to have been some form of garment.

211:2. *c.*80 by 65mm carbonised vegetable stems/fibres. Colour 10YR 2/1 Black

CLAY PIPES
by Joe Norton

Eight clay pipe bowls and three stems were recovered from modern disturbed deposits removed during mechanical clearance of the site.

Seventeenth-century pipes (fig. 25) Five of the bowls date from the middle of the seventeenth century to the beginning of the eighteenth century (fig. 25.1–5). None of these early bowls have any decorative features or makers' marks. The three earliest (50:25, 301:1 and 301:195) (fig. 40.1–3) have milling at the rim, a common feature of

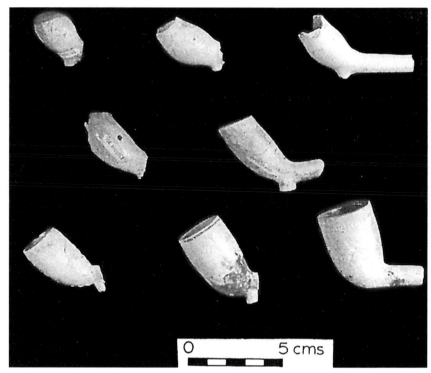

25 Clay pipes

this period. They range in date from 1620–1710. Pipe bowl 050:25 (fig. 25.1) between Oswald's types 4 and 5 (Oswald 1975, fig.3,G) Date:1620–1650. Pipe bowl 301:1 (fig. 25.2) Type 17 (ibid.,fig. 4,G). Date: 1640–1670. Pipe bowl 301:195 (fig.25.3) Type 18 (ibid., fig.4,G). Date: 1660–1680. Pipe bowl 301:194 (fig. 25.4) Incomplete spurred bowl. Date: 1690–1700. Pipe bowl 301:190 (fig. 25.5) Type 8 (ibid., fig.3,G). Date 1680–1710.

Nineteenth-century pipes The remaining three bowls date from the second half of the nineteenth century. Pipe bowl 301:117 (fig. 25.6). Oak leaves on the mould lines. Dates 1840–1880. Pipe bowl 301:2 (fig.25.7). On the back, in a circular frame, a cockerel with the legend 'While I live I'll crow', a similar pipe was found in Limerick (Lynch 1984, 313–4). Date: 1850–1880. Pipe bowl 301:3 (fig. 25.8). On the back, in an oval frame, the legend 'United Trade Association Dublin' with in centre a pair of clasped hands over 'Trade Mark'. This association was formed in Dublin in 1864 to encourage the use of Irish made goods. Date: 1860–1890.

DENDROCHRONOLOGICAL REPORT

by David Brown

The Paleoecology Centre, Queen's University Belfast, received three samples from Arran Quay, Dublin on 9 August 1990. The samples were labelled Q8183 to Q8185 for reference. Two samples, Q8183 and Q8184, were noted as coming from the same timber.

Q8183. Sample Number 1 (F53). Base plate of timber Revetment 1. This sample yielded 108 annual growth rings, including 27 sapwood rings when measured. The sapwood is not complete but from examination of the sample only a few rings appear to be missing. The centre of the tree is not present. The ring pattern obtained was compared against the standard Irish master. A significant correlation was found with an end date of AD 1301. The best estimated felling date for this tree would be AD 1305 or slightly later.

Q8185. Sample number 2 (F53). Base plate from timber Revetment 1. This sample yielded 153 annual growth rings, including 10 sapwood rings when measured. The sapwood is not complete. The centre of the tree is not present. The ring pattern obtained was compared against the standard Irish masters. Consistent correlation values were found, giving an end date of AD 1282. The best estimated felling date for this tree will be AD 1304 +/− 9. This is calculated by adding the Belfast sapwood estimate of 32 +/− 9 years to the date of the last heartwood ring of the sample.

Q8184. Sample number 3 (F54). Base plate from timber Revetment 2. This sample yielded 102 annual growth rings, including 7 sapwood rings when measured. The sapwood is not complete. The centre of the tree is not present. The ring pattern obtained was compared against the standard Irish masters. Consistent correlation values were found, giving an end date of AD 1279. The best estimated felling for this tree will be AD 1304 +/−9. This is calculated by adding the Belfast sapwood estimate of 32 +/− 9 years to the date for the last heartwood ring of the sample.

Conclusions As noted, samples Q8183 and Q8184 are from the same timber. Sample Q8185 matches well with these samples. The best estimate felling date for the two trees from this structure will be AD 1305. It is likely that the structure from Arran Quay was built from trees felled in the first decade of the fourteenth century.

THE MAMMAL BONE
by Finbar McCormick

Introduction The excavation at Arran Quay produced two distinct bone samples. The earlier, was dated from the early to late fourteenth century, and the later from the later fourteenth/early fifteenth to early seventeenth century. The earlier bones for the most part were from material dumped behind the wooden revetments. The material was probably derived from several different sources, not unlike the thirteenth-century material from the quayside at Shop Street, Drogheda (McCormick 1984, 209). The later phase material from Arran Quay consists of deposits dumped on the riverside of the quay walls. It is almost exclusively from the early fifteenth to the late sixteenth century, with a small sample of seventeenth-century material being present. The bones survived in very good condition and there was little evidence of water abrasion. A small proportion of the bone displayed gnawing marks implying that least some of the assemblage had been lying on the surface for a while before deposition and had not come directly from the kitchen table.

Methodology The minimum numbers of individuals (MNI) were calculated on the basis of the most frequent skeletal element present taking left and right side into consideration. No attempt, however, was made to increase MNI on the basis of bone size or state of epiphyseal fusion and tooth eruption, as this method is only valid for very small samples. The ageing data for tooth eruption is based on Higham (1967). The abbreviations used for bone measurements are those of von den Driesch (1976). A list of the bones and minimum numbers of individuals (MNI) is given in Tables 7 and 8 while the details of the metrical and ageing data are given at the end of the report.

Discussion Cattle, pig and sheep/goat comprised the great majority of the bones present with the other species being represented in only small numbers. The other domesticated species present were horse, dog and cat, while wild species were repre-sented by rabbit, hare, red and fallow deer. One piece of cetacean bone, a small whale or porpoise was present in the later phase. For the reasons outlined below it is assumed that the great majority of the caprovine bones are of sheep. Table 1 compares the High Street data with other animal bone assemblages from Dublin and two medieval samples from Drogheda and Waterford. Although there is considerable variation in the distribution of the main species present, a general trend can be identified. In the Scandinavian period in Dublin, as demonstrated by tenth- and early eleventh-century settlement in Fishamble Street, pig were the dominant animal present in terms of minimum numbers of individuals. Sheep played a very minor role, never accounting for more than 14% of the MNI total. After the Anglo-Norman settlement, however, there is an increase in the importance of sheep at the expense of pig. At Arran Quay sheep have risen to a level equal to cattle during the thirteenth- to fourteenth-century deposit, and they outnumber cattle in the fourteenth- to fifteenth-century levels. The increase in the incidence of sheep is not, however, as pronounced as noted in Patrick Street (A) Dublin, or in samples from Drogheda and Waterford, but the reason for this is unclear. The reasons for this increase in the keeping of sheep in urban sites in the east and south-east of Ireland must be considered in the context of changing agricultural practices after the Anglo-Norman settlement.

It must be recognized that sheep, unlike pig, could not be reared within the town but were instead supplied by outside producers. The Anglo-Normans established a manorial farming system, which differed greatly from the preceding native system. The new system generated a cash economy as rents were generally paid in money rather than by labour and tribute (Down 1987, 463). The generation of money, by the selling of agricultural surplus, became the motivating force in agricultural production. In this context sheep had a distinct advantage over cattle or pig. Firstly, the rural cash economy generated a great expansion in the production and export of grain (ibid., 460–61; O'Neill 1987, 20–29). The maintenance of productivity in arable farming necessitates continual manuring of the soil. Sheep dung is of higher quality than the dung of other domesticates being, for instance, richer in nitrogen, potassium and phosphorus than cattle dung (White 1970, 127–8). Thus, whenever there is an expansion in arable farming, there is often a corresponding increase in sheep rearing, as, for instance, in Iron Age England (Cunliffe 1974, 184). The Anglo-Normans in Ireland were aware of the qualities of sheep dung and the documentary sources provide evidence for the high regard in which it was held. In the earl of Norfolk's Irish estates in the late thirteenth century the tenants were obliged to fold their sheep on the lord's land rather than their own, thus depriving their land of enrichment (Down 1987, 473). Secondly, sheep were also of great 'cash crop' importance because of the value of wool, which, unlike other hides or furs and, of course, meat, could be repeatedly produced by the animal. Wool was one of the most important exports from medieval Ireland. Large herds were kept by the Cistercians, who became established in Ireland prior to the Anglo-Norman arrival. The extent and mechanics of the trade are discussed by O'Neill (1987, 58–64) who notes that the production of wool also provided opportunities for the generation of money on a very small scale. He states (ibid., 61) that 'by no means did all the wool exported come from the estates of the monasteries or the lands of wealthy lords … a great amount must have come from the smaller flocks of lesser farmers and peasants, who would have sold it to the nearest town'.

Table 1. Relative percentages of the MNIs of the three main domesticates from Arran Quay and a series of other urban sites (after Butler 1984, McCormick 1984, 1987; forthcoming). Abbreviations: C = Century: E = Early: M = Middle: L = Late.

Site	Date	Cattle	Sheep/Goat	Pig	N
DUBLIN					
Fishamble St (Plots 2 and 3)	10–E11 C	34.4	10.4	55.3	1062
Fishamble St (Bank to wall)	11–12 C	58.8	11.3	30.0	97
Ship Street	E12 C	47.8	13.0	39.1	23
High Street	12–E13 C	43.2	13.6	43.2	44
Wood Quay	13 C	40.0	36.0	24.0	917
Patrick St A	L13–L14 C	33.3	52.8	13.9	36
Patrick St B	L13–L14 C	33.3	23.5	43.1	51
Arran Quay Earlier	14 C	35.5	35.5	29.0	31
Arran Quay Later	15–16 C	34.0	42.4	23.0	144
DROGHEDA					
Shop Street	M–L13 C	27.8	55.6	16.7	36
WATERFORD					
High Street	L13–E14	14.7	47.4	37.9	95

Cattle

Introduction Cattle were by far the most important providers of meat at Arran Quay during both phases. Medieval domesticated animals were consistently smaller than their modern counterparts. By assuming a live animal weight of 450 kg for cattle, 23 kg for sheep and 80 kg for pig with a dressing-out weight of 50% for cattle and sheep and 80% for pig, the relative proportion of meat provided by the three main species at Arran Quay and other Dublin sites can be estimated (Table 2). Even during periods where they were greatly outnumbered by pigs or sheep, cattle were always, by far, the most important providers of meat. This is clearly demonstrated in Table 2 and fig. 1 which shows the relative proportions of meat supplied by the three main domesticates at Arran Quay and at Scandinavian-period Fishamble Street, where pig was the dominant species present and with Patrick Street (Site A) where sheep dominated (Table 1).

Table 2. Relative percentage of meat in terms of weight provided by the main domesticates.

		Cattle	*Sheep*	*Pig*
Arran Quay Early	MNI %	35.5	35.5	29.0
	Meat Wt %	77.9	4.1	18.1
Arran Quay Late	MNI %	34.0	42.4	23.0
	Meat Wt %	79.3	5.0	15.7
Fishamble St Plots	MNI %	34.4	10.4	55.3
	Meat Wt %	67.9	1.0	31.1
Patrick St, Site A.	MNI %	33.3	52.8	13.9
	Meat Wt %	82.9	7.3	9.8

Cattle: age/slaughter distribution The early phase contained only two cattle mandibulae, so the analysis of the age/slaughter pattern is confined to the later phase. The primary eruption data is shown in Table 9 and compared with other sites in Table 3. The cattle age distribution at Arran Quay is as expected in an Irish urban context during this period, with the peak in slaughter being for mature and old individuals. Table 3 shows that the slaughter pattern at Arran Quay was essentially similar to that on other Dublin sites, including the Scandinavian levels at Fishamble Street. This contrasted greatly, however, with the slaughter pattern noted at a rural Early Christian period site at Moynagh crannog, Co. Meath. It is clear that, in the case of the urban meat market, it was much more profitable for the producer to supply fully grown cattle than immature individuals. A similar age/slaughter pattern to Arran Quay has also been noted on other medieval urban sites in Ireland.

Table 3. Cattle age distribution from the late phase at Arran Quay and other sites (after Butler 1984: McCormick 1987; forthcoming). The ageing data is after Higham (1967).

Approx Age (in months)	*Moynagh*	*Fishamble St Plots 2–3*	*Patrick St Site B*	*Wood Quay*	*Arran Quay*
	N=1	N=262	N=17	N=216	N=23
0–7	4.1	6.1	11.8	0.92	8.7
7–13	11.2	8.8	–	4.16	4.3
13–24	41.0	12.2	17.7	10.17	8.7
24–36	18.6	19.5	17.7	15.74	13.0
36+	25.1	53.4	52.9	68.96	65.2

Sex/ratio The sex of cattle can be confidently identified on the basis of the meta-carpal, but only after the distal end has fused, i.e. in those animals older than 24–30 months of age. Multivariate analysis on large samples of metacarpals from Lagore and Fishamble Street suggests that those with distal widths (Bd) of greater than 57.5mm were male while those of less than 55.5mm were female. The early phase contained a very small sample of six distal metacarpals, five of which were female. In the later group, however, 91.1% of a sample of sixty-five were female. This is a much higher proportion than noted on other sites in Dublin. In the Scandinavian levels at Fishamble Street (N = 162) 76.5% were female while in the thirteenth-century Wood Quay 68% (N = 120) were female (Butler 1984). After this, however, there seems to be an increase in the proportion of females present with 80% in a small sample (N = 10) from late13th–14th century from Patrick Street and the present 91% noted at Arran Quay, which is mostly of a 15th-century date. As cattle of both sexes are born in roughly equal proportions this implies that the great majority of male cattle are killed off at an early age. This slaughter was undertaken by the rural beef producers as there is no evidence that young male cattle were brought to the urban meat market in significant quantities. It is clear that it was more economical for the beef producer to rear cows rather than males to maturity when limitations on the amount of grazing available prohibited the rearing of all calves to full size. After reaching the age of three years the cow could annually provide a calf and a season of milk while a fattening male produced no useful side products. Indeed, it also seems that early cows fattened at a faster rate than males. Lisle (1757, 7) stated that 'a cow-calf would make a very pretty beef at three years old ... [but] steers will not be beef till four or five years old, because they are so long growing; therefore it is only profitable in those countries to fat steers that plough them'. Clearly, therefore, the motivation for the rearing of males, with the exception of the small numbers needed for breeding, was very limited, especially as horse began to replace the ox for ploughing. The increase in cows in the cattle brought to the Dublin meat market as the medieval period progressed probably reflects the decline in the use of the ox for ploughing within the hinterland of Dublin. A decline in the use of ox for ploughing is also implied in the rather scanty historical evidence for the later middle ages in Ireland. During the thirteenth-century oxen generally far outnumbered horses as working animals within the area of Anglo-Norman settlement but by the late fifteenth-century evidence from Co. Meath indicates that horse have begun to outnumber ox for ploughing (Down 1987, 474).

Cattle size The metrical data shows that there was no significant difference in the cattle measurements between the earlier and late periods. As the sample from the early phase is rather small, and Irish assemblages of the fifteenth century are rare, only those of the later phase are presented in Table 10. Comparison of the metrical data from Arran Quay with those of other Dublin sites indicate that there is no significant difference in the size of cattle between the thirteenth and fifteenth century. The means of the measurements from the tenth- to eleventh-century settlement in Fishamble Street are consistently, but not significantly, larger than those present in Arran Quay, but this is almost certainly due to the higher proportion of males present in the Fishamble Street samples. There is, therefore, no evidence for change in the size of cattle in Dublin between the tenth and fifteenth century. 4.7% of a large sample from the early phase were polled (hornless) but this is probably not representative of the cattle population as a whole because of the atypical nature of the sample (see below). It was not possible to estimate the proportion of polled cattle on other Dublin sites but the incidence is less than the incidence of 7% noted at Moynagh.

Horn cores The early phase deposits contained an unusually large quantity of cattle horn cores that had clearly little to do with the remainder of the assemblage, which consisted almost exclusively of discarded food refuse. The MNI estimate on the basis of the horns was forty-eight compared with the eleven in the case of the post-cranial bones. They clearly represent an industrial deposit and could either represent waste from a hornworkers (MacGregor 1989) or from the tanning process. Serjeantson (1989) has shown that hides were often brought to the tannery with the horns attached. In an early twelfth century ditch-fill in Bakehouse Lane, Waterford, a large quantity of cattle horns were found in association with large quantities of antler (McCormick, forthcoming). But in this case it probably represented hornworking rather than tanning, as hornworking and antler working are likely, in this context, to have been undertaken by the same craftsman. A notable feature of the horns at Arran Quay is that the great majority of the cores are very porous and of young cattle. Only seven out of the ninety horn cores present were developed enough to provide metrical data. The cattle ageing data has already shown that the great majority of cattle present were mature or old so the horns clearly were not a by-product of the urban meat trade. They almost certainly, therefore, represent the by-produce of a rural age/slaughter pattern where, as already seen, there was significant killing off of younger males. They, therefore, represent rural animal produce exported to the town, independently of the beef trade. The horn-sheaths of calves are clearly of little value compared with those on mature horns, so it seems much more likely that they represent hides being sent to the town. More specifically, as calf skin provides the highest quality parchment, combining thinness and strength (Reed 1972, 126), it can be suggested that the horn assemblage at Arran Quay represents consignments of calf skins used for parchment making.

Pathological anomalies Only a small number of the bones displayed pathological anomolies. One metatarsal from the early phase and two from the later phase display spavin with slight eburnation and extosis along the edge of the proximal articulation. This is generally caused by pressure on the lower hind limb when the animals are used for traction. They probably represent old oxen that have been slaughtered once they have passed their useful working life. Also present is the distal end of a cattle metatarsal that displays extreme exostosis due either to trauma or penetrative infection, the former being the more likely. The articular surface is unaffected. The only other affected bone is a re-healed large mammal rib fragment.

Pig Pigs were probably kept by the inhabitants of the Arran Quay area. This is supported by the presence of a neonatal scapula in the later phase. The primary eruption data are shown in Table 11 while the data from the later phase are summarised and compared with data from other sites in Table 4. Pig is raised exclusively for its meat and with the exception of a few kept for breeding there is no economic advantage in keeping them alive after they have reached full size. The age slaughter distribution for pig is, therefore, rather similar on all sites with the peak in slaughter occurring in the second year. The higher proportions of pig killed during the first year in most Dublin sites, compared to rural Moynagh, may reflect the constraints on the space available to the urban pig breeder. Unfortunately, most of the pig mandibulae were broken so it was not possible to investigate if male and female had different age/slaughter patterns. The pigs were similar in size to those noted in other Scandinavian and medieval samples from Dublin. The measurements from the later phase at Arran Quay are summarised in Table 12. Pathological anomalies were noted only on two pig bones, both from the later phase. In the first example there is extensive exostosis along the dorsal edge of the proximal articulation of a metatarsal, accompanied by slight pitting of the articular surface. The anomaly is suggestive of an arthritic condition. The distal end of the bone is fused suggesting that a mature, if not old animal, is represented. The second consists of penetrative trauma with limited bony growth around the edge of the wound on the lateral edge of a tibia shaft, immediately above the distal end.

Table 4. *Pig age distribution from the late phase at Arran Quay and other sites (after Butler 1984; McCormick 1987, forthcoming. The ageing data is after Higham (1967).*

Approx Age (in months)	Moynagh Crannog	Fishamble St Plots 2–3	Fishamble St Bank to Wall	Patrick St Site B	Arran Quay
	N=241	N=965	N=51	N=32	N=47
0–12	10.3	29.2	11.8	31.2	21.3
12–23	73.4	45.1	64.6	37.5	51.1
23–29	12.0	22.6	23.4	31.2	23.4
30+	4.1	3.1	–	–	4.3

Sheep/goat No post-cranial goat bones were identified but, as is usually the case on Irish urban medieval sites, goat horns outnumbered those of sheep. In the early phase one sheep and two female goats were present while in the later phase five sheep and seven goats, the latter all female, were present. The high incidence of goat horn may be due to the independent import of horns to the site (see McCormick 1984, 211) but it is equally likely that the extreme hardness of goat cores compared with sheep, especially ewes, accounts for their very high survival rate. The presence of polled sheep, a 20% incidence in the small sample from the later phase being noted, also contributed to the under-representation of sheep horn cores. It can be confidently concluded that the great majority of the caprovine bone was sheep and contamination by goat was minimal. The fact that all the goat horns in the samples were female reflects the role of the goat as a provider of fresh milk within the town. The primary age/slaughter data is shown in Table 13 and summarised and compared with other sites in Table 5.

Table 5. Sheep age distribution from the later phase from Arran Quay and other sites (after McCormick 1987 and forthcoming). The ageing is after Higham (1967).

Approx Age (in months)	Moynagh Crannog	Fishamble St Plots	Waterford High St	Patrick St Site A	Arran Quay
	N=117	N=115	N=69	N=32	N=43
Date	7–9 C	10–E11 C	L13–E14 C	L13–L14 C	15–L16 C
0–11	12.8	16.5	5.7	3.1	6.9
12–26	59.8	51.3	21.7	50.0	46.5
26+	27.4	32.2	72.5	46.9	46.5

The sheep ageing data in Table 5 is beginning to suggest the following trend. In the pre-Norman samples there is a small but significant slaughter of sheep in the first year, a very distinct peak in slaughter in the second year, and with a moderate amount killed in their third and later years. It is interesting to note that the patterns for rural Moynagh and urban Fishamble Street are almost identical. The post-Norman period indicates a change in the age/slaughter pattern that may be attributable to the development of the wool trade. It has already been seen that this led to an expansion of sheep-keeping, reflected in the higher incidence of sheep in post-Norman assemblages. The development of the wool trade would have led to the slaughtering of sheep at an older age in order to exploit their wool producing capabilities to the utmost before slaughter for the pot. This may be reflected in the lower incidence of sheep slaughtered in the first year and higher proportion of older sheep present. The latter is most pronounced in thirteenth-century Waterford where over 70% were older than two years before slaughter. Examination of predominantly fourteenth-century sheep bones from Patrick Street, Dublin has shown an improvement in the size of sheep in Dublin, almost certainly due to the importation of improved wool bearing sheep types. This size increase is again reflected in the Arran Quay material (Table 6). No pathological anomalies were noted among the sheep bones.

Table 6. Comparison between sheep metapodial greatest lengths (GL) between Arran Quay (later phase) and Fishamble Street and Patrick Street

		N	Min.	Max.	Mean	S.D.
Metacarpals	Arran Quay	15	104.1	126.1	117.0	5.3
	Patrick	13	112.5	132.2	121.7	6.8
	Fishamble St	25	101.9	123.5	114.3	5.9
Metatarsal	Arran Quay	11	118.2	147.1	129.1	8.2
	Patrick St	13	114.5	146.3	130.6	9.6
	Fishamble St	13	102.7	129.9	119.0	7.0

Other Domesticates Small numbers of dog, cat and horse were present and the measurements of these are shown in Table 15. Many of the horse bones were broken but none displayed butchering marks. A mandible from the late phase, however, had a neat, drilled circular hole (5.9mm dia.) at the angle of the bone about 3cm from its edge. No explanation can be suggested for this feature. A complete metatarsal from the later phase (Table 15) produced an estimated withers height of 143cm which represents a horse of 14.1 hands (after Kiesewalter, in von den Driesch and Boessneck 1974, 333). There is presently no comparative material from medieval sites but the horse lies at the upper range of the horse size noted on Early Christian-period sites. Ponies as small as 12 hands have been noted at Moynagh and Lagore but the example from Arran Quay is similar in size to the Connemara pony which is generally between 13 and 14 hands high. The excavation also produced a reasonably large quantity of dog and cat bone. Some of the dog bones were broken but none displayed butchering marks. The great majority of the long bones were complete and most were mature animals, thus allowing the shoulder heights to be estimated. They were all medium-sized dogs, similar in height to a modern collie, with none of the small terrier-sized animals or lap-dogs whose presence was noted in Fishamble Street or medieval Waterford. The cat sample was too small for analysis of the age/slaughter pattern but immature individuals were present, indicating that they were being exploited for their skins (McCormick 1988).

Wild animals Wild animals were represented by small quantities of hare, rabbit, fallow and red deer, and a single cetacean bone. Fallow deer have not previously been recorded in medieval Dublin but documentary evidence records the importation of fallow deer to stock the king's forest park at Glencree, County Wicklow (McCormick, in press). Eighty deer, consisting of sixty does and twenty bucks, were brought to the park from Chester in 1244. Fallow deer do not thrive in the wild and it seems likely that the fallow deer is derived from that area. The survival of the deer to as late as the late fourteenth or fifteenth century is interesting. They seem to have become extinct by the seventeenth century as Richard Boyle needed to re-import them from Devon to stock his deer park at Lismore, County Waterford in 1617 (Grosart 1887, 172). Although no fallow deer have been found on other medieval Dublin sites they have been noted by the writer at Ferrycarraig and by Whelan (1979) at Ferns, both in the same county. Rabbit are also an Anglo-Norman introduction, rabbit warrens having been established on Lambay Island as early as 1191 (McNeill 1950, 79). Rabbit and hare have already been noted in Dublin at thirteenth-century Wood Quay (Butler 1984), and have also been recorded in Dublin deposits as late as the later seventeenth and early eighteenth century (Butler 1988, 314). The single cetacean bone, from the later phase, consisted of the vertebra centrum of a common dolphin (*Delphinus delphinus*).[3] Small quantities of cetacean bone have been noted on most Dublin excavations. Only at thirteenth- or fourteenth-century Patrick Street, however, has it also been possible to identify the cetaceans at species level where the chopped skull of an immature Pilot whale (*Globicephala melaena*) was noted.

---

3 I would like to thank Jerry Hermon of the National Museum of Scotland, Natural History Division, for identifying the dolphin bone.

Table 7. Arran Quay, Earlier Phase. Distribution of fragments and minimum numbers of individuals (MNI).

	Cattle	Horse	Sheep/Goat	Pig	Dog	Cat	Rabbit	Hare
Horn	95	0	3	0	0	0	0	0
Skull	15	0	3	6	0	0	0	0
Mandible	9	1	19	21	2	0	0	0
Teeth	2	1	0	4	0	0	0	0
Scapula	26	0	21	3	1	0	0	0
Humerus	14	0	18	5	3	5	0	0
Radius	16	1	14	8	1	0	0	0
Ulna	11	0	4	12	1	0	0	0
Metacarpal	18	0	13	4	1	0	0	0
Pelvis	15	0	22	4	0	1	1	0
Femur	15	0	12	2	0	4	1	0
Tibia	19	0	20	9	1	0	0	1
Astragalus	9	0	1	0	0	0	0	0
Calcaneus	18	0	1	4	0	0	0	0
Metatarsal	0	0	4	9	0	0	0	0
Phalanx I	15	0	0	1	0	0	0	0
Phalanx II	6	0	0	0	0	0	0	0
Phalanx III	11	0	0	0	0	0	0	0
Total	314	3	155	92	10	10	2	1
Total %	53.5	0.5	26.6	15.7	1.7	1.7	0.3	0.2
MNI	11	1	11	9	2	3	1	1
MNI %	28.2	2.6	28.2	23	5.1	7.7	2.6	2.6

Table 8. Arran Quay, Later Phase. Distribution of fragments and minimum numbers of individuals (MNI). The sample also contained one cetacean bone. Fal.=Fallow.

	Cattle	Horse	Sheep/Goat	Pig	Dog	Cat	Rabbit	Red Deer	Fal. Deer
Horn	26	0	13	0	0	0	0	0	0
Skull	32	0	7	33	0	0	0	0	0
Mandible	120	2	76	79	2	2	2	0	0
Teeth	23	1	0	9	0	0	0	0	0
Scapula	112	1	92	29	4	0	0	1	0
Humerus	56	0	62	43	2	3	0	0	0
Radius	28	1	70	33	2	1	0	0	0
Ulna	31	1	22	52	1	3	1	0	0
Metacarpal	146	0	61	15	7	0	0	0	1
Pelvis	83	0	69	11	0	1	3	0	0

→

Femur	79	1	29	11	9	4	4	0	0
Tibia	83	1	180	36	0	4	0	0	1
Fibula	0	0	0	9	0	0	0	0	0
Astragalus	30	0	0	2	0	0	0	0	0
Calcaneus	62	1	1	5	0	0	0	0	0
Metatarsal	188	1	48	28	2	0	0	0	0
Tarsals/Carpals	13	3	0	5	0	0	0	0	0
Phalanx I	75	2	0	1	0	0	0	0	0
Phalanx II	12	1	0	0	0	0	0	0	0
Phalanx III	21	0	0	0	0	0	0	0	0
Total	1120	16	730	401	29	18	10	1	2
Total %	50.3	0.7	30.1	16.5	1.2	0.7	0.4	0	0
MNI	49	1	61	34	5	4	2	1	1
MNI %	31	0.6	38.6	21.5	3.2	2.5	1.3	0.6	0.6

Table 9. Cattle tooth eruption data after Higham (1967) and wear state of M3 after Grant (1982), i.e., capitals in brackets.

Eruption Approx. age	State of tooth eruption N Stage and wear (In Months)		
4	M1 in primary eruption	5–6	2
7	M1 in primary wear, M2 unerupted	8–13	1
11	M2 in wear, M3 unerupted	18–24	1
12	M3 in primary eruption	24	1
13	M3 in secondary eruption	24–30	2
16	M3 in wear (E)	36	1
20+	M3 in wear (G)	40+	5
20+	M3 in wear (H)	40+	1
20+	M3 in wear (J)	40+	2
20+	M3 in wear (K)	40+	6
20+	M3 in wear (L)	40+	1

THE BIRD BONES
by Tanya O'Sullivan

A total of 283 bird bones were submitted for examination from the Arran Quay site, 66 came from the fourteenth-century levels (earlier phase) and 217 came from the fifteenth- to seventeenth-century levels (later phase). All of the bones were examined, measured and identified to species where possible.

Discussion The deposits from which the bones were uncovered were dumped behind the riverfront revetments in the earlier phase and outside the stone quay walls in the later phase. The deposits were brought into the site from elsewhere. Fowl outnumbered geese in both phases, fowl lower limb bones being four times more abundant than upper limb bones in the earlier phase and over twice as abundant in the later phase. This phenomenon is common on urban sites, and has been shown to indicate that the bulk of the material represents refuse from meals (Coy 1989, 35–40). The occurrence of cut marks on the distal tibio-tarsii (both phases), and fine shaft scratches on radii specimens (later phase) would lend support to this theory. The frequent observation of such fine scratches on limb bones from urban sites has led to the conclusion that they were the result of using knives at table, whereby the meat was scraped directly from the bone to the mouth by means of a knife (Bourdillon and Coy 1980, 118). Cut marks on the distal tibio-tarsii result from the removal of the lower limbs from the carcass before cooking (O'Sullivan 1990, 34). A number of immature fowl specimens were recovered from the later phase, indicating the possibility that fowl were reared for consumption on the site where the material was originally deposited. Further evidence for the rearing of fowl was the presence in the later phase of four male tarso-metatarsii with fully-grown spurs. Three tarso-metatarsii also from the later phase displayed spur scars on their shafts. This would indicate that caponisation was taking place.

It would appear that hens were present in small numbers during the earlier phase. By the later phase fowl rearing appears to have increased in popularity, hens would have supplemented the meat diet with eggs, and cocks and capons bred for the table. The upper limb bones of geese outnumber the lower limb bones by a factor of almost 3:1 in both the early and later phases. The high number of upper limb bones to lower limb bones in all of the goose species would normally support the theory that goose feathers were imported on the wing (goose feathers were widely sought after for use as quills and for fletching arrows), and that the majority of wing bones present on the site would be a reflection of this trade rather than as a result of goose breeding. However, many of the Arran Quay wing bones were incomplete, indicating that they may have been broken up for consumption (Maltby 1979, 72). It is possible that this fracturing was due to river action, because the majority of the bones had an intact shaft and were broken along the less resilient proximal and distal epiphyses. Taking this into account it is likely that the wing bones were indeed imported into the site. No immature goose specimens were recovered from either the early or the later phases, adding support to the theory that geese may not have been bred to any great degree on the site on which the material was originally deposited. The cut marks on the upper limb bones are consistent with the removal of the wings from the carcass. Butchery evidence on a tibio-tarsus in the later phase indicates that the occasional goose was eaten. It would appear that the utilisation of goose meat and goose bones increased from the early to the later phase. Only one raven was recovered from the site, unusual for an urban context. The absence of raven and other smaller species can be put down to poor survival rates, especially when subjected to river action over centuries.

Fourteenth-century bones (earlier phase) At least five species of bird were represented by the sample from the earlier phase. These included a minimum number of seven domestic fowl (Gallus Gallus), two domestic geese (Anser Anser), four pink-footed geese (Anser Brachyrhynchos), two white fronted geese (Anser Albifrons) and one raven (Corus Corax).

Table 1. Earlier phase (14th century)

Species	No. of Fragments	MNI.	MNI%
Dom. Fowl	24	7	46.6
Dom. Goose	4	2	13.3
Pink-footed Goose	10	4	26.6
White-fronted Goose	2	2	13.6
Raven	2	1	6.6
Unid.	24	—	—
Total	**66**	**16**	

Fowl butchery analysis

Tibio-tarsus: One bone displayed cuts on the internal condyle. Three specimens were cut across the external condyles, and one displayed a series of scratches (knife marks) in this area. Two bones were perforated in the proximal shaft region. None of the remaining skeletal elements displayed any evidence of butchery. **Fragmentation analysis** First of all it was necessary to look at the relative proportions of upper/lower limb bones. Upper limb fragments: humerus 1, radius 1, ulna 3, carpo-metacarpus 0–Total 5. Lower limb fragments: tibio-tarsus 11, femur 7, tarso-metatarsus 2–Total 20. **Tibio-tarsus:** Two bones had mid-shaft breaks, one was missing the distal end, and one was missing the proximal end. The remaining tibio-tarsii were complete. **Femur:** Two bones were broken in the mid-shaft region, with the distal ends missing. A further specimen was broken in this area but with the proximal end missing. The remaining specimens were complete. The remaining fowl skeletal elements were complete.

Age analysis One immature specimen was present. The remaining fowl skeletal elements were mature.

Goose (all breeds) butchery analysis

Humerus: One bone displayed cuts across its internal and external condyles. **Carpo-metacarpus**: One bone displayed a minor cut mark on the proximal joint surface. **Scapula:** One specimen had a series of scratches (knife marks) on the shaft. None of the remaining bones displayed evidence of butchery. **Fragmentation analysis** First of all it was necessary to look at the relative proportions of upper/lower limb bones. Upper limb fragments: humerus 2, radius 1, ulna 0, carpo-metacarpus 7–Total 10. Lower limb fragments: femurs 0, tibio-tarsus 3, tarso-metatarsus 0–Total 3. **Tibio-tarsus:** One specimen was broken mid-shaft and was missing its proximal end, one consisted of a shaft only, and one was complete. **Humerus:** One bone had a fracture in the upper shaft region, and was missing the distal end. The other specimen was complete. The remainder of the skeletal elements were complete. **Age analysis** All of the complete bones were mature. No definite signs of immaturity could be ascertained from the fragmented specimens.

15th–17th century (later phase) bones Only five species could be identified in the sample from the later phase, despite the fact that over four times the number of bones were recovered from this phase. Large numbers of single species were noted, as well as a high percentage of fragmented and unidentifiable specimens. The sample consisted of a minimum number of fourteen domestic fowl (Gallus Gallus), four domestic geese (Anser Anser), ten pink-footed geese (Anser Brachyrhynchos), seven white fronted geese (Anser Albifrons), and one brent goose (Branta Bernicla).

Table 2. Later phase (15th to 17th century)

Species Present	No. of Fragments	MNI	% MNI
Dom. Fowl	99	14	38.8
Dom. Goose	11	4	11.1
Pink-footed Goose	44	10	27.7
White-fronted Goose	29	7	19.4
Brent Goose	1	1	2.7
Unid.	33	—	—

Fowl butchery analysis

Tibio-tarsus: Seven fowl tibio-tarsii displayed cut marks on both external and internal condyles. One bone had a series of fine scratches on the upper shaft. One radius and one femur displayed scratches in the proximal shaft area. Butchery marks were not evident on the humeri, the carpo-metacarpi, the coracoids, the tarso-metatarsii, or on the remains of the pelvis or sternum. **Fragmentation analysis** First of all it was necessary to look at the relative proportions of upper/lower limb bones. Upper limb bones: humerus 8, radius 6, ulna 6, carpo-metacarpus 1–Total 21. Lower limb bones: tibio-tarsus 32, femur 11, tarso-metatarsus 10–Total 53. **Tibio-tarsus:** Five bones were broken in the mid to lower shaft region with the distal end missing. Eleven bones were broken in the mid to upper shaft region with the proximal end missing. The remaining specimens were complete. **Humerus:** All the humeri specimens, save two, were missing both proximal and distal ends. One bone was broken in the mid-shaft region and was missing the proximal end. The final specimen was similarly fractured but was without its distal end. **Femur:** Four femurs were broken in the mid-shaft region and were minus the distal ends. The remaining specimens were complete. **Sternum:** Only apex sterni and keel fragments were present. **Pelvis:** Only acetabulum fragments were present. The ulnae, carpo-metacarpi, radii, tarso-metatarsii, scapulae and coracoids were all complete. **Age analysis: tibio-tarsus:** Two immature bones were present. **ulna:** One immature bone was present. **humerus:** Five immature bones were present. The carpo-metacarpii, radii, femurs, tarso-metatarsii, scapulae and coracoids were all mature.

Geese (all breeds) butchery analysis: tibio-tarsus: Two bones show evidence of having their internal condyles sliced off. One bone displayed a puncture mark on its shaft. **ulna:** One bone has cut marks across the distal condyles. Two bones displayed a series of scratches on the upper shaft, and two further bones were cut in this area.

humerus: Two bones had perforations in the upper shaft region, and two humeri had scratches (knife marks) in this region. **carpo-metacarpus:** One bone displayed a proximal cut mark, another was perforated in the mid-shaft area. **radius:** One bone was perforated in the upper shaft region. One bone had scratches (knife marks) in this area. **coracoid:** Two bones were perforated on their glenoid and sternal facets. The femurs, tarso-metatarsii, sterni, and pelvic bones displayed no evidence of butchery marks. **Fragmentation analysis** It was necessary first of all to look at the relative proportions of the upper/lower limb bone fragments. **Upper limb fragments:** humerus 28, radius 20, ulna 11, carpo-metacarpus 5–Total 64. **Lower limb fragments:** tibio-tarsus 12, femurs 0, tarso-metatarsus 0–Total 12. **Tibio-tarsus:** Four bones were broken mid-shaft with distal ends missing. The remaining tibio-tarsii were complete. **Ulna:** Five bones were broken mid-shaft, with their proximal ends missing, and four bones were broken mid-shaft, with the distal ends missing. The remainder were complete. **Humerus:** Two bones had mid-shaft fractures with the distal ends missing, four bones had similar fractures with the proximal ends missing. The remaining specimens consisted of shafts only. **Radius:** Six bones were broken in the mid-shaft area, with the proximal ends missing. Four bones were similarly broken but missing their distal ends. The remaining specimens were complete. The other skeletal elements present were complete. One coracoid and one ulna displayed evidence of gnawing on the proximal surfaces.

Results of age analysis: tibio-tarsus: No definite evidence of immaturity in the tibio-tarsii specimens. **ulna:** No definite evidence of immaturity in the ulna specimens. **humerus:** Four mature proximal joint surfaces were present, and two mature distal joint surfaces. As the distal epiphyses of the humerus fuse at an earlier stage to the proximal, it can be assumed that the latter two bones represent mature individuals. The remaining specimens were lacking their joint surfaces, so estimates of age were not possible. **radius:** Six mature distal joint surfaces, and five mature proximal joint surfaces were present. The proximal epiphyses of the radius fuse at an earlier stage than the distal so in this case it can be assumed that the distal joint surfaces came from three mature bones. The five proximal joint surfaces may come from younger birds. The remaining complete skeletal elements were mature.

THE FISH BONE
by Sheila Hamilton-Dyer

Introduction A quantity of fish bone was recovered from the riverside of the quay walls. The bones appeared to be mostly head bones of large fish, possibly waste from the production of stockfish. The sample of over 1,000 fragments was taken from context 117. No sieving had been carried out for small bone retrieval. The methods used for identification and recording were based on the FRU (Faunal Remains Unit, Southampton) method 86 system, with some modifications (see FRU archive, and SH-D archive file BONESTRU). Identifications were made primarily using the modern comparative collections of S. Hamilton-Dyer and the FRU. Fish nomenclature follows Wheeler (1978).

Results 1,109 fish bone fragments were examined. This total excludes approximately 50 small fragments, which were judged to have been recently broken off other bones. A small number of bones have been counted as 1 where they are broken parts of the same element. Eight species of fish were identified. These were ling, *Molva molva*, and cod, *gadus morhua*; together with a few bones of conger eel, *conger conver*; flatfish, (plaice, *pleuronectes platessa*, and flounder, *platichthys flesus*); and one fragment each of hake, *merluccius merluccius*; bass, *dicentrarchus labrax*; and a sea-bream, probably the red sea-bream, *pagellus bogeraveo*. The distribution of anatomical elements is uneven. The major species ling and cod were represented mainly by head bones. Of a total of 148 cod bones from at least 12 individuals there were only 25 precaudal vertebrae and 2 caudal vertebra, nor were there any cleithra, the large curved bone behind the gill opening, although there were 4 supra-cleithra. Ling bones had a similar distribution but with a slightly higher representation of these non-head bones (Table 1). The presence of some ling precaudal vertebra may be a result of differing butchery practices between the cod and the slimmer ling. Four bones only showed definite butchery marks, all of them ling. The cut elements were two ectopterygoid, a maxilla and a cleithrum. The minimum number of individuals was calculated as 27 ling, 12 cod, 4 flatfish (one plaice, one flounder, two not identified to species), 3 conger, 1 hake, 1 bass and 1 sea bream. Ling and cod were best represented by dentaries and articulars; with a very close correlation between numbers of left and right elements. The lower numbers for other elements is probably due to the taphonomic biases of smaller size and/or fragility; however, it is interesting to note that the sturdy pre-maxilla and quadrate are not as well represented, at about half the numbers in the case of ling. Otoliths were notable by their almost total absence, one of ling only being recovered. There are several possible explanations. Without sieving they may simply be missed; the single find here was less than 1cm in length. Otoliths are often missing even from sites with an extensive sieving programme, probably due to destruction in the soil as they are calcareous. A more interesting possibility is extraction for use as medicines, a practice that seems to have been carried out in England and France between the fourteenth and eighteenth centuries (J. Desse, pers. comm).

Size Much of the material was extremely well preserved and, like the mammal bone, showed little sign of water damage. This enables measurements to be taken on most of the major skeletal elements. The measurements were taken on the basio-occipital, vomer, proatlas, atlas, maxilla, premaxilla, dentary, articular, quadrate, opercular, and also the anal pterygiophore of flatfish. These were taken in millimetres to one decimal place using a vernier calliper. The measurements mainly follow Morales and Rosenlund 1979; additional measurements are described in archive. The bones were also compared for size with modern skeletons in the collections of S. Hamilton-Dyer and the FRU. The measurements indicate a selected population rather than the full natural range. Comparison with the modern material indicates that most of the cod and ling were of about 1 metre total length, representing fish of approximately 8–10kg. Some of the ling were considerably larger than the largest modern specimen compared, which had a total length of 1.16m. The three conger were of two different sizes, two were similar to a recent specimen of 1.15m (2.72kg), the other was much larger, comparable with a specimen of nearly 2 metres and 15kg. The flatfish were of about 30–35cm, an average size today.

Discussion Although a lack of sieving could be responsible for the low numbers of the smaller species, it does not explain the almost total absence of vertebrae of the ling and cod as these bones would be quite large. The concentration on ling and cod heads indicates a primarily industrial activity resulting in the dumping of a select category, possibly a single episode. This deposit may represent the waste from preparation of 'stockfish': salted and dried cod and related species. Ling preserved in this way, beheaded and split open, can still be obtained in Scandinavia. Although not until an Act of Parliament in 1542 gave free entry for fish imported from Ireland, Scotland, Orkney, the Shetlands, Iceland and Newfoundland (Cutting 1955), use of and trade in stockfish was already taking place all over medieval Europe. Taking the weights of modern fish of this length as a guide, these bones give a conservative estimate of 300kg of whole fish. Again this large quantity points towards an industrial explanation for this deposit, rather than a domestic one. Ling are not shallow water fish and would not have been caught in the local waters of the Irish Sea. Today they are found at depths up to 600m in a band stretching from northern Norway and Iceland, down the west of the British Isles as far as Biscay. The range of cod is more extensive, both in area and depth, and could have been caught more locally. If traded as stockfish the cod and ling would have already been beheaded; the implication from this material is that whole, fresh fish were arriving at Dublin from one of the fishing grounds around Ireland. The hake and sea bream may have been incidental catches with the cod and ling but the other minor species are probably of local inshore origin. They are perhaps even unconnected with the head dumping episode, and it could even be argued that as none have butchery marks they may be the remains of fish living at the quayside. This is perhaps most likely for the flatfish, which are commonly found in shallow estuarine waters.

Table 1. Anatomical Distribution (NB. Excludes 50 fragments, probably broken off other elements but includes joined bones recorded as one in database, for example, Conger articular, joined with and recorded as dentary).

	Conger	Cod	Ling	Gadidae	Hake	Bass	Sea-bream	Flatfish
Supraoccipital	–	–	5	–	–	–	–	–	5
Basioccipital	–	1	8	–	–	–	–	–	9
Parasphenoid	–	3	17	–	–	–	–	–	20
Frontal	–	1	23	–	–	–	–	–	24
Vomer	–	2	5	–	–	–	–	–	7
other neurocranial	–	1	2	91	–	–	–	–	94
premaxilla	1	9	17	–	–	–	–	–	27
maxilla	–	13	28	–	–	–	–	–	41
dentary	3	22	50	–	–	–	–	–	75
articular	3	11	54	–	–	–	–	–	68
ceratohyal	–	9	45	–	–	–	–	–	54
other hyal	–	6	19	2	–	–	–	–	27
branchial	–	–	–	85	–	–	–	–	85
branchial ray	–	–	–	201	–	–	–	–	201
pharyngeal	–	–	–	9	–	–	–	–	9

Table 1. (continued)

	Conger	Cod	Ling	Gadidae	Hake	Bass	Sea-bream	Flatfish
quadrate	–	1	10	–	–	–	–	11
hyomandibular	1	8	16	–	–	–	–	25
preoperculum	–	9	21	–	–	1	–	31
operculum	–	6	13	–	–	–	–	19
other opercular	–	8	11	–	–	–	–	19
post temporal	–	–	–	9	–	–	–	9
other head bones	–	7	45	–	–	–	–	52
cleithrum	–	–	1	–	–	–	2	3
supra cleithrum	–	4	13	–	–	–	–	17
anal pterygiophore	–	–	–	–	–	–	4	4
atlas	–	–	8	–	–	–	–	8
precaudal vertebra	–	25	131	–	–	–	–	156
first caudal vertebra	–	–	–	–	–	1	1	2
caudal vertebra	–	2	–	–	1	–	3	6
otolith	–	–	1	–	–	–	–	1
Total	8	148	543	397	1	1	1 10	1109

BIBLIOGRAPHY

Alexander, J. and Binski, P. (eds) 1987 *Age of chivalry – Art in Plantagenet England, 1200–1400*. London.

Allan, J.P. 1984 *Medieval and post-medieval finds from Exeter, 1971–1980*.

Ayers, B.S. 1979 Excavations at Chapel Lane, Staith, 1978. *East Riding Arch.* 5.

Barnard, F.P. 1981 *The casting counter and the counting board*. Castlebary.

Bayley, J. et al. 1984 A medieval mirror from Heybridge, Essex, Exhibits at Ballots 2. *Antiq. Jn* 64, 2, 399–402.

Biddle, M. 1990 *Object and economy in medieval Winchester*, Winchester Studies 7, Artefacts from Medieval Winchester Part II , 2 vols, Oxford.

Bourdillon, J. and Coy, J.P. 1980 The animal bones. In P. Holdsworth (ed.), *Excavations at Melbourne Street, Southampton, 1971–76*. C.B.A. Research Rep. 33,118.

Bradley, J. and Manning, C. 1981 Excavations at Duiske abbey, Graiguenamanagh Co. Kilkenny. *R.I.A. Proc.* 81C, 397–426.

Callender, J. G. 1924 Fourteenth-century brooches and other ornaments in the National Museum of Antiquities of Scotland. *Soc. Antiqs Scot. Proc.* 58.

Campbell, K. 1985 A medieval tile kiln site at Magdelene Street, Drogheda. *Louth Arch. and Hist. Soc. Jn*, 21, 48–54.

Carville, G. 1972 The urban property of the Cistercians in medieval Ireland. *Studia Monastica* 14, 35–47.

Clarke, H. and Carter, A. 1977 *Excavations in Kings Lynn, 1963–1970*. Soc. Med. Arch. Monograph. Ser. No. 7.

Clarke, H.B. 1978. *Dublin c.840 to c.1540: The medieval town in the modern city*. Friends of Medieval Dublin/Ordnance Survey Dublin. 2nd edn, R.I.A., 2002.

Cosgrove, A. ed. 1988 *Dublin through the ages.* Dublin.

Coy, J.P. 1989 The provision of fowl and fish for towns. In D. Serjeantson and T. Waldron (eds), *Diet and crafts in towns – the evidence of animal remains from the Roman to the post-medieval periods.* B.A.R. Brit. Ser., 199, 25–40.

Craig, M. 1980 *Dublin 1660–1860.* Dublin.

Crowfoot, E. 1990 The textiles. In M. Biddle (ed.), *Object and economy in medieval Winchester,* 467–94.

Cunliffe, B. 1971 *Excavations at Fishbourne 1961–1969.* Vol. II The finds. Rept of the Research Comm. of Soc. Antiqs of London, No. XXVII.

Cutting, C.L. 1955 Fish saving. *A history of fish processing from ancient to modern times.* London.

Daniels, R. 1991 Medieval Hartlepool: evidence of and from the waterfront. In G.L. Good, R.H. Jones, and M.W. Ponsford (eds), *Waterfront archaeology.* Proceedings of the Third International Conference, Bristol, 1988. C.B.A. Research Report No. 74, 43–50.

Davey, P. 1961 *History of building materials.* London.

De Courcy, J.W. 1984 Medieval banks of the Liffey estuary. In J. Bradley (ed.), *Viking Dublin exposed. The Wood Quay saga.* 164–6.

De Courcy, J.W. 1990 A bridge in its time: the river Liffey crossing at Church Street in Dublin. *R.I.A. Proc.,* 90C, 243–57.

Dunleavy, M. 1988 A classification of early Irish combs. *R.I.A. Proc.* 88C, 341–422.

Dunning, G.C. 1975 Roof fittings. In C. Platt and R. Coleman-Smith (eds), *Excavations in medieval Southampton, 1953–1969, ii, 186–96.* Leicester

Eagan, G. and Pritchard, F. 1991. *Dress accessories c.1150–1450. medieval finds from excavations in London.* London.

Eames, E.S. and Fanning, T. 1988 *Irish medieval tiles.* R.I.A. Dublin.

Eames, E.S. 1980 *Catalogue of the medieval lead-glazed earthenware tiles in the Department of Medieval and Later Antiquities, British Museum.* 2 vols. London.

Evans, J. 1922 *Magical jewels.* Oxford.

Ford, B. 1987 Copper alloy objects. In P. Holdsworth (ed.) *Excavations in the medieval burgh of Perth, 1979–1981.* Edinburgh, 121–30.

Gaimster, D. 1987 The supply of Rhenish stoneware to London, 1350–1600. *The London Archaeologist,* 5, no. 13, 339–47.

Gilbert, J.T. and R.M. 1889–1944 *Calendar of ancient records of Dublin.* 19 vols. Dublin.

Gilbert, J.T. 1854–9 *A history of the city of Dublin.* 3 vols. London.

Good, G.L. and Tabraham, C.J. 1981 Excavations at Threave Castle, Galloway, 1974–78. *Medieval Archaeology.* 25,90–140.

Good, G.L. 1987 The excavation of two docks at Narrow Quay, Bristol, 1978–9. *Post-Medieval Archaeology.* 21, 25–126.

Good, G.L., Jones, R.H. and Ponsford, M.W. (eds) 1991 *Waterfront archaeology.* Proc. of the Third International Conference, Bristol, 1988. C.B.A. Research Report No. 74 Oxford.

Gowen, M. 1990 Unpublished report on archaeological testing at Arran Quay, Dublin. Lodged with Dúchas: the Heritage Service.

Gwynn, A. and Hadcock, R.N. 1988 *Medieval religious houses. Ireland.* 2nd edn. Dublin.

Gwynn, A. 1990 The first bishops of Dublin. In H.B. Clarke (ed.) 1990b *Medieval Dublin. The living city.* Dublin, 37–61.

Hare, J.N. 1985 *Battle Abbey–the eastern range and the excavations of 1978–80.* Hist. Build. and Mon. Comm Eng. Arch. Rep. No. 2.

Hayden, A. 1989 Excavations at Bakehouse Lane, Waterford. Unpublished report lodged with Dúchas: the Heritage Service.

Hayden, A. 1993 Excavations at Cornmarket and Bridge Street Upper, Dublin. Unpublished report lodged with Dúchas: the Heritage Service.

Hayden, A. 1997 The small finds. In C. Walsh 1997 *Archaeological excavations at Patrick Street, Nicholas Street and Winetavern Street, Dublin*. Dingle.

Hayden, A. 1991 Excavations at St Stephen's leper hospital, Dublin. Unpublished report lodged with Dúchas: the Heritage Service.

Henderson, C.G. 1981 Exeter. In G. Milne and B. Hobley (eds) *Waterfront archaeology in Britain and Northern Europe*. C.B.A. Research Report 41 London, 119–22.

Hillam, J. and Morgan, R.A. 1981 What value is dendrochronology to waterfront archaeology? In G. Milne and B. Hobley (eds) *Waterfront archaeology in Britain and Northern Europe*. C.B.A. Research Report 41 London, 39–46.

Hobley, B. 1981. The London waterfront–the exception or the rule? In G. Milne and B. Hobley (eds) *Waterfront archaeology in Britain and Northern Europe*. C.B.A. Research Report 41 London, 1–9.

Holdsworth, P. ed. 1987 *Excavations in the medieval burgh of Perth 1979–1981*. Soc. Ant. Scot. Monograph Ser. no. 5. Edinburgh.

Hurley, M. 1989 Excavations at Grand Parade II Cork. *Jn. Cork Arch. Hist. Soc.* 94, 27–45.

Hurley, M. 1993 Kyrls Quay/North Main Street, Cork. In Bennett (ed.) *Excavations 1992, summary accounts of archaeological excavations in Ireland*, O.I.A.

Hurley, M.F., Scully, O.M.B. and McCutcheon, S.W.J. 1997 *Late Viking Age and medieval Waterford excavations 1986–1992*. Waterford.

Hurst, J.G. 1974 Sixteenth- and seventeenth-century pottery imported from the Stonge. In V.I. Evison, H. Hodges and J.G. Hurst (eds), *Medieval pottery from excavations: studies presented to Gerald Clough Dunning*. London.

Hurst, J.G. 1977 Imported Spanish pottery. *Medieval Archaeology*. 21, 68–105.

Hurst, J.G., Neal, D.S., van Beuningen H.J.E. 1986 *Rotterdam papers 6. Pottery produced and traded in north-west Europe, 1350–1650*. Rotterdam.

Jones, R.H. 1991 Industry and environment in medieval Bristol. In G.L. Good, R.H. Jones, and M.W. Ponsford (eds) *Waterfront Archaeology*. Proceedings of the Third International Conference, Bristol, 1988. C.B.A. Research Report No 74, 19–26.

Lang, J.T. 1988 *Viking-Age decorated wood. A study of its ornament and style*. Medieval Dublin Excavations 1962–81, Ser.B, vol 1. R.I.A., Dublin.

Lindh, J. 1991 Aspects of sea-level changes, fishing, and fish processing in Tønsberg in the Middle Ages. In G.L. Good, R.H. Jones, and M.W. Ponsford (eds) *Waterfront archaeology*. Proceedings of the Third International Conference, Bristol, 1988. C.B.A. Research Report No. 74, 67–75.

Lydon, J.F. 1988 The medieval city. In A. Cosgrove (ed.), *Dublin through the ages*. Dublin, 25–45.

Lynch, A. 1984 Excavations of the medieval town defences at Charlotte's Quay, Limerick. *R.I.A. Proc.* 84C, 281–331.

MacGregor, A. 1985 *Bone, antler, ivory and horn: the technology of skeletal materials since the Roman period*. London.

MacGregor, A. 1989 Bone, antler and horn industries in the urban context. In D. Serjeantson and T. Waldron (eds) *Diet and crafts in towns – the evidence of animal remains from the Roman to the post medieval periods*. B.A.R. Brit. Ser. 199, 107–28.

MacMahon, M. 1988 Archaeological excavations at the site of the Four Courts extension, Inns Quay, Dublin. *R.I.A. Proc.* 88C, 271–319.

MacMahon, M. 1991 Archaeological excavations at Bridge Street Lower, Dublin. *R.I.A. Proc.* 91C, 3–71.

Marsden, P. 1981 Early shipping and the waterfronts of London. In G. Milne and B. Hobley (eds) *Waterfront archaeology in Britain and Northern Europe*. C.B.A. Research Report 41 London, 10–16.

McCullough, N. 1989 *Dublin. An urban history*. Dublin.

McGrail, S. 1981 Medieval boats, ships and landing places. In G. Milne and B. Hobley (eds) *Waterfront archaeology in Britain and Northern Europe*. C.B.A. Research Report 41 London, 17–23.

McNeill, C. ed. 1950. *Calendar of Archbishop Alen's register*. Dublin.

Milne, G. and Milne, C. 1978 Excavations on the Thames Waterfront at Trig Lane, London, 1974–76. *Medieval Archaeology* 22, 84–104.

Milne, G. and Milne, C. 1982. *Medieval waterfront development at Trig Lane, London*. London and Middlesex Arch. Soc. Special Paper no. 3 London.

Milne, G. 1981. Medieval riverfront reclamation in London. In G. Milne and B. Hobley (eds) *Waterfront archaeology in Britain and Northern Europe*. C.B.A. Research Report 41 London, 32–6.

Mitchell, G.F. 1987. *Archaeology and environment in early Dublin*. Med. Dub. Exc. 1962–81 Ser. C, Vol. 1. R.I.A. Dublin.

Mitchener, M. 1988 *The medieval period and Nuremberg*, Vol. 1, London.

Morales, A. and Rosenlund, K. 1979 *Fish bone measurements*. Steenstrupia, Copenhagen.

Newton, S. 1980 *Fashion in the age of the Black Prince*. Woodbridge.

Oakley, G.E. 1978 The copper alloy objects. In J.H. Williams, Excavations on Greyfriars, Northampton, 1972. *Northampton Arch.*, 13, 147–31.

Oakley, G.E. 1979 The copper alloy objects. In J.H. Williams 1979 *St Peter's Street Northampton, Excavations, 1973–1976*, 248–64.

Ó Ríordáin, B. 1990 The High Street excavations. In H.B. Clarke (ed.) 1990a Medieval Dublin. *The making of a metropolis. Dublin, 165–72*.

Orton, C. 1982 Pottery evidence for the dating of the revetments. In G. Milne and C. Milne (eds) *Medieval waterfront development at Trig Lane, London*. London and Middlesex Arch. Soc. Special Paper no. 3 London.

O'Sullivan, B. 1990 The Dominicans in medieval Dublin. In H.B. Clarke (ed.) 1990b *Medieval Dublin. The living city*. Dublin, 83–99.

O'Sullivan, T. 1990 The exploitation of birds in Viking Dublin. Unpublished M.A. thesis, National University of Ireland.

Oswald, A. 1975 *Clay pipes for the archaeologist*. B.A.R. Int. Ser.,14. Oxford.

Platt, C. and Coleman-Smith, R. 1975. *Excavations in medieval Southampton, 1953–1969*. 2 vols. Leicester.

Platt, C., Coleman-Smith, R. 1975 *Excavations in medieval Southampton, 1953–69*. Leicester.

Potter, G. 1991 The medieval bridge and waterfront at Kingston-upon-Thames. In G.J. Good, R.H. Jones, and M.W. Ponsford (eds) 1991 *Waterfront archaeology*. Proceedings of the Third International Conference, Bristol, 1988. Oxford, 137–49.

Robinson, D. 1987 The plant remains. In P. Holdsworth (ed.) *Excavations in the medieval burgh of Perth 1979–1981*. Edinburgh, 199–209.

Schofield, J. 1975 Seal House. *Current Archaeology*. 5, 54–7.

Simms, A. 1990. Medieval Dublin in a European context: from proto-town to chartered town. In H.B. Clarke (ed.) 1990a *Medieval Dublin. The making of a metropolis*. Dublin, 37–51.

Stalley, R. 1987 *The Cistercian monasteries of Ireland*. London and Newhaven.

Stronkova, O. 1954 *Gothic woman's fashion*. Prague.

Swan, L. 1991 Wood Quay found at Usher's Quay! *Archaeology Ireland* 5, no. 2,6.

Sweetman, P.D. 1978 Archaeological excavations at Trim Castle, Co. Meath, 1971–74. *R.I.A. Proc.* 78C, 127–98.

Sweetman, P.D. 1979 Archaeological excavations at Ferns Castle, Co. Wexford. *R.I.A. Proc.* 79C, 217–45.

Sweetman, P.D. 1984 Archaeological excavations at Shop Street, Drogheda, Co. Louth. *R.I.A. Proc.* 84C, 171–224.

Taton Brown, T. 1974 Excavations at the Custom House site, City of London, 1973. *Trans. London Middlesex Arch. Soc.* 25,117–219.

Wallace, P.F. and Ó Floinn, R. 1988 *Dublin 1000–discovery and excavation in Dublin, 1842–1981.* Dublin.

Wallace, P.F. 1981 Dublin's waterfront at Wood Quay, 900–1317. In G. Milne and B. Hobley (eds) *Waterfront archaeology in Britain and Northern Europe.* London, 109–18.

Wallace, P.F. 1982 Carpentry in Ireland AD 900–1300–The Wood Quay Evidence. In S. McGrail (ed.) *Woodworking techniques before AD 1500. Papers presented to a symposium at Greenwich in September, 1980,* 263–99.

Wallace, P.F. 1985 The archaeology of Anglo-Norman Dublin. In H.B. Clarke and a. Simms, (eds) *The comparative history of urban origins in non-Roman Europe.* Oxford, 379–410.

Walsh, C. 1997 *Archaeological excavations at Patrick Street, Nicholas Street and Winetavern Street, Dublin.* Dingle.

Walton, P. 1988 Caulking, cordage and textiles. In *The origins of the Newcastle quayside, Newcastle,* 78–91.

Warburton, J., Whitelaw, J. and Walsh, R. 1818 *History of the city of Dublin,* London.

Ward-Perkins 1967. *Medieval catalogue – London Museum.* 2nd. ed.. London.

Watt, S.L. and Rahtz, P.A. 1983 The finds. In S.M. Hurst and S.M. Wright (eds) *Bordesley abbey II.* B.A.R. Brit. Ser. 111, 129–206.

Went, A.E.J. 1990 Fisheries of the river Liffey. In H.B. Clarke (ed.) *Medieval Dublin. The living city.* Dublin, 182–91.

Wheeler, A. and Jones, A.K.G. 1976 Fish remains. In A. Rogerson (ed.) *Excavations on Fullers Hill, Great Yarmouth.* Sheffield.

White, N.B. ed. 1943 *Extents of Irish monastic possessions, 1540–1541,* Dublin.

Williams, J.H. 1979 *St Peter's Street Northampton, Excavations, 1973–1976.* Northampton.

Wincott Heckett, E. 1990. The textiles. In M. Hurley Excavations at Grand Parade Cork II part 2. *Jn. Cork Hist. & Arch. Soc.,* 95, 81–86.

Wincott Heckett, E. forthcoming. Textiles, animal hair and yarn from a Viking pit, High Street, Dublin'.

Wren, J, 1987 The medieval crested tiles from urban sites in Leinster. Unpublished M.A. Thesis, N.U.I.

Wren, J. 1997 The roof tiles. In C. Walsh, *Archaeological excavations at Patrick Street, Nicholas Street and Winetavern Street, Dublin.* Dingle.

Wren, J. forthcoming (a). The roof tiles. In A. Lynch. Excavations at Tintern Abbey, Co. Wexford.

Wren, J. forthcoming (b). The roof tiles. In A. Lynch and C. Manning Excavations at Dublin Castle.

St Patrick's cathedral, Dublin, and its prebendal churches: gothic architectural relationships

MICHAEL O'NEILL

This study attempts to analyse the influence of St Patrick's cathedral on the architecture of the parish churches with which it had a tithing relationship. The prebendal income of the secular canons in St Patrick's was derived mainly from the tithes of parishes impropriated to them. In return for the tithes, the canons were responsible for employing a vicar in the parish to provide cure of souls, saying mass on Sundays and feast days, and the provision of the other sacraments.[1] What will be studied here is whether, by architectural patronage on behalf of the canons, or by a more general association, the parish churches show any sign of architectural influence deriving from the cathedral.

In the parishes impropriated to St Patrick's, the canons, like other impropriators, were responsible for the upkeep of the chancels of the churches in those parishes.[2] Visitations were generally carried out on a tri-annual basis in the medieval period, and, in the case of St Patrick's, Monck Mason recorded the mechanics of two visitations. In 1304, the archbishop reserved the privileges granted by his predecessors to the dean and chapter, and particularly the exemption of their prebendal churches from visitations of the archdeacon or dean. The dean and chapter were required to appoint some out of their canons or other priests, to examine the conditions of the chancels of those churches and the conduct of the ministers officiating there, and report to the chapter if anything should be wanting in the necessary repair of buildings, ornaments or books, or defective in their ministers. He further stipulated that fines might be levied for defects; they were, however, to be appropriated solely to sustention of the fabric of the cathedral.[3] In 1468, during a visitation of the

1 Henry A. Jefferies, *Priests and prelates of Armagh in the age of reformations, 1518–1558* (Dublin, 1997), 28–32. 2 This division of responsibilities is made explicit in the legislation of the provincial council of Cashel in 1453. This is printed in D. Wilkins (ed.), *Concilia Magnae Britanniae et Hiberniae A.D. 446–1717* (London, 1737), vol. 3, 565 *et seq.* Some of the statutes are translated in J. Begley, *The diocese of Limerick* (Dublin, 1906), I, 289–94. See also Michael A.J. Burrows, 'Fifteenth-century Irish provincial legislation and pastoral care', in W.J. Sheils and Diana Wood (eds), *The churches, Ireland and the Irish*, Studies in Church History, vol. 25 (Oxford, 1989), 55–67. 3 William Monck Mason, *The history and antiquities of the collegiate church of St Patrick near Dublin* (Dublin, 1820), 116.

chapter-house by Archbishop Michael Tregury, the dean reported that he had visited the canons, petty canons and vicars choral; that all the prebends were visited except those which lay in the Irish territory, or on the marches of the Pale, so that he dared not visit them on account of the war in those parts; and, except, also, Howth and Malahide.[4]

Another piece of evidence is from the very end of the period under review. In the inquisition held upon the dissolution of the cathedral on 27 January 1547, we learn that the total value of the deanery (including tithes, etc. from Clondalkin, Esker, Rathcoole and Tallaght) amounted to £246 9s. 9d., from which only £6 was deducted for repair of chancels. Thus, less than 3% of the income was required for structural and other repair work in these parish churches.[5] This indicates that these particular buildings were in good repair in the mid-sixteenth century. The situation had changed considerably within the century that followed. In Archbishop Bulkeley's report of his visitation of Dublin in 1630 he noted that Clondalkin parish church was indifferently repaired, Esker was altogether ruinous, Rathcoole church was in good repair, the chancel was not mentioned so it may have been out of repair, and in Tallaght the church and chancel were in good repair and 'decent'.[6]

One explicit instance of architectural patronage is recorded in 1502. Thomas Rochfort, precentor (elected dean in 1505), being, by right of his dignity, possessed of half the prebend of Lusk, made a donation on 8 April 1502 to that church of a large table of alabaster, to serve for the high altar, with three images, one of the Saviour, placed in the middle, with St Maculin, the patron saint of Lusk, on the right hand, and St Patrick on the left.[7] This suggests that a major reordering of the chancel interior took place at this date.

The medieval parish churches associated with St Patrick's, like the vast majority of medieval parish churches in Ireland, have fared very badly. The majority are now in ruins with most of the cut-stone details of windows and doors missing. Some medieval fabric survives at Aderrig, Artane, Baldongan, Balrothery, Crumlin, Esker, Finglas, Kilmactalway, Lusk, Malahide, Maynooth, Mulhuddart, Newcastle Lyons, St Audeon's, St Brigid's (The Ward), St Margaret's, Swords, and Tallaght.[8] Of these, only the medieval naves of Newcastle Lyons and St Audeon's remain in use. The medieval towers at

4 Monck Mason, *Collegiate church of St Patrick*, 136.   5 Monck Mason, *Collegiate church of St Patrick*, 26–31.   6 M.V. Ronan, 'Archbishop Bulkeley's visitation of Dublin, 1630', *Archivium Hibernicum* (1941), 71–3.   7 Monck Mason, *Collegiate church of St Patrick*, 142 (Obits of Luske, TCD MS E.3.10).   8 Baldongan, Balrothery, Finglas, Lusk, Malahide and Swords are discussed by Mary McMahon, *Medieval church sites of North Dublin: a heritage trail* (Dublin, 1991). Aderrig, Crumlin, Esker, Kilmactalway, Newcastle and Tallaght are discussed by Máirín Ní Mharcaigh, 'The medieval parish churches of south-west County Dublin', *RIA Proc.*, 97C, 5 (1997), 245–96. Finglas and St Margaret's are discussed by Michael Brown, Majella McLoughlin, Moira Cassidy and Dara Larkin in *Finglas through the ages* (Dublin, 1991), 35–8.

Plate 1 St Patrick's cathedral. View of Nave and choir (National Library of Ireland)

Crumlin, Lusk, Maynooth, Swords, and Tallaght, are incorporated into or stand near the site of parish churches rebuilt in the eighteenth and nineteenth centuries.

Even a cursory glance at the architecture of these buildings will reveal that the majority have later medieval features and raises the question of what architectural relationship they could have to St Patrick's cathedral. There, the main fabric of the building dates to *c.*1225–55 which includes the choir, transepts and nave (plate 1). Between *c.*1262 and *c.*1270 the eastern bays of the cathedral were remodelled with the addition of a two-bay aisled retrochoir and a two-bay aisled Lady Chapel.[9] The thirteenth-century architecture is most closely related to other buildings of cathedral rank, particularly with

9 The medieval architecture of St Patrick's is discussed by J.H. Bernard, *The cathedral church of Saint Patrick* (London, 1903); Michael O'Neill, 'Design sources for St Patrick's cathedral, Dublin, and its relationship to Christ Church cathedral', *RIA Proc.*, 100C, 6, (2000) 207–56; Edwin C. Rae, 'The medieval fabric of the cathedral church of St Patrick in Dublin', *RSAI Jn.*, 109 (1979), 29–73; Roger Stalley, 'Irish Gothic and English Fashion', in James Lydon (ed.), *The English in medieval Ireland: proceedings of the first joint meeting of the Royal Irish Academy and the British Academy* (Dublin, 1982).

Plate 2 St Patrick's cathedral, nave (J. Cruise, National Gallery of Ireland).

Plate 3 Newtown Trim, Co. Meath. Elevation of west bay of nave.

nearly Christ Church cathedral.[10] The two-tier nave elevation (incorrectly restored as a three-storey elevation in the nineteenth century) may have influenced the upper nave elevation of Newtown Trim cathedral in County Meath (plates 2, 3).[11] The west elevation there, with the thirteenth-century door (the square-headed west window is a later insertion) and the clasping buttresses at the corners, may also have echoed the original west front (excluding the aisles) of St Patrick's cathedral, presumably similar to the north transept elevation as recorded in 1739 (plate 9).

It is difficult to find influences from St Patrick's on other nearby parish church buildings of this period. This situation is in marked contrast to the south of the country where there was a distinct school of architecture operating in the mid-thirteenth century. There, a common stock of architectural features is found in the Cistercian monastery at Graiguenamanagh, St Mary's parish church in New Ross, Cashel cathedral, St Mary's parish church in Youghal, and Cloyne cathedral.[12] The two parish churches mentioned above are located in important walled port towns of the medieval period, and it is difficult to avoid the impression that they were deliberately built to be large and impressive buildings. They have good cut-stone details, particularly in the rear arches of windows and door surrounds, and in features such as pisciane and aumbries. Even here, however, the elaborate foliate capitals and deeply moulded soffit roll bundles articulating the arcades and the elaborate choir and nave elevations of St Patrick's and Christ Church cathedral are absent.

However, apart from the financial inability or lack of desire to emulate the expensive details of cathedral architecture in the parish churches associated with St Patrick's, there may be another underlying factor. One aspect of the building history of St Patrick's is instructive in this regard. Following the foundation of the collegiate establishment in 1191, and the subsequent development of the secular chapter explicitly on the model of Salisbury cathedral after 1216 if not before, to include the offices of dean, precentor, chancellor and treasurer, the old parish church of St Patrick's in Insula continued to be used.[13] It is likely that it was the elevation of St Patrick's

10 The most recent discussion of the architecture of Christ Church cathedral is by Roger Stalley in Kenneth Milne (ed.), *Christ Church cathedral, Dublin: a history* (Dublin, 2000), 53–74, 95–128, 218–36, 353–73.   11 Richard de la Corner was bishop of Meath in the middle decades of the thirteenth century. He had formerly been a secular canon in St Patrick's cathedral.   12 Graiguenamanagh is discussed in Roger Stalley, *The Cistercian monasteries of Ireland* (London and New Haven, 1987), 99–103 and passim; St Mary's New Ross in Roger Stalley, *Architecture and sculpture in Ireland, 1150–1350* (Dublin, 1971), 81–3; Cashel cathedral in Colm Hourihane, *Gothic art in Ireland, 1169–1550: enduring vitality* (London, 2003), 35–64; St Mary's, Youghal in Rev. Samuel Hayman, 'The ecclesiastical antiquities of Youghal. No. 1: St Mary's collegiate church', *Proceedings and Transactions of the Kilkenny and South-East of Ireland Archaeological Society*, 3 (1854–5), 96–119. Both St Mary's in Youghal and Cloyne cathedral deserve a modern study.   13 White, *Dignitas Decani*, no. 2; Aubrey Gwynn, 'Henry of London, archbishop of Dublin', *Studies* (1949),

chapter to cathedral rank that prompted the building campaign from *c.*1225 onwards. Two cathedrals in one diocese, one secular and one regular, were also found at Wells and Bath, Lichfield and Coventry and at Canterbury. The rivalry between the cathedral chapters in Dublin has been discussed by Geoffrey Hand,[14] and the architectural competition that ensued between the two cathedrals throughout the thirteenth century has been discussed by me.[15]

The fact that the canons were apparently satisfied to use the pre-Norman parish church of St Patrick's in Insula for more than thirty-five years may be symptomatic of an underlying phenomenon–that in many cases the church buildings also found on the newly created manors (be they episcopal or otherwise) continued to be used, and some at least were only substantially rebuilt in the fourteenth and fifteenth centuries. Late twelfth to mid thirteenth-century details are rare enough in the medieval parish churches in the Pale, where the intensive settlement by the Anglo-Normans and their role in parish formation would make one expect to find buildings of this date. And where one does find details from this period, there are invariably later medieval additions to the churches (for example, at Cruicetown, Ardsallagh and Ballygarth in County Meath), which indicates that the late-medieval building campaigns did not necessarily sweep away earlier Anglo-Norman structures. This apparent continuity of use of the inherited church buildings may go some way to explain the lack of influence of the thirteenth-century cathedral on the prebendal churches as much as the prohibitive cost of elaborate elevations or cut-stone embellishment in the churches.

Unlike the ruined parish churches enumerated above, which are fossilised, so to speak, in their late-medieval form, St Patrick's cathedral continues to be used, and later medieval additions, particularly window tracery, were 'returned' to their thirteenth-century form during two major restoration campaigns in the mid-nineteenth century.[16] Fortunately, physical evidence in the building from the later fourteenth century onwards, combined with documentary evidence, eighteenth- and early nineteenth-century views, and important pre-restoration plans and elevations, can be used to evaluate the later work on the cathedral, some of which was destroyed in the nineteenth century.[17] On the

295–304, at p. 279; H.J. Lawlor, *Fasti,* 2–5; H.S. Sweetman, (ed.), *Calendar of documents relating to Ireland, 1171–1307,* 5 vols (London, 1875–86), i, 189. The offices of precentor, chancellor and treasurer were constituted in 1214, the office of dean not until 1220–1, when the archbishop nominated his own nephew, Master William fitz Guido (*Dignitas decani,* no. 3; *Fasti,* 39). **14** Geoffrey Hand, 'The rivalry of the cathedral chapters in medieval Dublin', *RSAI Jn.,* 92 (1962), 193–206. **15** Michael O'Neill, 'Design sources', 221–7. **16** Michael O'Neill, '*Marks of unheeded dilapidation': the nineteenth and early twentieth century restorations.* St Patrick's cathedral 800 Series, no. 3 (Dublin, 1991), and in 'St Patrick's cathedral in Dublin and its place in the history of Irish medieval architecture' (unpublished Ph.D. thesis, University of Dublin, 1995), chap. 2. **17** These include drawings of the north, south and west elevations by J. Blaymires dating to 1739; a series of elevations by the architect John Bowden dating to 1820; and the important detailed elevations of the north, south and west elevations drawn by Richard Cromwell Carpenter in 1845 prior to his planned restoration.

basis of this evidence it will be possible to argue that this later work had a significant influence on the architecture of the later parish churches in the Pale.

According to Grace's annals, in 1362 there was an accidental fire in St Patrick's caused by John the Sexton.[18] In 1363 a petition from Archbishop Minot sought aid for 'the repair of the church of St Patrick, Dublin, which by negligence and fire has so greatly suffered that the tower and bells are destroyed',[19] and the petition was granted before the year was out. According to Sir James Ware, 'Minot repaired part of St Patrick's church, which had been destroyed by an accidental fire; and built a very high steeple of hewed stone about the year 1370'.[20] Minot used as his seal the device of a bishop holding a steeple in his hand. He was archbishop from 1363 to 1375, so we can assume that Minot's tower was completed in this period. Ware records a rather bizarre detail. He says that in 1367, after the burning of St Patrick's church, sixty 'idle and straggling fellows' were taken up, and obliged to assist in repairing the church and building the steeple, and they were subsequently banished out of the diocese in 1376.[21]

A third document may also relate to the building. A 1394 entry in the papal registers refers to those who would 'give alms for the repair of the church of Dublin, whose bell-tower has fallen and thrown down a great part of the church'.[22] Edwin Rae argued that this entry cannot be a belated answer to Minot's petition of 1363 as that request was granted.[23] The entry raises two further problems. Firstly, unlike the earlier petition, it is not specifically related to St Patrick's, but rather to 'the church of Dublin'. If it in fact relates to Christ Church cathedral, there is no archaeological or other documentary evidence to support such a catastrophe as having taken place in that building. The tower is over the crossing there and, had it fallen, one would expect to find some evidence of this collapse either in the transepts or the nave or in views of the long choir.[24] At St Patrick's, on the other hand, where the tower is at the northwest end of the cathedral, there is significant remodelling of the four western bays of the north nave arcade, and the west front has been substantially remodelled when compared to the elevation of the north transept gable as recorded by Blaymires, which shows essentially a thirteenth-century gable elevation (plate 9). If 'the church of Dublin' referred to in the 1394

These are all now housed in the Representative Church Body Library in Breamor Park, Churchtown, Dublin 14.   18 Richard Butler (ed.), *Jacobi Grace, Kilkenniensis, Annales Hiberniae* (Dublin, 1842), 152.   19 W.H. Bliss (ed.), *Calendar of entries in the papal registers elating to Great Britain and Ireland. Petitions to the pope. Vol. I, AD 1342–1419* (London, 1896), 467.   20 Sir James Ware, *The whole works of Sir James Ware concerning Ireland. Revised and updated (by Walter Harris)* (Dublin, 1739), 333.   21 Ware, *The whole works*, 333.   22 W.H. Bliss and J.A. Twemlow (eds), *Calendar of entries in the papal registers relating to Great Britain and Ireland. Papal letters. Vol. IV, AD 1362–1404* (London, 1902), 506.   23 Rae, 'The medieval fabric', 65.   24 I wish to thank Mr Stuart Kinsella for discussing this problem with me.

Plate 4 St Patrick's cathedral. Exterior north nave elevation (R.C. Carpenter, 1845. RCB Library).

entry refers to a cathedral in Dublin, then St Patrick's cathedral must be the more likely candidate, even though it suggests, if we follow Ware, that part of the tower repaired by Minot *c.*1370 collapsed in less than thirty years.

The treatment of the four western bays on the north nave elevation are different from those further east and there are some obvious differences between them (plate 10). While the eastern pair of arches spring from a higher level than the three bays to the east, they are under the string course which divides the arcade from the upper elevation. Secondly, the piers are aligned with the opposite pair on the south elevation. In contrast, the final two bays spring from a slightly higher level, forcing the string course over the arcade to step up over these bays. These bays are also wider than those to the east, the western pier is not aligned with that on the opposite elevation, and there is a deep respond against the west wall. However, it is important not to overstate these differences. The treatment of the arch soffits of the four bays is practically identical, and the piers may well be aligned with the foundations of the thirteenth-century ones they replace. It seems clear from the 1363 document that a bell-tower already

Plate 5 Bristol Cathedral. Lady Chapel windows, (after J. Bony).

existed on the site and the curious misalignment of Minot's tower may reflect the existing orientation of the previous structure.

Turning to the exterior, as recorded on Carpenter's invaluable pre-restoration elevations, what is most striking is the variety of the window forms of the nave and Minot's tower (plates 4, 6, 7). Five different window forms are recorded. These include two thirteenth-century lancet forms, those at clerestory level with colonettes rising from bases and moulded capitals supporting the outer order in the eastern bays of the nave and the narrow tall plain lancet at aisle level nearest the tower. A third form was found at clerestory level lighting the fifth and sixth bay of the nave, that is, over the eastern pair of the remodelled arcade arches discussed above. This tracery form also lit the ground floor of Minot's tower. These windows are of two lights with Y-tracery in their heads with elongated trefoil cusping in the head of each light. The spandrel between the lights is uncusped and a form of dog-tooth decorates the jambs and continues around the pointed heads of the two clerestory lights.[25] The fourth

25 The two western clerestory windows are blocked from view by Minot's tower on all views and elevations known.

Plate 6 St Patrick's cathedral. West Front (R.C. Carpenter, 1845, RCB Library).

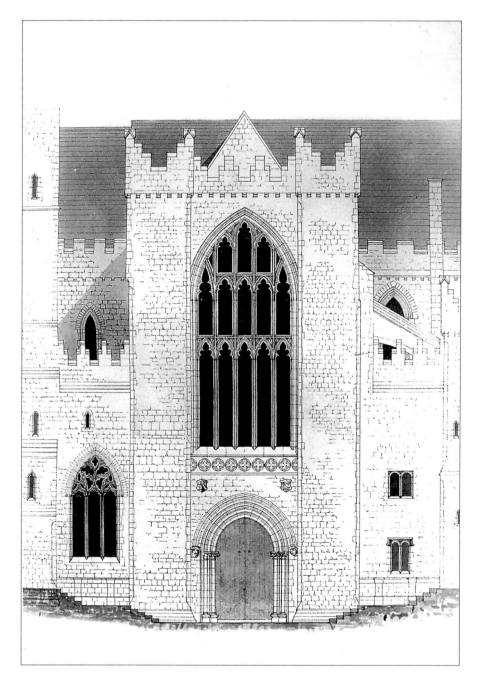

Plate 7 St Patrick's cathedral. West Front (R.C. Carpenter, detail).

Plate 8 St Patrick's cathedral. South elevation of South Transept and Choir (R.C. Carpenter, 1845. RCB Library).

form, which lit both the north and south nave aisles, was less steeply pointed, the cusped pairs of lights were more depressed and there was an elongated quatrefoil in the spandrel above. The jambs were not decorated, in contrast to those at clerestory level. Both these window forms are closely related to the choir aisle windows at Bristol cathedral (plate 5), and a recent study has convincingly re-dated the completion of this work to the 1340s.[26] The fifth window type, in a two light form at belfry level in Minot's tower and in three-light form at the west end of the north aisle, is markedly different (plates 6, 7). The heads of the individual lights below springing level are significantly depressed and have quinfoil cusping with elongated daggers decorating the pointed heads. The spandrel between the lights at belfry stage has an elon-gated quatrefoil, while the three-light nave aisle west window has mouchettes over the lower central light and two elongated daggers under a quatrefoil in the head of the window.

26 Richard K. Morris, 'European prodigy or regional eccentric? The rebuilding of St Augustine's abbey church, Bristol', '*Almost the richest city': Bristol in the middle ages. British Archaeological Association Conference Transactions*, 19 (1997), 41–56.

Attempting to tie in the evidence of the building with the available documentary evidence might suggest the following sequence for work in the nave in the later fourteenth century. The work undertaken by Archbishop Minot from the 1360s onwards, included rebuilding the bell tower, but also apparently the four western bays of the nave. He also remodelled many of the windows in both north and south nave aisles, and at least two of the windows at clerestory level on the north side. These Y-traceried windows found at Bristol *c.*1340 would not seem out of place in Dublin thirty years later. It may be that following the hiatus of the Black Death they were an accessible and reasonably up-to-date source of influence. The fact that these window forms were at clerestory level and also at ground-floor level in Minot's tower would suggest a similar *c.*1370 date for the western nave arcade. However, we cannot discount the possibility that these window forms were introduced after 1394. The details of the nave arcade soffit rolls could as easily date to the 1390s as the 1360s and 1370s, however unattractive the notion might be of the introduction of fifty year-old tracery forms over these arcades. The 1394 document implies extensive damage caused by the collapse of a tower. The turrets articulating the west front of the cathedral and the turreted corners of Minot's tower, both rising to crow-stepped battlements and the similar late curvilinear tracery at belfry level and at the west end of the north aisle seem to point to the later date. In the English West Country, curvilinear tracery had a long afterlife and was found in combination with perpendicular detailing.[27]

It may be that the late fourteenth-century work on the nave and west front was a protracted and under-funded affair. Apart from the income derived from indulgences, it seems that the main source of funding for maintaining the cathedral fabric was from the fines derived from irregularities discovered during visitations, and the level of these fines was apparently capped in the early fourteenth century.[28] Leaving aside the problem of precisely dating the work at St Patrick's, what is readily apparent is that there was an extensive building campaign at St Patrick's in the latter part of the fourteenth century. It is tempting to regard the activity here as the first major architectural campaign undertaken in the region in the aftermath of the Black Death. Indeed it will be argued below that St Patrick's was at the fountainhead of the great rebuilding campaigns undertaken in the Pale which coincided with and were predicated on the economic upturn in the fifteenth century.

Three buildings in County Meath, although having no prebendal relationship with St Patrick's, are clearly indebted architecturally to it. The first is the

---

27 Richard K. Morris, 'Worcester nave: from decorated to perpendicular', *Medieval art and architecture at Worcester cathedral. British Archaeological Association Conference Transactions 1978*, 116–43, 116 and note 1.   **28** Monck Mason, *Collegiate church of St Patrick*, 116. The proxies to be paid were fixed at ten marks, for the cathedral, the prebendal churches and those appropriated to the economy.

Plate 9 St Patrick's cathedral. North elevation (J. Blaymires, 1739. RCB Library).

Yellow Steeple at Trim, which was part of the Augustinian abbey of St Mary's, which is similar to Minot's tower, with turreted corners and having multiple weathered string courses marking the stages of the tower (plates 6, 7, 9, 11). There are slight offsets at each of these stages. The surviving two-light belfry stage window with transom is curiously uncusped and, with the rather pitiable curvilinear pattern in its head, we cannot dismiss the possibility that it is a later insertion.[29] The good-quality limestone split-stone rubble coursing and the surviving square-headed lights indicate a date contemporary with or slightly later than Minot's tower. Leask remarked that the walls of the Yellow Steeple tower are not battered but rise vertically,[30] which is a feature of earlier fourteenth-century towers in the Pale including Ardmulchan and Skreen in County Meath and Swords, Baldongan and Tallaght in County Dublin.

The two other buildings are the Plunkett churches at Killeen and Dunsany. Edwin Rae pointed out the similarity of the turreted west gable at St Patrick's and the treatment of the west ends at both these manorial churches (plate 12).[31] An examination of the better-preserved fabric of Killeen shows that the indebtedness to St Patrick's is far more extensive. The three-light west window

---

29 The coursing over the window is irregular and of smaller rubble blocks than the rest of the build.   **30** Harold Leask, *Irish churches and monastic buildings. Vol. 2, gothic architecture to A.D. 1400* (Dundalk, 1967), 183.   **31** Rae, 'The medieval fabric', 32.

Plate 11 Yellow Steeple, Trim, Co. Meath.

Plate 10a
St Patrick's
cathedral.
Nave elevation,
north side.

Plate 10b
St Patrick's
cathedral.
Nave elevation,
north side.

Plate 12 Dunsany, Co. Meath. West Front.

Plate 13 Killeen, Co. Meath. Chancel, nave and west window.

Plate 14 Killeen, Co. Meath. Nave windows   **Plate 15** St Audeon's nave.

there is almost an exact replica of the west window of the north aisle in St
Patrick's (plates 7, 13). Even though the central light and the head of the
window is damaged it is fairly clear that it also had mouchettes over the
central light, surmounted by two large daggers and a quatrefoil. The two-light
Y-traceried nave windows follow exactly the treatment of the belfry windows
at Minot's tower above the transoms and have the same elongated trefoil in
the spandrel between the lights (plate 14). The quinfoil cusping in the heads
of the two-light window under a square head is similar to the treatment of the
Y-traceried windows below the springing of the head of each light in the
other nave windows.

There were single blind lights under square heads found on Minot's tower
and, again, St Patrick's may be responsible for introducing this perpendicular
style feature of square-headed lights into the parish church architecture of
the Pale. The north and south nave doors are also closely modelled on the
doorway into Minot's Tower from the nave of the cathedral. The crow-
stepped battlements over the choir at Killeen also echo the treatment of the
west gable at St Patrick's. It is practically certain that one or more masons
who worked on Minot's tower and the west front of St Patrick's held a later
commission in Killeen. Killeen was completed by 1445 and is unlikely to have

started before 1403 when Christopher Plunkett became lord of Killeen by right of his wife Joan de Cusack, the last heiress of that line. Plunkett had held the post of vice-deputy in the Dublin administration and it is tempting to see his architectural patronage introducing the latest style from the capital into the general Pale area.

St Audoen's was linked with the cathedral since 1218 when its tithes were appropriated to the treasurer as his 'dignity' in addition to his prebendal income from Clonkeen (Kill-o'-the-Grange). St Audoen's was made a separate prebend in 1467 and half the prebend of Lusk was granted to the treasurer in exchange. The mouldings of the nave arcade soffits are generally similar to those of the western bays in the north nave arcade in St Patrick's (plate 15). The compound pier arcade at St Audoen's is very different to the octagonal plan of the St Patrick arcade piers, but the moulded capitals on the engaged colonettes are apparently not dissimilar to the corbel capitals under the central soffit order in St Patrick's as recorded by Parker.[32] While this might indicate an early fifteenth-century date for this arcade, we have to take cognisance of the fact that a guild or fraternity of St Anne's was founded there in December 1430 by letters patent of King Henry VI, and the fraternity was also empowered to have a chantry of six priests, one in the chapel of St Anne, when built, one in the Lady Chapel, and at four other named altars.[33]

Twin-aisled naves and chancels are surprisingly common in County Dublin in the medieval period. In addition to the fifteenth-century arcade at St Audoen's, there were twin aisles at Balrothery,[34] Clondalkin nave,[35] Finglas, Howth, Lusk, and Swords. The medieval church at Lusk is one of the more unfortunate losses as the east end remained in use until a storm in January 1839 destroyed the roof of the whole building. A description from 1833 depicted it as having two long aisles divided by a range of seven arches, the western ones being blocked up at that time.[36] An earlier description by Austin Cooper, in 1783, stated that the east part of the south aisle only was in use. The blocked arches meant that the whole north aisle was in darkness and was 'a waste, only used as a burial place in the same manner as the churchyard; consequently it is all rubbish, bones, skulls, etc., the church is only preserved entire by a good roof covering the whole'.[37] There are several views of this church, the most valuable being a view of the south elevation from the *Irish Penny Magazine* of 11 May 1833 (plate 16). What is most striking is the

32 John Henry Parker, 'Notes on the architecture of Ireland. St Patrick's Dublin', *The Gentlemen's Magazine*, Jan. 1864, 14–19 and figures.   **33** Henry F. Berry, 'History of the religious guild of S. Anne, in S. Audoen's church, Dublin, 1430–1740, taken from the records in the Haliday Collection', *RIA Proc.*, 25C (1904–5), 21–106, at p. 22. **34** National Library of Ireland, Topographical prints and drawings, ET 1991 TX 1 and 1976 TX 123.   **35** Ní Mharcaigh, 'Churches of south-west County Dublin', 254–5, and plates V, VI.   **36** D'Alton, *History of the county of Dublin*, 414–25, esp. 414–15.   **37** Austin Cooper, quoted in 'Proceedings', *RSAI Jn.*, 4 (1914), 253.

Plate 16 Lusk (*Irish Penny Magazine* 1833)

variety of window forms including Y-tracery under pointed heads, perhaps related to the clerestory windows in St Patrick's nave or those on Minot's tower, and a three-light form under a square head which was very likely similar to a two-light window in Kilsharvan, County Meath (plate 17).[38] It is interesting that a record from 1467 shows that one portion of the tithes of Lusk was appropriated to the precentor of St Patrick's and the other to the treasurer. This may have prompted some rebuilding, culminating in the massive western tower build and the reordering of the chancel in 1503. In 1847 the modern church was built and is attached to the massive late medieval west tower.[39]

A twin-aisled nave and chancel with a fourteenth-century arcade survives at Howth, and it is tempting to assume that this basic plan obtained at Lusk also. Good sixteenth-century windows in limestone survive in the east gable of the north aisle and in the west gable of the south aisle, recessed behind the

38 Du Noyer recorded a similar window form at Bellewstown, County Meath (Royal Irish Academy collection). There was a similar three-light window in the north wall of the chancel at Lusk, recorded in the *Irish Penny Magazine*, no. 19, vol. 1 (11 May 1833), 145. These three locations are very close geographically.   **39** D'Alton, *History of the County of Dublin*, 414–25; Weston St John Joyce, *The Neighbourhood of Dublin*, 3rd edn (Dublin, 1920).

Plate 17
Kilsharvan,
Co. Meath.
Window.

Plate 18
Howth, north
aisle looking
west.

Plate 18a Howth, window at west end
of north aisle.

Plate 19 Newcastle Lyons, Co. Dublin.
Nave window.

massive western gable structure with the triple-stepped belfry over (plate 18).
Unfortunately, the fourteenth-century aisle windows in sandstone have not
survived; one was inserted at a later date over the west gable of the north aisle.
This treatment of the cusping of what survives of this double-light window
echoes the treatment of the clerestory windows in St Patrick's nave (plates 4,
18a). The east window of the south aisle consists of three graduated lancets
under a pointed arch; the simple cusping and the graduated form would
suggest an early fourteenth-century date.

The archdeacon of Glendalough held the tithes of Newcastle Lyons after
1467.[40] The two-light windows of the south side of the nave have more
depressed and rounded heads than those at nave aisle level in St Patrick's
(plate 19). They are, however, similar to the quinfoil cusping under the transoms
of the two-light windows at belfry stage in Minot's tower, and would indicate a
late fourteenth- or early fifteenth-century date for the nave. The ruined chancel
is somewhat later, as indicated by the two-light cusped windows with blank
spandrels between the lights and a square hood mould over. The three-light

---

40 Monck Mason, *Collegiate church of St Patrick*, 136.

Plate 20 Newcastle Lyons,
Co. Dublin. East window.

Plate 21 Killeen, Co. Meath.
East window.

east window of the chancel is now placed at the east end of the nave (plate 20). It is an interesting variation on the west window of the north nave aisle in St Patrick's. At Newcastle Lyons the central light is carried up into the head of the arch and springs from the same level as the outer lights. Elongated quatrefoils are placed in the spandrels over the lights and each of these in turn is surmounted by pairs of mouchettes with a quatrefoil in the apex of the window arch. This is a very accomplished design and we cannot dismiss the possibility that the west window of the nave in St Patrick's had the same tracery design. The east window at Killeen also carried up the central light, but here a form of switch-line tracery is used to decorate the head, and mouchettes are avoided in the tracery design (plate 21). As the chancel fabric was the responsibility of the holder of the tithes, the choice of the design of the east window at Newcastle Lyons may reflect the explicit architectural patronage of a member of the cathedral chapter of St Patrick's.

One curious feature of the west front of St Patrick's, which appears in all views prior to the 1830s, is a single bell-cote apparently with a stepped gable over and some views show a trefoil-headed aperture (plate 22). This would seem to be a totally redundant feature given the presence of a massive bell

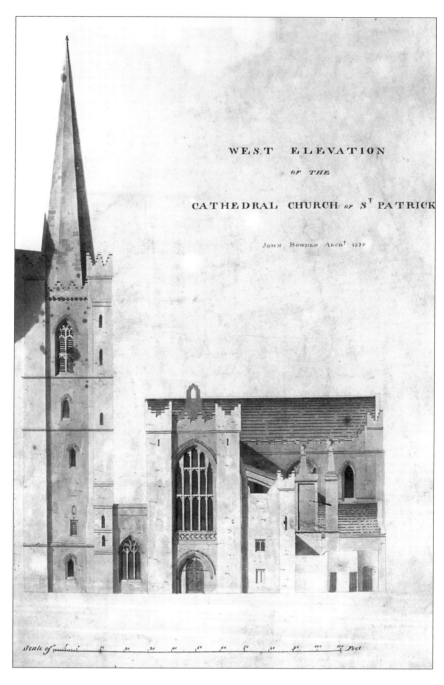

Plate 22 St Patrick's cathedral. West font (J. Bowden, 1820. RCB Library).

Plate 23 Esker,
Co. Dublin.
West front.

tower directly to the north. Monck Mason recorded that in 1443 the dean and chapter wished to erect a large bell in their cathedral, and that they might be enabled to perform this and to execute certain repairs, the archbishop, on 19 November, granted an indulgence of 40 days to all persons who should contribute to those good works.[41] So perhaps Minot's tower did not house a bell or bells before this date, necessitating the bell-cote on the west gable. While such a feature on the west gable of a cathedral seems rather gauche, single, double and treble bell-cotes in a variety of configurations became *de*

41 Ibid., 132.

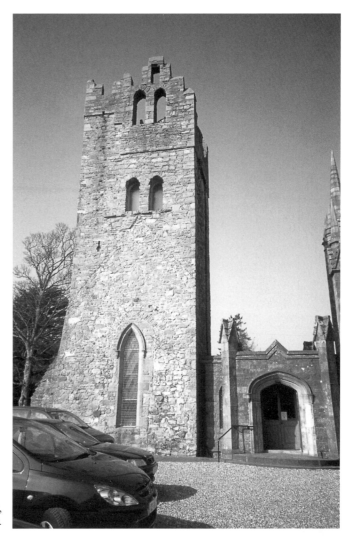

Plate 24 Tallaght,
Co. Dublin. Tower.

rigueur on the west gables of the parish churches in the Pale and beyond
during the fifteenth and sixteenth centuries. The presence of pairs of
buttresses with offsets on the west gables of Esker, Malahide, Mulhuddard
and at Donaghmore in County Meath, with elaborate bell-cotes surviving
over two of these, may ultimately relate back to two features of the west front
of St Patrick's, namely the deeper buttress with multiple offsets against the
stair turret of Minot's tower and the bell-cote over the west gable (plate 23).
Equally odd, perhaps, is the triple bell-cote on the tower at Tallaght (plate 24),
the double or perhaps triple bell-cote at Baldongan and the single bell-cote at
Balrothery, which seem to indicate that these were essentially residential and

Plate 25 Swords, Co. Dublin. Tower.

Plate 26 Lusk, Co. Dublin. Tower.

defensive towers rather than strictly belfry towers. Only those at Swords and the later tower at Lusk give the impression that the belfry stage actually housed bells (plates 25, 26).

A chapel dedicated to St Michael in the nave of St Patrick's cathedral is recorded in 1495.[42] It is likely that the chapel was at the west end of the south nave aisle, where a late medieval two-bay vaulted structure with large ribs supported on dumbbell-type capitals is inserted in the western bays.[43] The round-headed pairs of lights under square heads lighting the areas below and above the lower vault are likely to be of this date (plates 7, 22). Round-headed pairs of lights become popular in the Pale area throughout the sixteenth century (at Ballygarth, Platin and Slane in County Meath, for example). The round-headed lights at ground floor and at belfry level in the massive western tower at Lusk may indicate a similar date for this tower (plates 16, 26). Two bequests for 'the erection of the belfry', recorded in Berry's register of wills dating from 1457 to 1483, would also seem to date the tower to the late fifteenth century or later.[44] Round-headed lights under square heads are also

---

42 Ibid., 9, note i.   43 O'Neill, 'Design sources', 217–18 for a discussion of this feature. 44 Henry F. Berry, *Register of wills and inventories of the diocese of Dublin in the time of Archbishops Tregury and Walton, 1457–1483* (Dublin, 1898), 67, 111 and 126. In 1476 Nicholas Wygth left 6s. 8d. 'for the erection of a belfry at Lusk'; in 1474 Joan Usberne left

Plate 27 St Audeon's. Portlester Chapel from choir.

found in the Portlester Chapel in St Audeon's, indicating an early sixteenth-century or later remodelling of a chapel apparently built in 1455 (plate 27).

The final window form to be discussed lit the third bay of the south aisle of the choir. It had a pair of round-headed uncusped lights with super-mullions under a pointed head (plate 8). A similar two-light window was recorded by Grose at Macetown, County Meath and a three-light version survives in the east gable of Malahide chancel (plate 28). The 1547 inquisition at the dissolution of the cathedral records that the chancel at Malahide had been recently repaired which might indicate a mid-sixteenth century date for the window.[45] Macetown was in repair in 1622,[46] but was in ruin by 1685,[47] and

20d 'for the erection of a belfry at Lusk'. Contrast this with Robert Walsh who left 2s. 8d. 'to the works of the belfry of Swords', which implies that the belfry there already existed. **45** Monck Mason, *Collegiate church of St Patrick*, 79: 'repairing of the chancel, defrayed by the farmer'. **46** C.E. Elrington and J.H. Todd (eds), *The whole works of … James Ussher*, 17 vols (Dublin, 1847–64), vol. 1, Appendix V, 'A certificate of the state and revenues of the bishoppricke of Meath and Clonemackenosh', li–cxxv. **47** C.C. Ellison, 'Bishop Dopping's visitation book 1682–1685', *Ríocht na Midhe*, v, no. 1 (1971), 28–39; v, no. 2 (1972), 3–13; v, no. 3 (1973), 3–11; v, no. 4 (1974), 98–103; v, no. 5 (1975), 3–13. Philippe Loupes, 'Bishop Dopping's visitation of the diocese of Meath 1693', *Studia Hibernica*, 24 (1984–8), 127–51.

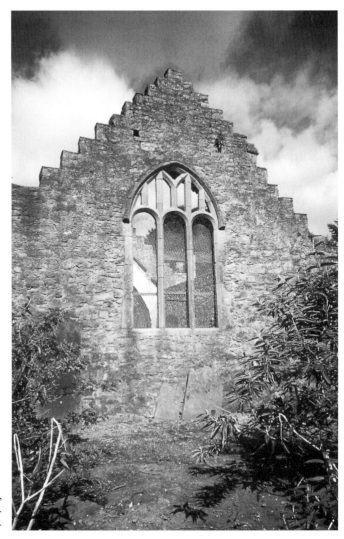

Plate 28 Malahide,
Co. Dublin.
East window.

Malahide was reported to be ruinous in 1630.[48] The likelihood is that these windows date to the first half of the sixteenth century but a late sixteenth- or early seventeenth-century date cannot be excluded.

In conclusion, it seems apparent that work undertaken at St Patrick's cathedral from the late fourteenth century onwards significantly influenced fifteenth-century parish church-building in the Pale, particularly window tracery design and elements derived from the massing of the west gable and Minot's tower. Sixteenth-century window forms are also apparently copied

48 M.V. Ronan, 'Archbishop Bulkeley's visitation of Dublin, 1630', *Archivium Hibernicum* (1941), 67–8.

from the cathedral. It is the fortuitous survival of the Carpenter pre-restoration elevations in combination with an analysis of the standing fabric that confirms the importance of St Patrick's for understanding aspects of late Gothic architecture in the Pale. Had any of the later medieval fabric at St Mary's Cistercian abbey and other regular institutions in Dublin survived, the analysis outlined above might have to be modified. Having entered that caveat, St Patrick's would appear to have been at the head of one stream of architectural influence in the Pale throughout the fifteenth century and into the next.

ACKNOWLEDGEMENTS

I wish to thank Dr Seán Duffy for the opportunity to present a version of this paper to the Friends of Medieval Dublin Symposium in May 2003.

BIBLIOGRAPHY

Bernard, J.H. 1903 *The cathedral church of St Patrick, Dublin*. London.
Berry, H.F. (ed.) 1898 *Register of wills and inventories of the diocese of Dublin in the time of Archbishops Tregury and Walton, 1457–1483*. Dublin.
Bliss, W.H. (ed.) 1896 *Calendar of entries in the papal registers relating to Great Britain and Ireland. Petitions to the pope. Vol. I, AD 1342–1419*. London.
Bliss, W.H. and Twemlow, J.A. (eds) 1902 *Calendar of entries in the papal registers relating to Great Britain and Ireland. Papal Letters Vol. IV, AD 1362–1404*. London.
Butler, R. (ed.) 1842 *Jacobi Grace, Kilkenniensis, Annales Hiberniae*. Dublin.
D'Alton, J. 1838 *The history of the county of Dublin*. Dublin.
Gwynn, A. 1949 Henry of London, archbishop of Dublin. In *Studies*, 295–304.
Hand, G. 1962 The rivalry of the cathedral chapters in medieval Dublin. In *RSAI Jn.*, 92, 193–206.
—1964 The medieval chapters of St Patrick's cathedral, Dublin. 1. The early period (*c*.1219–*c*.1279). In *Reportorium Novum*, 3, no. 2, 229–48.
Harbison, P. 1975 *Guide to the national monuments in the Republic of Ireland, including a selection of other monuments not in state care*. Dublin.
—2000 *Cooper's Ireland: drawings and notes from an eighteenth-century gentleman*. Dublin.
Hayman, S. 1854–55 The ecclesiastical antiquities of Youghal. No. 1: St Mary's collegiate church. *Proceedings and Transactions of the Kilkenny and South-East of Ireland Archaeological Society*, 3, 96–119.
Hourihane, C. 2000 *The mason and his mark: masons' marks in the medieval Irish archbishoprics of Cashel and Dublin*. Oxford.
—2003 *Gothic art in Ireland, 1169–1550: enduring vitality*. London.
Joyce, W. St J. 1920 *The neighbourhood of Dublin*. Dublin.
Lawlor, H.J. 1930 *The fasti of St Patrick's cathedral, Dublin*. Dublin.
Leask, H.G. 1967 *Irish churches and monastic buildings. Vol.2, gothic architecture to A.D. 1400*. Dundalk.
—1960 *Irish monastic buildings. Vol.3, medieval gothic and last phases*. Dundalk.
McMahon, M. 1991 *Medieval church sites of North Dublin. A heritage trail*. Dublin.

Monck Mason, W. 1820 *The history and antiquities of the collegiate church of St Patrick near Dublin,* Dublin.

Morris, R.K. 1978 Worcester nave: from decorated to perpendicular. In *Medieval art and architecture at Worcester cathedral. British Archaeological Association Conference Transactions 1978,* 116–143.

—1997 European prodigy or regional eccentric? The rebuilding of St Augustine's abbey church, Bristol. In *'Almost the richest city': Bristol in the middle ages. British Archaeological Association Conference Transactions,* 19, 41–56.

Ní Mharcaigh, M. 1997 The medieval parish churches of south-west County Dublin. In *RIA Proc.,* 97C, 5, 245–296.

O'Neill, M. 1991 *'Marks of unheeded dilapidation': the nineteenth and early twentieth century restorations.* St Patrick's cathedral 800 Series, No. 3. Dublin.

—2000 Design sources for St Patrick's cathedral, Dublin, and its relationship to Christ Church cathedral. In *RIA Proc.,* 100C, 6, 207–256.

Rae, E.C. 1979 The medieval fabric of the cathedral church of St Patrick in Dublin. In *RSAI Jn.,* 109, 29–73.

Ronan, M.V. 1941 Royal visitation of Dublin. In *Archivium Hibernicum,* 1941, 1–55.

—1941 Archbishop Bulkeley's visitation of Dublin, 1630. In *Archivium Hibernicum,* 1941, 56–98.

Stalley, R. 1971 *Architecture and sculpture in Ireland, 1150–1350.* Dublin.

—1987 *The Cistercian monasteries of Ireland: an account of the history, art and architecture of the white monks in Ireland from 1142 to 1540.* London and New Haven.

White, N.B. 1957 *The 'Dignitas Decani' of St Patrick's cathedral Dublin.* Irish Manuscripts Commission. Dublin.

God's Jesters and the festive culture of
medieval Ireland

ALAN J. FLETCHER

I

This essay has an interrelated, twofold purpose, and, necessarily, it will work by inference. It will present a Latin text that in the field of literary studies is known imperfectly, and that in the field of historical studies is hardly known at all, in order that it may exemplify an aspect of the festive culture of medieval Ireland that has largely been forgotten, and thus help to reinstate it in scholarly consciousness.[1] More particularly, since that culture was also arguably medieval Dublin's, the value of the text for supplementing our depleted understanding of the festive culture of the capital in the medieval period deserves wider recognition – hence its relevance to the concerns of the present volume.[2]

When the last of the great regular clerical orders, those of the friars, were sanctioned by the medieval church early in the thirteenth century, it was not very long after that Dublin started acquiring its first houses of mendicants. The Dominicans arrived in 1224, when they also settled in Drogheda, and soon they pushed out into the rest of the country, founding a house at Kilkenny in 1225, and another at Waterford in 1226.[3] The arrival of the Franciscans, though less clearly documented, may have been by a similar route, for while their earliest house has traditionally been held to have been that in Youghal, co. Cork, some doubt has been cast upon this tradition, and it is conceivable that they, too, arrived in Ireland through Dublin. Whatever the truth of that, it is nevertheless undisputable that Dublin was home to one of their earliest houses.[4]

1 The text has been most recently published by Paul Lehmann, *Parodie im mittelalter*, 2nd edn (Stuttgart: Hiersemann, 1963), pp 233–41, but this edition is deficient in a number of respects, and is not in fact new, but an (unacknowledged) reissue with minor adjustments of the nineteenth-century *editio princeps* of Thomas Wright and J. O. Halliwell (eds), *Reliquiæ antiquæ: scraps from ancient manuscripts, illustrating chiefly early English literature and the English language*, 2 vols (London: John Russell Smith, 1845), ii, 208ff.   2 For a corpus of material pertinent to early Dublin festive culture (between *c*.1157 and the death of King Henry VIII in 1547), see Alan J. Fletcher, *Drama and the performing arts in pre-Cromwellian Ireland: a repertory of sources and documents from the earliest times until c.1642* (Cambridge: Brewer, 2001), pp 220–38.   3 Aubrey Gwynn and R. Neville Hadcock, *Medieval religious houses: Ireland* (London: Longman, 1970; repr. Dublin, 1988), pp 218–19.   4 Francis J. Cotter, *The friars minor in Ireland from their arrival to 1400*, Franciscan Institute Publications, History Series 7 (New York: St Bonaventure University, 1994), pp 14–17.

In the case of those mendicant orders commissioned a little later in the thirteenth century and subsequent to the Dominican and Franciscan, the Carmelite order established its earliest Irish house at Leighlinbridge, co. Carlow, between 1265 and 1272, but its Dublin one followed very soon after 1274 (Drogheda's Carmelite house, not surprisingly, was again a near contemporary with Dublin's), and the first documentary evidence for an Irish house of Augustinian friars, in 1282, comes again from Dublin.[5] A less well-known order, the friars of the Sack, founded but one house in Ireland, in 1268, but once more it was in Dublin that it was established.[6]

As might be expected, then, the chief pattern of entry into Ireland for this new clerical regime of preachers and evangelists was from the east, through the port of Dublin, making Dublin a confluence-point of mendicant immigration and tradition. But additionally, no matter what conventual house they were usually attached to, friars were customarily peripatetic, and thus Dublin, as well as having intrinsic importance as the prime entry destination of the mendicant orders into the country, is likely to have been regularly visited by friars who were not otherwise normally based there. Indeed, interesting documentary evidence survives of friar mobility between the Irish provinces in the thirteenth century that begs for further study.[7] It was the tradition of the mendicant orders that their members travel on preaching tours, and they normally did so in pairs. This peripatetic aspect of their ministry also finds its corollary in the physical dimensions of many of the books that they produced. Characteristically, friars' books were of a small, portable format ideally suited to their owners' life on the road and to the needs of travelling light. A few medieval Irish examples survive of mendicant books that conform to this typical requirement of portability.[8] In company with these books is the manuscript containing the text with which this essay is concerned.

London, British Library, MS Harley 913, an eminently portable codex, is a trilingual anthology of texts in Hiberno-English, French, and Latin, that was compiled and copied, probably by one man, about 1330.[9] He was almost certainly a Franciscan, since some of the content of his manuscript is best explained as indicating compilation under Franciscan auspices.[10] Although, as

---

5 See Gwynn and Hadcock, *Medieval religious houses*, pp 282–92 and pp 293–305 respectively.   6 See Gwynn and Hadcock, *Medieval religious houses*, p. 306.   7 Compare, for example, the mobility of the thirteenth-century Friar Tomás Ó Cuinn, briefly noted in Alan J. Fletcher, 'Preaching in late-medieval Ireland: the English and the Latin tradition', in Alan J. Fletcher and Raymond Gillespie (eds), *Irish preaching, 700–1700* (Dublin: Four Courts Press, 2001), pp 56–80; see p. 56. (A new study of the history of the mendicant orders in Ireland, which will include consideration of mendicant mobility, is in preparation by Dr Colmán Ó Clabaigh, OSB.)   8 On friars' books of portable format, see David L. d'Avray, *The preaching of the friars: sermons diffused from Paris before 1300* (Oxford: Clarendon, 1985), pp 57–62; and for a survey of similar manuscripts produced in Ireland, see Fletcher, 'Preaching in late-medieval Ireland'.   9 See Michael Benskin, 'The hands of the Kildare poems manuscript', *Irish University Review*, 20 (1990), 163–93.   10 See, on its

Michael Benskin has argued, the likelihood is that the linguistic complexion of his written Hiberno-English locates in the Waterford area, this ought not deter us from regarding at least some of his anthology's content as a barometer of mendicant taste generally in the island at this date, including that taste as it would likewise have been manifest in Dublin, and for precisely the reasons outlined at the beginning of this essay: Dublin was the confluence-point of mendicant immigration and tradition, where some of the concerns and interests witnessed in Harley 913 would similarly have been current. Indeed, while some of the content of Harley 913 responded to topicalities within the Waterford area and whose relevance might therefore be thought to have been primarily local,[11] other of its materials would have given the collection a more broadly national appeal.[12] There was material in Harley 913 that would have interested any friar, no matter where in the country he was. Some of the manuscript's content also makes it clear that, had it not been for the sort of commerce between the friars of the Irish Franciscan custodies that was mentioned above, the compilation as we have it could never have been assembled. For example, one of its poems, close enough to Dublin by virtue of its author's provenance, is attributed to a certain Friar Michael of Kildare. (Indeed, Benskin's studies have clarified and demonstrated the extensiveness of the co. Kildare affiliation of some of the material in this manuscript, notwithstanding its probable assembly further to the south, in or around Waterford.)[13] So it seems reasonable to characterise Harley 913 as a compilation in which are found materials answering now to local, now to national, mendicant interests; they answered in the first place to those of the compiler, no doubt, but sometimes also to those of members of his order generally throughout Ireland.[14]

Further, there is reason to consider certain of the interests catered for in Harley 913 as indicative of mendicant taste at large and on an international scale, in as much as they chime with some of the foundational values of the

construction, Angela M. and Peter J. Lucas, 'Reconstructing a disarranged manuscript: the case of MS Harley 913, a medieval Hiberno-English miscellany', *Scriptorium*, 44 (1990), 286–99 (a small adjustment to their analysis is entered by Neil Cartlidge, 'Festivity, order, and community in fourteenth-century Ireland: the composition and contexts of BL MS Harley 913', *The Yearbook of English Studies*, 33 (2003), 33–52; see p. 49). 11 For example, the Middle English poem *Yung Men of Waterford*, though this is no longer extant in the manuscript (see Angela M. Lucas (ed.), *Anglo-Irish poems of the middle ages* (Blackrock, Columba Press, 1995), pp 17–18); or the Anglo-French poem on the walling of New Ross (Lucas, *Anglo-Irish poems*, pp 17–19). 12 Not only, of course, the comedic, festive material on which this article concentrates, but also the religious materials, including ones of particular concern to the Franciscan order (Michael Benskin, 'The style and authorship of the Kildare poems – (1) Pers of Bermingham', in J.L. MacKenzie and R. Todd (eds), *In other words: transcultural studies in philology, translation and lexicography* (Dordrecht, 1989), pp 57–75; see p. 57). 13 See Benskin, 'Style and authorship'; for some further reflection on its possible assembly, see Lucas, *Anglo-Irish poems*, pp 18–19. 14 For an attempt to characterise the thematic preoccupations and imaginative commitments of the Franciscan compiler of MS Harley 913, see Cartlidge, 'Composition and contexts of BL MS Harley 913'.

friars. From the beginning, it is clear that the mendicant orders cultivated joyous forms of spiritual expression, and there were those amongst their ranks who gained some skill in the performing arts. (In time, a distinctive association of the friars with worldly entertainment would supply their critics and detractors with a convenient weapon.) St Francis himself helped pave the way for this association, reputedly having recommended that his friars be the *joculatores Dei*, the 'jesters of God', by which we are to understand not only such things as jesters are traditionally known for, like a developed sense of humour and verbal wit, but also various kinds of performance skill, including skill in music.[15] However, the ethos of holy levity nurtured within the mendicant orders easily risked appearing not at all holy; when by the later fourteenth century in these islands anti-mendicant feeling was running high, instances like the parodic text presented below might well seem incriminating evidence, an instance of the degenerate taste that friars were now thought in some quarters to exhibit.

The *Mass of the Drinkers* (headed the *missa de potatoribus* in the manuscript) was most likely not an Irish composition but an import.[16] Nor was it even necessarily mendicant in origin.[17] These facts are immaterial in the present context, however; for, by appropriation in an Irish mendicant context, the *Mass* opens a window onto an aspect of the festive culture of the country for which we would otherwise have almost no direct evidence.[18] There are two other light-hearted Latin pieces in Harley 913, similarly imports, which immediately precede the *Mass of the Drinkers* and which further amplify the manuscript-compiler's comedic tastes: the *Abbot of Gloucester's Feast*, a dog-Latin treatment of an outrageous monastic drinking bout in the eponymous monastery,[19] and the *Hours of the Seven Sleepers*, like the *Mass of the Drinkers* another parodic liturgy, this time a ludicrous office for the Seven Sleepers of Ephesus.[20] Not only does the third item, the *Mass of the Drinkers*, illustrate the festive temperament of this early section of the manuscript particularly well, it also attracts attention on account of its potential performability; as earlier noted, performative, festive expression seems to have been embraced by the mendicants, but this aspect of their religious ethos has been insufficiently recognised in the Irish context. *The Mass of the Drinkers* helps correct the imbalance.

---

15 This was the term coined for them by St Francis in the *Speculum perfectionis* (cited in E.K. Chambers, *The mediæval stage*, 2 vols (Oxford: Oxford University Press, 1903), i, 46).   **16** The existence of a slightly earlier and related version of the *Mass of the Drinkers* from England (see the headnote to the explanatory notes to the text below, p. 286) perhaps suggests that the text came to Ireland with the friars.   **17** There are no indications that either the version in the earlier English manuscript (London, British Library, MS Harley 2851), or that in MS Harley 913, were authored by mendicants.   **18** Signs of the friars' taste for a racy style of preaching and of the strategically popular pitch of some of their sermons are to be glimpsed in certain of the mendicant preaching compilations from medieval Ireland (see Fletcher, 'Preaching in late-medieval Ireland'), but these make modest pickings.   **19** Edited by Wilhelm Meyer, 'Quondam fuit factus festus: ein Gedicht in Spottlatein', in *Nachrichten von der königlichen Gesellschaft der Wissenschaften zu Göttingen*, Philologisch-Historische Klasse (Göttingen, 1908), pp 406–29.   **20** Edited by Hans Walther, 'Zur lateinischen parodie des mittelalters', *Zeitschrift*

The text of the *Mass of the Drinkers* given below is newly edited from London, British Library, MS Harley 913.[21] Modern conventions of punctuation and capitalisation have been followed and abbreviations silently expanded. Explanatory notes and a translation are also provided for the reader's convenience, although since no English translation is capable of doing justice to the close liturgical parody which the Latin text achieves, the Latin deserves the reader's first attention. Because prior knowledge of the liturgical texts proper is essential for understanding the parody, these are supplied in the notes.

II

Incipit missa de potatoribus

Versus: Introibo ad altare Bachi. Responsus: Ad uinum qui letificat cor hominis.

Confiteor reo Bacho omnepotanti, et reo uino coloris rubei, et omnibus ciphis, et uobis potatoribus, me nimis gulose potasse per nimiam nauseam rei Bachi
5   dei mei potacione, sternutacione, ocitacione; maxima mea crupa, mea maxima crupa. Ideo precor beatissimum Bacum, et omnes ciphos eius, et uos fratres potatores, ut potetis pro me ad dominum reum Bachum, ut misereatur mei.

Misereatur uestri ciphipotens Bachus, et permittat uos perdere omnia uestimenta uestra, et perducat uos ad uiuam tabernam, qui bibit et potat per
10   omnia pocula poculorum. Stramen.

Crapulanciam et [absorbutionem] et perdicionem omnium uestimentorum nostrorum tribuat nobis ciph[ip]otens Bacus. Stramen.

Deus tuus conuersus letificabis nos. Et plebs tua potabitur in te.

Ostende nobis, Domine, leticiam tuam. Et potum tuum da nobis.

15   Domine, exaudi lamentacionem meam. Et perdicionem uestimentorum da nobis.

Dolus uobiscum. Et cum gemitu tuo.

Potemus. Oratio: Aufer a nobis, quesumus, Bache, cuncta uestimenta nostra, ut ad taberna[m] poculorum nudis corporibus mereamur introire, per omnia pocula poculorum. Stramen.

für deutsches Altertum, 84 (1952–3), 265–73.   21 Most recently edited by Paul Lehmann (ed.), *Die parodie im mittelalter*, 2nd edn (Stuttgart: Hiersemann, 1963), pp 233–41. However, see the headnote to the explanatory notes to the text below, p. 286, on the status of this edition.

20 Introitus. Lugeamus omnes in Decio diem mestum deplorantes sub honore
quadrati Decii, de cuius iactacione plangunt miseri et periurant filium Dei.

Versus: Beati qui habitant in taberna et meditabitur ibi die ac nocte.

Versus: Gloria pot[at]ori, et filio Londri.

Asiot. Ambisasiot. Treisasiot. Quinsiot. Quinsasiot. Sinsasiot. Quernisiot.
25 Quernisasiot. Deusasiot.

Versus: Dolus uobiscum. Et cum gemitu tuo.

Potemus. Oracio: |fol. 14| Deus, qui multitudinem rusticorum ad seruicium
clericorum uenire fecisti et militum, et inter nos et ipsos discordiam seminasti:
da nobis, quesumus, de eorum laboribus uiuere, et eorum uxoribus uti, et de
30 mortificacione eorum gaudere, per Dominum nostrum reum Bachum, qui bibit
et poculat, per omnia pocula poculorum. Stramen.

Lectio Actuum Apurtatricum: In diebus nullis, multitudinis bibencium erat
cor vnum et omnia communia. Nec quisquam eorum quod possidebat suum
esse dicebat. Sed qui uendebat spolia, afferebat ante pedes potatorum, et erant
35 illis omnia communia. Et erat quidam Londrus nomine, pessimus potator qui
accomodabat potatoribus ad ludum prout uestis ualebat. Et sic faciebat lucra et
dampna e poculo. Et eicientes eum extra tabernam lapidabant. Deiectio autem
fiebat uestimentorum eius, et diuidebatur potacio unicuique prout opus erat.

Responsus: Iacta cogitatum tuum in Decio et ipse te destruet. Versus: Ad
40 dolium enim potatorem inebriauit me. Asiat. Asiat.

Versus: Rorate ciphi desuper, et nubes pluant mustum; aperiatur terra et
germinet potatorem.

Dolus uobiscum. Et cum gemitu tuo.

Frequencia falsi ewangelii secundum Bachum. Fraus tibi, rustice.

45 In uerno tempore potatores loquebantur ad inuicem, 'Transeamus usque tabernam,
et uideamus hoc uerbum quod dictum est de dolio hoc'. Intrantes autem tabernam,
inuenerunt tabernariam et tres talos positos in disco. Gustantes autem de mero hoc,
cognouerunt, quia uerum erat quod dictum fuerat illis de dolio hoc. Et omnes qui
ibi aderant, inebriati sunt de hiis que data fuerant a potatoribus ad ipsos. Tabernaria
50 autem contemplabat uestes eorum, conferens in corde suo si ualerent. Et denudati
sunt potatores glorificantes Bachum; et malidicentes Decium.

Dolus uobiscum. Et cum gemitu tuo. | fol. 14v |

Potemus. Offertorium: Ciphi euacuant copiam Bachi, et os potatorum nauseant usque ad fundamentum.

55 Non cantatur Sanctus, nec Agnus Dei, sed pax detur cum gladiis et fustibus.

Pater noster qui es in ciphis, sanctificetur vinum istud. Adueniat Bachi potus, fiat tempestas tua sicut in vino et in taberna. Panem nostrum ad deuorandum da nobis hodie. Et dimitte nobis pocula magna, sicut et nos dimittimus potatoribus nostris. Et ne nos inducas in uini temptacionem. Sed libera nos a uestimento.

60 Communio: Gaudent anime potatorum qui Bachi uestigia sunt secuti, et quia pro eius amore uestes suas perdiderunt, imo cum Bacho in vini dolium.

Dolus uosbiscum. Et cum gemitu tuo.

Potemus. Deus qui tres quadratos decies Lx^{a}iij^{us} oculis illluminasti, tribue nobis, quesumus, ut nos qui uestigia eorum sequimur, iactacione quadrati
65 Decii a nostris pannis exuamur, per Dominum.

Dolus uobiscum, et cetera. Ite bursa uacua. Reo gratias.

Translation

Here begins the Mass of the Drinkers

Verse: I will go unto the altar of Bacchus. Response: Unto the wine that gladdens the heart of man.

I confess to the malefactor Bacchus the all-drinker, and to the culprit wine red in colour, and to all drinking cups, and to you [fellow] drunkards, that I have drunk exceedingly gluttonously through excessive vomiting of the malefactor Bacchus my god, by boozing, by sneezing, by yawning; by my very large rump, by my very large rump. Therefore I pray most blessed Bacchus, and all his goblets, and you [my] fellow drunkards, to drink to me to the lord Bacchus the malefactor, that he may have mercy on me.

May cup-mighty Bacchus have mercy on you, and allow you to lose all your clothes, and lead you to the living tavern, who drinks and swills, cups without end. Garbage.

May cup-mighty Bacchus grant you crapulence, gulping, and the loss of all your clothes. Garbage.

O your God, turn and you will gladden us. And your people will be drunk in you.

Reveal unto us your joy, o Lord. And grant us your drink.

Lord, hear my cry. And grant us the loss of our clothes.

The fraud be with you. And with your groaning.

Let us drink. Prayer: Take away from us, Bacchus, we pray, all our clothes, so that we may be worthy to enter the cup-tavern with bodies naked, cups without end. Garbage.

Introit. Let us all lament Decius's day of sadness, bewailing in honour of the quadrate Decius, over whose bragging wretches grieve and foreswear the son of God.

Verse: Blessed are they that dwell in the tavern, and will meditate there day and night.

Verse: Glory be to the drinker, and to the son of Londrus.

Asiot. Ambisasiot. Treisasiot. Quinsiot. Quinsasiot. Sinsasiot. Quernisiot. Quernisasiot. Deusasiot.

The fraud be with you. And with your groaning.

Let us drink. Prayer: O God, who has caused a multitude of rustics to come to the service of knighthood and clergy, and who has sown discord between them: grant us, we beseech you, to live off their labours, to use their wives, and to rejoice in their humiliation, by our Lord the malefactor Bacchus, who drinks and swills, cups without end. Garbage.

Lesson. The Acts of the (?) Female Strippers: In no days, a host of drinkers were of one heart and all things were held in common between them. Nor did any of them claim what they possessed as their own. But the one who sold the spoils brought [them] before the feet of the drinkers, and they owned everything in common. And there was a certain man, Londrus by name, the worst imbiber, who agreed with the drinkers upon a game of chance, as far as his clothes were worth. And thus he made his profits and losses from the cup.

And throwing him out of the tavern, they stoned him. His clothes, however, were cast off, and to each man was a drink distributed, according as he had need.

Response: Cast your thought upon Decius and he will destroy you. Verse: For he has made me drunk as a drinker to the wine jar. Asiat. Asiat.

Verse: Drop down, you cups, from above, and let the clouds pour down wine; let the earth open and give birth to the drinker.

The fraud be with you. And with your groaning.

The frequency of the false gospel according to Bacchus. Deceit to you, rustic.

In springtime, the drinkers spoke one to another, 'Let us go even unto the tavern, and see there this word that is spoken concerning this wine jar'. And, entering the tavern, they found the hostess of the tavern and three dice placed in a bowl. And tasting of this wine, they understood that what had been said to them about this wine jar was true. And all who were there were made drunk by these things which had been given to them by the drinkers. But the hostess of the tavern looked upon their clothes, revolving in her mind whether they were of any worth. And the drinkers, praising Bacchus, and cursing Decius, were stripped.

The fraud be with you. And with your groaning.

Let us drink. Offertory: Cups empty the supply of Bacchus, and they make the mouth of drinkers throw up right to the bottom.

(Let not Sanctus nor Agnus Dei be sung, but let the peace be given with swords and cudgels.)

Our father who are in cups, hallowed be your wine. Let the drink of Bacchus come, let your raging be done in wine as it is in the tavern. Give us this day our bread to devour. And forgive us our great cups, as we forgive our drinkers. And do not lead us into wine's temptation. But deliver us from our clothes.

Communion: The souls of drinkers who have followed the steps of Bacchus, indeed [who have gone] with Bacchus into the wine jar, rejoice, and because they have lost their clothes for his love.

The fraud be with you. And with your groaning.

Let us drink. O God, who has enlightened three quadrate ten times sixty-three eyes, grant us, we pray, that we who follow their steps, by bragging of the quadrate Decius may be removed from our clothes. By our Lord.

The fraud be with you, et cetera. Go with an empty purse. Thanks be to the malefactor.

NOTES

Errors in the edition of the *Mass of the Drinkers* by Paul Lehmann, *Parodie im Mittelalter*, 2nd edn (Stuttgart: Hiersemann, 1963), pp 233–41, and which are largely inherited from the *editio princeps* of Thomas Wright and J.O. Halliwell (eds), *Reliquiæ antiquæ. Scraps from ancient manuscripts, illustrating chiefly early English literature and the English language*, 2 vols (London: John Russell Smith, 1845), II, 208ff, are noted in the apparatus below. A related text of the *Mass of the Drinkers* is also to be found in a slightly earlier manuscript (dated to the late thirteenth century and after 1290 by A.G. Rigg, *A history of Anglo-Latin literature, 1066–1422* (Cambridge: Cambridge University Press, 1992), p. 238) that is preserved in London, British Library, MS Harley 2851. Variants from this version are printed in the editions of Wright and Halliwell, and of Lehmann. Lehmann has noted other versions of the *Mass of the Drinkers* in fifteenth- and sixteenth-century manuscripts held in Continental libraries. He cites these in his list of sources (Lehmann, *Parodie*, p. 233; he also provides a facing edition, with variants, based on one of them).

 The *Mass of the Drinkers* follows the order of a late medieval Mass quite closely. In the following notes, comparison has been made with that order as it would have been heard according to the rite of Sarum which, as in England, so also in Ireland at this date, was the most widely observed of the rites.

Line 2: Compare the antiphon, 'Introibo ad altare Dei, ad Deum qui laetificat juventutem meam', which occurs near the beginning of the Mass (Francis Henry Dickinson (ed.), *Missale ad usum insignis et præclaræ ecclesiæ Sarum* (Burntisland: E Prelo de Pitsligo; Oxford and London: J. Parker, 1861–83; repr. Farnborough: Gregg International, 1969), col. 579). No indications are given for the Kyrie, the Paternoster, and the Ave Maria, which would ordinarily follow this antiphon. (The relative *qui* in Line 2 has not been regularized as *quod*, as might be expected after neuter *vinum*.)

Lines 3–7: Compare the Confiteor uttered by the celebrant, 'Confiteor Deo, beatae Mariae, omnibus sanctis, et vobis; quia peccavi nimis cogitatione, locutione, et opere: mea culpa: precor sanctam Mariam, omnes sanctos Dei, et vos, orare pro me.' (Dickinson, *Missale*, col. 580).

Lines 8–10: Compare the response given to the Confiteor by the celebrant's ministers, 'Misereatur vestri omnipotens Deus, et dimittat vobis omnia peccata vestra; liberet vos ab omni malo; conservet et confirmet in bono; et ad vitam perducat aeternam.' (Dickinson, *Missale*, col. 580).

Line 9: uiuam] maiorem (Lehmann).

Lines 11–12: Compare the absolution declared by the celebrant, which itself follows his own response to the 'Misereatur': 'Absolutionem et remissionem omnium peccatorum vestrorum, spatium verae poenitentiae, et emendationem vitae, gratiam et consolationem Sancti Spiritus, tribuat vobis omnipotens et misericors Dominus.' (Dickinson, *Missale*, col. 580).

Line 11: absorbutionem] erased in MS, and suggested by comparison with the text in British Library, MS Harley 2851; nostrorum] vestrorum (Lehmann).

Line 12: nobis] vos (Lehmann); ciphipotens] ciphotens MS.

Lines 13–19: Compare the prayers that follow the penitential rite of confession given above: 'Deus tu conversus vivificabis nos. Et plebs tua laetabitur in te. Ostende nobis misericordiam tuam. Et salutare tuum da nobis. Domine, exaudi oracionem meam. Et clamor meus ad te veniat. Aufer a nobis, Domine Deus, cunctas iniquitates nostras, ut ad sancta sanctorum puris mentibus mereamur introire. Per Christum Dominum nostrum.' (J. Wickham Legg (ed.), *The Sarum missal edited from three early manuscripts* (Oxford: Clarendon, 1916), p. 217; I have standardised spelling and punctuation from Legg's edition here and elsewhere in these notes.)

Lines 14–15: Et potum tuum ... lamentacionem meam] omitted in Lehmann.

Lines 18: tabernam] taberna MS.

Lines 20–1: This introit parodies a prayer formula heard at the office of the Mass on certain saints' days; compare, for example, the formula as applied on the feast of St Agatha: 'Gaudeamus omnes in Domino diem festum celebrantes sub honore Agathae martyris de cuius passione gaudent angeli et collaudant filium Dei' (Legg, *Sarum missal*, p. 251).

Line 23: The line mocks the doxology, 'Gloria Patri, et Filio, et Spiritui Sancto'; po[ta]tori] potori MS.

Lines 24–5: Each item in this string of words seems to be a burlesque confection of a gambling term with a (pseudo–liturgical?) termination –iot. The gambling terms are for throws in hazard, a medieval dice game, where 'as' is a score of one, 'ambesas' a score of two (that is, a 'double one'), and so forth.

Line 26: As before (line 16 above) and elsewhere here (lines 43, 52, 62 and 66 below), this is a parody of the formula 'Dominus vobiscum' and response, 'Et cum spiritu tuo.'

Lines 27–31: This prayer does not parody any for a particular occasion, but is constructed from common prayer formulas diverted to parodic ends (for example, 'Deus, qui', 'da nobis, quesumus', 'per Dominum nostrum', and 'qui bibit et poculat, per omnia pocula poculorum', the latter parodying 'qui vivit et regnat, per omnia secula seculorum').

Line 29 nobis] omitted in Lehmann.

Line 30 reum] omitted in Lehmann.

Line 32: This reading from the 'Actuum Apurtatricum' gives pause for thought. The reading itself burlesques extracts of the Acts of the Apostles, as a comparison with Acts 4:32 and Acts 7:57 demonstrates (see the following note), but the word

Apurtatricum is problematic. Its grammatical morphology is such as to suggest that it is based on some such form as *apertatrix*, although I have not noticed this noun in any of the standard lexicons of medieval Latin. Like its masculine cognate, *apertor* (a word which, conversely, is attested), the feminine *apertatrix* presumably had the meaning of one who 'lays bare' or 'reveals'. In the case of *apertor*, the 'revealing' or 'laying bare' was often intended in a metaphorical sense (that is, one who 'clarifies' or 'makes plain'), but in the parodic context of the *Mass of the Drinkers*, it is conceivable that the *apertatrices* were grossly literal. I have therefore ventured the translation 'female strippers'. I am indebted to Dr Helen Conrad O'Briain for discussion on this point.

Lines 32–8: Essentially, a parodic joining together of Acts 4:32 with Acts 7:57 and with Acts 4:35: 'In diebus illis, multitudinis autem credentium erat cor unum et anima una: nec quisquam eorum quae possidebat, aliquid suum esse dicebat, sed erant illis omnia communia.' (Acts 4:32); 'Et eicientes eum extra civitatem, lapidabant.' (Acts 7:57); 'Dividebatur autem singulis prout cuique opus erat.' (Acts 4:35). Acts 4:32 and 35 was heard as part of the epistle at Mass on the Vigil of the Ascension (Dickinson, *Missale*, col. 410), and Acts 7:57 as part of the epistle at Mass on the feast of St Stephen Protomartyr (Dickinson, *Missale*, col. 63).

Line 35 Londrus] Londrum (Lehmann).

Lines 36–7 Et sic faciebat lucra et dampna e poculo] omitted in Lehmann.

Line 39: Compare 'Iacta super Dominum curam tuam et ipse te enutriet: et non dabit in aeternum fluctuationem iusto' (Psalm 54:23, heard on a weekly basis in the context of a recitation of the whole of this psalm at matins of the fourth feria; F. Procter and C. Wordsworth (eds), *Breviarium ad usum insignis ecclesiæ Sarum*, 3 vols (Cambridge: Cambridge University Press, 1879–86), II, col. 114).

Lines 41–2: Compare the Advent antiphon, 'Rorate celi desuper, et nubes pluant iustum; aperiatur terra et germinet Salvatorem' (Legg, *Sarum missal*, p. 18), heard at the office for the fourth feria of each of the weeks of Advent.

Lines 45–51: Compare Luke 2:15–20, which is also the gospel lection for the second Mass on Christmas morning, at dawn (Dickinson, *Missale*, col. 57): 'Pastores loquebantur ad invicem, "Transeamus usque Bethlehem, et videamus hoc verbum, quod factum est, quod Dominus ostendit nobis." Et venerunt festinantes: et invenerunt Mariam, et Ioseph, et infantem positum in praesepio. Videntes autem cognoverunt de verbo, quod dictum erat illis de puero hoc. Et omnes qui audierunt, mirati sunt: et de his quae dicta erant a pastoribus ad ipsos. Maria autem conservabat omnia verba haec, conferens in corde suo. Et reversi sunt pastores glorificantes Deum in omnibus quae audierant et viderant, sicut dictum est ad illos.'

Lines 53–4: Compare 'Celi enarrant gloriam Dei, et opera manuum eius annunciat firmamentum' (Psalm 18:2), used as a gradual verse on various occasions in the church year, but most frequently during the season of Advent, on Saturdays (Legg, *Sarum missal*, p. 20).

Line 55: This direction mimics a liturgical rubric; see further discussion of its significance in the last section of this essay below.

Lines 56–9: Compare the Paternoster: 'Pater noster, qui es in celo, sanctificetur nomen tuum. Adveniat regnum tuum. Fiat voluntas tua, sicut in celo et in terra. Panem nostrum quotidianum da nobis hodie, et dimitte nobis debita nostra, sicut et nos dimittimus debitoribus nostris. Et ne nos inducas in temptacionem, sed libera nos a malo. Amen.'

Lines 60–1: I have not noticed a specific liturgical model for this communion prayer.

Line 60 Gaudent] Gaudeant (Lehmann).

Lines 63–5: Prayers organised around the formula 'Deus qui ...' + second person singular imperative + 'per Dominum' are common in the liturgy. Compare, for example, that used at the office for Mass on the feast of St Francis: 'Deus qui ecclesiam tuam beati Francisci meritis fetu nove prole amplificas, tribue nobis ex eius imitacione terrena despicere et celestium donorum semper participacione gaudere. Per Dominum.' (Legg, *Sarum missal*, p. 331.)

Line 63: I am unable to explain the apparent nonsense of the numerals in this line.

Line 66: The dismissal after Mass was 'Ite, missa est.' The response was 'Deo gratias.'

III

Although the carnivalesque prospect that its performability extends gives the *Mass of the Drinkers* much of its appeal, there is no evidence that it was ever staged in Ireland in some sort of actual mock liturgy. The only performance of which we can be certain is the notional one that would have occurred in the minds of readers of this section of the manuscript and, on the assumption that he was imaginatively engaged with the material he was copying, also in the mind of the Franciscan compiler himself. While actual mock liturgies had certainly been conducted in the middle ages – those accompanying the Feast of Fools are probably the most famous – no clear evidence forces the conclusion that the *Mass of the Drinkers* was ever so conducted.[22]

Yet for various reasons it seems best to leave the question of some actual mock liturgical performance open. After all, the *Mass* offered an effective script from which any such performance could be put together, and at least a notional performance seems invited by the inclusion of a rubric calling for physical, pseudo-liturgical action: *Non cantatur Sanctus, nec Agnus Dei, sed pax detur cum gladiis et fustibus* ('Let not the Sanctus nor Agnus Dei be sung, but

22 The most adequate survey of the Feast of Fools in these islands remains that of Chambers, *Mediæval stage*, i, 274–335. Our knowledge of the feast is also heavily dependent on the witness of Continental (principally French) sources; for an edition of the Feast of Fools liturgy celebrated on the feast of the Circumcision in the cathedral church of Sens, see H. Villetard (ed.), *Office de Pierre de Corbeil*, Bibliothèque musicologique 4 (Paris, 1907).

let the peace be given with swords and cudgels'; line 55). This 'peace' gesture that ludicrously subverts itself by its very violence could, of course, be considered no more than an amusing twist in the literary fiction, an action to be imagined solely, but it is also an action in keeping with what is known of the actual knockabout that attended the Feast of Fools and that its excoriators described in their accounts of the feast's antics.[23] Similarly, the *Mass*'s emphasis on boozing and gambling, while again explicable simply as a literary Goliardic trope, also corresponds to the spirit of the historical Feast of Fools, during which both of these indulgences seem to have been licensed in reality. Likewise it might be noted that three of the parodies that the *Mass* introduces depend upon allusions to real-time liturgies which fell either within, or shortly before, the festive season during which the Feast of Fools held sway.[24]

As a blueprint for either notional, or real, performance, then, may be how best to conceive the *Mass of the Drinkers*. At the very least, in order to realise to full advantage the burlesque that the *Mass* contrives, it begs for an oral delivery of some sort. While its outrageousness remains intact even in an exclusively private, mental reading, which is how it is likely to be received today, a public hearing, conversely, would bring it very close to the oral event that it was dedicated to parodying, namely, the liturgy of the Mass. Thus it seems reasonable to suppose that, whether treated to a full-blown mock liturgical enactment or not, in its day some sort of oral rendition would nevertheless have afforded the *Mass of the Drinkers* its most fitting medium and provided the next best thing.[25]

And as a riotous counterpoint to the sobriety that more usually seems taken for granted, or which stands by default, in historical accounts of the arrival of the friars in Ireland, this text makes salutary reading. It connects medieval Waterford with medieval Dublin via the common mendicant culture that presides at the appropriation of its text in Harley 913. Further, it connects both these places with one of the more robust, if underrepresented, aspects of early mendicant culture in Ireland generally. Finally, it connects Ireland with festive traditions for which medieval Europe, not Ireland, is more usually known. And all this happens on two folios of a manuscript that, having in the past been given such short and imperfect shrift, have barely been recognised.

---

23 Chambers, *Mediæval stage*, i, 274–335. 24 Three of the liturgical parodies in the *Mass of the Drinkers* fall near, or just before, the traditional date of the Feast of Fools, whose occasion coincided with the feast of the Circumcision on 1 January: (1) the parody of part of the epistle reading for the Feast of St Stephen Protomartyr between lines 32–8; (2) the parody of the Advent antiphon between lines 41–2; and (3) the parody of the gospel for the second Mass of Christmas morning between lines 45–51. 25 An oral delivery during reading, too, would have been quite consistent with what is known about medieval reading habits; see Joyce Coleman, *Public reading and the reading public in late medieval England and France* (Cambridge and New York: Cambridge University Press, 1996).

Robert Ware's telling tale: a medieval Dublin story and its significance

RAYMOND GILLESPIE

In 1678 the Dubliner Robert Ware, second son of the antiquarian Sir James Ware, wrote a work which he entitled 'The history and antiquities of Dublin'.[1] It was a double first. For Dublin, it was the first narrative history of the city, although there had been a few earlier attempts at urban chronicles. In the fifteenth century a chronicle may have been kept in the office of the Recorder of the city, listing on one side of a roll the names of the mayor and bailiffs and on the other significant events of that year.[2] In its present form the roll ends in 1534 but a fragment of what may be a continuation, since it details events in the city in the 1550s in a format similar to the older roll, survives among the papers of Robert's father, Sir James Ware.[3] Sometime in the later sixteenth century the older roll seems to have been resurrected, transcribed and new entries added bringing events up to 1566.[4] While the genre of the town chronicle would continue into the eighteenth century, it became less popular over time.[5] As the city chronicle ceased to be kept in Dublin nothing rose to replace it. Richard Stanihurst's account of the city in 1577 for Raphael Holinshed's *Chronicles of England, Scotland and Ireland* stands more in the tradition of topographical writing than as an historical account of the city.[6] Thus, when Robert Ware composed something resembling a narrative account of the city's past in 1678 it filled a distinct lacuna for the non-Dubliner who wished to become acquainted with the history of the city.

For Ware himself writing the history of Dublin was also a first. It was his first substantial work and it may be that his unpublished history of the Dublin churches and religious houses and his translation of his father's annals of Ireland were done about the same time.[7] Such works undoubtedly laid the

1 This now survives in four copies. The original manuscript is in the Public Library, Armagh. An eighteenth-century copy is British Library, Add. MS 4823. Two copies were made for the nineteenth-century antiquarian J.T. Gilbert, and are now Dublin Public Libraries, Gilbert Library, MSS 74–5, 76. 2 Trinity College, Dublin, MS 543/12/14. For the suggestion that its origin lay in the Recorder's office, see Alan J. Fletcher, *Drama and the performing arts in pre-Cromwellian Ireland* (Cambridge, 2001), pp 81–2. 3 British Library, Add. MS 4822, ff 113–3v. 4 Trinity College, Dublin, MS 591, ff 1–28. 5 D.R. Woolf, *Reading history in early modern England* (Cambridge, 2000), pp 64–74. 6 Liam Miller and Eileen Power (eds), *Holinshed's Irish chronicle* (Dublin, 1979), pp 39–51. 7 British

foundations for Robert Ware's more polemical writings of the 1680s. Beginning with his *Historical collections of the church in Ireland*, published in London in 1681, Ware, a deeply conservative Irish Protestant, attacked both Catholicism and the dissent of the 1650s, in a series of ten works published in both Dublin and London before 1690.[8] The history of Dublin predated these controversial publications although the later developments are clearly discernable. When describing the taking of Wexford by Diarmait Mac Murchada (Dermot MacMurrough), based on Giraldus Cambrensis's *Expugnatio Hibernica*, he observed in a marginal note: 'In those days subjects were more observant of their king than the pretended saints of this age now'; he adds that 'not observing these precepts was the occasion of so many divisions in our late king's time'.[9] The origin of Robert Ware's history of Dublin probably lay in his acquisition of the manuscript collection of his father, Sir James Ware, on the latter's death in 1666. Robert claimed of his history

> My scope is only to comply with those inducements which have been often vehemently urged unto me for the publishing in the best method I can such observations of my deceased father, Sir James Ware kt, and other particulars of moment relating to the city of Dublin since the conquest of Ireland as I find in the several volumes of these manuscripts which he was pleased to bequeath unto me as a legacy of great price and for the regulation and conduct of myself in this undertaking I shall look up no other pole, not have any other scope than the impartial representation of truth out of authentic memorials compiled with the secure warranty of faithful dealing.[10]

It is certainly true that Sir James Ware's manuscript collection was probably the finest in private hands in seventeenth-century Ireland.[11] It offered considerable riches for the historian of medieval Dublin since it included the registers of a number of religious houses such as the Victorine canons of St Thomas, the Cistercian house of St Mary, the hospital of St John the Baptist and manuscripts from Christ Church cathedral. In addition, Sir James had compiled his own notes of historical source material drawn from extensive reading in the archives of institutions where he was well known.

By the standards of even contemporary antiquarian scholarship Robert did not make as much use of all this as he might. He was reluctant to explore the medieval heritage of Dublin in the detail that his sources would have permitted. Instead, a good deal of his history, as with Stanihurst's earlier

Library, Add. MS 4813; *The antiquities and history of Ireland by the right honourable Sir James Ware* (Dublin, 1705), sig a2v. 8 Wing W847A–853. 9 Armagh Public Library, 'Ware's history and antiquities', p. 6. 10 Armagh Public Library, 'Ware's history and antiquities', p. 1. 11 William O'Sullivan, 'A finding list of Sir James Ware's manuscripts', in *RIA Proc.*, 97C, (1997), pp 69–99.

work, is taken up with topographical description and events much closer to his own day. He does, however, give considerable space to the Anglo-Norman seizure of the city taken from Giraldus's *Expugnatio*, but in the main he was uninterested in earlier developments. For Robert Ware, the Anglo-Norman conquest was 'the establishment thereof in the peaceable possession of the British nation' and from henceforth 'it [the city] hath flourished every day more and more saving in time of war and usurpations', before reaching its present perfection when its growth was 'so considerable for convenient and stately edifices and ornaments public and private and ever changing as it hath been since his Majesties late happy restoration'.[12] At one point, however, Robert Ware does engage at length with the medieval past of the city. Describing the Tholsel, the city's most significant secular public building, he included a long story which casts a good deal of light on the city's past and present. Of the Tholsel, he noted

> This structure was founded by Richard Mutton, first mayor of Dublin and last provost thereof. History reporteth of him that John Heath, provost of Dublin, going from the priory of the Blessed Trinity to the Abbey of Our Lady found a [*blank in MS*] in the way wherein this Richard lay wrapt up in a mutton skin from which consideration he was surnamed Mutton. The provost out of motives of Christian charity had him brought to the same abbey where he caused him to be christened and thereupon raised a sufficient allowance for his maintenance. The prior also of the Holy Trinity so soon as he was capable of letters taught him and instructed him according to his capacitie. He coming to some measure of learning the city bound him an apprentice and he being a thrifty young man he did so thrive in the progress of a few years that the said John Heath who first took care of him from his infancy continuing his indulgence towards him bestowed his daughter on him (though his only child) which made him with credit and riches begin to flourish in the world. Insomuch that by the favour of fortune and his own credit he became one of the provosts of this city and afterwards pursuant to the grant of Henry the third, king of England, he was elected mayor and in that office continued seven years together which was during the remainder of his life, and it is probable that he might longer have continued that administration had not death prevented him.
>
> About half a year before his death he began to build the Tholsel but before he had half finished that work, leaving his only daughter, Margery, behind him he charged her on his death bed to see it finished saying that all he had gotten was by the city and that in memory thereof

12 Armagh Public Library, 'Ware's history and antiquities', pp 16, 18.

he built the same as a monument of his gratitude and his affection to the city for an assembly or meeting place.

This work she performed according to his will. Others say that Margery herself founded it but in an old registery of Saint Mary Abbey, Dublin, I find authority for what I have written though both had to do in the structure thereof.[13]

This story undoubtedly has a core of truth. Most of the people mentioned are identifiable. While nothing is known of John Heath, Richard Muton was provost of Dublin in 1221–2 and again for the half year 1228–9. Following the granting of a charter to the city by Henry III in 1229, which created the Dublin mayoralty, Muton was appointed first mayor of the city in 1230.[14] His name appears throughout the 1230s and early 1240s on the witness lists to Dublin deeds, the last being in 1245 and he presumably died in the late 1240s.[15] Moreover, his daughter Margery can probably be identified with Margareta Motyn who appears in the Book of Obits of Christ Church and seems to have been associated with the cathedral confraternity.[16]

Apart from the historicity of the main actors, the story as Robert Ware tells it seems to have little value. It is replete with problems, not least with its chronology. According to Ware's version of events, Muton was mayor for seven years. Yet, in fact, he was mayor for only one year. The story seems to imply that Muton died shortly after his period of office whereas, on the evidence of witness lists appended to deeds, he survived at least another twenty years. Even more serious is the chronological gap between the last appearance of Muton in a deed of 1245 and the actual date of construction of the Tholsel to replace the older guildhall, probably in the first decade of the fourteenth century.[17]

Chronological inaccuracies are not the only difficulties here. That part of the story which provides an etymology for Richard's surname is contrived, particularly since the Muton family were probably well established in Dublin,

13 Armagh Public Library, 'Ware's history and antiquities', pp 60–1. 14 Philomena Connolly and Geoffrey Martin (eds), *The Dublin guild merchant roll, c.1190–1265* (Dublin, 1992), p. 111; J.T. and Lady Gilbert (eds), *Calendar of ancient records of Dublin*, 19 vols (Dublin, 1889–1944), i, p. 82. 15 M.J. McEnery and Raymond Refaussé (eds), *Christ Church deeds* (Dublin, 2001), nos 39, 47, 482–4, 485, 488, 489; Gilbert (ed.), *Cal. anc. rec. Dublin*, i, p. 85; J.T. Gilbert (ed.), *Cartularies of St Mary's Abbey, Dublin*, 2 vols (London, 1884–6), i, pp 35, 431; E. St John Brooks (ed.), *Register of the hospital of S. John the Baptist without the Newgate, Dublin* (Dublin, 1936), pp 17, 20, 39, 55, 91, 95, 101, 102, 111, 114–5, 129, 187, 191, 194. There are also a number of undated deeds witnessed by Muton. 16 J.C. Crosthwaite (ed.), *The book of obits and martyrology of the cathedral church of the Holy Trinity, Dublin* (Dublin, 1844), p. 25. Reprinted in Raymond Refaussé with Colm Lennon (eds), *The registers of Christ Church cathedral, Dublin* (Dublin, 1998), p. 57. This may also be Margery wife of Philip Motun who granted property in the city in 1285, Brooks (ed.), *Reg. S. John the Baptist, Dublin*, p. 129–30. 17 H.B. Clarke, *Dublin part 1, to 1610*, Irish Historic Towns Atlas, no. 11 (Dublin, 2002), p. 23.

the undated part of the guild merchant roll containing both an Arnoldus Muton of Bordeaux and a Walter Muton.[18] It is therefore tempting to dismiss the whole event as an invention by Robert Ware. This view might well be strengthened by two facts. First, Ware claimed that the source of his story was 'an old registery of Saint Mary Abbey, Dublin', and yet, while the document relating to St Mary's can almost certainly be identified as the cartulary then in Robert Ware's possession, there is nothing resembling this story in it. Secondly, Ware was certainly involved in other forgeries. In later life he was responsible for a number of forgeries of anti-Catholic tracts, using blank pages in his father's manuscript collection to give them a semblance of authenticity.[19]

It would, however, be rash to dismiss this story altogether. A number of features suggest that it was not a Robert Ware forgery. Muton was a rather obscure historical figure by the seventeenth century and he does not feature in any of the earlier works on Dublin's history, such as that of Stanihurst, and therefore it would have been difficult for Ware to have discovered him without a great deal of archival work. Moreover, Ware's other forgeries are all stories attached to significant figures: to attach a story to a relatively minor person would be unusual. On another occasion, Robert Ware seems to have been led astray by his own story, which would seem unlikely if it were a deliberate forgery. When discussing the charter of 1229, Ware noted that the first mayor of Dublin continued in office for seven years, the source for which incorrect statement can only be his own story of Muton.[20]

The key to understanding Robert Ware's story lies not in the historical persons he mentions but rather in the historicised narrative itself. The narrative is composed of easily identified folkloristic motifs recorded in the standard international index. The story is one of a foundling hero (L111.2) who is rescued by a merchant (R131.7 or N851, merchant as helper). The abandoned child is raised by poor folk (e.g. S351.2), in this case religious under vow of poverty, and the poor boy marries a rich girl (L161.1).[21] There are other features of the story which suggest such a folkloristic structure. The finding of the child at the edge of the city invites the invocation of liminality, frequent in such stories, while the story has some elements of the patterning which might be associated with tale types such as saint's lives or hero tales.[22] In the case of Ware's tale, a series of folkloristic motifs seems to have attached itself in a patterned way to a historical figure, in the same way that by the early seventeenth century a whole international tale-type (AT1651) attached

---

18 Connolly and Martin (eds), *Dublin merchant guild roll*, p. 20. A Roger Muton appears in *c.*1249–50 and a Philip in 1285 (Brooks (ed.), *Reg. S. John the Baptist, Dublin*, pp 27, 129). 19 T.E. Bridgett, *Blunders and forgeries* (London, 1890). 20 Armagh Public Library, 'Ware's history and antiquities', p. 50. 21 The numbers are from Stith Thompson, *Motif index of folk literature*, 6 vols (Bloomington, 1955–8). 22 For example, the discussion in Tomás Ó Cathasaigh (ed.), *The heroic biography of Cormac Mac Airt* (Dublin, 1977), pp 1–8.

itself to Richard Whittington of Gloucestershire, lord mayor of London 1397–8, 1406–7 and 1419–20, and benefactor of the city, to create the story of Dick Whittington and his cat.[23]

However, the result of a similar process in Dublin was not a story primarily about a major individual but rather a local legend about the founding of a building that was still visible in the landscape when the story was retold.[24] Such stories were not unusual in sixteenth- and seventeenth-century Dublin. Richard Stanihurst recorded a number of such origin-legends in his work on the city. Stanihurst told a story of how, after the death of Robin Hood, Little John had come to Dublin and engaged in an archery contest, shooting an arrow into a mole hill which became known as 'Little John hys shot'. This left 'behind him a monument, rather by his posterity to be wondered than possibly by any man living to be counterscored'.[25] The story was clearly transmitted orally since in the telling the Kirklees in Yorkshire of the written legend, where Robin Hood died, has become Bricklies in Scotland.[26]

This folkloric quality of the origin legend of the Tholsel makes it very difficult to date. It is possible that some parts of it, such as the association of Muton and the Tholsel, are old and that the story was elaborated over time. Speculation as to when it may have taken the form in which Robert Ware recorded it can be little more than guesswork. One indication may be found in Ware's claim that he found the story among the records of St Mary's abbey. Certainly there is nothing among the surviving muniments of the abbey, which were in Robert Ware's hands in the late seventeenth century, to match this story. It may be that Ware heard the story but, because oral testimony was falling out of fashion as evidence among antiquarians in the late seventeenth century, he invented a documentary provenance for it to give it more status.[27] It may also be that the reference was real and that the document Robert Ware saw has since been lost. This is not improbable since religious houses in the late middle ages were well known for propagating oral traditions which bolstered their position or raised their local status.[28] Given that three significant institutions feature in Ware's story, the city itself, St Mary's abbey and the priory

23 Caroline Barron, 'Richard Whittington: the man and the myth', in A.E.J. Hollaender and W. Kellaway (eds), *Studies in London history presented to Philip Jones* (London, 1969), pp 197–284 and, for a shorter discussion, Richard Barber, *Living legends* (London, 1980), pp 41–65. The story of Whittington, though without the cat, may have been known in Dublin since it was included in Richard Grafton's sixteenth-century chronicle, which seems to have been in the Stanihurst library since it was used by Edmund Campion in his history of Ireland which drew on the books in the Stanihurst library.   24 For this class of stories, see Jacqueline Simpson, 'The local legend: a product of popular culture' in *Rural History*, ii (1991), pp 25–36.   25 For a number of these stories, Miller and Power (eds), *Holinshed's Irish chronicle*, pp 50–1, 68–9.   26 For the literary tradition, see J.C. Holt, *Robin Hood* (2nd ed. London, 1989), pp 25–8.   27 For the status of oral evidence, see D.R. Woolf, 'The "common voice": history, folklore and oral tradition in early modern England', *Past and Present*, no. 120 (Aug 1988), pp 26–51.   28 Adam Fox, *Oral and literate culture in*

of Holy Trinity, a good guess as to the origin of the story in this form might be found at a point when all three institutions were under pressure and required a linked local legend to bolster their position. The best candidate for such a set of events would be in the aftermath of the Lambert Simnel fiasco in 1487, when the abbot of St Mary's and the prior of Christ Church were both attainted, though pardoned, and the city forced to repent publicly its actions.[29]

The story told by Robert Ware about Richard Muton is a complex local legend containing historical personages and folkloric themes and patterns that may have been the result of both popular tradition and political manipulation. As a result, it was capable of carrying many meanings and explanations for a variety of audiences. There were, for instance, meanings extracted from the story that related to immediate political developments in Dublin and may have been the occasion for its recording. In the same year that Ware wrote his history, Muton's Tholsel was demolished and replaced with a grander building. Robert Ware specifically juxtaposed the life of the original builder, Muton, with that of the rebuilder, John Smith, mayor 1678–9:

> it is worthy of observation that the builder of the Tholsel and he in whose time it was totally demolished [John Smith] should agree so well in one commendable qualification. And some may conjecture that the aged Tholsel expected a dissolution when it could no longer be subservient to the ancient rules and constitution of the city … whilst with an expectation we may too long look for the creation of a new one [Tholsel] by so sufficient a founder without the contribution of the whole city.[30]

In this episode the demolition of the old Tholsel is seen as a metaphor for the demolition of the 'ancient constitution' of the city following from the imposition of the 'New rules' on the Irish urban corporations in 1672. Ware, with his strong Protestant views, no doubt approved of the 'New rules' whose main function was to exclude Catholics from urban office, but they also increased the power of central government at the expense of the city.

While the demolition of the Tholsel and the changing political position of the city may help to explain why Robert Ware found this story relevant and interesting, they do not exhaust the lessons that might be learned from the legend of Richard Muton. Like the story of Richard Whittington, it may simply tell of the importance of towns in promoting social mobility, and encourage those living outside the urban centres to move there. For those

England, 1500–1700 (Oxford, 2000), pp 227–42, which also argues that towns invented 'charter myths'. **29** Kenneth Milne (ed.), *Christ Church cathedral, Dublin: a history* (Dublin, 2000), pp 85–6. Christ Church may have feared legal action against it and the reorganisation of its records may have resulted: see Raymond Gillespie, 'The archives of Christ Church cathedral, Dublin', in *Irish Archives* v no. 2 (Winter 1998), pp 8–9. **30** Armagh Public Library, 'Ware's history and antiquities', pp 53–4.

already within the town the story probably carried other messages about the nature of urban society. It was a tale in which Richard Muton certainly played a part but the meat of the story was in explaining why the Tholsel, a familiar sight for those who listened to the story, had been built. The Tholsel, as Ware explained, was the physical embodiment of the privileges of the city. It was the place where 'the administration of justice and all the principal functions of the mayor, sheriffs and commons of the city of Dublin were exercised'.[31] The Tholsel was the place where, in the fifteenth and sixteenth centuries, the mayor was elected, where the records of the city were kept, where the merchant's guild met and where the town clock, an important attribute of a civic sensibility, was located.[32]

The Tholsel may have conveyed even clearer messages in its iconography. In 1550, the corporation paid 'for lym and collors for the armys making on the Tholsel dore'.[33] What the arms were is not specified but it seems highly probable that they were the arms of the city, possibly painted in celebration of the recent charter. More tantalising is the reference in the corporation accounts of 1545 to money 'payd to James paynt[er] for the story that he payntyd in the cowrt house of the Tollsell'.[34] What the picture was is not recorded but in English town halls at this point portraits of the mayors were becoming more common and this may be what was painted. Alternatively, it may have been a scene from the city's history like Coventry's sixteenth-century portrait of Lady Godiva.[35] Such displays of civic status in the Tholsel could be impressive for bystanders. Moreover, within the Tholsel the mayor was the embodiment of the city. The ordinances in the Chain Book specified that if one reviled the mayor outside the Tholsel the fine was 40s. but if the same action was performed within the Tholsel the fine was £10.[36] It is likely that the desire to link the building of the Tholsel with the mayoralty established under the 1229 charter lies behind the attribution of the building to Muton, despite its chronological impossibility.[37]

When read in this way the values of Muton were some of the civic values of the city of Dublin, and the story was meant to convey appropriate rules for urban living. A rather similar process of associating an early mayor with a civic institution depicting a particular set of values seems to have been at work in late-medieval Chester, which had strong connections with Dublin. According to

---

31 Ibid., pp 59–60.   32 Gilbert (eds), *Cal. anc. rec. Dublin*, i, pp 272, 275, 312, 323, 338, 339, 413, 463. For the importance of the clock as a marker of urban civility see Raymond Gillespie, 'Describing Dublin: Francis Place's visit, 1698–9', in Adele Dalsimer (ed.), *Visualizing Ireland* (Winchester MA, 1993), p. 112.   33 Dublin City Archives, MR/35, p. 87.   34 Dublin City Archives, MR/35, p. 36.   35 Robert Tittler, *Architecture and power: the town hall and the English urban community, 1500–1640* (Oxford, 1991), pp 152, 153–4. 36 J.T. Gilbert (ed.), *Historic and municipal documents of Ireland, 1172–1320* (London, 1870), p. 232.   37 For origin myths associated with town halls, see Tittler, *Architecture and power*, pp 150–3.

one tradition on the origin of the civic-sponsored cycle of mystery plays, the patron was Sir John Arneway, mayor between 1268 and 1276, but the plays were probably fourteenth-century in date.[38] The message which the story conveyed is not historical but rather a story of harmonious church and civic collaboration, which figures in the plays themselves. In this case urban mythology, perhaps slightly earlier than Robert Ware's story, served the same function as the linking of Muton and his building.

Some of the attributes necessary for urban living set out in the story of Richard Muton are clear. Wealth was one, but another was the sort of generosity which supposedly impelled Muton to build the Tholsel. Robert Ware is clear that the building of the Tholsel had been a generous act. Such generosity was intimately linked to the practice of hospitality. Ware noted 'and we may presume that Richard Muton who built the Tholsel of the city of Dublin was no less to be commended for his hospitality in regard that he had the honour to be chosen first mayor and continued in that office for seven years altogether'.[39] Generosity was a well-established attribute of Dublin's mayors. Richard Stanihurst in the 1570s had written of the hospitality and generosity of the mayors and continued that 'the greater part of the city is generally addicted to such [hospitality]'.[40] Robert Ware clearly approved of this sort of activity and included in his work a chapter on the 'hospitality of Dublin' and related some of the stories reported by Stanihurst.[41] The activities received official recognition in 1667 when the corporation increased the annual grant from the treasury to the mayor, that he 'might be the better enabled to keep such hospitality as might be suitable to the credit of the mayor and the dignity of the city'.[42] In addition to the hospitality provided by the mayor, the corporation also provided feasts in the Tholsel at particular points in the year with mayoral 'drinkings', and feasts were provided for the Lord Deputy, visiting nobility and, on occasion, visiting mayors such as those from Drogheda or Wexford.[43] Religious and trade guilds also had annual feasts. In Ware's own time certain identifiable groups within the city, such as the Welsh immigrant community, met for special feasts.[44]

Such celebrations of hospitality and generosity were an essential part of urban sociability. They provided a mechanism to demonstrate that neighbourliness was important to the community and the regular meetings served to

---

38 R.M. Luiansky and David Mills, *The Chester mystery cycle: essays and documents* (Chapel Hill and London, 1983), pp 166–8, deals with the origins of the Chester cycle. I am very grateful to Alan Fletcher for drawing this parallel to my attention.   39 Armagh Public Library, 'Ware's history and antiquities', p. 53.   40 Ibid., p. 42.   41 Ibid., pp 84–7.   42 Gilbert (ed.), *Cal. anc. rec. Dublin*, iv, p. 430.   43 Alan J. Fletcher, *Drama, performance and polity in pre-Cromwellian Ireland* (Cork, 2000), pp 147–8, 386–8;Gilbert (ed.), *Cal. anc. rec. Dub.*, i, pp 406, 484; Dublin City Archives, MR/35, pp 15, 28, 32, 55, 58, 79, 85, 93, 121, 150.   44 Historic Manuscripts Commission, *Report on the manuscripts of the earl of Egmont*, 2 vols (London, 1905–9), ii, p. 25.

reduce social conflict and enhance solidarity.[45] Parish feasts, such as Ware described in St Audoen's and St Werburgh's parish, fulfilled similar functions.[46] By the 1670s, this was an important function since the city was growing at an unprecedented rate. As Sir Paul Davys observed in 1664: 'it is a wonder how buildings increase in all parts of this city'.[47] In this period of rapid change, social networks needed to be formed around a series of urban symbols and institutions.[48] Robert Ware's history of Dublin and the stories it contains took on the role of explaining the city to those who lived in it. There runs through his work a good deal of the civic pride of a third-generation Dubliner exemplified by the universal context in which he locates the city. In discussing the setting of the city, for example, he wrote of

> a fair and beautiful bowling green in Oxmanton on the north part of the city thought to be one of the fairest in Christendom, being nobly embellished with walks and walls set round with choice fruit trees. There is Saint Stephen's Green on the edge of Dublin and within the liberties thereof which is not only superior to Moorfields at London but also not inferior to the Prato in Florence, nor the Prato delle Valle in Padua, which is there accompted a wonderful object of beauty and place of ravishing delight.[49]

However, the history went further than simply telling the inhabitants what their city was like. It tried to teach them how to behave in that city. Ware tried to convey civic values such as piety, hospitality and good deeds by imbedding their history in chapters of his longer work. He urged the new urban residents of the city to return to basic urban values. He urged them to stop wasting their money on 'vain fashions' in furniture and clothing and to spend their money instead on the more old-fashioned traits of urban life such as hospitality and employing their money in trading.[50]

Robert Ware's story of Richard Muton and the Tholsel is not a simple tale. It carried a number of complex messages not only about Ware's world but also

---

45 Felicity Heal, *Hospitality in early modern England* (Oxford, 1990), pp 300–51. 46 British Library, Add. MS 4813, ff 31v, 33v–4. 47 Bodleian Library, Oxford, Carte MS 33, f. 626. 48 For the example of religion, see Raymond Gillespie, 'Religion in urban society: the case of early modern Dublin', in Peter Clark and Raymond Gillespie (eds), *Two capitals: London and Dublin, 1500–1840. Proceedings of the British Academy*, 107 (Oxford, 2001), pp 234–8. 49 Armagh Public Library, 'Ware's history and antiquities', p. 19. Sir William Petty also compared Dublin with Venice, Paris, Rome and Amsterdam but many made comparisons with London; see Raymond Gillespie, 'Dublin 1600–1700: a city and its hinterlands', in Peter Clark and Bernard Lepetit (eds), *Capital cities and their hinterlands in early modern Europe* (Aldershot, 1996), pp 84–5. 50 Armagh Public Library, 'Ware's history and antiquities', pp 48–51. The parallel is clear here with the contemporary work by Richard Lawrence, *The interest of Ireland in its trade and wealth stated* (Dublin, 1682), which urged similar traits.

about what it meant to live in late-medieval Dublin. It conveyed the importance of civic values in an age of change. Moreover, it is not unique. Robert Ware's Dublin works have a number of such didactic legends in which folkloric themes blend with historical fact to explain the realities of late-medieval Dublin life. His description of the walls and towers of Dublin is littered with stories of historical events which occurred at particular points, in the same way that Stanihurst's lists of streets in Dublin form three distinct walks around the city punctuated by stories about the places encountered.[51] Ware also told stories, usually improbable ones, of how names came to be associated with particular sites. Fishamble Street, for instance, 'was anciently called Bough Street as is supposed from the wattles or boughs of trees wherewith the houses were first built'. The double dedication of Christ Church and Holy Trinity he explained as 'the church of the Holy Trinity, vulgarly called Christ's Church being in great decay was repaired by one Crite, a merchant of Dublin, and hence called Chrite church'.[52] Again, in his history of the Dublin churches Robert Ware recorded of the Baltinglass monument in St John's that 'one of the sons is reddish, people did respond that it changed so after he had killed one of his brothers which that son for whom that statute was made did kill one of his brothers but I suppose that statue was of reddish in the face at the first setting up of that same monument'.[53]

Local legends such as these were validated by the very landscape and buildings to which they became attached. Such buildings, in effect, became symbols of what it meant to be an urban dweller. To walk around the streets of late-medieval Dublin was to know how to be a Dubliner. Ware's Dublin, however, was a world full of change. When Robert Ware died his history, together with other papers, passed into the hands of one of his relatives, Walter Harris. In 1766 Harris published another history of the city using Robert Ware's work as a basis for his own. The story of Richard Muton does not appear in Harris's work. The reason is not hard to discern. Muton's Tholsel had long gone from the landscape and what Harris wrote about was the new building, erected in the late 1670s.[54] That building contained its own messages of urban civility and so the story of Muton was allowed to die, the very physical evidence which vouched for its veracity having been removed from the landscape.[55] Each generation needs its own stories.

---

51 Armagh Public Library, 'Ware's history and antiquities', pp 20–34; Miller and Power (eds), *Holinshed's Irish chronicle*, pp 46–8.   52 Armagh Public Library, 'Ware's history and antiquities', pp 39, 94.   53 British Library, Add Ms 4813, ff 34v–5.   54 Walter Harris, *The history and antiquities of the city of Dublin* (Dublin, 1766), p. 472.   55 Gillespie, 'Describing Dublin', pp 110–12.